Numerical Computing
with MATLAB

REVISED REPRINT

Numerical Computing
with MATLAB

REVISED REPRINT

Cleve B. Moler
The MathWorks, Inc.

Society for Industrial and Applied Mathematics
Philadelphia

Published by the Society for Industrial and Applied Mathematics.

10 9 8 7 6 5 4 3 2 1

Library of Congress Cataloging-in-Publication Data

Moler, Cleve B.
    Numerical computing with MATLAB / Cleve B. Moler.
        p. cm.
    Includes bibliographical references and index.
    ISBN 978-0-898716-60-3 (pbk.)
        1. Numerical analysis—Data processing. 2. MATLAB. I. Title.

QA297.M625 2004
518'.0285—dc22   2004045360

Contents

Preface

Numerical Computing with MATLAB is a textbook for an introductory course in numerical methods, MATLAB, and technical computing. The emphasis is on informed use of mathematical software. We want you learn enough about the mathematical functions in MATLAB that you will be able to use them correctly, appreciate their limitations, and modify them when necessary to suit your own needs. The topics include

- introduction to MATLAB,
- linear equations,
- interpolation,
- zero finding,
- least squares,
- quadrature,
- ordinary differential equations,
- random numbers,
- Fourier analysis,
- eigenvalues and singular values,
- partial differential equations.

George Forsythe initiated a software-based numerical methods course at Stanford University in the late 1960s. The textbooks by Forsythe, Malcolm, and Moler [20] and Kahaner, Moler, and Nash [34] that evolved from the Stanford course were based upon libraries of Fortran subroutines.

This textbook is based upon MATLAB. NCM, a collection of over 70 M-files, forms an essential part of the book. Many of the over 200 exercises involve modifying and extending the programs in NCM. The book also makes extensive use of computer graphics, including interactive graphical expositions of numerical algorithms.

The prerequisites for the course, and the book, include

- calculus,
- some familiarity with ordinary differential equations,

ix

- some familiarity with matrices,

- some computer programming experience.

If you've never used MATLAB before, the first chapter will help you get started. If you're already familiar with MATLAB, you can glance over most of the first chapter quickly. Everyone should read the section in the first chapter about floating-point arithmetic.

There is probably too much material here for a one-quarter or one-semester course. Plan to cover the first several chapters and then choose the portions of the last four chapters that interest you.

Make sure that the NCM collection is installed on your network or your personal computer as you read the book. The software is available from a Web site devoted to the book [44]:

```
http://www.mathworks.com/moler
```

There are three types of NCM files:

- gui files: interactive graphical demonstrations;

- tx files: textbook implementations of built-in MATLAB functions;

- others: miscellaneous files, primarily associated with exercises.

When you have NCM available,

```
ncmgui
```

produces the figure shown on the next page. Each thumbnail plot is actually a push button that launches the corresponding gui.

This book would not have been possible without the people at The MathWorks and at SIAM. Both groups are professional, creative, and delightful to work with. They have been especially supportive of this book project. Out of the many friends and colleagues who have made specific contributions, I want to mention five in particular. Kathryn Ann Moler has used early drafts of the book several times in courses at Stanford and has been my best critic. Tim Davis and Charlie Van Loan wrote especially helpful reviews. Lisl Urban did an immaculate editing job. My wife Patsy has lived with my work habits and my laptop and loves me anyway. Thanks, everyone.

This revised reprint includes a change in the section on Google PageRank that improves the handling of web pages with no out links, a short new section in the Random Numbers chapter, removal of material on inline and feval, and correction of a few dozen minor typographical errors.

Cleve Moler
April 20, 2008

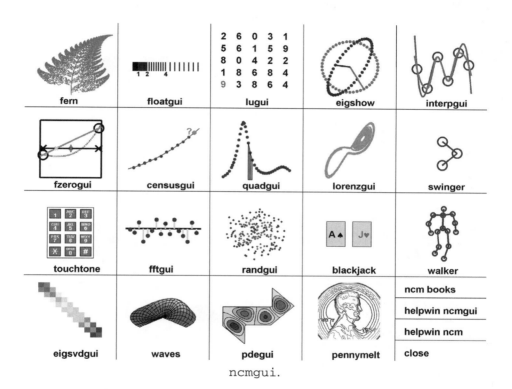

ncmgui.

Chapter 1

Introduction to MATLAB

This book is an introduction to two subjects: MATLAB and numerical computing. This first chapter introduces MATLAB by presenting several programs that investigate elementary, but interesting, mathematical problems. If you already have some experience programming in another language, we hope that you can see how MATLAB works by simply studying these programs.

If you want a more comprehensive introduction, an on-line manual from The Math-Works is available. Select **Help** in the toolbar atop the MATLAB command window, then select **MATLAB Help** and **Getting Started**. A PDF version is available under **Printable versions**. The document is also available from The MathWorks Web site [44]. Many other manuals produced by The MathWorks are available on line and from the Web site.

A list of over 600 MATLAB-based books by other authors and publishers, in several languages, is available at [45]. Three introductions to MATLAB are of particular interest here: a relatively short primer by Sigmon and Davis [55], a medium-sized, mathematically oriented text by Higham and Higham [31], and a large, comprehensive manual by Hanselman and Littlefield [29].

You should have a copy of MATLAB close at hand so you can run our sample programs as you read about them. All of the programs used in this book have been collected in a directory (or folder) named

```
NCM
```

(The directory name is the initials of the book title.) You can either start MATLAB in this directory or use

```
pathtool
```

to add the directory to the MATLAB path.

1.1 The Golden Ratio

What is the world's most interesting number? Perhaps you like π, or e, or 17. Some people might vote for ϕ, the *golden ratio*, computed here by our first MATLAB statement.

1

```
phi = (1 + sqrt(5))/2
```

This produces

```
phi =
    1.6180
```

Let's see more digits.

```
format long
phi
```

```
phi =
   1.61803398874989
```

This didn't recompute ϕ, it just displayed 15 significant digits instead of 5.

The golden ratio shows up in many places in mathematics; we'll see several in this book. The golden ratio gets its name from the golden rectangle, shown in Figure 1.1. The golden rectangle has the property that removing a square leaves a smaller rectangle with the same shape.

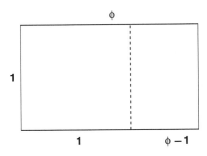

Figure 1.1. *The golden rectangle.*

Equating the aspect ratios of the rectangles gives a defining equation for ϕ:

$$\frac{1}{\phi} = \frac{\phi - 1}{1}.$$

This equation says that you can compute the reciprocal of ϕ by simply subtracting one. How many numbers have that property?

Multiplying the aspect ratio equation by ϕ produces the polynomial equation

$$\phi^2 - \phi - 1 = 0.$$

The roots of this equation are given by the quadratic formula:

$$\phi = \frac{1 \pm \sqrt{5}}{2}.$$

The positive root is the golden ratio.

If you have forgotten the quadratic formula, you can ask MATLAB to find the roots of the polynomial. MATLAB represents a polynomial by the vector of its coefficients, in descending order. So the vector

```
p = [1 -1 -1]
```

represents the polynomial

$$p(x) = x^2 - x - 1.$$

The roots are computed by the `roots` function.

```
r = roots(p)
```

produces

```
r =
   -0.61803398874989
    1.61803398874989
```

These two numbers are the only numbers whose reciprocal can be computed by subtracting one.

You can use the Symbolic Toolbox, which connects MATLAB to a computer algebra system, to solve the aspect ratio equation without converting it to a polynomial. The equation is represented by a character string. The `solve` function finds two solutions.

```
r = solve('1/x = x-1')
```

produces

```
r =
[ 1/2*5^(1/2)+1/2]
[ 1/2-1/2*5^(1/2)]
```

The `pretty` function displays the results in a way that resembles typeset mathematics.

```
pretty(r)
```

produces

```
    [        1/2        ]
    [1/2 5       + 1/2]
    [                   ]
    [               1/2]
    [1/2 - 1/2 5        ]
```

The variable `r` is a vector with two components, the symbolic forms of the two solutions. You can pick off the first component with

```
phi = r(1)
```

which produces

```
phi =
1/2*5^(1/2)+1/2
```

This expression can be converted to a numerical value in two different ways. It can be evaluated to any number of digits using variable-precision arithmetic with the vpa function.

```
vpa(phi,50)
```

produces 50 digits.

```
1.6180339887498948482045868343656381177203091798058
```

It can also be converted to double-precision floating point, which is the principal way that MATLAB represents numbers, with the double function.

```
phi = double(phi)
```

produces

```
phi =
    1.61803398874989
```

The aspect ratio equation is simple enough to have closed-form symbolic solutions. More complicated equations have to be solved approximately. In MATLAB an *anonymous function* is a convenient way to define an object that can be used as an argument to other functions. The statement

```
f = @(x) 1./x-(x-1)
```

defines $f(x) = 1/x - (x - 1)$ and produces

```
f =
    @(x) 1./x-(x-1)
```

The graph of $f(x)$ over the interval $0 \le x \le 4$ shown in Figure 1.2 is obtained with

```
ezplot(f,0,4)
```

The name ezplot stands for "easy plot," although some of the English-speaking world would pronounce it "e-zed plot." Even though $f(x)$ becomes infinite as $x \to 0$, ezplot automatically picks a reasonable vertical scale.

The statement

```
phi = fzero(f,1)
```

looks for a zero of $f(x)$ near $x = 1$. It produces an approximation to ϕ that is accurate to almost full precision. The result can be inserted in Figure 1.2 with

```
hold on
plot(phi,0,'o')
```

The following MATLAB program produces the picture of the golden rectangle shown in Figure 1.1. The program is contained in an M-file named goldrect.m, so issuing the command

```
goldrect
```

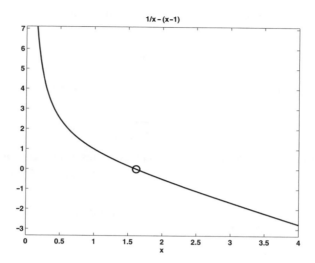

Figure 1.2. $f(\phi) = 0$.

runs the script and creates the picture.

```
% GOLDRECT   Plot the golden rectangle

phi = (1+sqrt(5))/2;
x = [0 phi phi 0 0];
y = [0 0 1 1 0];
u = [1 1];
v = [0 1];
plot(x,y,'b',u,v,'b--')
text(phi/2,1.05,'\phi')
text((1+phi)/2,-.05,'\phi - 1')
text(-.05,.5,'1')
text(.5,-.05,'1')
axis equal
axis off
set(gcf,'color','white')
```

The vectors x and y each contain five elements. Connecting consecutive (x_k, y_k) pairs with straight lines produces the outside rectangle. The vectors u and v each contain two elements. The line connecting (u_1, v_1) with (u_2, v_2) separates the rectangle into the square and the smaller rectangle. The plot command draws these lines—the $x - y$ lines in solid blue and the $u - v$ line in dashed blue. The next four statements place text at various points; the string '\phi' denotes the Greek letter. The two axis statements cause the scaling in the x and y directions to be equal and then turn off the display of the axes. The last statement sets the background color of gcf, which stands for *get current figure*, to white.

A *continued fraction* is an infinite expression of the form

$$a_0 + \cfrac{1}{a_1 + \cfrac{1}{a_2 + \cfrac{1}{a_3 + \cdots}}}.$$

If all the a_k's are equal to 1, the continued fraction is another representation of the golden ratio:

$$\phi = 1 + \cfrac{1}{1 + \cfrac{1}{1 + \cfrac{1}{1 + \cdots}}}.$$

The following MATLAB function generates and evaluates truncated continued fraction approximations to ϕ. The code is stored in an M-file named goldfract.m.

```
function goldfract(n)
%GOLDFRACT    Golden ratio continued fraction.
%   GOLDFRACT(n) displays n terms.

p = '1';
for k = 1:n
    p = ['1+1/(' p ')'];
end
p

p = 1;
q = 1;
for k = 1:n
    s = p;
    p = p + q;
    q = s;
end
p = sprintf('%d/%d',p,q)

format long
p = eval(p)

format short
err = (1+sqrt(5))/2 - p
```

The statement

```
goldfract(6)
```

produces

```
p =
1+1/(1+1/(1+1/(1+1/(1+1/(1+1/(1))))))

p =
21/13
```

```
p =
    1.61538461538462

err =
    0.0026
```

The three p's are all different representations of the same approximation to ϕ.

The first p is the continued fraction truncated to six terms. There are six right parentheses. This p is a string generated by starting with a single '1' (that's goldfract(0)) and repeatedly inserting the string '1+1/(' in front and the string ')' in back. No matter how long this string becomes, it is a valid MATLAB expression.

The second p is an "ordinary" fraction with a single integer numerator and denominator obtained by collapsing the first p. The basis for the reformulation is

$$1 + \frac{1}{\frac{p}{q}} = \frac{p+q}{p}.$$

So the iteration starts with

$$\frac{1}{1}$$

and repeatedly replaces the fraction

$$\frac{p}{q}$$

with

$$\frac{p+q}{p}.$$

The statement

```
p = sprintf('%d/%d',p,q)
```

prints the final fraction by formatting p and q as decimal integers and placing a '/' between them.

The third p is the same number as the first two p's, but is represented as a conventional decimal expansion, obtained by having the MATLAB eval function actually do the division expressed in the second p.

The final quantity err is the difference between p and ϕ. With only 6 terms, the approximation is accurate to less than 3 digits. How many terms does it take to get 10 digits of accuracy?

As the number of terms n increases, the truncated continued fraction generated by goldfract(n) theoretically approaches ϕ. But limitations on the size of the integers in the numerator and denominator, as well as roundoff error in the actual floating-point division, eventually intervene. Exercise 1.3 asks you to investigate the limiting accuracy of goldfract(n).

1.2 Fibonacci Numbers

Leonardo Pisano Fibonacci was born around 1170 and died around 1250 in Pisa in what is now Italy. He traveled extensively in Europe and Northern Africa. He wrote several mathematical texts that, among other things, introduced Europe to the Hindu-Arabic notation for numbers. Even though his books had to be transcribed by hand, they were widely circulated. In his best known book, *Liber Abaci*, published in 1202, he posed the following problem:

> *A man put a pair of rabbits in a place surrounded on all sides by a wall. How many pairs of rabbits can be produced from that pair in a year if it is supposed that every month each pair begets a new pair which from the second month on becomes productive?*

Today the solution to this problem is known as the *Fibonacci sequence*, or *Fibonacci numbers*. There is a small mathematical industry based on Fibonacci numbers. A search of the Internet for "Fibonacci" will find dozens of Web sites and hundreds of pages of material. There is even a Fibonacci Association that publishes a scholarly journal, the *Fibonacci Quarterly*.

If Fibonacci had not specified a month for the newborn pair to mature, he would not have a sequence named after him. The number of pairs would simply double each month. After n months there would be 2^n pairs of rabbits. That's a lot of rabbits, but not distinctive mathematics.

Let f_n denote the number of pairs of rabbits after n months. The key fact is that the number of rabbits at the end of a month is the number at the beginning of the month plus the number of births produced by the mature pairs:

$$f_n = f_{n-1} + f_{n-2}.$$

The initial conditions are that in the first month there is one pair of rabbits and in the second there are two pairs:

$$f_1 = 1, \quad f_2 = 2.$$

The following MATLAB function, stored in the M-file `fibonacci.m`, produces a vector containing the first n Fibonacci numbers.

```
function f = fibonacci(n)
% FIBONACCI  Fibonacci sequence
% f = FIBONACCI(n) generates the first n Fibonacci numbers.
f = zeros(n,1);
f(1) = 1;
f(2) = 2;
for k = 3:n
  f(k) = f(k-1) + f(k-2);
end
```

With these initial conditions, the answer to Fibonacci's original question about the size of the rabbit population after one year is given by

```
fibonacci(12)
```

This produces

```
   1
   2
   3
   5
   8
  13
  21
  34
  55
  89
 144
 233
```

The answer is 233 pairs of rabbits. (It would be 4096 pairs if the number doubled every month for 12 months.)

Let's look carefully at `fibonacci.m`. It's a good example of how to create a MATLAB function. The first line is

```
function f = fibonacci(n)
```

The first word on the first line says this is a `function` M-file, not a script. The remainder of the first line says this particular function produces one output result, `f`, and takes one input argument, `n`. The name of the function specified on the first line is not actually used, because MATLAB looks for the name of the M-file, but it is common practice to have the two match. The next two lines are comments that provide the text displayed when you ask for `help`.

```
   help fibonacci
```

produces

```
   FIBONACCI   Fibonacci sequence
   f = FIBONACCI(n) generates the first n Fibonacci numbers.
```

The name of the function is in uppercase because historically MATLAB was case insensitive and ran on terminals with only a single font. The use of capital letters may be confusing to some first-time MATLAB users, but the convention persists. It is important to repeat the input and output arguments in these comments because the first line is not displayed when you ask for `help` on the function.

The next line

```
   f = zeros(n,1);
```

creates an n-by-1 matrix containing all zeros and assigns it to `f`. In MATLAB, a matrix with only one column is a column vector and a matrix with only one row is a row vector.

The next two lines,

```
   f(1) = 1;
   f(2) = 2;
```

provide the initial conditions.

The last three lines are the `for` statement that does all the work.

```
for k = 3:n
   f(k) = f(k-1) + f(k-2);
end
```

We like to use three spaces to indent the body of `for` and `if` statements, but other people prefer two or four spaces, or a tab. You can also put the entire construction on one line if you provide a comma after the first clause.

This particular function looks a lot like functions in other programming languages. It produces a vector, but it does not use any of the MATLAB vector or matrix operations. We will see some of these operations soon.

Here is another Fibonacci function, `fibnum.m`. Its output is simply the nth Fibonacci number.

```
function f = fibnum(n)
% FIBNUM   Fibonacci number.
% FIBNUM(n) generates the nth Fibonacci number.
if n <= 1
   f = 1;
else
   f = fibnum(n-1) + fibnum(n-2);
end
```

The statement

```
fibnum(12)
```

produces

```
ans =
   233
```

The `fibnum` function is *recursive*. In fact, the term *recursive* is used in both a mathematical and a computer science sense. The relationship $f_n = f_{n-1} + f_{n-2}$ is known as a *recursion relation* and a function that calls itself is a *recursive function*.

A recursive program is elegant, but expensive. You can measure execution time with `tic` and `toc`. Try

```
tic, fibnum(24), toc
```

Do *not* try

```
tic, fibnum(50), toc
```

Now compare the results produced by `goldfract(6)` and `fibonacci(7)`. The first contains the fraction 21/13 while the second ends with 13 and 21. This is not just a coincidence. The continued fraction is collapsed by repeating the statement

```
p = p + q;
```

while the Fibonacci numbers are generated by

```
f(k) = f(k-1) + f(k-2);
```

In fact, if we let ϕ_n denote the golden ratio continued fraction truncated at n terms, then

$$\frac{f_{n+1}}{f_n} = \phi_n.$$

In the infinite limit, the ratio of successive Fibonacci numbers approaches the golden ratio:

$$\lim_{n \to \infty} \frac{f_{n+1}}{f_n} = \phi.$$

To see this, compute 40 Fibonacci numbers.

```
n = 40;
f = fibonacci(n);
```

Then compute their ratios.

```
f(2:n)./f(1:n-1)
```

This takes the vector containing `f(2)` through `f(n)` and divides it, element by element, by the vector containing `f(1)` through `f(n-1)`. The output begins with

```
2.00000000000000
1.50000000000000
1.66666666666667
1.60000000000000
1.62500000000000
1.61538461538462
1.61904761904762
1.61764705882353
1.61818181818182
```

and ends with

```
1.61803398874990
1.61803398874989
1.61803398874990
1.61803398874989
1.61803398874989
```

Do you see why we chose n = 40? Use the up arrow key on your keyboard to bring back the previous expression. Change it to

```
f(2:n)./f(1:n-1) - phi
```

and then press the Enter key. What is the value of the last element?

The population of Fibonacci's rabbit pen doesn't double every month; it is multiplied by the golden ratio every month.

It is possible to find a closed-form solution to the Fibonacci number recurrence relation. The key is to look for solutions of the form

$$f_n = c\rho^n$$

for some constants c and ρ. The recurrence relation

$$f_n = f_{n-1} + f_{n-2}$$

becomes

$$\rho^2 = \rho + 1.$$

We've seen this equation before. There are two possible values of ρ, namely ϕ and $1 - \phi$. The general solution to the recurrence is

$$f_n = c_1\phi^n + c_2(1 - \phi)^n.$$

The constants c_1 and c_2 are determined by initial conditions, which are now conveniently written

$$f_0 = c_1 + c_2 = 1,$$
$$f_1 = c_1\phi + c_2(1 - \phi) = 1.$$

Exercise 1.4 asks you to use the MATLAB backslash operator to solve this 2-by-2 system of simultaneous linear equations, but it is actually easier to solve the system by hand:

$$c_1 = \frac{\phi}{2\phi - 1},$$
$$c_2 = -\frac{(1 - \phi)}{2\phi - 1}.$$

Inserting these in the general solution gives

$$f_n = \frac{1}{2\phi - 1}(\phi^{n+1} - (1 - \phi)^{n+1}).$$

This is an amazing equation. The right-hand side involves powers and quotients of irrational numbers, but the result is a sequence of integers. You can check this with MATLAB, displaying the results in scientific notation.

```
format long e
n = (1:40)';
f = (phi.^(n+1) - (1-phi).^(n+1))/(2*phi-1)
```

The .^ operator is an element-by-element power operator. It is not necessary to use ./ for the final division because (2*phi-1) is a scalar quantity. The computed result starts with

```
f =
    1.000000000000000e+000
    2.000000000000000e+000
```

```
3.000000000000000e+000
5.000000000000001e+000
8.000000000000002e+000
1.300000000000000e+001
2.100000000000000e+001
3.400000000000001e+001
```

and ends with

```
5.702887000000007e+006
9.227465000000011e+006
1.493035200000002e+007
2.415781700000003e+007
3.908816900000005e+007
6.324598600000007e+007
1.023341550000001e+008
1.655801410000002e+008
```

Roundoff error prevents the results from being exact integers, but

```
f = round(f)
```

finishes the job.

1.3   Fractal Fern

The M-files `fern.m` and `finitefern.m` produce the "Fractal Fern" described by Michael Barnsley in *Fractals Everywhere* [6]. They generate and plot a potentially infinite sequence of random, but carefully choreographed, points in the plane. The command

```
fern
```

runs forever, producing an increasingly dense plot. The command

```
finitefern(n)
```

generates n points and a plot like Figure 1.3. The command

```
finitefern(n,'s')
```

shows the generation of the points one at a time. The command

```
F = finitefern(n);
```

generates, but does not plot, n points and returns an array of zeros and ones for use with sparse matrix and image-processing functions.

The NCM collection also includes `fern.png`, a 768-by-1024 color image with half a million points that you can view with a browser or a paint program. You can also view the file with

```
F = imread('fern.png');
image(F)
```

Figure 1.3. *Fractal fern.*

If you like the image, you might even choose to make it your computer desktop background. However, you should really run `fern` on your own computer to see the dynamics of the emerging fern in high resolution.

The fern is generated by repeated transformations of a point in the plane. Let x be a vector with two components, x_1 and x_2, representing the point. There are four different transformations, all of them of the form

$$x \rightarrow Ax + b,$$

with different matrices A and vectors b. These are known as *affine transformations*. The most frequently used transformation has

$$A = \begin{pmatrix} 0.85 & 0.04 \\ -0.04 & 0.85 \end{pmatrix}, \; b = \begin{pmatrix} 0 \\ 1.6 \end{pmatrix}.$$

This transformation shortens and rotates x a little bit, then adds 1.6 to its second component. Repeated application of this transformation moves the point up and to the right, heading toward the upper tip of the fern. Every once in a while, one of the other three transformations is picked at random. These transformations move the point into the lower subfern on the right, the lower subfern on the left, or the stem.

Here is the complete fractal fern program.

```
function fern
%FERN  MATLAB implementation of the Fractal Fern
```

```
%Michael Barnsley, Fractals Everywhere, Academic Press,1993
%This version runs forever, or until stop is toggled.
%See also: FINITEFERN.

shg
clf reset
set(gcf,'color','white','menubar','none', ...
  'numbertitle','off','name','Fractal Fern')
x = [.5; .5];
h = plot(x(1),x(2),'.');
darkgreen = [0 2/3 0];
set(h,'markersize',1,'color',darkgreen,'erasemode','none');
axis([-3 3 0 10])
axis off
stop = uicontrol('style','toggle','string','stop', ...
  'background','white');
drawnow

p = [ .85 .92 .99 1.00];
A1 = [ .85 .04; -.04 .85]; b1 = [0; 1.6];
A2 = [ .20 -.26; .23 .22]; b2 = [0; 1.6];
A3 = [-.15 .28; .26 .24]; b3 = [0; .44];
A4 = [ 0  0 ; 0 .16];

cnt = 1;
tic
while ~get(stop,'value')
  r = rand;
  if r < p(1)
    x = A1*x + b1;
  elseif r < p(2)
    x = A2*x + b2;
  elseif r < p(3)
    x = A3*x + b3;
  else
    x = A4*x;
  end
  set(h,'xdata',x(1),'ydata',x(2));
  cnt = cnt + 1;
  drawnow
end
t = toc;
s = sprintf('%8.0f points in %6.3f seconds',cnt,t);
text(-1.5,-0.5,s,'fontweight','bold');
set(stop,'style','pushbutton','string','close', ...
  'callback','close(gcf)')
```

Let's examine this program a few statements at a time.

```
shg
```

stands for "show graph window." It brings an existing graphics window forward, or creates a new one if necessary.

```
clf reset
```

resets most of the figure properties to their default values.

```
set(gcf,'color','white','menubar','none', ...
    'numbertitle','off','name','Fractal Fern')
```

changes the background color of the figure window from the default gray to white and provides a customized title for the window.

```
x = [.5; .5];
```

provides the initial coordinates of the point.

```
h = plot(x(1),x(2),'.');
```

plots a single dot in the plane and saves a *handle*, h, so that we can later modify the properties of the plot.

```
darkgreen = [0 2/3 0];
```

defines a color where the red and blue components are zero and the green component is two-thirds of its full intensity.

```
set(h,'markersize',1,'color',darkgreen,'erasemode','none');
```

makes the dot referenced by h smaller, changes its color, and specifies that the image of the dot on the screen should not be erased when its coordinates are changed. A record of these old points is kept by the computer's graphics hardware (until the figure is reset), but MATLAB itself does not remember them.

```
axis([-3 3 0 10])
axis off
```

specifies that the plot should cover the region

$$-3 \le x_1 \le 3, \;\; 0 \le x_2 \le 10,$$

but that the axes should not be drawn.

```
stop = uicontrol('style','toggle','string','stop', ...
    'background','white');
```

creates a toggle user interface control, labeled 'stop' and colored white, in the default position near the lower left corner of the figure. The handle for the control is saved in the variable stop.

```
drawnow
```

causes the initial figure, including the initial point, to actually be plotted on the computer screen.

The statement

```
p = [ .85   .92   .99   1.00];
```

sets up a vector of probabilities. The statements

```
A1 = [ .85   .04;  -.04   .85];   b1 = [0; 1.6];
A2 = [ .20  -.26;   .23   .22];   b2 = [0; 1.6];
A3 = [-.15   .28;   .26   .24];   b3 = [0; .44];
A4 = [  0     0 ;    0    .16];
```

define the four affine transformations. The statement

```
cnt = 1;
```

initializes a counter that keeps track of the number of points plotted. The statement

```
tic
```

initializes a stopwatch timer. The statement

```
while ~get(stop,'value')
```

begins a while loop that runs as long as the 'value' property of the stop toggle is equal to 0. Clicking the stop toggle changes the value from 0 to 1 and terminates the loop.

```
r = rand;
```

generates a *pseudorandom* value between 0 and 1. The compound if statement

```
if r < p(1)
    x = A1*x + b1;
elseif r < p(2)
    x = A2*x + b2;
elseif r < p(3)
    x = A3*x + b3;
else
    x = A4*x;
end
```

picks one of the four affine transformations. Because p(1) is 0.85, the first transformation is chosen 85% of the time. The other three transformations are chosen relatively infrequently.

```
set(h,'xdata',x(1),'ydata',x(2));
```

changes the coordinates of the point h to the new (x_1, x_2) and plots this new point. But get(h,'erasemode') is 'none', so the old point also remains on the screen.

```
cnt = cnt + 1;
```

counts one more point.

```
drawnow
```

tells MATLAB to take the time to redraw the figure, showing the new point along with all the old ones. Without this command, nothing would be plotted until `stop` is toggled.

```
end
```

matches the `while` at the beginning of the loop. Finally,

```
t = toc;
```

reads the timer.

```
s = sprintf('%8.0f points in %6.3f seconds',cnt,t);
text(-1.5,-0.5,s,'fontweight','bold');
```

displays the elapsed time since `tic` was called and the final count of the number of points plotted. Finally,

```
set(stop,'style','pushbutton','string','close', ...
    'callback','close(gcf)')
```

changes the control to a push button that closes the window.

1.4 Magic Squares

MATLAB stands for *Matrix Laboratory*. Over the years, MATLAB has evolved into a general-purpose technical computing environment, but operations involving vectors, matrices, and linear algebra continue to be its most distinguishing feature.

Magic squares provide an interesting set of sample matrices. The command `help magic` tells us the following:

```
MAGIC(N) is an N-by-N matrix constructed from the integers
1 through N^2 with equal row, column, and diagonal sums.
Produces valid magic squares for all N > 0 except N = 2.
```

Magic squares were known in China over 2,000 years before the birth of Christ. The 3-by-3 magic square is known as *Lo Shu*. Legend has it that Lo Shu was discovered on the shell of a turtle that crawled out of the Lo River in the 23rd century B.C. Lo Shu provides a mathematical basis for *feng shui*, the ancient Chinese philosophy of balance and harmony. MATLAB can generate Lo Shu with

```
A = magic(3)
```

which produces

```
A =
      8      1      6
      3      5      7
      4      9      2
```

The command

```
sum(A)
```

sums the elements in each column to produce

```
    15      15      15
```

The command

```
sum(A')'
```

transposes the matrix, sums the columns of the transpose, and then transposes the results to produce the row sums

```
    15
    15
    15
```

The command

```
sum(diag(A))
```

sums the main diagonal of A, which runs from upper left to lower right, to produce

```
    15
```

The opposite diagonal, which runs from upper right to lower left, is less important in linear algebra, so finding its sum is a little trickier. One way to do it makes use of the function that "flips" a matrix "upside-down."

```
sum(diag(flipud(A)))
```

produces

```
    15
```

This verifies that A has equal row, column, and diagonal sums.

Why is the magic sum equal to 15? The command

```
sum(1:9)
```

tells us that the sum of the integers from 1 to 9 is 45. If these integers are allocated to 3 columns with equal sums, that sum must be

```
sum(1:9)/3
```

which is 15.

There are eight possible ways to place a transparency on an overhead projector. Similarly, there are eight magic squares of order three that are rotations and reflections of A. The statements

```
for k = 0:3
   rot90(A,k)
   rot90(A',k)
end
```

display all eight of them.

```
8    1    6         8    3    4
3    5    7         1    5    9
4    9    2         6    7    2

6    7    2         4    9    2
1    5    9         3    5    7
8    3    4         8    1    6

2    9    4         2    7    6
7    5    3         9    5    1
6    1    8         4    3    8

4    3    8         6    1    8
9    5    1         7    5    3
2    7    6         2    9    4
```

These are all the magic squares of order three.

Now for some linear algebra. The determinant of our magic square,

```
det(A)
```

is

```
    -360
```

The inverse,

```
X = inv(A)
```

is

```
X =
    0.1472   -0.1444    0.0639
   -0.0611    0.0222    0.1056
   -0.0194    0.1889   -0.1028
```

The inverse looks better if it is displayed with a rational format.

```
format rat
X
```

shows that the elements of X are fractions with det(A) in the denominator.

```
X =
     53/360      -13/90       23/360
    -11/180        1/45       19/180
     -7/360       17/90      -37/360
```

The statement

```
format short
```

restores the output format to its default.

Three other important quantities in computational linear algebra are *matrix norms*, *eigenvalues*, and *singular values*. The statements

```
r = norm(A)
e = eig(A)
s = svd(A)
```

produce

```
r =
     15

e =
    15.0000
     4.8990
    -4.8990

s =
    15.0000
     6.9282
     3.4641
```

The magic sum occurs in all three because the vector of all ones is an eigenvector and is also a left and right singular vector.

So far, all the computations in this section have been done using floating-point arithmetic. This is the arithmetic used for almost all scientific and engineering computation, especially for large matrices. But for a 3-by-3 matrix, it is easy to repeat the computations using symbolic arithmetic and the Symbolic Toolbox. The statement

```
A = sym(A)
```

changes the internal representation of A to a symbolic form that is displayed as

```
A =
[ 8, 1, 6]
[ 3, 5, 7]
[ 4, 9, 2]
```

Now commands like

```
sum(A), sum(A')', det(A), inv(A), eig(A), svd(A)
```

produce symbolic results. In particular, the eigenvalue problem for this matrix can be solved exactly, and

```
e =
[            15]
[   2*6^(1/2)]
[  -2*6^(1/2)]
```

A 4-by-4 magic square is one of several mathematical objects on display in *Melancolia*, a Renaissance etching by Albrecht Dürer. An electronic copy of the etching is available in a MATLAB data file.

```
load durer
whos
```

produces

```
X          648x509       2638656  double array
caption      2x28            112  char array
map        128x3            3072  double array
```

The elements of the matrix X are indices into the gray-scale color map named map. The image is displayed with

```
image(X)
colormap(map)
axis image
```

Click the magnifying glass with a "+" in the toolbar and use the mouse to zoom in on the magic square in the upper right-hand corner. The scanning resolution becomes evident as you zoom in. The commands

```
load detail
image(X)
colormap(map)
axis image
```

display a higher resolution scan of the area around the magic square.

The command

```
A = magic(4)
```

produces a 4-by-4 magic square.

```
A =
    16     2     3    13
     5    11    10     8
     9     7     6    12
     4    14    15     1
```

The commands

```
sum(A), sum(A'), sum(diag(A)), sum(diag(flipud(A)))
```

yield enough 34's to verify that A is indeed a magic square.

The 4-by-4 magic square generated by MATLAB is not the same as Dürer's magic square. We need to interchange the second and third columns.

```
A = A(:,[1 3 2 4])
```

changes A to

```
A =
    16       3       2      13
     5      10      11       8
     9       6       7      12
     4      15      14       1
```

Interchanging columns does not change the column sums or the row sums. It usually changes the diagonal sums, but in this case both diagonal sums are still 34. So now our magic square matches the one in Dürer's etching. Dürer probably chose this particular 4-by-4 square because the date he did the work, 1514, occurs in the middle of the bottom row.

We have seen two different 4-by-4 magic squares. It turns out that there are 880 different magic squares of order 4 and 275305224 different magic squares of order 5. Determining the number of different magic squares of order 6 or larger is an unsolved mathematical problem.

The determinant of our 4-by-4 magic square, det(A), is 0. If we try to compute its inverse

```
inv(A)
```

we get

```
Warning: Matrix is close to singular or badly scaled.
         Results may be inaccurate.
```

So some magic squares represent singular matrices. Which ones? The *rank* of a square matrix is the number of linearly independent rows or columns. An n-by-n matrix is singular if and only if its rank is less than n.

The statements

```
for n = 1:24, r(n) = rank(magic(n)); end
[(1:24)'  r']
```

produce a table of order versus rank.

```
     1       1
     2       2
     3       3
     4       3
     5       5
     6       5
     7       7
     8       3
     9       9
    10       7
    11      11
    12       3
    13      13
```

```
14        9
15       15
16        3
17       17
18       11
19       19
20        3
21       21
22       13
23       23
24        3
```

Look carefully at this table. Ignore $n = 2$ because `magic(2)` is not really a magic square. What patterns do you see? A bar graph makes the patterns easier to see.

```
bar(r)
title('Rank of magic squares')
```

produces Figure 1.4.

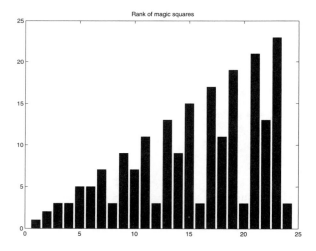

Figure 1.4. *Rank of magic squares.*

The rank considerations show that there are three different kinds of magic squares:

- *Odd* order: n is odd.
- *Singly even* order: n is a multiple of 2, but not 4.
- *Doubly even* order: n is a multiple of 4.

Odd-ordered magic squares, $n = 3, 5, 7, \ldots,$ have full rank n. They are nonsingular and have inverses. Doubly even magic squares, $n = 4, 8, 12, \ldots,$ have rank three no matter how large n is. They might be called *very singular*. Singly even magic squares, $n = 6, 10, 14, \ldots,$

have rank $n/2 + 2$. They are also singular, but have fewer row and column dependencies than the doubly even squares.

If you have MATLAB Version 6 or later, you can look at the M-file that generates magic squares with

```
edit magic.m
```

or

```
type magic.m
```

You will see the three different cases in the code.

The different kinds of magic squares also produce different three-dimensional surface plots. Try the following for various values of n.

```
surf(magic(n))
axis off
set(gcf,'doublebuffer','on')
cameratoolbar
```

Double buffering prevents flicker when you use the various camera tools to move the viewpoint. The following code produces Figure 1.5.

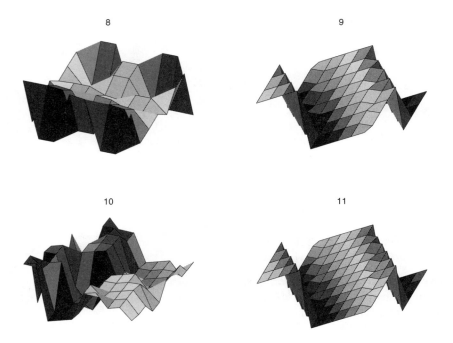

Figure 1.5. *Surface plots of magic squares.*

```
for n = 8:11
   subplot(2,2,n-7)
   surf(magic(n))
   title(num2str(n))
   axis off
   view(30,45)
   axis tight
end
```

1.5 Cryptography

This section uses a cryptography example to show how MATLAB deals with text and character strings. The cryptographic technique, which is known as a *Hill cipher*, involves arithmetic in a *finite field*.

Almost all modern computers use the ASCII character set to store basic text. ASCII stands for *American Standard Code for Information Interchange*. The character set uses 7 of the 8 bits in a byte to encode 128 characters. The first 32 characters are nonprinting control characters, such as tab, backspace, and end-of-line. The 128th character is another nonprinting character that corresponds to the Delete key on your keyboard. In between these control characters are 95 printable characters, including a space, 10 digits, 26 lowercase letters, 26 uppercase letters, and 32 punctuation marks.

MATLAB can easily display all the printable characters in the order determined by their ASCII encoding. Start with

```
x = reshape(32:127,32,3)'
```

This produces a 3-by-32 matrix.

```
x =
    32    33    34  ...    61    62    63
    64    65    66  ...    93    94    95
    96    97    98  ...   125   126   127
```

The char function converts numbers to characters. The statement

```
c = char(x)
```

produces

```
c =
 !"#$%&'()*+,-./0123456789:;<=>?
@ABCDEFGHIJKLMNOPQRSTUVWXYZ[\]^_
'abcdefghijklmnopqrstuvwxyz{|}~
```

We have cheated a little bit because the last element of x is 127, which corresponds to the nonprinting delete character, and we have not shown the last character in c. You can try this on your computer and see what is actually displayed.

The first character in c is blank, indicating that

```
char(32)
```

is the same as

```
' '
```

The last printable character in c is the *tilde*, indicating that

```
char(126)
```

is the same as

```
'~'
```

The characters representing digits are in the first line of c. In fact,

```
d = char(48:57)
```

displays a 10-character string

```
d =
0123456789
```

This string can be converted to the corresponding numerical values with `double` or `real`. The statement

```
double(d) - '0'
```

produces

0	1	2	3	4	5	6	7	8	9

Comparing the second and third lines of c, we see that the ASCII encoding of the lowercase letters is obtained by adding 32 to the ASCII encoding of the uppercase letters. Understanding this encoding allows us to use vector and matrix operations in MATLAB to manipulate text.

The ASCII standard is often extended to make use of all eight bits in a byte, but the characters that are displayed depend on the computer and operating system you are using, the font you have chosen, and even the country you live in. Try

```
char(reshape(160:255,32,3)')
```

and see what happens on your machine.

Our encryption technique involves *modular arithmetic*. All the quantities involved are integers and the result of any arithmetic operation is reduced by taking the remainder or *modulus* with respect to a prime number p. The functions $rem(x,y)$ and $mod(x,y)$ both compute the remainder if x is divided by y. They produce the same result if x and y have the same sign; the result also has that sign. But if x and y have opposite signs, then $rem(x,y)$ has the same sign as x, while $mod(x,y)$ has the same sign as y. Here is a table:

```
x = [37 -37 37 -37]';
y = [10 10 -10 -10]';
r = [ x   y   rem(x,y) mod(x,y)]
```

produces

```
   37      10       7       7
  -37      10      -7       3
   37     -10       7      -3
  -37     -10      -7      -7
```

We have chosen to encrypt text that uses the entire ASCII character set, not just the letters. There are 95 such characters. The next larger prime number is $p = 97$, so we represent the p characters by the integers $0:p-1$ and do arithmetic mod p.

The characters are encoded two at a time. Each pair of characters is represented by a 2-vector, x. For example, suppose the text contains the pair of letters 'TV'. The ASCII values for this pair of letters are 84 and 86. Subtracting 32 to make the representation start at 0 produces the column vector

$$x = \begin{pmatrix} 52 \\ 54 \end{pmatrix}.$$

The encryption is done with a 2-by-2 matrix-vector multiplication over the integers mod p. The symbol $\equiv$ is used to indicate that two integers have the same remainder, modulo the specified prime:

$$y \equiv Ax, \ \text{mod} \ p,$$

where A is the matrix

$$A = \begin{pmatrix} 71 & 2 \\ 2 & 26 \end{pmatrix}.$$

For our example, the product Ax is

$$Ax = \begin{pmatrix} 3800 \\ 1508 \end{pmatrix}.$$

If this is reduced mod p, the result is

$$y = \begin{pmatrix} 17 \\ 53 \end{pmatrix}.$$

Converting this back to characters by adding 32 produces '1U'.

Now comes the interesting part. Over the integers modulo p, the matrix A is its own inverse. If

$$y \equiv Ax, \ \text{mod} \ p,$$

then

$$x \equiv Ay, \ \text{mod} \ p.$$

In other words, in arithmetic mod p, A^2 is the identity matrix. You can check this with MATLAB.

```
p = 97;
A = [71 2; 2 26]
I = mod(A^2,p)
```

produces

```
A =
      71        2
       2       26


I =
       1        0
       0        1
```

This means that the encryption process is its own inverse. The same function can be used to both encrypt and decrypt a message.

The M-file crypto.m begins with a preamble.

```
function y = crypto(x)
% CRYPTO Cryptography example.
% y = crypto(x) converts an ASCII text string into another
% coded string.  The function is its own inverse, so
%   crypto(crypto(x)) gives x back.
% See also: ENCRYPT.
```

A comment precedes the statement that assigns the prime p.

```
% Use a two-character Hill cipher with arithmetic
% modulo 97, a prime.
p = 97;
```

Choose two characters above ASCII 128 to expand the size of the character set from 95 to 97.

```
c1 = char(169);
c2 = char(174);
x(x==c1) = 127;
x(x==c2) = 128;
```

The conversion from characters to numerical values is done by

```
x = mod(real(x-32),p);
```

Prepare for the matrix-vector product by forming a matrix with two rows and lots of columns.

```
n = 2*floor(length(x)/2);
X = reshape(x(1:n),2,n/2);
```

All this preparation has been so that we can do the actual finite field arithmetic quickly and easily.

```
% Encode with matrix multiplication modulo p.
A = [71 2; 2 26];
Y = mod(A*X,p);
```

Reshape into a single row.

```
y = reshape(Y,1,n);
```

If `length(x)` is odd, encode the last character

```
if length(x) > n
    y(n+1) = mod((p-1)*x(n+1),p);
end
```

Finally, convert the numbers back to characters.

```
y = char(y+32);
y(y==127) = c1;
y(y==128) = c2;
```

Let's follow the computation of `y = crypto('Hello world')`. We begin with a character string.

```
x = 'Hello world'
```

This is converted to an integer vector.

```
x =
    40   69   76   76   79    0   87   79   82   76   68
```

`length(x)` is odd, so the reshaping temporarily ignores the last element

```
X =
    40   76   79   87   82
    69   76    0   79   76
```

A conventional matrix-vector multiplication `A*X` produces an intermediate matrix.

```
    2978     5548     5609     6335     5974
    1874     2128      158     2228     2140
```

Then the `mod(.,p)` operation produces

```
Y =
    68   19   80   30   57
    31   91   61   94    6
```

This is rearranged to a row vector.

```
y =
    68   31   19   91   80   61   30   94   57    6
```

Now the last element of `x` is encoded by itself and attached to the end of `y`.

```
y =
    68   31   19   91   80   61   30   94   57    6   29
```

Finally, `y` is converted back to a character string to produce the encrypted result.

```
y = 'd?3{p]>~Y&='
```

If we now compute `crypto(y)`, we get back our original `'Hello world'`.

1.6   The 3n + 1 Sequence

This section describes a famous unsolved problem in number theory. Start with any positive integer n. Repeat the following steps:

- If $n = 1$, stop.

- If n is even, replace it with $n/2$.

- If n is odd, replace it with $3n + 1$.

For example, starting with $n = 7$ produces

$$7, 22, 11, 34, 17, 52, 26, 13, 40, 20, 10, 5, 16, 8, 4, 2, 1.$$

The sequence terminates after 17 steps. Note that whenever n reaches a power of 2, the sequence terminates in $\log_2 n$ more steps.

   The unanswered question is, does the process *always* terminate? Or is there some starting value that causes the process to go on forever, either because the numbers get larger and larger, or because some periodic cycle is generated?

   This problem is known as the $3n + 1$ problem. It has been studied by many eminent mathematicians, including Collatz, Ulam, and Kakatani, and is discussed in a survey paper by Jeffrey Lagarias [36].

   The following MATLAB code fragment generates the sequence starting with any specified n.

```
y = n;
while n > 1
   if rem(n,2)==0
      n = n/2;
   else
      n = 3*n+1;
   end
   y = [y n];
end
```

We don't know ahead of time how long the resulting vector y is going to be. But the statement

```
y = [y n];
```

automatically increases length(y) each time it is executed.

   In principle, the unsolved mathematical problem is, Can this code fragment run forever? In actual fact, floating-point roundoff error causes the calculation to misbehave whenever $3n + 1$ becomes greater than 2^{53}, but it is still interesting to investigate modest values of n.

   Let's embed our code fragment in a GUI. The complete function is in the M-file threenplus1.m. For example, the statement

```
threenplus1(7)
```

produces Figure 1.6.

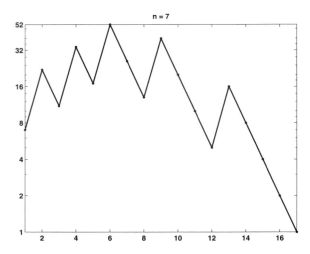

Figure 1.6. `threenplus1`.

The M-file begins with a preamble containing the function header and the `help` information.

```
function threenplus1(n)
% ''Three n plus 1''.
% Study the 3n+1 sequence.
% threenplus1(n) plots the sequence starting with n.
% threenplus1 with no arguments starts with n = 1.
% uicontrols decrement or increment the starting n.
% Is it possible for this to run forever?
```

The next section of code brings the current graphics window forward and resets it. Two push buttons, which are the default `uicontrols`, are positioned near the bottom center of the figure at pixel coordinates `[260,5]` and `[300,5]`. Their size is 25 by 22 pixels and they are labeled with `'<'` and `'>'`. If either button is subsequently pushed, the `'callback'` string is executed, calling the function recursively with a corresponding `'-1'` or `'+1'` string argument. The `'tag'` property of the current figure, `gcf`, is set to a characteristic string that prevents this section of code from being reexecuted on subsequent calls.

```
if ~isequal(get(gcf,'tag'),'3n+1')
   shg
   clf reset
   uicontrol( ...
       'position',[260 5 25 22], ...
       'string','<', ...
       'callback','threenplus1(''-1'')');
   uicontrol( ...
       'position',[300 5 25 22], ...
       'string','>', ...
```

```
        'callback','threeplus1('' +1'')');
      set(gcf,'tag','3n+1');
   end
```

The next section of code sets n. If nargin, the number of input arguments, is 0, then n is set to 1. If the input argument is either of the strings from the push button callbacks, then n is retrieved from the 'userdata' field of the figure and decremented or incremented. If the input argument is not a string, then it is the desired n. In all situations, n is saved in 'userdata' for use on subsequent calls.

```
if nargin == 0
   n = 1;
elseif isequal(n,'-1')
   n = get(gcf,'userdata') - 1;
elseif isequal(n,'+1')
   n = get(gcf,'userdata') + 1;
end
if n < 1, n = 1; end
set(gcf,'userdata',n)
```

We've seen the next section of code before; it does the actual computation.

```
y = n;
while n > 1
   if rem(n,2)==0
      n = n/2;
   else
      n = 3*n+1;
   end
   y = [y n];
end
```

The final section of code plots the generated sequence with dots connected by straight lines, using a logarithmic vertical scale and customized tick labels.

```
semilogy(y,'.-')
axis tight
ymax = max(y);
ytick = [2.^(0:ceil(log2(ymax))-1) ymax];
if length(ytick) > 8, ytick(end-1) = []; end
set(gca,'ytick',ytick)
title(['n = ' num2str(y(1))]);
```

1.7 Floating-Point Arithmetic

Some people believe that

- numerical analysis is the study of floating-point arithmetic;

- floating-point arithmetic is unpredictable and hard to understand.

We intend to convince you that both of these assertions are false. Very little of this book is actually about floating-point arithmetic. But when the subject does arise, we hope you will find floating-point arithmetic is not only computationally powerful, but also mathematically elegant.

If you look carefully at the definitions of fundamental arithmetic operations like addition and multiplication, you soon encounter the mathematical abstraction known as real numbers. But actual computation with real numbers is not very practical because it involves limits and infinities. Instead, MATLAB and most other technical computing environments use floating-point arithmetic, which involves a finite set of numbers with finite precision. This leads to the phenomena of *roundoff*, *underflow*, and *overflow*. Most of the time, it is possible to use MATLAB effectively without worrying about these details, but, every once in a while, it pays to know something about the properties and limitations of floating-point numbers.

Twenty years ago, the situation was far more complicated than it is today. Each computer had its own floating-point number system. Some were binary; some were decimal. There was even a Russian computer that used trinary arithmetic. Among the binary computers, some used 2 as the base; others used 8 or 16. And everybody had a different precision. In 1985, the IEEE Standards Board and the American National Standards Institute adopted the ANSI/IEEE Standard 754-1985 for Binary Floating-Point Arithmetic. This was the culmination of almost a decade of work by a 92-person working group of mathematicians, computer scientists, and engineers from universities, computer manufacturers, and microprocessor companies.

All computers designed since 1985 use IEEE floating-point arithmetic. This doesn't mean that they all get exactly the same results, because there is some flexibility within the standard. But it does mean that we now have a machine-independent model of how floating-point arithmetic behaves.

MATLAB has traditionally used the IEEE double-precision format. There is a single-precision format that saves space, but that isn't much faster on modern machines. MATLAB 7 will have support for single-precision arithmetic, but we will deal exclusively with double precision in this book. There is also an extended-precision format, which is optional and therefore is one of the reasons for lack of uniformity among different machines.

Most nonzero floating-point numbers are normalized. This means they can be expressed as

$$x = \pm(1 + f) \cdot 2^e.$$

The quantity f is the fraction or mantissa and e is the exponent. The fraction satisfies

$$0 \leq f < 1$$

and must be representable in binary using at most 52 bits. In other words, $2^{52} f$ is an integer in the interval

$$0 \leq 2^{52} f < 2^{52}.$$

The exponent e is an integer in the interval

$$-1022 \leq e \leq 1023.$$

The finiteness of f is a limitation on *precision*. The finiteness of e is a limitation on *range*. Any numbers that don't meet these limitations must be approximated by ones that do.

Double-precision floating-point numbers are stored in a 64-bit word, with 52 bits for f, 11 bits for e, and 1 bit for the sign of the number. The sign of e is accommodated by storing $e + 1023$, which is between 1 and $2^{11} - 2$. The 2 extreme values for the exponent field, 0 and $2^{11} - 1$, are reserved for exceptional floating-point numbers that we will describe later.

The entire fractional part of a floating-point number is not f, but $1 + f$, which has 53 bits. However, the leading 1 doesn't need to be stored. In effect, the IEEE format packs 65 bits of information into a 64-bit word.

The program `floatgui` shows the distribution of the positive numbers in a model floating-point system with variable parameters. The parameter t specifies the number of bits used to store f. In other words, $2^t f$ is an integer. The parameters e_{min} and e_{max} specify the range of the exponent, so $e_{min} \le e \le e_{max}$. Initially, `floatgui` sets $t = 3$, $e_{min} = -4$, and $e_{max} = 3$ and produces the distribution shown in Figure 1.7.

Figure 1.7. `floatgui`.

Within each binary interval $2^e \le x \le 2^{e+1}$, the numbers are equally spaced with an increment of 2^{e-t}. If $e = 0$ and $t = 3$, for example, the spacing of the numbers between 1 and 2 is $1/8$. As e increases, the spacing increases.

It is also instructive to display the floating-point numbers with a logarithmic scale. Figure 1.8 shows `floatgui` with `logscale` checked and $t = 5$, $e_{min} = -4$, and $e_{max} = 3$. With this logarithmic scale, it is more apparent that the distribution in each binary interval is the same.

A very important quantity associated with floating-point arithmetic is highlighted in red by `floatgui`. MATLAB calls this quantity eps, which is short for *machine epsilon*.

eps *is the distance from* 1 *to the next larger floating-point number.*

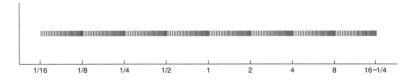

Figure 1.8. `floatgui(logscale)`.

For the `floatgui` model floating-point system, eps = `2^(-t)`.

Before the IEEE standard, different machines had different values of eps. Now, for IEEE double-precision,

eps = `2^(-52)`.

The approximate decimal value of eps is $2.2204 \cdot 10^{-16}$. Either eps $/2$ or eps can be called the roundoff level. The maximum relative error incurred when the result of an arithmetic operation is rounded to the nearest floating-point number is eps $/2$. The maximum relative spacing between numbers is eps. In either case, you can say that the roundoff level is about 16 decimal digits.

A frequent instance of roundoff occurs with the simple MATLAB statement

```
t = 0.1
```

The mathematical value t stored in t is not exactly 0.1 because expressing the decimal fraction $1/10$ in binary requires an infinite series. In fact,

$$\frac{1}{10} = \frac{1}{2^4} + \frac{1}{2^5} + \frac{0}{2^6} + \frac{0}{2^7} + \frac{1}{2^8} + \frac{1}{2^9} + \frac{0}{2^{10}} + \frac{0}{2^{11}} + \frac{1}{2^{12}} + \cdots.$$

After the first term, the sequence of coefficients 1, 0, 0, 1 is repeated infinitely often. Grouping the resulting terms together four at a time expresses $1/10$ in a base 16, or *hexadecimal*, series.

$$\frac{1}{10} = 2^{-4} \cdot \left(1 + \frac{9}{16} + \frac{9}{16^2} + \frac{9}{16^3} + \frac{9}{16^4} + \cdots\right)$$

Floating-point numbers on either side of $1/10$ are obtained by terminating the fractional part of this series after 52 binary terms, or 13 hexadecimal terms, and rounding the last term up or down. Thus

$$t_1 < 1/10 < t_2,$$

where

$$t_1 = 2^{-4} \cdot \left(1 + \frac{9}{16} + \frac{9}{16^2} + \frac{9}{16^3} + \cdots + \frac{9}{16^{12}} + \frac{9}{16^{13}}\right),$$

$$t_2 = 2^{-4} \cdot \left(1 + \frac{9}{16} + \frac{9}{16^2} + \frac{9}{16^3} + \cdots + \frac{9}{16^{12}} + \frac{10}{16^{13}}\right).$$

It turns out that $1/10$ is closer to t_2 than to t_1, so t is equal to t_2. In other words,

$$t = (1 + f) \cdot 2^e,$$

where

$$f = \frac{9}{16} + \frac{9}{16^2} + \frac{9}{16^3} + \cdots + \frac{9}{16^{12}} + \frac{10}{16^{13}},$$
$$e = -4.$$

The MATLAB command

```
format hex
```

causes t to be displayed as

```
3fb999999999999a
```

The characters a through f represent the hexadecimal "digits" 10 through 15. The first three characters, 3 fb, give the hexadecimal representation of decimal 1019, which is the value of the biased exponent $e + 1023$ if e is -4. The other 13 characters are the hexadecimal representation of the fraction f.

In summary, the value stored in t is very close to, but not exactly equal to, 0.1. The distinction is occasionally important. For example, the quantity

```
0.3/0.1
```

is not exactly equal to 3 because the actual numerator is a little less than 0.3 and the actual denominator is a little greater than 0.1.

Ten steps of length t are not precisely the same as one step of length 1. MATLAB is careful to arrange that the last element of the vector

```
0:0.1:1
```

is exactly equal to 1, but if you form this vector yourself by repeated additions of 0.1, you will miss hitting the final 1 exactly.

What does the floating-point approximation to the golden ratio look like?

```
format hex
phi = (1 + sqrt(5))/2
```

produces

```
phi =
    3ff9e3779b97f4a8
```

The first hex digit, 3, is 0011 in binary. The first bit is the sign of the floating-point number; 0 is positive, 1 is negative. So phi is positive. The remaining bits of the first three hex digits contain $e + 1023$. In this example, 3 ff in base 16 is $3 \cdot 16^2 + 15 \cdot 16 + 15 = 1023$ in decimal. So

$$e = 0.$$

In fact, any floating-point number between 1.0 and 2.0 has $e = 0$, so its hex output begins with 3ff. The other 13 hex digits contain f. In this example,

$$f = \frac{9}{16} + \frac{14}{16^2} + \frac{3}{16^3} + \cdots + \frac{10}{16^{12}} + \frac{8}{16^{13}}.$$

With these values of f and e,

$$(1 + f)2^e \approx \phi.$$

Another example is provided by the following code segment.

```
format long
a = 4/3
b = a - 1
c = 3*b
e = 1 - c
```

With exact computation, e would be 0. But with floating-point, the output produced is

```
a =
   1.33333333333333
b =
   0.33333333333333
c =
   1.00000000000000
e =
   2.220446049250313e-016
```

It turns out that the only roundoff occurs in the division in the first statement. The quotient cannot be exactly 4/3, except on that Russian trinary computer. Consequently the value stored in a is close to, but not exactly equal to, 4/3. The subtraction b = a - 1 produces a b whose last bit is 0. This means that the multiplication 3*b can be done without any roundoff. The value stored in c is not exactly equal to 1, and so the value stored in e is not 0. Before the IEEE standard, this code was used as a quick way to estimate the roundoff level on various computers.

The roundoff level eps is sometimes called "floating-point zero," but that's a misnomer. There are many floating-point numbers much smaller than eps. The smallest positive normalized floating-point number has $f = 0$ and $e = -1022$. The largest floating-point number has f a little less than 1 and $e = 1023$. MATLAB calls these numbers realmin and realmax. Together with eps, they characterize the standard system.

	Binary	Decimal
eps	2^(-52)	2.2204e-16
realmin	2^(-1022)	2.2251e-308
realmax	(2-eps)*2^1023	1.7977e+308

If any computation tries to produce a value larger than realmax, it is said to *overflow*. The result is an exceptional floating-point value called *infinity* or Inf. It is represented by taking $e = 1024$ and $f = 0$ and satisfies relations like 1/Inf = 0 and Inf+Inf = Inf.

If any computation tries to produce a value that is undefined even in the real number system, the result is an exceptional value known as Not-a-Number, or NaN. Examples include 0/0 and Inf-Inf. NaN is represented by taking $e = 1024$ and f nonzero.

If any computation tries to produce a value smaller than realmin, it is said to *underflow*. This involves one of the optional, and controversial, aspects of the IEEE standard. Many, but not all, machines allow exceptional denormal or subnormal floating-point numbers in the interval between realmin and eps*realmin. The smallest positive subnormal number is about 0.494e-323. Any results smaller than this are set to 0. On machines without subnormals, any results less than realmin are set to 0. The subnormal numbers fill in the gap you can see in the floatgui model system between 0 and the smallest positive number. They do provide an elegant way to handle underflow, but their practical importance for MATLAB-style computation is very rare. Denormal numbers are represented by taking $e = -1023$, so the biased exponent $e + 1023$ is 0.

MATLAB uses the floating-point system to handle integers. Mathematically, the numbers 3 and 3.0 are the same, but many programming languages would use different representations for the two. MATLAB does not distinguish between them. We sometimes use the term *flint* to describe a floating-point number whose value is an integer. Floating-point operations on flints do not introduce any roundoff error, as long as the results are not too large. Addition, subtraction, and multiplication of flints produce the exact flint result if it is not larger than 2^{53}. Division and square root involving flints also produce a flint if the result is an integer. For example, sqrt(363/3) produces 11, with no roundoff.

Two MATLAB functions that take apart and put together floating-point numbers are log2 and pow2.

```
help log2
help pow2
```

produces

```
[F,E] = LOG2(X) for a real array X, returns an array F
of real numbers, usually in the range 0.5 <= abs(F) < 1,
and an array E of integers, so that X = F .* 2.^E.
Any zeros in X produce F = 0 and E = 0.

X = POW2(F,E) for a real array F and an integer array E
computes X = F .* (2 .^ E).  The result is computed quickly
by simply adding E to the floating-point exponent of F.
```

The quantities F and E used by log2 and pow2 predate the IEEE floating-point standard and so are slightly different from the f and e we are using in this section. In fact, f = 2*F-1 and e = E-1.

```
[F,E] = log2(phi)
```

produces

```
F =
    0.80901699437495
E =
       1
```

Then

```
phi = pow2(F,E)
```

gives back

```
phi =
    1.61803398874989
```

As an example of how roundoff error affects matrix computations, consider the 2-by-2 set of linear equations

$$17x_1 + 5x_2 = 22,$$
$$1.7x_1 + 0.5x_2 = 2.2.$$

The obvious solution is $x_1 = 1, x_2 = 1$. But the MATLAB statements

```
A = [17 5; 1.7 0.5]
b = [22; 2.2]
x = A\b
```

produce

```
x =
   -1.0588
    8.0000
```

Where did this come from? Well, the equations are singular, but consistent. The second equation is just 0.1 times the first. The computed x is one of infinitely many possible solutions. But the floating-point representation of the matrix A is not exactly singular because A(2,1) is not exactly 17/10.

The solution process subtracts a multiple of the first equation from the second. The multiplier is mu = 1.7/17, which turns out to be the floating-point number obtained by truncating, rather than rounding, the binary expansion of 1/10. The matrix A and the right-hand side b are modified by

```
A(2,:) = A(2,:) - mu*A(1,:)
b(2)   = b(2)   - mu*b(1)
```

With exact computation, both A(2,2) and b(2) would become zero, but with floating-point arithmetic, they both become nonzero multiples of eps.

```
A(2,2)  = (1/4)*eps
        = 5.5511e-17
  b(2)  = 2*eps
        = 4.4408e-16
```

MATLAB notices the tiny value of the new A(2,2) and displays a message warning that the matrix is close to singular. It then computes the solution of the modified second equation by dividing one roundoff error by another.

```
x(2)  = b(2)/A(2,2)
      = 8
```

This value is substituted back into the first equation to give

```
x(1)  = (22 - 5*x(2))/17
      = -1.0588
```

The details of the roundoff error lead MATLAB to pick out one particular solution from among the infinitely many possible solutions to the singular system.

Our final example plots a seventh-degree polynomial.

```
x = 0.988:.0001:1.012;
y = x.^7-7*x.^6+21*x.^5-35*x.^4+35*x.^3-21*x.^2+7*x-1;
plot(x,y)
```

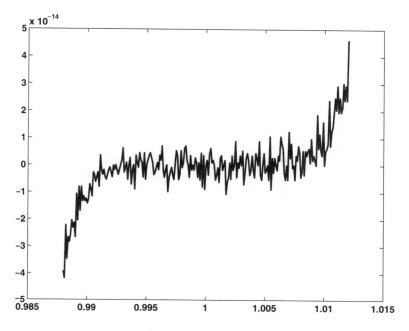

Figure 1.9. *Is this a polynomial?*

The resulting plot in Figure 1.9 doesn't look anything like a polynomial. It isn't smooth. You are seeing roundoff error in action. The y-axis scale factor is tiny, 10^{-14}. The tiny values of y are being computed by taking sums and differences of numbers as large as $35 \cdot 1.012^4$. There is severe subtractive cancellation. The example was contrived by using the Symbolic Toolbox to expand $(x-1)^7$ and carefully choosing the range for the x-axis to be near $x = 1$. If the values of y are computed instead by

```
y = (x-1).^7;
```

then a smooth (but very flat) plot results.

1.8 Further Reading

Additional information about floating-point arithmetic and roundoff error can be found in Higham [33] and Overton [49].

Exercises

1.1. Which of these familiar rectangles is closest to a golden rectangle? Use MATLAB to do the calculations with an element-by-element vector division, `w./h`.

    • 3-by-5 inch index card,

- 8.5-by-11 inch U.S. letter paper,
- 8.5-by-14 inch U.S. legal paper,
- 9-by-12 foot rug,
- 9:16 "letterbox" TV picture,
- 768-by-1024 pixel computer monitor.

1.2. ISO standard A4 paper is commonly used throughout most of the world, except in the United States and Canada. Its dimensions are 210 by 297 mm. This is not a golden rectangle, but the aspect ratio is close to another familiar irrational mathematical quantity. What is that quantity? If you fold a piece of A4 paper in half, what is the aspect ratio of each of the halves? Modify the M-file `goldrect.m` to illustrate this property.

1.3. How many terms in the truncated continued fraction does it take to approximate ϕ with an error less than 10^{-10}? As the number of terms increases beyond this roundoff, error eventually intervenes. What is the best accuracy you can hope to achieve with double-precision floating-point arithmetic and how many terms does it take?

1.4. Use the MATLAB *backslash* operator to solve the 2-by-2 system of simultaneous linear equations

$$c_1 + c_2 = 1,$$
$$c_1\phi + c_2(1 - \phi) = 1$$

for c_1 and c_2. You can find out about the backslash operator by taking a peek at the next chapter of this book, or with the commands

```
help \
help slash
```

1.5. The statement

```
semilogy(fibonacci(18),'-o')
```

makes a logarithmic plot of Fibonacci numbers versus their index. The graph is close to a straight line. What is the slope of this line?

1.6. How does the execution time of `fibnum(n)` depend on the execution time for `fibnum(n-1)` and `fibnum(n-2)`? Use this relationship to obtain an approximate formula for the execution time of `fibnum(n)` as a function of n. Estimate how long it would take your computer to compute `fibnum(50)`. Warning: You probably do not want to actually run `fibnum(50)`.

1.7. What is the index of the largest Fibonacci number that can be represented *exactly* as a MATLAB double-precision quantity without roundoff error? What is the index of the largest Fibonacci number that can be represented *approximately* as a MATLAB double-precision quantity without overflowing?

1.8. Enter the statements

```
A = [1 1; 1 0]
X = [1 0; 0 1]
```

Then enter the statement

```
X = A*X
```

Now repeatedly press the up arrow key, followed by the Enter key. What happens? Do you recognize the matrix elements being generated? How many times would you have to repeat this iteration before X overflows?

1.9. Change the fern color scheme to use pink on a black background. Don't forget the stop button.

1.10. (a) What happens if you resize the figure window while the fern is being generated? Why?

(b) The M-file `finitefern.m` can be used to produce printed output of the fern. Explain why printing is possible with `finitefern.m` but not with `fern.m`.

1.11. Flip the fern by interchanging its x- and y-coordinates.

1.12. What happens to the fern if you change the only nonzero element in the matrix A4?

1.13. What are the coordinates of the lower end of the fern's stem?

1.14. The coordinates of the point at the upper tip end of the fern can be computed by solving a certain 2-by-2 system of simultaneous linear equations. What is that system and what are the coordinates of the tip?

1.15. The fern algorithm involves repeated random choices from four different formulas for advancing the point. If the kth formula is used repeatedly by itself, without random choices, it defines a deterministic trajectory in the (x, y) plane. Modify `finitefern.m` so that plots of each of these four trajectories are superimposed on the plot of the fern. Start each trajectory at the point $(-1, 5)$. Plot o's connected with straight lines for the steps along each trajectory. Take as many steps as are needed to show each trajectory's limit point. You can superimpose several plots with

```
plot(...)
hold on
plot(...)
plot(...)
hold off
```

1.16. Use the following code to make your own Portable Network Graphics file from the fern. Then compare your image with one obtained from `ncm/fern.png`.

```
bg = [0 0 85];      % Dark blue background
fg = [255 255 255]; % White dots
sz = get(0,'screensize');
rand('state',0)
X = finitefern(500000,sz(4),sz(3));
d = fg - bg;
R = uint8(bg(1) + d(1)*X);
G = uint8(bg(2) + d(2)*X);
B = uint8(bg(3) + d(3)*X);
F = cat(3,R,G,B);
imwrite(F,'myfern.png','png','bitdepth',8)
```

1.17. Modify `fern.m` or `finitefern.m` so that it produces *Sierpinski's triangle*. Start at

$$x = \begin{pmatrix} 0 \\ 0 \end{pmatrix}.$$

At each iterative step, the current point x is replaced with $Ax + b$, where the matrix A is always

$$A = \begin{pmatrix} 1/2 & 0 \\ 0 & 1/2 \end{pmatrix}$$

and the vector b is chosen at random with equal probability from among the three vectors

$$b = \begin{pmatrix} 0 \\ 0 \end{pmatrix}, \quad b = \begin{pmatrix} 1/2 \\ 0 \end{pmatrix}, \quad \text{and} \quad b = \begin{pmatrix} 1/4 \\ \sqrt{3}/4 \end{pmatrix}.$$

1.18. `greetings(phi)` generates a seasonal holiday fractal that depends upon the parameter `phi`. The default value of `phi` is the golden ratio. What happens for other values of `phi`? Try both simple fractions and floating-point approximations to irrational values.

1.19. `A = magic(4)` is singular. Its columns are linearly dependent. What do `null(A)`, `null(A,'r')`, `null(sym(A))`, and `rref(A)` tell you about that dependence?

1.20. Let `A = magic(n)` for `n = 3, 4`, or `5`. What does

```
p = randperm(n); q = randperm(n); A = A(p,q);
```

do to

```
sum(A)
sum(A')'
sum(diag(A))
sum(diag(flipud(A)))
rank(A)
```

1.21. The character `char(7)` is a control character. What does it do?

1.22. What does `char([169 174])` display on your computer?

1.23. What fundamental physical law is hidden in this string?

```
s = '/b_t3{$H~MO6JTQI>v~#3GieW*l(p,nF'
```

1.24. Find the two files `encrypt.m` and `gettysburg.txt`. Use `encrypt` to encrypt `gettysburg.txt`. Then decrypt the result. Use `encrypt` to encrypt itself.

1.25. With the NCM directory on your path, you can read the text of Lincoln's Gettysburg Address with

```
fp = fopen('gettysburg.txt');
G = char(fread(fp))'
fclose(fp);
```

(a) How many characters are in the text?
(b) Use the `unique` function to find the unique characters in the text.

(c) How many blanks are in the text? What punctuation characters, and how many of each, are there?

(d) Remove the blanks and the punctuation and convert the text to all upper- or lowercase. Use the `histc` function to count the number of letters. What is the most frequent letter? What letters are missing?

(e) Use the `bar` function as described in `help histc` to plot a histogram of the letter frequencies.

(f) Use `get(gca,'xtick')` and `get(gca,'xticklabel')` to see how the *x*-axis of the histogram is labeled. Then use

```
set(gca,'xtick',...,'xticklabel',...)
```

to relabel the *x*-axis with the letters in the text.

1.26. If x is the character string consisting of just two blanks,

```
x = '  '
```

then `crypto(x)` is actually equal to x. Why does this happen? Are there any other two-character strings that `crypto` does not change?

1.27. Find another 2-by-2 integer matrix A for which

```
mod(A*A,97)
```

is the identity matrix. Replace the matrix in `crypto.m` with your matrix and verify that the function still works correctly.

1.28. The function `crypto` works with 97 characters instead of 95. It can produce output, and correctly handle input, that contains two characters with ASCII values greater than 127. What are these characters? Why are they necessary? What happens to other characters with ASCII values greater than 127?

1.29. Create a new `crypto` function that works with just 29 characters: the 26 lowercase letters, plus blank, period, and comma. You will need to find a 2-by-2 integer matrix A for which `mod(A*A,29)` is the identity matrix.

1.30. The graph of the $3n + 1$ sequence has a particular characteristic shape if the starting *n* is 5, 10, 20, 40, ..., that is, *n* is five times a power of 2. What is this shape and why does it happen?

1.31. The graphs of the $3n + 1$ sequences starting at $n = 108$, 109, and 110 are very similar to each other. Why?

1.32. Let $L(n)$ be the number of terms in the $3n + 1$ sequence that starts with *n*. Write a MATLAB function that computes $L(n)$ *without* using any vectors or unpredictable amounts of storage. Plot $L(n)$ for $1 \leq n \leq 1000$. What is the maximum value of $L(n)$ for *n* in this range, and for what value of *n* does it occur? Use `threenplus1` to plot the sequence that starts with this particular value of *n*.

1.33. Modify `floatgui.m` by changing its last line from a comment to an executable statement and changing the question mark to a simple expression that counts the number of floating-point numbers in the model system.

1.34. Explain the output produced by

```
t = 0.1
n = 1:10
e = n/10 - n*t
```

1.35. What does each of these programs do? How many lines of output does each program produce? What are the last two values of x printed?

```
x = 1; while 1+x > 1, x = x/2, pause(.02), end

x = 1; while x+x > x, x = 2*x, pause(.02), end

x = 1; while x+x > x, x = x/2, pause(.02), end
```

1.36. Which familiar real numbers are approximated by floating-point numbers that display the following values with format hex?

```
4059000000000000
3f847ae147ae147b
3fe921fb54442d18
```

1.37. Let $\mathcal{F}$ be the set of all IEEE double-precision floating-point numbers, except NaNs and Infs, which have biased exponent 7ff (hex), and denormals, which have biased exponent 000 (hex).
(a) How many elements are there in $\mathcal{F}$?
(b) What fraction of the elements of $\mathcal{F}$ are in the interval $1 \leq x < 2$?
(c) What fraction of the elements of $\mathcal{F}$ are in the interval $1/64 \leq x < 1/32$?
(d) Determine by random sampling approximately what fraction of the elements x of $\mathcal{F}$ satisfy the MATLAB logical relation

```
x*(1/x) == 1
```

1.38. The classic quadratic formula says that the two roots of the quadratic equation

$$ax^2 + bx + c = 0$$

are

$$x_1, x_2 = \frac{-b \pm \sqrt{b^2 - 4ac}}{2a}.$$

Use this formula in MATLAB to compute both roots for

$$a = 1, \quad b = -100000000, \quad c = 1.$$

Compare your computed results with

```
roots([a b c])
```

What happens if you try to compute the roots by hand or with a hand calculator? You should find that the classic formula is good for computing one root, but not the other. So use it to compute one root accurately and then use the fact that

$$x_1 x_2 = \frac{c}{a}$$

to compute the other.

1.39. The power series for $\sin x$ is

$$\sin x = x - \frac{x^3}{3!} + \frac{x^5}{5!} - \frac{x^7}{7!} + \cdots.$$

This MATLAB function uses the series to compute $\sin x$.

```
function s = powersin(x)
% POWERSIN.  Power series for sin(x).
% POWERSIN(x) tries to compute sin(x)
% from a power series
s = 0;
t = x;
n = 1;
while s+t ~= s;
   s = s + t;
   t = -x.^2/((n+1)*(n+2)).*t;
   n = n + 2;
end
```

What causes the `while` loop to terminate?
Answer the following questions for $x = \pi/2$, $11\pi/2$, $21\pi/2$, and $31\pi/2$:

How accurate is the computed result?

How many terms are required?

What is the largest term in the series?

What do you conclude about the use of floating-point arithmetic and power series to evaluate functions?

1.40. *Steganography* is the technique of hiding messages or other images in the low-order bits of the data for an image. The MATLAB image function has a hidden image that contains other hidden images. To see the top-level image, just execute the single command

```
image
```

Then, to improve its appearance,

```
colormap(gray(32))
truesize
axis ij
axis image
axis off
```

But that's just the beginning. The NCM program `stegano` helps you continue the investigation.

(a) How many images are hidden in the `cdata` for the default image?

(b) What does this have to do with the structure of floating-point numbers?

1.41. *Prime spirals.* A Ulam prime spiral is a plot of the location of the prime numbers using a numbering scheme that spirals outward from the center of a grid. Our NCM file `primespiral(n,c)` generates an *n*-by-*n* prime spiral starting with the number *c* in the center. The default is $c = 1$. Figure 1.10 is `primespiral(7)` and Figure 1.11 is `primespiral(250)`.

43	44	45	46	**47**	48	49
42	21	22	**23**	24	25	26
41	20	**7**	8	9	10	27
40	**19**	6	1	**2**	**11**	28
39	18	**5**	4	**3**	12	**29**
38	**17**	16	15	14	**13**	30
37	36	35	34	33	32	**31**

Figure 1.10. `primespiral(7)`.

The concentration of primes on some diagonal segments is remarkable, and not completely understood. The value of the element at position (i, j) is a piecewise quadratic function of i and j, so each diagonal segment represents a mini-theorem about the distribution of primes. The phenomenon was discovered by Stanislaw Ulam in 1963 and appeared on the cover of *Scientific American* in 1964. There are a number of interesting Web pages devoted to prime spirals. Start with [52] and [66].

(a) The MATLAB demos directory contains an M-file `spiral.m`. The integers from 1 to n^2 are arranged in a spiral pattern, starting in the center of the matrix. The code in `demos/spiral.m` is not very elegant. Here is a better version.

```
function S = spiral(n)
%SPIRAL SPIRAL(n) is an n-by-n matrix with elements
%   1:n^2 arranged in a rectangular spiral pattern.
S = [];
for m = 1:n
    S = rot90(S,2);
    S(m,m) = 0;
    p = ???
    v = (m-1:-1:0);
    S(:,m) = p-v';
    S(m,:) = p+v;
```

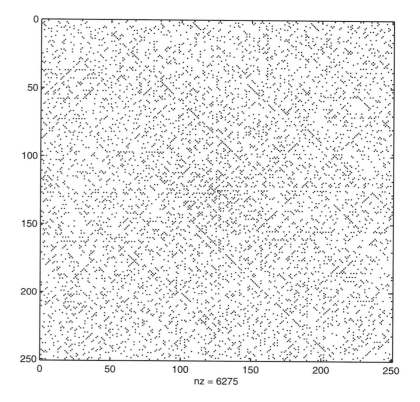

Figure 1.11. `primespiral(250)`.

```
    end
if mod(n,2)==1
    S = rot90(S,2);
end
```

What value should be assigned to p each time through the loop so that this function generates the same matrices as `spiral.m` in the `demos` directory?

(b) Why do half of the diagonals of `spiral(n)` contain no primes?

(c) Let `S = spiral(2*n)` and let `r1` and `r2` be rows that go nearly halfway across the middle of the matrix:

```
    r1 = S(n+1,1:n-2)
    r2 = S(n-1,n+2:end)
```

Why do these rows contain no primes?

(d) There is something particularly remarkable about

```
    primespiral(17,17)
    primespiral(41,41)
```

What is it?

(e) Find values of n and c, both less than 50, and not equal to 17 or 41, so that

    [S,P] = primespiral(n,c)

contains a diagonal segment with 8 or more primes.

1.42. *Triangular numbers* are integers of the form $n(n + 1)/2$. The term comes from the fact that a triangular grid with n points on a side has a total of $n(n+1)/2$ points. Write a function trinums (m) that generates all the triangular numbers less than or equal to m. Modify primespiral to use your trinums and become trinumspiral.

1.43. Here is a puzzle that does not have much to do with this chapter, but you might find it interesting nevertheless. What familiar property of the integers is represented by the following plot?

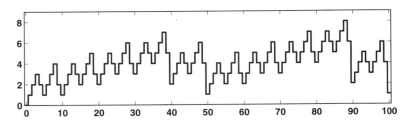

1.44. In the Gregorian calendar, a year y is a *leap year* if and only if

$$(\text{mod}(y,4) \ == \ 0) \ \& \ (\text{mod}(y,100) \ \text{\textasciitilde}= \ 0) \ | \ (\text{mod}(y,400) \ == \ 0)$$

Thus 2000 was a leap year, but 2100 will not be a leap year. This rule implies that the Gregorian calendar repeats itself every 400 years. In that 400-year period, there are 97 leap years, 4800 months, 20871 weeks, and 146097 days. The MATLAB functions datenum, datevec, datestr, and weekday use these facts to facilitate computations involving calendar dates. For example, either of the statements

    [d,w] = weekday('Aug. 17, 2003')

and

    [d,w] = weekday(datenum([2003 8 17]))

tells me that my birthday was on a Sunday in 2003.

Use MATLAB to answer the following questions.

(a) On which day of the week were you born?

(b) In a 400-year Gregorian calendar cycle, which weekday is the most likely for your birthday?

(c) What is the probability that the 13th of any month falls on a Friday? The answer is close to, but not exactly equal to, 1/7.

1.45. *Biorhythms* were very popular in the 1960s. You can still find many Web sites today that offer to prepare personalized biorhythms, or that sell software to compute them. Biorhythms are based on the notion that three sinusoidal cycles influence our lives. The physical cycle has a period of 23 days, the emotional cycle has a period of 28 days, and the intellectual cycle has a period of 33 days. For any individual, the cycles are initialized at birth. Figure 1.12 is my biorhythm, which begins on August 17, 1939, plotted for an eight-week period centered around the date this is being written, October 19, 2003. It shows that my intellectual power reached a peak yesterday, that my physical strength and emotional wellbeing will reach their peaks within 6 h of each other on the same day next week, and that all three cycles will be at their low point within a few days of each other early in November.

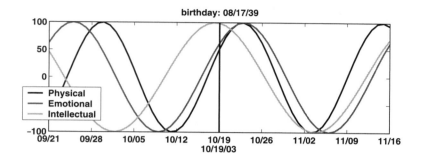

Figure 1.12. *My biorhythm.*

The date and graphics functions in MATLAB make the computation and display of biorhythms particularly convenient. Dates are represented by their *date number*, which is the number of days since the zeroth day of a theoretical calendar year zero. The function datenum returns the date number for any given date and time. For example, datenum('Oct. 19, 2003') is 731873. The expression fix(now) returns the date number of the current date.

The following code segment is part of a program that plots a biorhythm for an eight-week period centered on the current date.

```
t0 = datenum(mybirthday);
t1 = fix(now);
t = (t1-28):1:(t1+28);
y = 100*[sin(2*pi*(t-t0)/23)
         sin(2*pi*(t-t0)/28)
         sin(2*pi*(t-t0)/33)];
plot(t,y)
```

(a) Complete this program, using your own birthday, and the line, datetick, title, datestr, and legend functions. Your program should produce something like Figure 1.12.

(b) All three cycles started at zero when you were born. How long does it take until all three simultaneously return to that initial condition? How old were you, or will you be, on that date? Plot your biorhythm near that date. You should find the lcm function helpful.

(c) Is it possible for all three cycles to reach their maximum or minimum at exactly the same time?

Chapter 2

Linear Equations

One of the problems encountered most frequently in scientific computation is the solution of systems of simultaneous linear equations. This chapter covers the solution of linear systems by Gaussian elimination and the sensitivity of the solution to errors in the data and roundoff errors in the computation.

2.1 Solving Linear Systems

With matrix notation, a system of simultaneous linear equations is written

$$Ax = b.$$

In the most frequent case, when there are as many equations as unknowns, A is a given square matrix of order n, b is a given column vector of n components, and x is an unknown column vector of n components.

Students of linear algebra learn that the solution to $Ax = b$ can be written $x = A^{-1}b$, where A^{-1} is the inverse of A. However, in the vast majority of practical computational problems, it is unnecessary and inadvisable to actually compute A^{-1}. As an extreme but illustrative example, consider a system consisting of just one equation, such as

$$7x = 21.$$

The best way to solve such a system is by division:

$$x = \frac{21}{7} = 3.$$

Use of the matrix inverse would lead to

$$x = 7^{-1} \times 21 = 0.142857 \times 21 = 2.99997.$$

The inverse requires more arithmetic—a division and a multiplication instead of just a division—and produces a less accurate answer. Similar considerations apply to systems of more than one equation. This is even true in the common situation where there are several systems of equations with the same matrix A but different right-hand sides b. Consequently, we shall concentrate on the direct solution of systems of equations rather than the computation of the inverse.

2.2   The MATLAB Backslash Operator

To emphasize the distinction between solving linear equations and computing inverses, MATLAB has introduced nonstandard notation using *backward slash* and *forward slash* operators, "\" and "/".

If A is a matrix of any size and shape and B is a matrix with as many rows as A, then the solution to the system of simultaneous equations

$$AX = B$$

is denoted by

$$X = A \backslash B.$$

Think of this as dividing both sides of the equation by the coefficient matrix A. Because matrix multiplication is not commutative and A occurs on the left in the original equation, this is *left division*.

Similarly, the solution to a system with A on the right and B with as many columns as A,

$$XA = B,$$

is obtained by *right division*,

$$X = B/A.$$

This notation applies even if A is not square, so that the number of equations is not the same as the number of unknowns. However, in this chapter, we limit ourselves to systems with square coefficient matrices.

2.3   A 3-by-3 Example

To illustrate the general linear equation solution algorithm, consider an example of order three:

$$\begin{pmatrix} 10 & -7 & 0 \\ -3 & 2 & 6 \\ 5 & -1 & 5 \end{pmatrix} \begin{pmatrix} x_1 \\ x_2 \\ x_3 \end{pmatrix} = \begin{pmatrix} 7 \\ 4 \\ 6 \end{pmatrix}.$$

This, of course, represents the three simultaneous equations

$$10x_1 - 7x_2 = 7,$$
$$-3x_1 + 2x_2 + 6x_3 = 4,$$
$$5x_1 - x_2 + 5x_3 = 6.$$

The first step of the solution algorithm uses the first equation to eliminate x_1 from the other equations. This is accomplished by adding 0.3 times the first equation to the second equation and subtracting 0.5 times the first equation from the third equation. The coefficient 10 of x_1 in the first equation is called the first *pivot* and the quantities -0.3 and 0.5, obtained by dividing the coefficients of x_1 in the other equations by the pivot, are called the *multipliers*. The first step changes the equations to

$$\begin{pmatrix} 10 & -7 & 0 \\ 0 & -0.1 & 6 \\ 0 & 2.5 & 5 \end{pmatrix} \begin{pmatrix} x_1 \\ x_2 \\ x_3 \end{pmatrix} = \begin{pmatrix} 7 \\ 6.1 \\ 2.5 \end{pmatrix}.$$

The second step might use the second equation to eliminate x_2 from the third equation. However, the second pivot, which is the coefficient of x_2 in the second equation, would be -0.1, which is smaller than the other coefficients. Consequently, the last two equations are interchanged. This is called *pivoting*. It is not actually necessary in this example because there are no roundoff errors, but it is crucial in general:

$$\begin{pmatrix} 10 & -7 & 0 \\ 0 & 2.5 & 5 \\ 0 & -0.1 & 6 \end{pmatrix} \begin{pmatrix} x_1 \\ x_2 \\ x_3 \end{pmatrix} = \begin{pmatrix} 7 \\ 2.5 \\ 6.1 \end{pmatrix}.$$

Now the second pivot is 2.5 and the second equation can be used to eliminate x_2 from the third equation. This is accomplished by adding 0.04 times the second equation to the third equation. (What would the multiplier have been if the equations had not been interchanged?)

$$\begin{pmatrix} 10 & -7 & 0 \\ 0 & 2.5 & 5 \\ 0 & 0 & 6.2 \end{pmatrix} \begin{pmatrix} x_1 \\ x_2 \\ x_3 \end{pmatrix} = \begin{pmatrix} 7 \\ 2.5 \\ 6.2 \end{pmatrix}.$$

The last equation is now

$$6.2x_3 = 6.2.$$

This can be solved to give $x_3 = 1$. This value is substituted into the second equation:

$$2.5x_2 + (5)(1) = 2.5.$$

Hence $x_2 = -1$. Finally, the values of x_2 and x_3 are substituted into the first equation:

$$10x_1 + (-7)(-1) = 7.$$

Hence $x_1 = 0$. The solution is

$$x = \begin{pmatrix} 0 \\ -1 \\ 1 \end{pmatrix}.$$

This solution can be easily checked using the original equations:

$$\begin{pmatrix} 10 & -7 & 0 \\ -3 & 2 & 6 \\ 5 & -1 & 5 \end{pmatrix} \begin{pmatrix} 0 \\ -1 \\ 1 \end{pmatrix} = \begin{pmatrix} 7 \\ 4 \\ 6 \end{pmatrix}.$$

The entire algorithm can be compactly expressed in matrix notation. For this example, let

$$L = \begin{pmatrix} 1 & 0 & 0 \\ 0.5 & 1 & 0 \\ -0.3 & -0.04 & 1 \end{pmatrix}, \ U = \begin{pmatrix} 10 & -7 & 0 \\ 0 & 2.5 & 5 \\ 0 & 0 & 6.2 \end{pmatrix}, \ P = \begin{pmatrix} 1 & 0 & 0 \\ 0 & 0 & 1 \\ 0 & 1 & 0 \end{pmatrix}.$$

The matrix L contains the multipliers used during the elimination, the matrix U is the final coefficient matrix, and the matrix P describes the pivoting. With these three matrices, we have

$$LU = PA.$$

In other words, the original coefficient matrix can be expressed in terms of products involving matrices with simpler structure.

2.4   Permutation and Triangular Matrices

A *permutation matrix* is an identity matrix with the rows and columns interchanged. It has exactly one 1 in each row and column; all the other elements are 0. For example,

$$P = \begin{pmatrix} 0 & 0 & 0 & 1 \\ 1 & 0 & 0 & 0 \\ 0 & 0 & 1 & 0 \\ 0 & 1 & 0 & 0 \end{pmatrix}.$$

Multiplying a matrix A on the left by a permutation matrix to give PA permutes the rows of A. Multiplying on the right, AP, permutes the columns of A.

MATLAB can also use a *permutation vector* as a row or column index to rearrange the rows or columns of a matrix. Continuing with the P above, let p be the vector

```
p = [4 1 3 2]
```

Then P*A and A(p,:) are equal. The resulting matrix has the fourth row of A as its first row, the first row of A as its second row, and so on. Similarly, A*P and A(:,p) both produce the same permutation of the columns of A. The P*A notation is closer to traditional mathematics, PA, while the A(p,:) notation is faster and uses less memory.

Linear equations involving permutation matrices are trivial to solve. The solution to

$$Px = b$$

is simply a rearrangement of the components of b:

$$x = P^T b.$$

An *upper triangular* matrix has all its nonzero elements above or on the main diagonal. A *unit lower triangular* matrix has ones on the main diagonal and all the rest of its nonzero elements below the main diagonal. For example,

$$U = \begin{pmatrix} 1 & 2 & 3 & 4 \\ 0 & 5 & 6 & 7 \\ 0 & 0 & 8 & 9 \\ 0 & 0 & 0 & 10 \end{pmatrix}$$

is upper triangular, and

$$L = \begin{pmatrix} 1 & 0 & 0 & 0 \\ 2 & 1 & 0 & 0 \\ 3 & 5 & 1 & 0 \\ 4 & 6 & 7 & 1 \end{pmatrix}$$

is unit lower triangular.

Linear equations involving triangular matrices are also easily solved. There are two variants of the algorithm for solving an n-by-n upper triangular system $Ux = b$. Both begin by solving the last equation for the last variable, then the next-to-last equation for the next-to-last variable, and so on. One subtracts multiples of the columns of U from b.

```
x = zeros(n,1);
for k = n:-1:1
    x(k)  = b(k)/U(k,k);
    i  = (1:k-1)';
    b(i)  = b(i) - x(k)*U(i,k);
end
```

The other uses inner products between the rows of U and portions of the emerging solution x.

```
x = zeros(n,1);
for k = n:-1:1
    j = k+1:n;
    x(k)  = (b(k) - U(k,j)*x(j))/U(k,k);
end
```

2.5 LU Factorization

The algorithm that is almost universally used to solve square systems of simultaneous linear equations is one of the oldest numerical methods, the systematic elimination method, generally named after C. F. Gauss. Research in the period 1955 to 1965 revealed the importance of two aspects of Gaussian elimination that were not emphasized in earlier work: the search for pivots and the proper interpretation of the effect of rounding errors.

In general, Gaussian elimination has two stages, the *forward elimination* and the *back substitution*. The forward elimination consists of $n-1$ steps. At the kth step, multiples of the kth equation are subtracted from the remaining equations to eliminate the kth variable. If the coefficient of x_k is "small," it is advisable to interchange equations before this is done. The elimination steps can be simultaneously applied to the right-hand side, or the interchanges and multipliers saved and applied to the right-hand side later. The back substitution consists of solving the last equation for x_n, then the next-to-last equation for x_{n-1}, and so on, until x_1 is computed from the first equation.

Let $P_k, k = 1, \ldots, n-1$, denote the permutation matrix obtained by interchanging the rows of the identity matrix in the same way the rows of A are interchanged at the kth step of the elimination. Let M_k denote the unit lower triangular matrix obtained by inserting the negatives of the multipliers used at the kth step below the diagonal in the kth column of the identity matrix. Let U be the final upper triangular matrix obtained after the $n-1$ steps. The entire process can be described by one matrix equation,

$$U = M_{n-1}P_{n-1} \cdots M_2 P_2 M_1 P_1 A.$$

It turns out that this equation can be rewritten

$$L_1 L_2 \cdots L_{n-1} U = P_{n-1} \cdots P_2 P_1 A,$$

where L_k is obtained from M_k by permuting and changing the signs of the multipliers below the diagonal. So, if we let

$$L = L_1 L_2 \cdots L_{n-1},$$
$$P = P_{n-1} \cdots P_2 P_1,$$

then we have

$$LU = PA.$$

The unit lower triangular matrix L contains all the multipliers used during the elimination and the permutation matrix P accounts for all the interchanges.

For our example

$$A = \begin{pmatrix} 10 & -7 & 0 \\ -3 & 2 & 6 \\ 5 & -1 & 5 \end{pmatrix},$$

the matrices defined during the elimination are

$$P_1 = \begin{pmatrix} 1 & 0 & 0 \\ 0 & 1 & 0 \\ 0 & 0 & 1 \end{pmatrix}, \quad M_1 = \begin{pmatrix} 1 & 0 & 0 \\ 0.3 & 1 & 0 \\ -0.5 & 0 & 1 \end{pmatrix},$$

$$P_2 = \begin{pmatrix} 1 & 0 & 0 \\ 0 & 0 & 1 \\ 0 & 1 & 0 \end{pmatrix}, \quad M_2 = \begin{pmatrix} 1 & 0 & 0 \\ 0 & 1 & 0 \\ 0 & 0.04 & 1 \end{pmatrix}.$$

The corresponding L's are

$$L_1 = \begin{pmatrix} 1 & 0 & 0 \\ 0.5 & 1 & 0 \\ -0.3 & 0 & 1 \end{pmatrix}, \quad L_2 = \begin{pmatrix} 1 & 0 & 0 \\ 0 & 1 & 0 \\ 0 & -0.04 & 1 \end{pmatrix}.$$

The relation $LU = PA$ is called the *LU factorization* or the *triangular decomposition* of A. It should be emphasized that nothing new has been introduced. Computationally, elimination is done by row operations on the coefficient matrix, not by actual matrix multiplication. LU factorization is simply Gaussian elimination expressed in matrix notation.

With this factorization, a general system of equations

$$Ax = b$$

becomes a pair of triangular systems

$$Ly = Pb,$$
$$Ux = y.$$

2.6   Why Is Pivoting Necessary?

The diagonal elements of U are called *pivots*. The kth pivot is the coefficient of the kth variable in the kth equation at the kth step of the elimination. In our 3-by-3 example, the pivots are 10, 2.5, and 6.2. Both the computation of the multipliers and the back substitution require divisions by the pivots. Consequently, the algorithm cannot be carried out if any of the pivots are zero. Intuition should tell us that it is a bad idea to complete the computation if any of the pivots are nearly zero. To see this, let us change our example slightly to

$$\begin{pmatrix} 10 & -7 & 0 \\ -3 & 2.099 & 6 \\ 5 & -1 & 5 \end{pmatrix} \begin{pmatrix} x_1 \\ x_2 \\ x_3 \end{pmatrix} = \begin{pmatrix} 7 \\ 3.901 \\ 6 \end{pmatrix}.$$

The $(2, 2)$ element of the matrix has been changed from 2.000 to 2.099, and the right-hand side has also been changed so that the exact answer is still $(0, -1, 1)^T$. Let us assume that the solution is to be computed on a hypothetical machine that does decimal floating-point arithmetic with five significant digits.

The first step of the elimination produces

$$\begin{pmatrix} 10 & -7 & 0 \\ 0 & -0.001 & 6 \\ 0 & 2.5 & 5 \end{pmatrix} \begin{pmatrix} x_1 \\ x_2 \\ x_3 \end{pmatrix} = \begin{pmatrix} 7 \\ 6.001 \\ 2.5 \end{pmatrix}.$$

The $(2, 2)$ element is now quite small compared with the other elements in the matrix. Nevertheless, let us complete the elimination without using any interchanges. The next step requires adding $2.5 \cdot 10^3$ times the second equation to the third:

$$(5 + (2.5 \cdot 10^3)(6))x_3 = (2.5 + (2.5 \cdot 10^3)(6.001)).$$

On the right-hand side, this involves multiplying 6.001 by $2.5 \cdot 10^3$. The result is $1.50025 \cdot 10^4$, which cannot be exactly represented in our hypothetical floating-point number system. It must be rounded to $1.5002 \cdot 10^4$. The result is then added to 2.5 and rounded again. In other words, both of the 5's shown in italics in

$$(5 + 1.5000 \cdot 10^4)x_3 = (2.5 + 1.50025 \cdot 10^4)$$

are lost in roundoff errors. On this hypothetical machine, the last equation becomes

$$1.5005 \cdot 10^4 x_3 = 1.5004 \cdot 10^4.$$

The back substitution begins with

$$x_3 = \frac{1.5004 \cdot 10^4}{1.5005 \cdot 10^4} = 0.99993.$$

Because the exact answer is $x_3 = 1$, it does not appear that the error is too serious. Unfortunately, x_2 must be determined from the equation

$$-0.001x_2 + (6)(0.99993) = 6.001,$$

which gives

$$x_2 = \frac{1.5 \cdot 10^{-3}}{-1.0 \cdot 10^{-3}} = -1.5.$$

Finally, x_1 is determined from the first equation,

$$10x_1 + (-7)(-1.5) = 7,$$

which gives
$$x_1 = -0.35.$$
Instead of $(0, -1, 1)^T$, we have obtained $(-0.35, -1.5, 0.99993)^T$.

Where did things go wrong? There was no "accumulation of rounding error" caused by doing thousands of arithmetic operations. The matrix is not close to singular. The difficulty comes from choosing a small pivot at the second step of the elimination. As a result, the multiplier is $2.5 \cdot 10^3$, and the final equation involves coefficients that are 10^3 times as large as those in the original problem. Roundoff errors that are small if compared to these large coefficients are unacceptable in terms of the original matrix and the actual solution.

We leave it to the reader to verify that if the second and third equations are interchanged, then no large multipliers are necessary and the final result is accurate. This turns out to be true in general: If the multipliers are all less than or equal to one in magnitude, then the computed solution can be proved to be satisfactory. Keeping the multipliers less than one in absolute value can be ensured by a process known as *partial pivoting*. At the kth step of the forward elimination, the pivot is taken to be the largest (in absolute value) element in the unreduced part of the kth column. The row containing this pivot is interchanged with the kth row to bring the pivot element into the (k, k) position. The same interchanges must be done with the elements of the right-hand side b. The unknowns in x are not reordered because the columns of A are not interchanged.

2.7 `lutx, bslashtx, lugui`

We have three functions implementing the algorithms discussed in this chapter. The first function, `lutx`, is a readable version of the built-in MATLAB function `lu`. There is one outer `for` loop on k that counts the elimination steps. The inner loops on i and j are implemented with vector and matrix operations, so that the overall function is reasonably efficient.

```
function [L,U,p] = lutx(A)
%LU Triangular factorization
%   [L,U,p] = lutx(A) produces a unit lower triangular
%   matrix L, an upper triangular matrix U, and a
%   permutation vector p, so that L*U = A(p,:).

[n,n] = size(A);
p = (1:n)'

for k = 1:n-1

    % Find largest element below diagonal in k-th column
    [r,m] = max(abs(A(k:n,k)));
    m = m+k-1;

    % Skip elimination if column is zero
    if (A(m,k) ~= 0)
```

```
      % Swap pivot row
      if (m ~= k)
         A([k m],:) = A([m k],:);
         p([k m]) = p([m k]);
      end

      % Compute multipliers
      i = k+1:n;
      A(i,k) = A(i,k)/A(k,k);

      % Update the remainder of the matrix
      j = k+1:n;
      A(i,j) = A(i,j) - A(i,k)*A(k,j);
   end
end

% Separate result
L = tril(A,-1) + eye(n,n);
U = triu(A);
```

Study this function carefully. Almost all the execution time is spent in the statement

```
      A(i,j) = A(i,j) - A(i,k)*A(k,j);
```

At the kth step of the elimination, i and j are index vectors of length n-k. The operation A(i,k)*A(k,j) multiplies a column vector by a row vector to produce a square, rank one matrix of order n-k. This matrix is then subtracted from the submatrix of the same size in the bottom right corner of A. In a programming language without vector and matrix operations, this update of a portion of A would be done with doubly nested loops on i and j.

The second function, bslashtx, is a simplified version of the built-in MATLAB backslash operator. It begins by checking for three important special cases: lower triangular, upper triangular, and symmetric positive definite. Linear systems with these properties can be solved in less time than a general system.

```
function x = bslashtx(A,b)
% BSLASHTX   Solve linear system (backslash)
% x = bslashtx(A,b) solves A*x = b

[n,n] = size(A);
if isequal(triu(A,1),zeros(n,n))
   % Lower triangular
   x = forward(A,b);
   return
elseif isequal(tril(A,-1),zeros(n,n))
   % Upper triangular
   x = backsubs(A,b);
   return
```

```
elseif isequal(A,A')
   [R,fail] = chol(A);
   if ~fail
      % Positive definite
      y = forward(R',b);
      x = backsubs(R,y);
      return
   end
end
```

If none of the special cases is detected, bslashtx calls lutx to permute and factor the coefficient matrix, then uses the permutation and factors to complete the solution of a linear system.

```
% Triangular factorization
[L,U,p] = lutx(A);

% Permutation and forward elimination
y = forward(L,b(p));

% Back substitution
x = backsubs(U,y);
```

The bslashtx function employs subfunctions to carry out the solution of lower and upper triangular systems.

```
function x = forward(L,x)
% FORWARD. Forward elimination.
% For lower triangular L, x = forward(L,b) solves L*x = b.
[n,n] = size(L);
for k = 1:n
   j = 1:k-1;
   x(k) = (x(k) - L(k,j)*x(j))/L(k,k);
end

function x = backsubs(U,x)
% BACKSUBS.  Back substitution.
% For upper triangular U, x = backsubs(U,b) solves U*x = b.
[n,n] = size(U);
for k = n:-1:1
   j = k+1:n;
   x(k) = (x(k) - U(k,j)*x(j))/U(k,k);
end
```

A third function, lugui, shows the steps in LU decomposition by Gaussian elimination. It is a version of lutx that allows you to experiment with various pivot selection strategies. At the kth step of the elimination, the largest element in the unreduced portion of the kth column is shown in magenta. This is the element that partial pivoting would ordinarily select as the pivot. You can then choose among four different pivoting strategies:

- Pick a pivot. Use the mouse to pick the magenta element, or any other element, as pivot.

- Diagonal pivoting. Use the diagonal element as the pivot.

- Partial pivoting. Same strategy as lu and lutx.

- Complete pivoting. Use the largest element in the unfactored submatrix as the pivot.

The chosen pivot is shown in red and the resulting elimination step is taken. As the process proceeds, the emerging columns of L are shown in green and the emerging rows of U in blue.

2.8 Effect of Roundoff Errors

The rounding errors introduced during the solution of a linear system of equations almost always cause the computed solution—which we now denote by x_*—to differ somewhat from the theoretical solution $x = A^{-1}b$. In fact, if the elements of x are not floating-point numbers, then x_* cannot equal x. There are two common measures of the discrepancy in x_*: the *error*,

$$e = x - x_*,$$

and the *residual*,

$$r = b - Ax_*.$$

Matrix theory tells us that, because A is nonsingular, if one of these is zero, the other must also be zero. But they are not necessarily both "small" at the same time. Consider the following example:

$$\begin{pmatrix} 0.780 & 0.563 \\ 0.913 & 0.659 \end{pmatrix} \begin{pmatrix} x_1 \\ x_2 \end{pmatrix} = \begin{pmatrix} 0.217 \\ 0.254 \end{pmatrix}.$$

What happens if we carry out Gaussian elimination with partial pivoting on a hypothetical three-digit decimal computer? First, the two rows (equations) are interchanged so that 0.913 becomes the pivot. Then the multiplier

$$\frac{0.780}{0.913} = 0.854 \text{ (to three places)}$$

is computed. Next, 0.854 times the new first row is subtracted from the new second row to produce the system

$$\begin{pmatrix} 0.913 & 0.659 \\ 0 & 0.001 \end{pmatrix} \begin{pmatrix} x_1 \\ x_2 \end{pmatrix} = \begin{pmatrix} 0.254 \\ 0.001 \end{pmatrix}.$$

Finally, the back substitution is carried out:

$$x_2 = \frac{0.001}{0.001} = 1.00 \text{ (exactly)},$$

$$x_1 = \frac{0.254 - 0.659x_2}{0.913}$$
$$= -0.443 \text{ (to three places)}.$$

Thus the computed solution is

$$x_* = \begin{pmatrix} -0.443 \\ 1.000 \end{pmatrix}.$$

To assess the accuracy without knowing the exact answer, we compute the residuals (exactly):

$$r = b - Ax_* = \begin{pmatrix} 0.217 - ((0.780)(-0.443) + (0.563)(1.00)) \\ 0.254 - ((0.913)(-0.443) + (0.659)(1.00)) \end{pmatrix}$$

$$= \begin{pmatrix} -0.000460 \\ -0.000541 \end{pmatrix}.$$

The *residuals* are less than 10^{-3}. We could hardly expect better on a three-digit machine. However, it is easy to see that the exact solution to this system is

$$x = \begin{pmatrix} 1.000 \\ -1.000 \end{pmatrix}.$$

So the components of our computed solution actually have the wrong signs; the *error* is larger than the solution itself.

Were the small residuals just a lucky fluke? You should realize that this example is highly contrived. The matrix is very close to being singular and is *not* typical of most problems encountered in practice. Nevertheless, let us track down the reason for the small residuals.

If Gaussian elimination with partial pivoting is carried out for this example on a computer with six or more digits, the forward elimination will produce a system something like

$$\begin{pmatrix} 0.913000 & 0.659000 \\ 0 & -0.000001 \end{pmatrix} \begin{pmatrix} x_1 \\ x_2 \end{pmatrix} = \begin{pmatrix} 0.254000 \\ 0.000001 \end{pmatrix}.$$

Notice that the sign of $U_{2,2}$ differs from that obtained with three-digit computation. Now the back substitution produces

$$x_2 = \frac{0.000001}{-0.000001} = -1.00000,$$

$$x_1 = \frac{0.254 - 0.659x_2}{0.913}$$

$$= 1.00000,$$

the exact answer. On our three-digit machine, x_2 was computed by dividing two quantities, both of which were on the order of rounding errors and one of which did not even have the correct sign. Hence x_2 can turn out to be almost anything. Then this arbitrary value of x_2 was substituted into the first equation to obtain x_1.

We can reasonably expect the residual from the first equation to be small—x_1 was computed in such a way as to make this certain. Now comes a subtle but crucial point. We can also expect the residual from the second equation to be small, *precisely because the matrix is so close to being singular*. The two equations are very nearly multiples of one another, so any pair (x_1, x_2) that nearly satisfies the first equation will also nearly satisfy the second. If the matrix were known to be exactly singular, we would not need the second equation at all—any solution of the first would automatically satisfy the second.

In Figure 2.1, the exact solution is marked with a circle and the computed solution with an asterisk. Even though the computed solution is far from the exact intersection, it is close to both lines because they are nearly parallel.

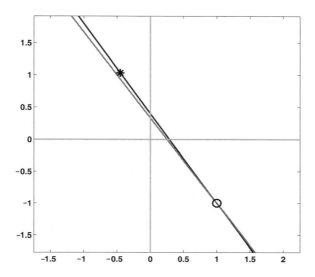

Figure 2.1. *The computed solution, marked by an asterisk, shows a large error, but a small residual.*

Although this example is contrived and atypical, the conclusion we reached is not. It is probably the single most important fact that we have learned about matrix computation since the invention of the digital computer:

> *Gaussian elimination with partial pivoting is guaranteed to produce small residuals.*

Now that we have stated it so strongly, we must make a couple of qualifying remarks. By "guaranteed" we mean it is possible to prove a precise theorem that assumes certain technical details about how the floating-point arithmetic system works and that establishes certain inequalities that the components of the residual must satisfy. If the arithmetic units work some other way or if there is a bug in the particular program, then the "guarantee" is void. Furthermore, by "small" we mean on the order of roundoff error *relative to* three quantities: the size of the elements of the original coefficient matrix, the size of the elements of the coefficient matrix at intermediate steps of the elimination process, and the size of the elements of the computed solution. If any of these are "large," then the residual will not necessarily be small in an absolute sense. Finally, even if the residual is small, we have made no claims that the error will be small. The relationship between the size of the residual and the size of the error is determined in part by a quantity known as the *condition number* of the matrix, which is the subject of the next section.

2.9   Norms and Condition Numbers

The coefficients in the matrix and right-hand side of a system of simultaneous linear equations are rarely known exactly. Some systems arise from experiments, and so the coefficients are subject to observational errors. Other systems have coefficients given by formulas that involve roundoff error in their evaluation. Even if the system can be stored exactly in the computer, it is almost inevitabe that roundoff errors will be introduced during its solution. It can be shown that roundoff errors in Gaussian elimination have the same effect on the answer as errors in the original coefficients.

Consequently, we are led to a fundamental question. If perturbations are made in the coefficients of a system of linear equations, how much is the solution altered? In other words, if $Ax = b$, how can we measure the sensitivity of x to changes in A and b?

The answer to this question lies in making the idea of *nearly singular* precise. If A is a singular matrix, then for some b's a solution x will not exist, while for others it will not be unique. So if A is nearly singular, we can expect small changes in A and b to cause very large changes in x. On the other hand, if A is the identity matrix, then b and x are the same vector. So if A is nearly the identity, small changes in A and b should result in correspondingly small changes in x.

At first glance, it might appear that there is some connection between the size of the pivots encountered in Gaussian elimination with partial pivoting and *nearness to singularity*, because if the arithmetic could be done exactly, all the pivots would be nonzero if and only if the matrix is nonsingular. To some extent, it is also true that if the pivots are small, then the matrix is *close to singular*. However, when roundoff errors are encountered, the converse is no longer true—a matrix might be close to singular even though none of the pivots are small.

To get a more precise, and reliable, measure of nearness to singularity than the size of the pivots, we need to introduce the concept of a *norm* of a vector. This is a single number that measures the general size of the elements of the vector. The family of vector norms known as l_p depends on a parameter p in the range $1 \leq p \leq \infty$:

$$\|x\|_p = \left(\sum_{i=1}^{n} |x_i|^p \right)^{1/p}.$$

We almost always use $p = 1$, $p = 2$, or $\lim p \to \infty$:

$$\|x\|_1 = \sum_{i=1}^{n} |x_i|,$$

$$\|x\|_2 = \left(\sum_{i=1}^{n} |x_i|^2 \right)^{1/2},$$

$$\|x\|_\infty = \max_i |x_i|.$$

The l_1-norm is also known as the *Manhattan* norm because it corresponds to the distance traveled on a grid of city streets. The l_2-norm is the familiar Euclidean distance. The l_∞-norm is also known as the *Chebyshev* norm.

The particular value of p is often unimportant and we simply use $\|x\|$. All vector norms have the following basic properties associated with the notion of distance:

$$\|x\| > 0 \text{ if } x \neq 0,$$
$$\|0\| = 0,$$
$$\|cx\| = |c| \|x\| \text{ for all scalars } c,$$
$$\|x + y\| \leq \|x\| + \|y\| \text{ (the } triangle\ inequality\text{)}.$$

In MATLAB, $\|x\|_p$ is computed by norm(x,p), and norm(x) is the same as norm(x,2). For example,

```
x = (1:4)/5
norm1 = norm(x,1)
norm2 = norm(x)
norminf = norm(x,inf)
```

produces

```
x =
    0.2000    0.4000    0.6000    0.8000

norm1 =
    2.0000

norm2 =
    1.0954

norminf =
    0.8000
```

Multiplication of a vector x by a matrix A results in a new vector Ax that can have a very different norm from x. This change in norm is directly related to the sensitivity we want to measure. The range of the possible change can be expressed by two numbers:

$$M = \max \frac{\|Ax\|}{\|x\|},$$
$$m = \min \frac{\|Ax\|}{\|x\|}.$$

The max and min are taken over all nonzero vectors x. Note that if A is singular, then $m = 0$. The ratio M/m is called the *condition number* of A:

$$\kappa(A) = \frac{\max \frac{\|Ax\|}{\|x\|}}{\min \frac{\|Ax\|}{\|x\|}}.$$

The actual numerical value of $\kappa(A)$ depends on the vector norm being used, but we are usually only interested in order of magnitude estimates of the condition number, so the particular norm is usually not very important.

Consider a system of equations

$$Ax = b$$

and a second system obtained by altering the right-hand side:

$$A(x + \delta x) = b + \delta b.$$

We think of δb as being the error in b and δx as being the resulting error in x, although we need not make any assumptions that the errors are small. Because $A(\delta x) = \delta b$, the definitions of M and m immediately lead to

$$\|b\| \leq M \|x\|$$

and

$$\|\delta b\| \geq m \|\delta x\|.$$

Consequently, if $m \neq 0$,

$$\frac{\|\delta x\|}{\|x\|} \leq \kappa(A) \frac{\|\delta b\|}{\|b\|}.$$

The quantity $\|\delta b\| / \|b\|$ is the *relative* change in the right-hand side, and the quantity $\|\delta x\| / \|x\|$ is the *relative* error caused by this change. The advantage of using relative changes is that they are *dimensionless*, that is, they are not affected by overall scale factors.

This shows that the condition number is a relative error magnification factor. Changes in the right-hand side can cause changes $\kappa(A)$ times as large in the solution. It turns out that the same is true of changes in the coefficient matrix itself.

The condition number is also a measure of nearness to singularity. Although we have not yet developed the mathematical tools necessary to make the idea precise, the condition number can be thought of as the reciprocal of the relative distance from the matrix to the set of singular matrices. So, if $\kappa(A)$ is large, A is close to singular.

Some of the basic properties of the condition number are easily derived. Clearly, $M \geq m$, and so

$$\kappa(A) \geq 1.$$

If P is a permutation matrix, then the components of Px are simply a rearrangement of the components of x. It follows that $\|Px\| = \|x\|$ for all x, and so

$$\kappa(P) = 1.$$

In particular, $\kappa(I) = 1$. If A is multiplied by a scalar c, then M and m are both multiplied by the same scalar, and so

$$\kappa(cA) = \kappa(A).$$

If D is a diagonal matrix, then

$$\kappa(D) = \frac{\max |d_{ii}|}{\min |d_{ii}|}.$$

These last two properties are two of the reasons that $\kappa(A)$ is a better measure of nearness to singularity than the determinant of A. As an extreme example, consider a 100-by-100 diagonal matrix with 0.1 on the diagonal. Then $\det(A) = 10^{-100}$, which is usually regarded as a small number. But $\kappa(A) = 1$, and the components of Ax are simply 0.1 times the corresponding components of x. For linear systems of equations, such a matrix behaves more like the identity than like a singular matrix.

The following example uses the l_1-norm:

$$A = \begin{pmatrix} 4.1 & 2.8 \\ 9.7 & 6.6 \end{pmatrix},$$

$$b = \begin{pmatrix} 4.1 \\ 9.7 \end{pmatrix},$$

$$x = \begin{pmatrix} 1 \\ 0 \end{pmatrix}.$$

Clearly, $Ax = b$, and

$$\|b\| = 13.8, \quad \|x\| = 1.$$

If the right-hand side is changed to

$$\tilde{b} = \begin{pmatrix} 4.11 \\ 9.70 \end{pmatrix},$$

the solution becomes

$$\tilde{x} = \begin{pmatrix} 0.34 \\ 0.97 \end{pmatrix}.$$

Let $\delta b = b - \tilde{b}$ and $\delta x = x - \tilde{x}$. Then

$$\|\delta b\| = 0.01,$$
$$\|\delta x\| = 1.63.$$

We have made a fairly small perturbation in b that completely changes x. In fact, the relative changes are

$$\frac{\|\delta b\|}{\|b\|} = 0.0007246,$$
$$\frac{\|\delta x\|}{\|x\|} = 1.63.$$

Because $\kappa(A)$ is the maximum magnification factor,

$$\kappa(A) \geq \frac{1.63}{0.0007246} = 2249.4.$$

We have actually chosen the b and δb that give the maximum, and so, for this example with the l_1-norm,

$$\kappa(A) = 2249.4.$$

It is important to realize that this example is concerned with the *exact* solutions to two slightly different systems of equations and that the method used to obtain the solutions is irrelevant. The example is constructed to have a fairly large condition number so that the effect of changes in b is quite pronounced, but similar behavior can be expected in any problem with a large condition number.

The condition number also plays a fundamental role in the analysis of the roundoff errors introduced during the solution by Gaussian elimination. Let us assume that A and b have elements that are exact floating-point numbers, and let x_* be the vector of floating-point numbers obtained from a linear equation solver such as the function we shall present in the next section. We also assume that exact singularity is not detected and that there are no underflows or overflows. Then it is possible to establish the following inequalities:

$$\frac{\|b - Ax_*\|}{\|A\|\|x_*\|} \leq \rho\epsilon,$$

$$\frac{\|x - x_*\|}{\|x_*\|} \leq \rho\kappa(A)\epsilon.$$

Here ϵ is the relative machine precision eps and ρ is defined more carefully later, but it usually has a value no larger than about 10.

The first inequality says that the *relative residual* can usually be expected to be about the size of roundoff error, no matter how badly conditioned the matrix is. This was illustrated by the example in the previous section. The second inequality requires that A be nonsingular and involves the exact solution x. It follows directly from the first inequality and the definition of $\kappa(A)$ and says that the *relative error* will also be small if $\kappa(A)$ is small but might be quite large if the matrix is nearly singular. In the extreme case where A is singular but the singularity is not detected, the first inequality still holds but the second has no meaning.

To be more precise about the quantity ρ, it is necessary to introduce the idea of a *matrix norm* and establish some further inequalities. Readers who are not interested in such details can skip the remainder of this section. The quantity M defined earlier is known as the norm of the matrix. The notation for the matrix norm is the same as for the vector norm:

$$\|A\| = \max \frac{\|Ax\|}{\|x\|}.$$

It is not hard to see that $\|A^{-1}\| = 1/m$, so an equivalent definition of the condition number is

$$\kappa(A) = \|A\|\|A^{-1}\|.$$

Again, the actual numerical values of the matrix norm and condition number depend on the underlying vector norm. It is easy to compute the matrix norms corresponding to the l_1 and l_∞ vector norms. In fact, it is not hard to show that

$$\|A\|_1 = \max_j \sum_i |a_{i,j}|,$$

$$\|A\|_\infty = \max_i \sum_j |a_{i,j}|.$$

Computing the matrix norm corresponding to the l_2 vector norm involves the singular value decomposition (SVD), which is discussed in a later chapter. MATLAB computes matrix norms with norm(A,p) for p = 1, 2, or inf.

The basic result in the study of roundoff error in Gaussian elimination is due to J. H. Wilkinson. He proved that the computed solution x_* exactly satisfies

$$(A + E)x_* = b,$$

where E is a matrix whose elements are about the size of roundoff errors in the elements of A. There are some rare situations where the intermediate matrices obtained during Gaussian elimination have elements that are larger than those of A, and there is some effect from accumulation of rounding errors in large matrices, but it can be expected that if ρ is defined by

$$\frac{\|E\|}{\|A\|} = \rho\epsilon,$$

then ρ will rarely be bigger than about 10.

From this basic result, we can immediately derive inequalities involving the residual and the error in the computed solution. The residual is given by

$$b - Ax_* = Ex_*,$$

and hence

$$\|b - Ax_*\| = \|Ex_*\| \leq \|E\|\|x_*\|.$$

The residual involves the product Ax_*, so it is appropriate to consider the *relative residual*, which compares the norm of $b - Ax$ to the norms of A and x_*. It follows directly from the above inequalities that

$$\frac{\|b - Ax_*\|}{\|A\|\|x_*\|} \leq \rho\epsilon.$$

If A is nonsingular, the error can be expressed using the inverse of A by

$$x - x_* = A^{-1}(b - Ax_*),$$

and so

$$\|x - x_*\| \leq \|A^{-1}\|\|E\|\|x_*\|.$$

It is simplest to compare the norm of the error with the norm of the computed solution. Thus the *relative error* satisfies

$$\frac{\|x - x_*\|}{\|x_*\|} \leq \rho\|A\|\|A^{-1}\|\epsilon.$$

Hence

$$\frac{\|x - x_*\|}{\|x_*\|} \leq \rho\kappa(A)\epsilon.$$

The actual computation of $\kappa(A)$ requires knowing $\|A^{-1}\|$. But computing A^{-1} requires roughly three times as much work as solving a single linear system. Computing the l_2 condition number requires the SVD and even more work. Fortunately, the exact value of $\kappa(A)$ is rarely required. Any reasonably good estimate of it is satisfactory.

MATLAB has several functions for computing or estimating condition numbers.

- `cond(A)` or `cond(A,2)` computes $\kappa_2(A)$. Uses `svd(A)`. Suitable for smaller matrices where the geometric properties of the l_2-norm are important.

- cond(A,1) computes $\kappa_1(A)$. Uses inv(A). Less work than cond(A,2).

- cond(A,inf) computes $\kappa_\infty(A)$. Uses inv(A). Same as cond(A',1).

- condest(A) estimates $\kappa_1(A)$. Uses lu(A) and a recent algorithm of Higham and Tisseur [32]. Especially suitable for large, sparse matrices.

- rcond(A) estimates $1/\kappa_1(A)$. Uses lu(A) and an older algorithm developed by the LINPACK and LAPACK projects. Primarily of historical interest.

2.10   Sparse Matrices and Band Matrices

Sparse matrices and band matrices occur frequently in technical computing. The *sparsity* of a matrix is the fraction of its elements that are zero. The MATLAB function nnz counts the number of nonzeros in a matrix, so the sparsity of A is given by

```
density  = nnz(A)/prod(size(A))
sparsity = 1 - density
```

A *sparse matrix* is a matrix whose sparsity is nearly equal to 1.

The *bandwidth* of a matrix is the maximum distance of the nonzero elements from the main diagonal.

```
[i,j] = find(A)
bandwidth = max(abs(i-j))
```

A *band matrix* is a matrix whose bandwidth is small.

As you can see, both sparsity and bandwidth are matters of degree. An n-by-n diagonal matrix with no zeros on the diagonal has sparsity $1 - 1/n$ and bandwidth 0, so it is an extreme example of both a sparse matrix and a band matrix. On the other hand, an n-by-n matrix with no zero elements, such as the one created by rand(n,n), has sparsity equal to zero and bandwidth equal to $n - 1$, and so is far from qualifying for either category.

The MATLAB sparse data structure stores the nonzero elements together with information about their indices. The sparse data structure also provides efficient handling of band matrices, so MATLAB does not have a separate band matrix storage class. The statement

```
S = sparse(A)
```

converts a matrix to its sparse representation. The statement

```
A = full(S)
```

reverses the process. However, most sparse matrices have orders so large that it is impractical to store the full representation. More frequently, sparse matrices are created by

```
S = sparse(i,j,x,m,n)
```

This produces a matrix S with

```
[i,j,x] = find(S)
[m,n]   = size(S)
```

Most MATLAB matrix operations and functions can be applied to both full and sparse matrices. The dominant factor in determining the execution time and memory requirements for sparse matrix operations is the number of nonzeros, nnz(S), in the various matrices involved.

A matrix with bandwidth equal to 1 is known as a *tridiagonal* matrix. It is worthwhile to have a specialized function for one particular band matrix operation, the solution of a tridiagonal system of simultaneous linear equations:

$$\begin{pmatrix} b_1 & c_1 \\ a_1 & b_2 & c_2 \\ & a_2 & b_3 & c_3 \\ & & \ddots & \ddots & \ddots \\ & & & a_{n-2} & b_{n-1} & c_{n-1} \\ & & & & a_{n-1} & b_n \end{pmatrix} \begin{pmatrix} x_1 \\ x_2 \\ x_3 \\ \vdots \\ x_{n-1} \\ x_n \end{pmatrix} = \begin{pmatrix} d_1 \\ d_2 \\ d_3 \\ \vdots \\ d_{n-1} \\ d_n \end{pmatrix}.$$

The function tridisolve is included in the NCM directory. The statement

```
x = tridisolve(a,b,c,d)
```

solves the tridiagonal system with subdiagonal a, diagonal b, superdiagonal c, and right-hand side d. We have already seen the algorithm that tridisolve uses; it is Gaussian elimination. In many situations involving tridiagonal matrices, the diagonal elements dominate the off-diagonal elements, so pivoting is unnecessary. Furthermore, the right-hand side is processed at the same time as the matrix itself. In this context, Gaussian elimination without pivoting is also known as the *Thomas algorithm*.

The body of tridisolve begins by copying the right-hand side to a vector that will become the solution.

```
x = d;
n = length(x);
```

The forward elimination step is a simple for loop.

```
for j = 1:n-1
    mu = a(j)/b(j);
    b(j+1) = b(j+1) - mu*c(j);
    x(j+1) = x(j+1) - mu*x(j);
end
```

The mu's would be the multipliers on the subdiagonal of L if we were saving the LU factorization. Instead, the right-hand side is processed in the same loop. The back substitution step is another simple loop.

```
x(n) = x(n)/b(n);
for j = n-1:-1:1
    x(j) = (x(j)-c(j)*x(j+1))/b(j);
end
```

Because tridisolve does not use pivoting, the results might be inaccurate if abs(b) is much smaller than abs(a)+abs(c). More robust, but slower, alternatives that do use pivoting include generating a full matrix with `diag`:

```
T = diag(a,-1) + diag(b,0) + diag(c,1);
x = T\d
```

or generating a sparse matrix with `spdiags`:

```
S = spdiags([a b c],[-1 0 1],n,n);
x = S\d
```

2.11   PageRank and Markov Chains

One of the reasons why Google™ is such an effective search engine is the PageRank™ algorithm developed by Google's founders, Larry Page and Sergey Brin, when they were graduate students at Stanford University. PageRank is determined entirely by the link structure of the World Wide Web. It is recomputed about once a month and does not involve the actual content of any Web pages or individual queries. Then, for any particular query, Google finds the pages on the Web that match that query and lists those pages in the order of their PageRank.

Imagine surfing the Web, going from page to page by randomly choosing an outgoing link from one page to get to the next. This can lead to dead ends at pages with no outgoing links, or cycles around cliques of interconnected pages. So, a certain fraction of the time, simply choose a random page from the Web. This theoretical random walk is known as a *Markov chain* or *Markov process*. The limiting probability that an infinitely dedicated random surfer visits any particular page is its PageRank. A page has high rank if other pages with high rank link to it.

Let W be the set of Web pages that can be reached by following a chain of hyperlinks starting at some root page, and let n be the number of pages in W. For Google, the set W actually varies with time. In June 2004, their value of n was over 4 billion. Today, Google does not reveal how many pages they reach. Let G be the *n-by-n connectivity matrix* of a portion of the Web, that is, $g_{ij} = 1$ if there is a hyperlink to page i from page j and $g_{ij} = 0$ otherwise. The matrix G can be huge, but it is very sparse. Its jth column shows the links on the jth page. The number of nonzeros in G is the total number of hyperlinks in W.

Let r_i and c_j be the row and column sums of G:

$$r_i = \sum_j g_{ij}, \quad c_j = \sum_i g_{ij}.$$

The quantities r_j and c_j are the *in-degree* and *out-degree* of the jth page. Let p be the probability that the random walk follows a link. A typical value is $p = 0.85$. Then $1 - p$ is the probability that some arbitrary page is chosen and $\delta = (1 - p)/n$ is the probability that a particular random page is chosen. Let A be the n-by-n matrix whose elements are

$$a_{ij} = \begin{cases} pg_{ij}/c_j + \delta & : \quad c_j \neq 0 \\ 1/n & : \quad c_j = 0. \end{cases}$$

Notice that A comes from scaling the connectivity matrix by its column sums. The jth column is the probability of jumping from the jth page to the other pages on the Web. Most of the elements of A are equal to δ, the probability of jumping from one page to another without following a link. If $n = 4 \cdot 10^9$ and $p = 0.85$, then $\delta = 3.75 \cdot 10^{-11}$.

The matrix A is the transition probability matrix of the Markov chain. Its elements are all strictly between zero and one and its column sums are all equal to one. An important result in matrix theory known as the *Perron–Frobenius theorem* applies to such matrices. It concludes that a nonzero solution of the equation

$$x = Ax$$

exists and is unique to within a scaling factor. If this scaling factor is chosen so that

$$\sum_i x_i = 1,$$

then x is the *state vector* of the Markov chain and is Google's PageRank. The elements of x are all positive and less than one.

The vector x is the solution to the singular, homogeneous linear system

$$(I - A)x = 0.$$

For modest n, an easy way to compute x in MATLAB is to start with some approximate solution, such as the PageRanks from the previous month, or

```
x = ones(n,1)/n
```

Then simply repeat the assignment statement

```
x = A*x
```

until successive vectors agree to within a specified tolerance. This is known as the *power method* and is about the only possible approach for very large n. In practice, the matrices G and A are never actually formed. One step of the power method would be done by one pass over a database of Web pages, updating weighted reference counts generated by the hyperlinks between pages.

The best way to compute PageRank in MATLAB is to take advantage of the particular structure of the Markov matrix. Here is an approach that preserves the sparsity of G. The transition matrix can be written

$$A = pGD + ez^T,$$

where D is the diagonal matrix formed from the reciprocals of the outdegrees,

$$d_{jj} = \begin{cases} 1/c_j & : & c_j \neq 0 \\ 0 & : & c_j = 0, \end{cases}$$

e is the n-vector of all ones, and z is the vector with components

$$z_j = \begin{cases} \delta & : & c_j \neq 0 \\ 1/n & : & c_j = 0. \end{cases}$$

The rank-one matrix ez^T accounts for the random choices of Web pages that do not follow links. The equation

$$x = Ax$$

can be written

$$(I - pGD)x = \gamma e,$$

where

$$\gamma = z^T x.$$

We do not know the value of γ because it depends upon the unknown vector x, but we can temporarily take $\gamma = 1$. As long as p is strictly less than one, the coefficient matrix $I - pGD$ is nonsingular and the equation

$$(I - pGD)x = e$$

can be solved for x. Then the resulting x can be rescaled so that

$$\sum_i x_i = 1.$$

Notice that the vector z is not actually involved in this calculation.

The following MATLAB statements implement this approach

```
c = sum(G,1);
k = find(c~=0);
D = sparse(k,k,1./c(k),n,n);
e = ones(n,1);
I = speye(n,n);
x = (I - p*G*D)\e;
x = x/sum(x);
```

The power method can also be implemented in a way that does not actually form the Markov matrix and so preserves sparsity. Compute

```
G = p*G*D;
z = ((1-p)*(c~=0) + (c==0))/n;
```

Start with

```
x = e/n
```

Then repeat the statement

```
x = G*x + e*(z*x)
```

until x settles down to several decimal places.

It is also possible to use an algorithm known as *inverse iteration*.

```
A = p*G*D + delta
x = (I - A)\e
x = x/sum(x)
```

At first glance, this appears to be a very dangerous idea. Because $I - A$ is theoretically singular, with exact computation some diagonal element of the upper triangular factor of $I - A$ should be zero and this computation should fail. But with roundoff error, the computed matrix I - A is probably not exactly singular. Even if it is singular, roundoff during Gaussian elimination will most likely prevent any exact zero diagonal elements. We know that Gaussian elimination with partial pivoting always produces a solution with a small residual, relative to the computed solution, even if the matrix is badly conditioned. The vector obtained with the backslash operation, (I - A)\e, usually has very large components. If it is rescaled by its sum, the residual is scaled by the same factor and becomes very small. Consequently, the two vectors x and A*x equal each other to within roundoff error. In this setting, solving the singular system with Gaussian elimination blows up, but it blows up in exactly the right direction.

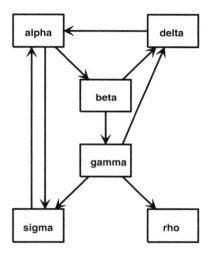

Figure 2.2. *A tiny Web.*

Figure 2.2 is the graph for a tiny example, with $n = 6$ instead of $n = 4 \cdot 10^9$. Pages on the Web are identified by strings known as *uniform resource locators*, or *URLs*. Most URLs begin with http because they use the *hypertext transfer protocol*. In MATLAB, we can store the URLs as an array of strings in a *cell array*. This example involves a 6-by-1 cell array.

```
U = {'http://www.alpha.com'
     'http://www.beta.com'
     'http://www.gamma.com'
     'http://www.delta.com'
     'http://www.rho.com'
     'http://www.sigma.com'}
```

Two different kinds of indexing into cell arrays are possible. Parentheses denote subarrays, including individual cells, and curly braces denote the contents of the cells. If k is a scalar, then U(k) is a 1-by-1 cell array consisting of the kth cell in U, while U{k} is the string in that cell. Thus U(1) is a single cell and U{1} is the string 'http://www.alpha.com'. Think of mail boxes with addresses on a city street. B(502) is the box at number 502, while B{502} is the mail in that box.

We can generate the connectivity matrix by specifying the pairs of indices (i,j) of the nonzero elements. Because there is a link to beta.com from alpha.com, the (2,1) element of *G* is nonzero. The nine connections are described by

```
i = [ 2 6 3 4 4 5 6 1 1]
j = [ 1 1 2 2 3 3 3 4 6]
```

A sparse matrix is stored in a data structure that requires memory only for the nonzero elements and their indices. This is hardly necessary for a 6-by-6 matrix with only 27 zero entries, but it becomes crucially important for larger problems. The statements

```
n = 6
G = sparse(i,j,1,n,n);
full(G)
```

generate the sparse representation of an n-by-n matrix with ones in the positions specified by the vectors i and j and display its full representation.

```
0    0    0    1    0    1
1    0    0    0    0    0
0    1    0    0    0    0
0    1    1    0    0    0
0    0    1    0    0    0
1    0    1    0    0    0
```

The statement

```
c = full(sum(G))
```

computes the column sums

```
c =
     2    2    3    1    0    1
```

Notice that c(5) = 0 because the 5th page, labeled rho, has no out-links.

The statements

```
x = (I - p*G*D)\e
x = x/sum(x)
```

solve the sparse linear system to produce

```
x =
   0.3210
   0.1705
   0.1066
   0.1368
   0.0643
   0.2007
```

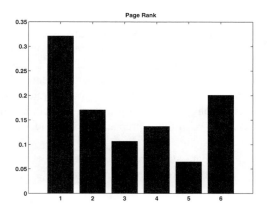

Figure 2.3. *Page Rank for the tiny Web*

The `bar` graph of x is shown in Figure 2.3. If the URLs are sorted in PageRank order and listed along with their in- and out-degrees, the result is

```
    page-rank   in   out   url
1    0.3210      2    2    http://www.alpha.com
6    0.2007      2    1    http://www.sigma.com
2    0.1705      1    2    http://www.beta.com
4    0.1368      2    1    http://www.delta.com
3    0.1066      1    3    http://www.gamma.com
5    0.0643      1    0    http://www.rho.com
```

We see that `alpha` has a higher PageRank than `delta` or `sigma`, even though they all have the same number of in-links. A random surfer will visit `alpha` over 32% of the time and `rho` only about 6% of the time.

For this tiny example with $p = .85$, the smallest element of the Markov transition matrix is $\delta = .15/6 = .0250$.

```
A =
   0.0250    0.0250    0.0250    0.8750    0.1667    0.8750
   0.4500    0.0250    0.0250    0.0250    0.1667    0.0250
   0.0250    0.4500    0.0250    0.0250    0.1667    0.0250
   0.0250    0.4500    0.3083    0.0250    0.1667    0.0250
   0.0250    0.0250    0.3083    0.0250    0.1667    0.0250
   0.4500    0.0250    0.3083    0.0250    0.1667    0.0250
```

Notice that the column sums of A are all equal to one.

Our collection of NCM programs includes `surfer.m`. A statement like

```
[U,G] = surfer('http://www.xxx.zzz',n)
```

starts at a specified URL and tries to surf the Web until it has visited n pages. If successful, it returns an n-by-1 cell array of URLs and an n-by-n sparse connectivity matrix. The function uses `urlread`, which was introduced in MATLAB 6.5, along with underlying Java utilities to access the Web. Surfing the Web automatically is a dangerous undertaking and this function must be used with care. Some URLs contain typographical errors and illegal characters. There is a list of URLs to avoid that includes `.gif` files and Web sites known to cause difficulties. Most importantly, `surfer` can get completely bogged down trying to read a page from a site that appears to be responding, but that never delivers the complete page. When this happens, it may be necessary to have the computer's operating system ruthlessly terminate MATLAB. With these precautions in mind, you can use `surfer` to generate your own PageRank examples.

   The statement

```
[U,G] = surfer('http://www.harvard.edu',500)
```

accesses the home page of Harvard University and generates a 500-by-500 test case. The graph generated in August 2003 is available in the NCM directory. The statements

```
load harvard500
spy(G)
```

produce a `spy` plot (Figure 2.4) that shows the nonzero structure of the connectivity matrix. The statement

```
pagerank(U,G)
```

computes page ranks, produces a bar graph (Figure 2.5) of the ranks, and prints the most highly ranked URLs in PageRank order.

   For the `harvard500` data, the dozen most highly ranked pages are

	page-rank	in	out	url
1	0.0843	195	26	http://www.harvard.edu
10	0.0167	21	18	http://www.hbs.edu
42	0.0166	42	0	http://search.harvard.edu:8765/
				custom/query.html
130	0.0163	24	12	http://www.med.harvard.edu
18	0.0139	45	46	http://www.gse.harvard.edu
15	0.0131	16	49	http://www.hms.harvard.edu
9	0.0114	21	27	http://www.ksg.harvard.edu
17	0.0111	13	6	http://www.hsph.harvard.edu
46	0.0100	18	21	http://www.gocrimson.com
13	0.0086	9	1	http://www.hsdm.med.harvard.edu
260	0.0086	26	1	http://search.harvard.edu:8765/
				query.html
19	0.0084	23	21	http://www.radcliffe.edu

The URL where the search began, www.harvard.edu, dominates. Like most universities, Harvard is organized into various colleges and institutes, including the Kennedy School of Government, the Harvard Medical School, the Harvard Business School, and the Radcliffe Institute. You can see that the home pages of these schools have high PageRank. With a different sample, such as the one generated by Google itself, the ranks would be different.

2.12   Further Reading

Further reading on matrix computation includes books by Demmel [18], Golub and Van Loan [26], Stewart [58, 59], and Trefethen and Bau [60]. The definitive references on Fortran matrix computation software are the LAPACK Users' Guide and Web site [2]. The MATLAB sparse matrix data structure and operations are described in [25]. Information available on Web sites about PageRank includes a brief explanation at Google [27], a technical report by Page, Brin, and colleagues [50], and a comprehensive survey by Langville and Meyer [37].

Exercises

2.1. Alice buys three apples, a dozen bananas, and one cantaloupe for $2.36. Bob buys a dozen apples and two cantaloupes for $5.26. Carol buys two bananas and three cantaloupes for $2.77. How much do single pieces of each fruit cost? (You might want to set `format bank`.)

2.2. What MATLAB function computes the reduced row echelon form of a matrix? What MATLAB function generates magic square matrices? What is the reduced row echelon form of the magic square of order six?

2.3. Figure 2.6 depicts a plane truss having 13 members (the numbered lines) connecting 8 joints (the numbered circles). The indicated loads, in tons, are applied at joints 2, 5, and 6, and we want to determine the resulting force on each member of the truss. For the truss to be in static equilibrium, there must be no net force, horizontally or vertically, at any joint. Thus, we can determine the member forces by equating the

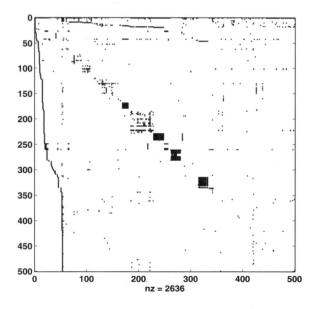

Figure 2.4. *Spy plot of the* `harvard500` *graph.*

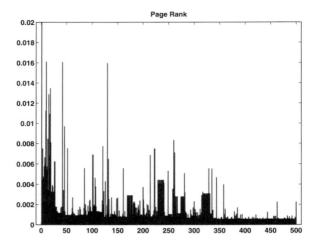

Figure 2.5. *PageRank of the* `harvard500` *graph.*

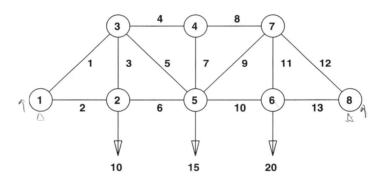

Figure 2.6. *A plane truss.*

horizontal forces to the left and right at each joint, and similarly equating the vertical forces upward and downward at each joint. For the eight joints, this would give 16 equations, which is more than the 13 unknown factors to be determined. For the truss to be statically determinate, that is, for there to be a unique solution, we assume that joint 1 is rigidly fixed both horizontally and vertically and that joint 8 is fixed vertically. Resolving the member forces into horizontal and vertical components and defining $\alpha = 1/\sqrt{2}$, we obtain the following system of equations for the member forces f_i:

$$\text{Joint 2:} \qquad f_2 = f_6,$$
$$f_3 = 10;$$
$$\text{Joint 3:} \quad \alpha f_1 = f_4 + \alpha f_5,$$

$$\alpha f_1 + f_3 + \alpha f_5 = 0;$$

Joint 4: $\quad f_4 = f_8,$

$$f_7 = 0;$$

Joint 5: $\alpha f_5 + f_6 = \alpha f_9 + f_{10},$

$$\alpha f_5 + f_7 + \alpha f_9 = 15;$$

Joint 6: $\quad f_{10} = f_{13},$

$$f_{11} = 20;$$

Joint 7: $\quad f_8 + \alpha f_9 = \alpha f_{12},$

$$\alpha f_9 + f_{11} + \alpha f_{12} = 0;$$

Joint 8: $\quad f_{13} + \alpha f_{12} = 0.$

Solve this system of equations to find the vector f of member forces.

2.4. Figure 2.7 is the circuit diagram for a small network of resistors.

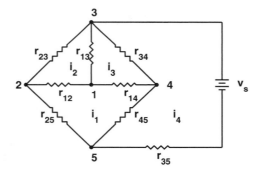

Figure 2.7. *A resistor network.*

There are five nodes, eight resistors, and one constant voltage source. We want to compute the voltage drops between the nodes and the currents around each of the loops.

Several different linear systems of equations can be formed to describe this circuit. Let $v_k, k = 1, \ldots, 4$, denote the voltage difference between each of the first four nodes and node number 5 and let $i_k, k = 1, \ldots, 4$, denote the clockwise current around each of the loops in the diagram. *Ohm's law* says that the voltage drop across a resistor is the resistance times the current. For example, the branch between nodes 1 and 2 gives

$$v_1 - v_2 = r_{12}(i_2 - i_1).$$

Using the *conductance*, which is the reciprocal of the resistance, $g_{kj} = 1/r_{kj}$, Ohm's law becomes

$$i_2 - i_1 = g_{12}(v_1 - v_2).$$

The voltage source is included in the equation

$$v_3 - v_s = r_{35}i_4.$$

Kirchhoff's voltage law says that the sum of the voltage differences around each loop is zero. For example, around loop 1,

$$(v_1 - v_4) + (v_4 - v_5) + (v_5 - v_2) + (v_2 - v_1) = 0.$$

Combining the voltage law with Ohm's law leads to the *loop* equations for the currents:

$$Ri = b.$$

Here i is the current vector,

$$i = \begin{pmatrix} i_1 \\ i_2 \\ i_3 \\ i_4 \end{pmatrix},$$

b is the source voltage vector,

$$b = \begin{pmatrix} 0 \\ 0 \\ 0 \\ v_s \end{pmatrix},$$

and R is the resistance matrix,

$$\begin{pmatrix} r_{25} + r_{12} + r_{14} + r_{45} & -r_{12} & -r_{14} & -r_{45} \\ -r_{12} & r_{23} + r_{12} + r_{13} & -r_{13} & 0 \\ -r_{14} & -r_{13} & r_{14} + r_{13} + r_{34} & -r_{34} \\ -r_{45} & 0 & -r_{34} & r_{35} + r_{45} + r_{34} \end{pmatrix}.$$

Kirchhoff's current law says that the sum of the currents at each node is zero. For example, at node 1,

$$(i_1 - i_2) + (i_2 - i_3) + (i_3 - i_1) = 0.$$

Combining the current law with the conductance version of Ohm's law leads to the *nodal* equations for the voltages:

$$Gv = c.$$

Here v is the voltage vector,

$$v = \begin{pmatrix} v_1 \\ v_2 \\ v_3 \\ v_4 \end{pmatrix},$$

c is the source current vector,

$$c = \begin{pmatrix} 0 \\ 0 \\ g_{35} v_s \\ 0 \end{pmatrix},$$

and G is the conductance matrix,

$$\begin{pmatrix} g_{12}+g_{13}+g_{14} & -g_{12} & -g_{13} & -g_{14} \\ -g_{12} & g_{12}+g_{23}+g_{25} & -g_{23} & 0 \\ -g_{13} & -g_{23} & g_{13}+g_{23}+g_{34}+g_{35} & -g_{34} \\ -g_{14} & 0 & -g_{34} & g_{14}+g_{34}+g_{45} \end{pmatrix}.$$

You can solve the linear system obtained from the loop equations to compute the currents and then use Ohm's law to recover the voltages. Or you can solve the linear system obtained from the node equations to compute the voltages and then use Ohm's law to recover the currents. Your assignment is to verify that these two approaches produce the same results for this circuit. You can choose your own numerical values for the resistances and the voltage source.

2.5. The Cholesky algorithm factors an important class of matrices known as *positive definite* matrices. Andre-Louis Cholesky (1875–1918) was a French military officer involved in geodesy and surveying in Crete and North Africa just before World War I. He developed the method now named after him to compute solutions to the normal equations for some least squares data-fitting problems arising in geodesy. His work was posthumously published on his behalf in 1924 by a fellow officer, Benoit, in the *Bulletin Geodesique*.

A real symmetric matrix $A = A^T$ is *positive definite* if any of the following equivalent conditions hold:

- The *quadratic form*

$$x^T A x$$

  is positive for all nonzero vectors x.

- All *determinants* formed from symmetric submatrices of any order centered on the diagonal of A are positive.

- All *eigenvalues* $\lambda(A)$ are positive.

- There is a real matrix R such that

$$A = R^T R.$$

These conditions are difficult or expensive to use as the basis for checking if a particular matrix is positive definite. In MATLAB, the best way to check positive definiteness is with the chol function. See

```
help chol
```

(a) Which of the following families of matrices are positive definite?

```
M = magic(n)
H = hilb(n)
P = pascal(n)
I = eye(n,n)
R = randn(n,n)
R = randn(n,n); A = R' * R
R = randn(n,n); A = R' + R
R = randn(n,n); I = eye(n,n); A = R' + R + n*I
```

(b) If the matrix R is upper triangular, then equating individual elements in the equation $A = R^T R$ gives

$$a_{kj} = \sum_{i=1}^{k} r_{ik} r_{ij}, \ k \le j.$$

Using these equations in different orders yields different variants of the Cholesky algorithm for computing the elements of R. What is one such algorithm?

2.6. This example shows that a badly conditioned matrix does not necessarily lead to small pivots in Gaussian elimination. The matrix is the n-by-n upper triangular matrix A with elements

$$a_{ij} = \begin{cases} -1, \ i < j, \\ 1, \ i = j, \\ 0, \ i > j. \end{cases}$$

Show how to generate this matrix in MATLAB with eye, ones, and triu.
Show that

$$\kappa_1(A) = n2^{n-1}.$$

For what n does $\kappa_1(A)$ exceed 1/eps?
This matrix is not singular, so Ax cannot be zero unless x is zero. However, there are vectors x for which $\|Ax\|$ is much smaller than $\|x\|$. Find one such x.
Because this matrix is already upper triangular, Gaussian elimination with partial pivoting has no work to do. What are the pivots?
Use lugui to design a pivot strategy that will produce smaller pivots than partial pivoting. (Even these pivots do not completely reveal the large condition number.)

2.7. The matrix factorization

$$LU = PA$$

can be used to compute the determinant of A. We have

$$\det(L)\det(U) = \det(P)\det(A).$$

Because L is triangular with ones on the diagonal, $\det(L) = 1$. Because U is triangular, $\det(U) = u_{11}u_{22}\cdots u_{nn}$. Because P is a permutation, $\det(P) = +1$ if the number of interchanges is even and -1 if it is odd. So

$$\det(A) = \pm u_{11}u_{22}\cdots u_{nn}.$$

Modify the lutx function so that it returns four outputs.

```
function [L,U,p,sig] = lutx(A)
%LU Triangular factorization
%   [L,U,p,sig] = lutx(A) computes a unit lower triangular
%   matrix L, an upper triangular matrix U, a permutation
%   vector p, and a scalar sig, so that L*U = A(p,:) and
%   sig = +1 or -1 if p is an even or odd permutation.
```

Write a function `mydet(A)` that uses your modified `lutx` to compute the determinant of A. In MATLAB, the product $u_{11}u_{22}\cdots u_{nn}$ can be computed by the expression `prod(diag(U))`.

2.8. Modify the `lutx` function so that it uses explicit `for` loops instead of MATLAB vector notation. For example, one section of your modified program will read

```
% Compute the multipliers
for i = k+1:n
   A(i,k) = A(i,k)/A(k,k);
end
```

Compare the execution time of your modified `lutx` program with the original `lutx` program and with the built-in `lu` function by finding the order of the matrix for which each of the three programs takes about 10 s on your computer.

2.9. Let

$$
A = \begin{pmatrix} 1 & 2 & 3 \\ 4 & 5 & 6 \\ 7 & 8 & 9 \end{pmatrix}, \quad b = \begin{pmatrix} 1 \\ 3 \\ 5 \end{pmatrix}.
$$

(a) Show that the set of linear equations $Ax = b$ has infinitely many solutions. Describe the set of possible solutions.

(b) Suppose Gaussian elimination is used to solve $Ax = b$ using exact arithmetic. Because there are infinitely many solutions, it is unreasonable to expect one particular solution to be computed. What does happen?

(c) Use `bslashtx` to solve $Ax = b$ on an actual computer with floating-point arithmetic. What solution is obtained? Why? In what sense is it a "good" solution? In what sense is it a "bad" solution?

(d) Explain why the built-in backslash operator `x = A\b` gives a different solution from `x = bslashtx(A,b)`.

2.10. Section 2.4 gives two algorithms for solving triangular systems. One subtracts columns of the triangular matrix from the right-hand side; the other uses inner products between the rows of the triangular matrix and the emerging solution.

(a) Which of these two algorithms does `bslashtx` use?

(b) Write another function, `bslashtx2`, that uses the other algorithm.

2.11. The inverse of a matrix A can be defined as the matrix X whose columns x_j solve the equations

$$
Ax_j = e_j,
$$

where e_j is the jth column of the identity matrix.

(a) Starting with the function `bslashtx`, write a MATLAB function

```
X = myinv(A)
```

that computes the inverse of A. Your function should call `lutx` only once and should not use the built-in MATLAB backslash operator or `inv` function.

(b) Test your function by comparing the inverses it computes with the inverses obtained from the built-in `inv(A)` on a few test matrices.

2.12. If the built-in MATLAB lu function is called with only two output arguments

```
[L,U] = lu(A)
```

the permutations are incorporated into the output matrix L. The help entry for lu describes L as "psychologically lower triangular." Modify lutx so that it does the same thing. You can use

```
if nargout == 2, ...
```

to test the number of output arguments.

2.13. (a) Why is

```
M = magic(8)
lugui(M)
```

an interesting example?
(b) How is the behavior of lugui(M) related to rank(M)?
(c) Can you pick a sequence of pivots so that no roundoff error occurs in lugui(M)?

2.14. The pivot selection strategy known as *complete pivoting* is one of the options available in lugui. It has some slight numerical advantages over *partial pivoting*. At each state of the elimination, the element of largest magnitude in the entire unreduced matrix is selected as the pivot. This involves both row and column interchanges and produces two permutation vectors p and q so that

```
L*U = A(p,q)
```

Modify lutx and bslashtx so that they use complete pivoting.

2.15. The function golub in the NCM directory is named after Stanford professor Gene Golub. The function generates test matrices with random integer entries. The matrices are very badly conditioned, but Gaussian elimination without pivoting fails to produce the small pivots that would reveal the large condition number.
(a) How does condest(golub(n)) grow with increasing order n? Because these are random matrices you can't be very precise here, but you can give some qualitative description.
(b) What atypical behavior do you observe with the diagonal pivoting option in lugui(golub(n))?
(c) What is det(golub(n))? Why?

2.16. The function pascal generates symmetric test matrices based on Pascal's triangle.
(a) How are the elements of pascal(n+1) related to the binomial coefficients generated by nchoosek(n,k)?
(b) How is chol(pascal(n)) related to pascal(n)?
(c) How does condest(pascal(n)) grow with increasing order n?
(d) What is det(pascal(n))? Why?
(e) Let Q be the matrix generated by

```
Q = pascal(n);
Q(n,n) = Q(n,n) - 1;
```

How is chol(Q) related to chol(pascal(n))? Why?

(f) What is det(Q)? Why?

2.17. Play "Pivot Pickin' Golf" with pivotgolf. The goal is to use lugui to compute the LU decompositions of nine matrices with as little roundoff error as possible. The score for each hole is

$$\|R\|_\infty + \|L_\epsilon\|_\infty + \|U_\epsilon\|_\infty,$$

where $R = LU - PAQ$ is the residual and $\|L_\epsilon\|_\infty$ and $\|U_\epsilon\|_\infty$ are the nonzeros that should be zero in L and U.

(a) Can you beat the scores obtained by partial pivoting on any of the courses?

(b) Can you get a perfect score of zero on any of the courses?

2.18. The object of this exercise is to investigate how the condition numbers of random matrices grow with their order. Let R_n denote an n-by-n matrix with normally distributed random elements. You should observe experimentally that there is an exponent p so that

$$\kappa_1(R_n) = O(n^p).$$

In other words, there are constants c_1 and c_2 so that most values of $\kappa_1(R_n)$ satisfy

$$c_1 n^p \le \kappa_1(R_n) \le c_2 n^p.$$

Your job is to find p, c_1, and c_2.

The NCM M-file randncond.m is the starting point for your experiments. This program generates random matrices with normally distributed elements and plots their l_1 condition numbers versus their order on a loglog scale. The program also plots two lines that are intended to enclose most of the observations. (On a loglog scale, power laws like $\kappa = cn^p$ produce straight lines.)

(a) Modify randncond.m so that the two lines have the same slope and enclose most of the observations.

(b) Based on this experiment, what is your guess for the exponent p in $\kappa(R_n) = O(n^p)$? How confident are you?

(c) The program uses ('erasemode', 'none'), so you cannot print the results. What would you have to change to make printing possible?

2.19. For $n = 100$, solve this tridiagonal system of equations three different ways:

$$2x_1 - x_2 = 1,$$
$$-x_{j-1} + 2x_j - x_{j+1} = j, \ j = 2, \ldots, n-1,$$
$$-x_{n-1} + 2x_n = n.$$

(a) Use diag three times to form the coefficient matrix and then use lutx and bslashtx to solve the system.

(b) Use spdiags once to form a sparse representation of the coefficient matrix and then use the backslash operator to solve the system.

(c) Use tridisolve to solve the system.

(d) Use condest to estimate the condition of the coefficient matrix.

2.20. Use surfer and pagerank to compute PageRanks for some subset of the Web that you choose. Do you see any interesting structure in the results?

2.21. Suppose that U and G are the URL cell array and the connectivity matrix produced by `surfer` and that k is an integer. Explain what

```
U{k}, U(k), G(k,:), G(:,k), U(G(k,:)), U(G(:,k))
```

are.

2.22. The connectivity matrix for the `harvard500` data set has four small, almost entirely nonzero, submatrices that produce dense patches near the diagonal of the `spy` plot. You can use the zoom button to find their indices. The first submatrix has indices around 170 and the other three have indices in the 200s and 300s. Mathematically, a graph with every node connected to every other node is known as a *clique*. Identify the organizations within the Harvard community that are responsible for these near cliques.

2.23. A Web connectivity matrix G has $g_{ij} = 1$ if it is possible to get to page i from page j with one click. If you multiply the matrix by itself, the entries of the matrix G^2 count the number of different paths of length two to page i from page j. The matrix power G^p shows the number of paths of length p.
(a) For the `harvard500` data set, find the power p where the number of nonzeros stops increasing. In other words, for any q greater than p, `nnz(G^q)` is equal to `nnz(G^p)`.
(b) What fraction of the entries in G^p are nonzero?
(c) Use `subplot` and `spy` to show the nonzeros in the successive powers.
(d) Is there a set of interconnected pages that do not link to the other pages?

2.24. The function `surfer` uses a subfunction, `hashfun`, to speed up the search for a possibly new URL in the list of URLs that have already been processed. Find two different URLs on The MathWorks home page `http://www.mathworks.com` that have the same `hashfun` value.

2.25. Figure 2.8 is the graph of another six-node subset of the Web. In this example, there are two disjoint subgraphs.

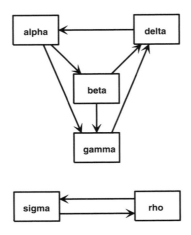

Figure 2.8. *Another tiny Web.*

(a) What is the connectivity matrix G?

(b) What are the PageRanks if the hyperlink transition probability p is the default value 0.85?

(c) Describe what happens with this example to both the definition of PageRank and the computation done by pagerank in the limit $p \to 1$.

2.26. The function pagerank(U,G) computes PageRanks by solving a sparse linear system. It then plots a bar graph and prints the dominant URLs.

(a) Create pagerank1(G) by modifying pagerank so that it just computes the PageRanks, but does not do any plotting or printing.

(b) Create pagerank2(G) by modifying pagerank1 to use inverse iteration instead of solving the sparse linear system. The key statements are

```
x = (I - A)\e
x = x/sum(x)
```

What should be done in the unlikely event that the backslash operation involves a division by zero?

(c) Create pagerank3(G) by modifying pagerank1 to use the power method instead of solving the sparse linear system. The key statements are

```
while termination_test
    x = A*x;
end
```

What is an appropriate test for terminating the power iteration?

(d) Use your functions to compute the PageRanks of the six-node example discussed in the text. Make sure you get the correct result from each of your three functions.

2.27. Here is yet another function for computing PageRank. This version uses the power method, but does not do any matrix operations. Only the link structure of the connectivity matrix is involved.

```
function [x,cnt] = pagerankpow(G)
% PAGERANKPOW  PageRank by power method.
% x = pagerankpow(G) is the PageRank of the graph G.
% [x,cnt] = pagerankpow(G)
%     counts the number of iterations.

% Link structure

[n,n] = size(G);
for j = 1:n
    L{j} = find(G(:,j));
    c(j) = length(L{j});
end

% Power method

p = .85;
```

```
delta = (1-p)/n;
x = ones(n,1)/n;
z = zeros(n,1);
cnt = 0;
while max(abs(x-z)) > .0001
    z = x;
    x = zeros(n,1);
    for j = 1:n
        if c(j) == 0
            x = x + z(j)/n;
        else
            x(L{j}) = x(L{j}) + z(j)/c(j);
        end
    end
    x = p*x + delta;
    cnt = cnt+1;
end
```

(a) How do the storage requirements and execution time of this function compare
with the three `pagerank` functions from exercise 2.26?
(b) Use this function as a template to write a function that computes PageRank in
some other programming language.

Chapter 3

Interpolation

Interpolation is the process of defining a function that takes on specified values at specified points. This chapter concentrates on two closely related interpolants: the piecewise cubic spline and the shape-preserving piecewise cubic named "pchip."

3.1 The Interpolating Polynomial

We all know that two points determine a straight line. More precisely, any two points in the plane, (x_1, y_1) and (x_2, y_2), with $x_1 \neq x_2$, determine a unique first-degree polynomial in x whose graph passes through the two points. There are many different formulas for the polynomial, but they all lead to the same straight line graph.

This generalizes to more than two points. Given n points in the plane, (x_k, y_k), $k = 1, \ldots, n$, with distinct x_k's, there is a unique polynomial in x of degree less than n whose graph passes through the points. It is easiest to remember that n, the number of data points, is also the number of coefficients, although some of the leading coefficients might be zero, so the degree might actually be less than $n - 1$. Again, there are many different formulas for the polynomial, but they all define the same function.

This polynomial is called the *interpolating* polynomial because it exactly reproduces the given data:

$$P(x_k) = y_k, \ k = 1, \ldots, n.$$

Later, we examine other polynomials, of lower degree, that only approximate the data. They are *not* interpolating polynomials.

The most compact representation of the interpolating polynomial is the *Lagrange* form

$$P(x) = \sum_k \left(\prod_{j \neq k} \frac{x - x_j}{x_k - x_j} \right) y_k.$$

There are n terms in the sum and $n - 1$ terms in each product, so this expression defines a polynomial of degree at most $n - 1$. If $P(x)$ is evaluated at $x = x_k$, all the products except the kth are zero. Furthermore, the kth product is equal to one, so the sum is equal to y_k and the interpolation conditions are satisfied.

For example, consider the following data set.

```
x = 0:3;
y = [-5   -6   -1   16];
```

The command

```
disp([x;   y])
```

displays

```
    0       1       2       3
   -5      -6      -1      16
```

The Lagrangian form of the polynomial interpolating these data is

$$P(x) = \frac{(x-1)(x-2)(x-3)}{(-6)}(-5) + \frac{x(x-2)(x-3)}{(2)}(-6)$$
$$+ \frac{x(x-1)(x-3)}{(-2)}(-1) + \frac{x(x-1)(x-2)}{(6)}(16).$$

We can see that each term is of degree three, so the entire sum has degree at most three. Because the leading term does not vanish, the degree is actually three. Moreover, if we plug in $x = 0, 1, 2$, or 3, three of the terms vanish and the fourth produces the corresponding value from the data set.

Polynomials are not usually represented in their Lagrangian form. More frequently, they are written as something like

$$x^3 - 2x - 5.$$

The simple powers of x are called *monomials*, and this form of a polynomial is said to be using the *power form*.

The coefficients of an interpolating polynomial using its power form,

$$P(x) = c_1 x^{n-1} + c_2 x^{n-2} + \cdots + c_{n-1} x + c_n,$$

can, in principle, be computed by solving a system of simultaneous linear equations

$$\begin{pmatrix} x_1^{n-1} & x_1^{n-2} & \cdots & x_1 & 1 \\ x_2^{n-1} & x_2^{n-2} & \cdots & x_2 & 1 \\ \cdots & \cdots & \cdots & \cdots & 1 \\ x_n^{n-1} & x_n^{n-2} & \cdots & x_n & 1 \end{pmatrix} \begin{pmatrix} c_1 \\ c_2 \\ \vdots \\ c_n \end{pmatrix} = \begin{pmatrix} y_1 \\ y_2 \\ \vdots \\ y_n \end{pmatrix}.$$

The matrix V of this linear system is known as a *Vandermonde* matrix. Its elements are

$$v_{k,j} = x_k^{n-j}.$$

The columns of a Vandermonde matrix are sometimes written in the opposite order, but polynomial coefficient vectors in MATLAB always have the highest power first.

The MATLAB function vander generates Vandermonde matrices. For our example data set,

```
V = vander(x)
```

generates

```
V =
         0        0        0        1
         1        1        1        1
         8        4        2        1
        27        9        3        1
```

Then

```
c = V\y'
```

computes the coefficients.

```
c =
     1.0000
     0.0000
    -2.0000
    -5.0000
```

In fact, the example data were generated from the polynomial $x^3 - 2x - 5$.

Exercise 3.6 asks you to show that Vandermonde matrices are nonsingular if the points x_k are distinct. But Exercise 3.19 asks you to show that a Vandermonde matrix can be very badly conditioned. Consequently, using the power form and the Vandermonde matrix is a satisfactory technique for problems involving a few well-spaced and well-scaled data points. But as a general-purpose approach, it is dangerous.

In this chapter, we describe several MATLAB functions that implement various interpolation algorithms. All of them have the calling sequence

$$v = interp(x,y,u)$$

The first two input arguments, x and y, are vectors of the same length that define the interpolating points. The third input argument, u, is a vector of points where the function is to be evaluated. The output v is the same length as u and has elements $v(k) = interp(x,y,u(k))$

Our first such interpolation function, polyinterp, is based on the Lagrange form. The code uses MATLAB array operations to evaluate the polynomial at all the components of u simultaneously.

```
function v = polyinterp(x,y,u)
n = length(x);
v = zeros(size(u));
for k = 1:n
   w = ones(size(u));
   for j = [1:k-1 k+1:n]
      w = (u-x(j))./(x(k)-x(j)).*w;
   end
   v = v + w*y(k);
end
```

To illustrate `polyinterp`, create a vector of densely spaced evaluation points.

```
u = -.25:.01:3.25;
```

Then

```
v = polyinterp(x,y,u);
plot(x,y,'o',u,v,'-')
```

creates Figure 3.1.

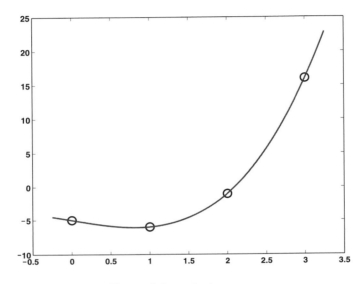

Figure 3.1. `polyinterp`.

The `polyinterp` function also works correctly with symbolic variables.   For example, create

```
symx = sym('x')
```

Then evaluate and display the symbolic form of the interpolating polynomial with

```
P = polyinterp(x,y,symx)
pretty(P)
```

which produces

```
-5 (-1/3 x + 1)(-1/2 x + 1)(-x + 1) - 6 (-1/2 x + 3/2)(-x + 2)x
-1/2 (-x + 3)(x - 1)x + 16/3 (x - 2)(1/2 x - 1/2)x
```

This expression is a rearrangement of the Lagrange form of the interpolating polynomial. Simplifying the Lagrange form with

```
P = simplify(P)
```

changes P to the power form

```
P =
   x^3-2*x-5
```

Here is another example, with a data set that is used by the other methods in this chapter.

```
x = 1:6;
y = [16 18 21 17 15 12];
disp([x; y])
u = .75:.05:6.25;
v = polyinterp(x,y,u);
plot(x,y,'o',u,v,'-');
```

produces

1	2	3	4	5	6
16	18	21	17	15	12

and Figure 3.2.

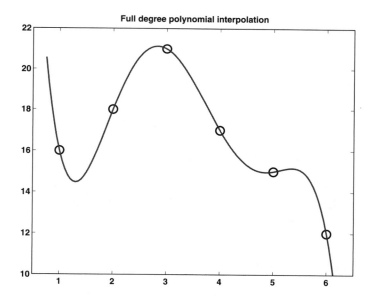

Figure 3.2. *Full-degree polynomial interpolation.*

Already in this example, with only six nicely spaced points, we can begin to see the primary difficulty with full-degree polynomial interpolation. In between the data points, especially in the first and last subintervals, the function shows excessive variation. It over-shoots the changes in the data values. As a result, full-degree polynomial interpolation is hardly ever used for data and curve fitting. Its primary application is in the derivation of other numerical methods.

3.2   Piecewise Linear Interpolation

You can create a simple picture of the data set from the last section by plotting the data
twice, once with circles at the data points and once with straight lines connecting the points.
The following statements produce Figure 3.3.

```
x = 1:6;
y = [16 18 21 17 15 12];
plot(x,y,'o',x,y,'-');
```

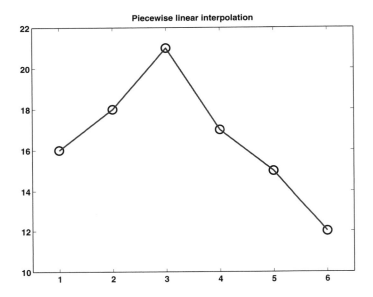

Figure 3.3. *Piecewise linear interpolation.*

To generate the lines, the MATLAB graphics routines use *piecewise linear* interpolation. The algorithm sets the stage for more sophisticated algorithms. Three quantities are
involved. The *interval index k* must be determined so that

$$x_k \leq x < x_{k+1}.$$

The *local variable, s*, is given by

$$s = x - x_k.$$

The *first divided difference* is

$$\delta_k = \frac{y_{k+1} - y_k}{x_{k+1} - x_k}.$$

With these quantities in hand, the interpolant is

$$L(x) = y_k + (x - x_k)\frac{y_{k+1} - y_k}{x_{k+1} - x_k}$$
$$= y_k + s\delta_k.$$

This is clearly a linear function that passes through (x_k, y_k) and (x_{k+1}, y_{k+1}).

The points x_k are sometimes called *breakpoints* or *breaks*. The piecewise linear interpolant $L(x)$ is a continuous function of x, but its first derivative, $L'(x)$, is not continuous. The derivative has a constant value, δ_k, on each subinterval and jumps at the breakpoints.

Piecewise linear interpolation is implemented in `piecelin.m`. The input u can be a vector of points where the interpolant is to be evaluated. In this case, the index k is actually a vector of indices. Read this code carefully to understand how k is computed.

```
function v = piecelin(x,y,u)
%PIECELIN   Piecewise linear interpolation.
%   v = piecelin(x,y,u) finds the piecewise linear L(x)
%   with L(x(j)) = y(j) and returns v(k) = L(u(k)).

%   First divided difference

    delta = diff(y)./diff(x);

%   Find subinterval indices k so that x(k) <= u < x(k+1)

    n = length(x);
    k = ones(size(u));
    for j = 2:n-1
        k(x(j) <= u) = j;
    end

%   Evaluate interpolant

    s = u - x(k);
    v = y(k) + s.*delta(k);
```

3.3   Piecewise Cubic Hermite Interpolation

Many of the most effective interpolation techniques are based on piecewise cubic polynomials. Let h_k denote the length of the kth subinterval:

$$h_k = x_{k+1} - x_k.$$

Then the first divided difference, δ_k, is given by

$$\delta_k = \frac{y_{k+1} - y_k}{h_k}.$$

Let d_k denote the slope of the interpolant at x_k:

$$d_k = P'(x_k).$$

For the piecewise linear interpolant, $d_k = \delta_{k-1}$ or δ_k, but this is not necessarily true for higher order interpolants.

Consider the following function on the interval $x_k \leq x \leq x_{k+1}$, expressed in terms of local variables $s = x - x_k$ and $h = h_k$:

$$P(x) = \frac{3hs^2 - 2s^3}{h^3} y_{k+1} + \frac{h^3 - 3hs^2 + 2s^3}{h^3} y_k$$
$$+ \frac{s^2(s-h)}{h^2} d_{k+1} + \frac{s(s-h)^2}{h^2} d_k.$$

This is a cubic polynomial in s, and hence in x, that satisfies four interpolation conditions, two on function values and two on the possibly unknown derivative values:

$$P(x_k) = y_k, \; P(x_{k+1}) = y_{k+1},$$
$$P'(x_k) = d_k, \; P'(x_{k+1}) = d_{k+1}.$$

Functions that satisfy interpolation conditions on derivatives are known as *Hermite* or *osculatory* interpolants, because of the higher order contact at the interpolation sites. ("Osculari" means "to kiss" in Latin.)

If we happen to know both function values and first derivative values at a set of data points, then piecewise cubic Hermite interpolation can reproduce those data. But if we are not given the derivative values, we need to define the slopes d_k somehow. Of the many possible ways to do this, we will describe two, which MATLAB calls pchip and spline.

3.4   Shape-Preserving Piecewise Cubic

The acronym pchip abbreviates "piecewise cubic Hermite interpolating polynomial." Although it is fun to say, the name does not specify which of the many possible interpolants is actually being used. In fact, spline interpolants are also piecewise cubic Hermite interpolating polynomials, but with different slopes. Our particular pchip is a shape-preserving, "visually pleasing" interpolant that was introduced into MATLAB fairly recently. It is based on an old Fortran program by Fritsch and Carlson [23] that is described by Kahaner, Moler, and Nash [34]. Figure 3.4 shows how pchip interpolates our sample data.

The key idea is to determine the slopes d_k so that the function values do not overshoot the data values, at least locally. If δ_k and δ_{k-1} have opposite signs or if either of them is zero, then x_k is a discrete local minimum or maximum, so we set

$$d_k = 0.$$

This is illustrated in the first half of Figure 3.5. The lower solid line is the piecewise linear interpolant. Its slopes on either side of the breakpoint in the center have opposite signs. Consequently, the dashed line has slope zero. The curved line is the shape-preserving interpolant, formed from two different cubics. The two cubics interpolate the center value and their derivatives are both zero there. But there is a jump in the second derivative at the breakpoint.

If δ_k and δ_{k-1} have the same sign and the two intervals have the same length, then d_k is taken to be the harmonic mean of the two discrete slopes:

$$\frac{1}{d_k} = \frac{1}{2}\left(\frac{1}{\delta_{k-1}} + \frac{1}{\delta_k}\right).$$

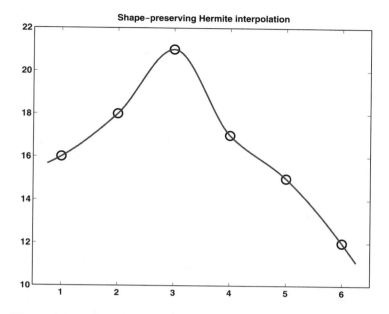

Figure 3.4. *Shape-preserving piecewise cubic Hermite interpolation.*

In other words, at the breakpoint, the reciprocal slope of the Hermite interpolant is the average of the reciprocal slopes of the piecewise linear interpolant on either side. This is shown in the other half of Figure 3.5. At the breakpoint, the reciprocal slope of the piecewise linear interpolant changes from 1 to 5. The reciprocal slope of the dashed line is 3, the average of 1 and 5. The shape-preserving interpolant is formed from the 2 cubics that interpolate the center value and that have slope equal to $1/3$ there. Again, there is a jump in the second derivative at the breakpoint.

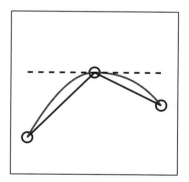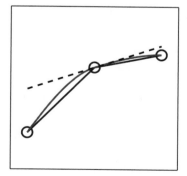

Figure 3.5. *Slopes for* `pchip`.

If δ_k and δ_{k-1} have the same sign, but the two intervals have different lengths, then d_k is a weighted harmonic mean, with weights determined by the lengths of the two intervals:

$$\frac{w_1 + w_2}{d_k} = \frac{w_1}{\delta_{k-1}} + \frac{w_2}{\delta_k},$$

where

$$w_1 = 2h_k + h_{k-1}, \; w_2 = h_k + 2h_{k-1}.$$

This defines the `pchip` slopes at interior breakpoints, but the slopes d_1 and d_n at either end of the data interval are determined by a slightly different, one-sided analysis. The details are in `pchiptx.m`.

3.5   Cubic Spline

Our other piecewise cubic interpolating function is a *cubic spline*. The term "spline" refers to an instrument used in drafting. It is a thin, flexible wooden or plastic tool that is passed through given data points and defines a smooth curve in between. The physical spline minimizes potential energy subject to the interpolation constraints. The corresponding mathematical spline must have a continuous second derivative and satisfy the same interpolation constraints. The breakpoints of a spline are also referred to as its *knots*.

The world of splines extends far beyond the basic one-dimensional, cubic, interpolatory spline we are describing here. There are multidimensional, high-order, variable knot, and approximating splines. A valuable expository and reference text for both the mathematics and the software is *A Practical Guide to Splines* by Carl de Boor [16]. De Boor is also the author of the `spline` function and the Spline Toolbox for MATLAB.

Figure 3.6 shows how `spline` interpolates our sample data.

The first derivative $P'(x)$ of our piecewise cubic function is defined by different formulas on either side of a knot x_k. Both formulas yield the same value d_k at the knots, so $P'(x)$ is continuous.

On the kth subinterval, the second derivative is a linear function of $s = x - x_k$:

$$P''(x) = \frac{(6h - 12s)\delta_k + (6s - 2h)d_{k+1} + (6s - 4h)d_k}{h^2}.$$

If $x = x_k$, $s = 0$ and

$$P''(x_k+) = \frac{6\delta_k - 2d_{k+1} - 4d_k}{h_k}.$$

The plus sign in x_k+ indicates that this is a one-sided derivative. If $x = x_{k+1}$, $s = h_k$ and

$$P''(x_{k+1}-) = \frac{-6\delta_k + 4d_{k+1} + 2d_k}{h_k}.$$

On the $(k - 1)$st interval, $P''(x)$ is given by a similar formula involving δ_{k-1}, d_k, and d_{k-1}. At the knot x_k,

$$P''(x_k-) = \frac{-6\delta_{k-1} + 4d_k + 2d_{k-1}}{h_{k-1}}.$$

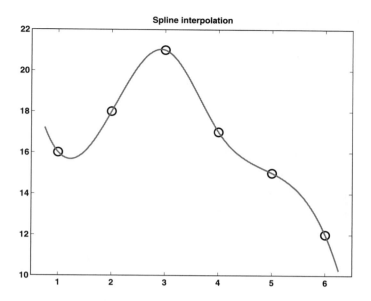

Figure 3.6. *Cubic spline interpolation.*

Requiring $P''(x)$ to be continuous at $x = x_k$ means that

$$P''(x_k+) = P''(x_k-).$$

This leads to the condition

$$h_k d_{k-1} + 2(h_{k-1} + h_k)d_k + h_{k-1}d_{k+1} = 3(h_k \delta_{k-1} + h_{k-1}\delta_k).$$

If the knots are equally spaced, so that h_k does not depend on k, this becomes

$$d_{k-1} + 4d_k + d_{k+1} = 3\delta_{k-1} + 3\delta_k.$$

Like our other interpolants, the slopes d_k of a spline are closely related to the differences δ_k. In the spline case, they are a kind of running average of the δ_k's.

The preceding approach can be applied at each interior knot x_k, $k = 2, \ldots, n-1$, to give $n-2$ equations involving the n unknowns d_k. As with `pchip`, a different approach must be used near the ends of the interval. One effective strategy is known as "not-a-knot." The idea is to use a single cubic on the first two subintervals, $x_1 \leq x \leq x_3$, and on the last two subintervals, $x_{n-2} \leq x \leq x_n$. In effect, x_2 and x_{n-1} are not knots. If the knots are equally spaced with all $h_k = 1$, this leads to

$$d_1 + 2d_2 = \frac{5}{2}\delta_1 + \frac{1}{2}\delta_2$$

and

$$2d_{n-1} + d_n = \frac{1}{2}\delta_{n-2} + \frac{5}{2}\delta_{n-1}.$$

The details if the spacing is not equal to one are in `splinetx.m`.

With the two end conditions included, we have n linear equations in n unknowns:

$$Ad = r.$$

The vector of unknown slopes is

$$d = \begin{pmatrix} d_1 \\ d_2 \\ \vdots \\ d_n \end{pmatrix}.$$

The coefficient matrix A is tridiagonal:

$$A = \begin{pmatrix} h_2 & h_2 + h_1 \\ h_2 & 2(h_1 + h_2) & h_1 \\ & h_3 & 2(h_2 + h_3) & h_2 \\ & & \ddots & \ddots & \ddots \\ & & & h_{n-1} & 2(h_{n-2} + h_{n-1}) & h_{n-2} \\ & & & & h_{n-1} + h_{n-2} & h_{n-2} \end{pmatrix}.$$

The right-hand side is

$$r = 3 \begin{pmatrix} r_1 \\ h_2\delta_1 + h_1\delta_2 \\ h_3\delta_2 + h_2\delta_3 \\ \vdots \\ h_{n-1}\delta_{n-2} + h_{n-2}\delta_{n-1} \\ r_n \end{pmatrix}.$$

The two values r_1 and r_n are associated with the end conditions.

If the knots are equally spaced with all $h_k = 1$, the coefficient matrix is quite simple:

$$A = \begin{pmatrix} 1 & 2 \\ 1 & 4 & 1 \\ & 1 & 4 & 1 \\ & & \ddots & \ddots & \ddots \\ & & & 1 & 4 & 1 \\ & & & & 2 & 1 \end{pmatrix}.$$

The right-hand side is

$$r = 3 \begin{pmatrix} \frac{5}{6}\delta_1 + \frac{1}{6}\delta_2 \\ \delta_1 + \delta_2 \\ \delta_2 + \delta_3 \\ \vdots \\ \delta_{n-2} + \delta_{n-1} \\ \frac{1}{6}\delta_{n-2} + \frac{5}{6}\delta_{n-1} \end{pmatrix}.$$

In our textbook function, `splinetx`, the linear equations defining the slopes are solved with the `tridisolve` function introduced in Chapter 2, Linear Equations. In the spline functions distributed with MATLAB and the Spline Toolbox, the slopes are computed by the MATLAB backslash operator

$$\texttt{d = A\textbackslash r}$$

Because most of the elements of A are zero, it is appropriate to store A in a *sparse* data structure. The backslash operator can then take advantage of the tridiagonal structure and solve the linear equations in time and storage proportional to n, the number of data points.

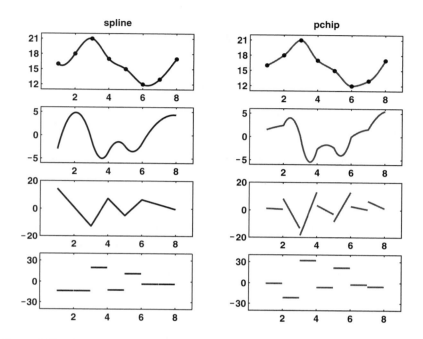

Figure 3.7. *The spline and* pchip *interpolants, and their first three derivatives.*

Figure 3.7 compares the spline interpolant, $s(x)$, with the pchip interpolant, $p(x)$. The difference between the functions themselves is barely noticeable. The first derivative of spline, $s'(x)$, is smooth, while the first derivative of pchip, $p'(x)$, is continuous, but shows "kinks." The spline second derivative $s''(x)$ is continuous, while the pchip second derivative $p''(x)$ has jumps at the knots. Because both functions are piecewise cubics, their third derivatives, $s'''(x)$ and $p'''(x)$, are piecewise constant. The fact that $s'''(x)$ takes on the same values in the first two intervals and the last two intervals reflects the "not-a-knot" spline end conditions.

3.6 pchiptx, splinetx

The M-files pchiptx and splinetx are both based on piecewise cubic Hermite interpolation. On the kth interval, this is

$$P(x) = \frac{3hs^2 - 2s^3}{h^3} y_{k+1} + \frac{h^3 - 3hs^2 + 2s^3}{h^3} y_k$$
$$+ \frac{s^2(s-h)}{h^2} d_{k+1} + \frac{s(s-h)^2}{h^2} d_k,$$

where $s = x - x_k$ and $h = h_k$. The two functions differ in the way they compute the slopes, d_k. Once the slopes have been computed, the interpolant can be efficiently evaluated using the power form with the local variable s:

$$P(x) = y_k + s d_k + s^2 c_k + s^3 b_k,$$

where the coefficients of the quadratic and cubic terms are

$$c_k = \frac{3\delta_k - 2d_k - d_{k+1}}{h},$$
$$b_k = \frac{d_k - 2\delta_k + d_{k+1}}{h^2}.$$

Here is the first portion of code for pchiptx. It calls an internal subfunction to compute the slopes, then computes the other coefficients, finds a vector of interval indices, and evaluates the interpolant. After the preamble, this part of the code for splinetx is the same.

```
function v = pchiptx(x,y,u)
%PCHIPTX   Textbook piecewise cubic Hermite interpolation.
%  v = pchiptx(x,y,u) finds the shape-preserving piecewise
%  P(x), with P(x(j)) = y(j), and returns v(k) = P(u(k)).
%
%  See PCHIP, SPLINETX.

% First derivatives

   h = diff(x);
   delta = diff(y)./h;
   d = pchipslopes(h,delta);

% Piecewise polynomial coefficients

   n = length(x);
   c = (3*delta - 2*d(1:n-1) - d(2:n))./h;
   b = (d(1:n-1) - 2*delta + d(2:n))./h.^2;

% Find subinterval indices k so that x(k) <= u < x(k+1)

   k = ones(size(u));
   for j = 2:n-1
       k(x(j) <= u) = j;
   end

% Evaluate interpolant

   s = u - x(k);
   v = y(k) + s.*(d(k) + s.*(c(k) + s.*b(k)));
```

The code for computing the pchip slopes uses the weighted harmonic mean at interior breakpoints and a one-sided formula at the endpoints.

```
function d = pchipslopes(h,delta)
%   PCHIPSLOPES  Slopes for shape-preserving Hermite cubic
%   pchipslopes(h,delta) computes d(k) = P'(x(k)).

%   Slopes at interior points
%   delta = diff(y)./diff(x).
%   d(k) = 0 if delta(k-1) and delta(k) have opposites
%          signs or either is zero.
%   d(k) = weighted harmonic mean of delta(k-1) and
%          delta(k) if they have the same sign.

   n = length(h)+1;
   d = zeros(size(h));
   k = find(sign(delta(1:n-2)).*sign(delta(2:n-1))>0)+1;
   w1 = 2*h(k)+h(k-1);
   w2 = h(k)+2*h(k-1);
   d(k) = (w1+w2)./(w1./delta(k-1) + w2./delta(k));

%   Slopes at endpoints

   d(1) = pchipend(h(1),h(2),delta(1),delta(2));
   d(n) = pchipend(h(n-1),h(n-2),delta(n-1),delta(n-2));

function d = pchipend(h1,h2,del1,del2)
%   Noncentered, shape-preserving, three-point formula.
   d = ((2*h1+h2)*del1 - h1*del2)/(h1+h2);
   if sign(d) ~= sign(del1)
      d = 0;
   elseif (sign(del1)~=sign(del2))&(abs(d)>abs(3*del1))
      d = 3*del1;
   end
```

The splinetx M-file computes the slopes by setting up and solving a tridiagonal system of simultaneous linear equations.

```
function d = splineslopes(h,delta);
%   SPLINESLOPES  Slopes for cubic spline interpolation.
%   splineslopes(h,delta) computes d(k) = S'(x(k)).
%   Uses not-a-knot end conditions.

%   Diagonals of tridiagonal system

   n = length(h)+1;
   a = zeros(size(h)); b = a; c = a; r = a;
```

```
a(1:n-2) = h(2:n-1);
a(n-1) = h(n-2)+h(n-1);
b(1) = h(2);
b(2:n-1) = 2*(h(2:n-1)+h(1:n-2));
b(n) = h(n-2);
c(1) = h(1)+h(2);
c(2:n-1) = h(1:n-2);

% Right-hand side

r(1) = ((h(1)+2*c(1))*h(2)*delta(1)+ ...
         h(1)^2*delta(2))/c(1);
r(2:n-1) = 3*(h(2:n-1).*delta(1:n-2)+ ...
             h(1:n-2).*delta(2:n-1));
r(n) = (h(n-1)^2*delta(n-2)+ ...
         (2*a(n-1)+h(n-1))*h(n-2)*delta(n-1))/a(n-1);

% Solve tridiagonal linear system

d = tridisolve(a,b,c,r);
```

3.7 `interpgui`

Figure 3.8 illustrates the tradeoff between smoothness and a somewhat subjective property
that we might call *local monotonicity* or *shape preservation*.

The piecewise linear interpolant is at one extreme. It has hardly any smoothness. It
is continuous, but there are jumps in its first derivative. On the other hand, it preserves the
local monotonicity of the data. It never overshoots the data and it is increasing, decreasing,
or constant on the same intervals as the data.

The full-degree polynomial interpolant is at the other extreme. It is infinitely differ-
entiable. But it often fails to preserve shape, particularly near the ends of the interval.

The `pchip` and spline interpolants are in between these two extremes. The spline
is smoother than `pchip`. The spline has two continuous derivatives, while `pchip` has only
one. A discontinuous second derivative implies discontinuous curvature. The human eye
can detect large jumps in curvature in graphs and in mechanical parts made by numerically
controlled machine tools. On the other hand, `pchip` is guaranteed to preserve shape, but
the spline might not.

The M-file `interpgui` allows you to experiment with the four interpolants discussed
in this chapter:

- piecewise linear interpolant,

- full-degree interpolating polynomial,

- piecewise cubic spline,

- shape-preserving piecewise cubic.

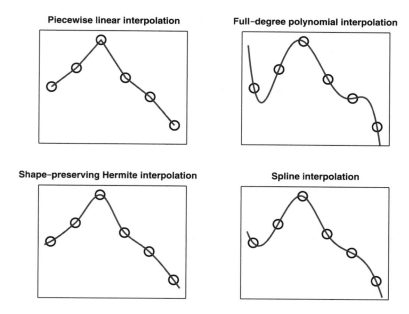

Figure 3.8. *Four interpolants.*

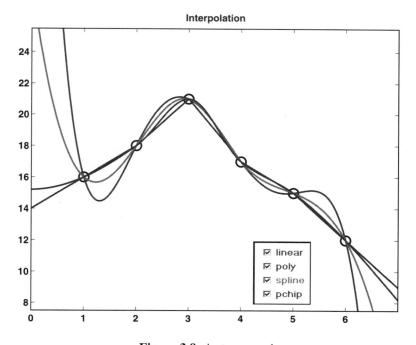

Figure 3.9. interpgui.

The program can be initialized in several different ways:

- With no arguments, `interpgui` starts with 8 zeros.

- With a scalar argument, `interpgui(n)` starts with n zeros.

- With one vector argument, `interpgui(y)` starts with equally spaced x's.

- With two arguments, `interpgui(x,y)` starts with a plot of y versus x.

After initialization, the interpolation points can be varied with the mouse. If x has been specified, it remains fixed. Figure 3.9 is the initial plot generated by our example data.

Exercises

3.1. Reproduce Figure 3.8, with four subplots showing the four interpolants discussed in this chapter.

3.2. Tom and Ben are twin boys born on October 27, 2001. Here is a table of their weights, in pounds and ounces, over their first few months.

```
%          Date           Tom        Ben
W  =  [10 27 2001         5 10       4  8
       11 19 2001         7  4       5 11
       12 03 2001         8 12       6  4
       12 20 2001        10 14       8  7
       01 09 2002        12 13      10  3
       01 23 2002        14  8      12  0
       03 06 2002        16 10      13 10];
```

You can use `datenum` to convert the date in the first three columns to a serial date number measuring time in days.

```
t = datenum(W(:,[3 1 2]));
```

Make a plot of their weights versus time, with circles at the data points and the `pchip` interpolating curve in between. Use `datetick` to relabel the time axis. Include a `title` and a `legend`. The result should look something like Figure 3.10.

3.3. (a) Interpolate these data by each of the four interpolants discussed in this chapter: `piecelin`, `polyinterp`, `splinetx`, and `pchiptx`. Plot the results for $-1 \leq x \leq 1$.

```
      x          y
   -1.00     -1.0000
   -0.96     -0.1512
   -0.65      0.3860
    0.10      0.4802
    0.40      0.8838
    1.00      1.0000
```

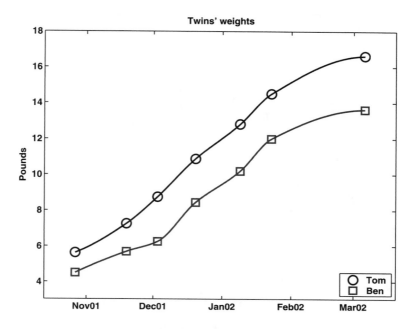

Figure 3.10. *Twins' weights.*

(b) What are the values of each of the four interpolants at $x = -0.3$? Which of these values do you prefer? Why?

(c) The data were actually generated from a low-degree polynomial with integer coefficients. What is that polynomial?

3.4. Make a plot of your hand. Start with

```
figure('position',get(0,'screensize'))
axes('position',[0 0 1 1])
[x,y] = ginput;
```

Place your hand on the computer screen. Use the mouse to select a few dozen points outlining your hand. Terminate the `ginput` with a carriage return. You might find it easier to trace your hand on a piece of paper and then put the paper on the computer screen. You should be able to see the `ginput` cursor through the paper. (Save these data. We will refer to them in other exercises later in this book.)

Now think of x and y as two functions of an independent variable that goes from one to the number of points you collected. You can interpolate both functions on a finer grid and plot the result with

```
n = length(x);
s = (1:n)';
t = (1:.05:n)';
u = splinetx(s,x,t);
```

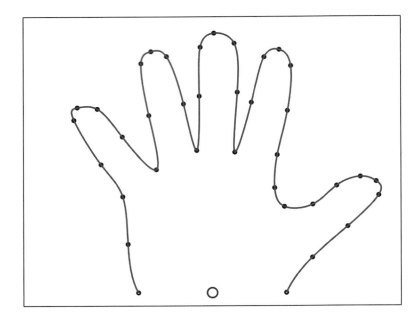

Figure 3.11. *A hand.*

```
v = splinetx(s,y,t);
clf reset
plot(x,y,'.',u,v,'-');
```

Do the same thing with `pchiptx`. Which do you prefer?

Figure 3.11 is the plot of my hand. Can you tell if it was done with `splinetx` or `pchiptx`?

3.5. The previous exercise uses the data index number as the independent variable for two-dimensional parametric interpolation. This exercise uses, instead, the angle θ from polar coordinates. In order to do this, the data must be centered so that they lie on a curve that is *starlike* with respect to the origin, that is, every ray emanating from the origin meets the data only once. This means that you must be able to find values x_0 and y_0 so that the MATLAB statements

```
x = x - x0
y = y - y0
theta = atan2(y,x)
r = sqrt(x.^2 + y.^2)
plot(theta,r)
```

produce a set of points that can be interpolated with a single-valued function, $r = r(\theta)$. For the data obtained by sampling the outline of your hand, the point (x_0, y_0) is located near the base of your palm. See the small circle in Figure 3.11. Furthermore, in order to use `splinetx` and `pchiptx`, it is also necessary to order the data so that `theta` is monotonically increasing.

Choose a subsampling increment, `delta`, and let

```
t = (theta(1):delta:theta(end))';
p = pchiptx(theta,r,t);
s = splinetx(theta,r,t);
```

Examine two plots:

```
plot(theta,r,'o',t,[p s],'-')
```

and

```
plot(x,y,'o',p.*cos(t),p.*sin(t),'-',...
          s.*cos(t),s.*sin(t),'-')
```

Compare this approach with the one used in the previous exercise. Which do you prefer? Why?

3.6. This exercise requires the Symbolic Toolbox.
   (a) What does `vandal(n)` compute and how does it compute it?
   (b) Under what conditions on `x` is the matrix `vander(x)` nonsingular?

3.7. Prove that the interpolating polynomial is unique. That is, if $P(x)$ and $Q(x)$ are two polynomials with degree less than n that agree at n distinct points, then they agree at all points.

3.8. Give convincing arguments that each of the following descriptions defines the *same* polynomial, the Chebyshev polynomial of degree five, $T_5(x)$. Your arguments can involve analytic proofs, symbolic computation, numeric computation, or all three. Two of the representations involve the golden ratio,

$$\phi = \frac{1 + \sqrt{5}}{2}.$$

(a) Power form basis:
$$T_5(x) = 16x^5 - 20x^3 + 5x.$$

(b) Relation to trigonometric functions:
$$T_5(x) = \cos\left(5\cos^{-1} x\right).$$

(c) Horner representation:
$$T_5(x) = ((((16x + 0)x - 20)x + 0)x + 5)x + 0.$$

(d) Lagrange form:
$$x_1, x_6 = \pm 1,$$
$$x_2, x_5 = \pm \phi/2,$$
$$x_3, x_4 = \pm(\phi - 1)/2,$$
$$y_k = (-1)^k, \quad k = 1, \dots, 6,$$
$$T_5(x) = \sum_k \left(\prod_{j \neq k} \frac{x - x_j}{x_k - x_j} \right) y_k.$$

(e) Factored representation:

$$z_1, z_5 = \pm\sqrt{(2+\phi)/4},$$
$$z_2, z_4 = \pm\sqrt{(3-\phi)/4},$$
$$z_3 = 0,$$
$$T_5(x) = 16 \prod_1^5 (x - z_k).$$

(f) Three-term recurrence:

$$T_0(x) = 1,$$
$$T_1(x) = x,$$
$$T_n(x) = 2x T_{n-1}(x) - T_{n-2}(x) \quad \text{for } n = 2, \ldots, 5.$$

3.9. The M-file `rungeinterp.m` provides an experiment with a famous polynomial interpolation problem due to Carl Runge. Let

$$f(x) = \frac{1}{1 + 25x^2},$$

and let $P_n(x)$ denote the polynomial of degree $n-1$ that interpolates $f(x)$ at n equally spaced points on the interval $-1 \le x \le 1$. Runge asked whether, as n increases, $P_n(x)$ converges to $f(x)$. The answer is yes for some x, but no for others.
(a) For what x does $P_n(x) \to f(x)$ as $n \to \infty$?
(b) Change the distribution of the interpolation points so that they are not equally spaced. How does this affect convergence? Can you find a distribution so that $P_n(x) \to f(x)$ for all x in the interval?

3.10. We skipped from piecewise linear to piecewise cubic interpolation. How far can you get with the development of piecewise quadratic interpolation?

3.11. Modify `splinetx` and `pchiptx` so that, if called with two output arguments, they produce both the value of the interpolant and its first derivative. That is,

        [v,vprime] = pchiptx(x,y,u)

and

        [v,vprime] = splinetx(x,y,u)

compute $P(u)$ and $P'(u)$.

3.12. Modify `splinetx` and `pchiptx` so that, if called with only two input arguments, they produce PP, the piecewise polynomial structure produced by the standard MATLAB functions `spline` and `pchip` and used by `ppval`.

3.13. (a) Create two functions `perpchip` and `perspline` by modifying `pchiptx` and `splinetx` to replace the one-sided and not-a-knot end conditions with *periodic* boundary conditions. This requires that the given data have

$$y_n = y_1$$

and that the resulting interpolant be periodic. In other words, for all x,

$$P(x + \Delta) = P(x),$$

where

$$\Delta = x_n - x_1.$$

The algorithms for both `pchip` and spline involve calculations with y_k, h_k, and δ_k to produce slopes d_k. With the periodicity assumption, all of these quantities become periodic functions, with period $n - 1$, of the subscript k. In other words, for all k,

$$y_k = y_{k+n-1},$$
$$h_k = h_{k+n-1},$$
$$\delta_k = \delta_{k+n-1},$$
$$d_k = d_{k+n-1}.$$

This makes it possible to use the same calculations at the endpoints that are used at the interior points in the nonperiodic situation. The special case code for the end conditions can be eliminated and the resulting M-files are actually much simpler. For example, the slopes d_k for `pchip` with equally spaced points are given by

$$d_k = 0 \text{ if } \text{sign}(\delta_{k-1}) \neq \text{sign}(\delta_k),$$

$$\frac{1}{d_k} = \frac{1}{2}\left(\frac{1}{\delta_{k-1}} + \frac{1}{\delta_k}\right) \text{ if } \text{sign}(\delta_{k-1}) = \text{sign}(\delta_k).$$

With periodicity, these formulas can also be used at the endpoints where $k = 1$ and $k = n$ because

$$\delta_0 = \delta_{n-1} \text{ and } \delta_n = \delta_1.$$

For spline, the slopes satisfy a system of simultaneous linear equations for $k = 2, \ldots, n - 1$:

$$h_k d_{k-1} + 2(h_{k-1} + h_k)d_k + h_{k-1}d_{k+1} = 3(h_k\delta_{k-1} + h_{k-1}\delta_k).$$

With periodicity, this becomes

$$h_1 d_{n-1} + 2(h_{n-1} + h_1)d_1 + h_{n-1}d_2 = 3(h_1\delta_{n-1} + h_{n-1}\delta_1)$$

at $k = 1$ and

$$h_n d_{n-1} + 2(h_{n-1} + h_1)d_n + h_{n-1}d_2 = 3(h_1\delta_{n-1} + h_{n-1}\delta_1)$$

at $k = n$. The resulting matrix has two nonzero elements outside the tridiagonal structure. The additional nonzero elements in the first and last rows are $A_{1,n-1} = h_1$ and $A_{n,2} = h_{n-1}$.

(b) Demonstrate that your new functions work correctly on

```
x = 0:pi/4:2*pi;
y = cos(x);
u = 0:pi/50:2*pi;
v = your_function(x,y,u);
plot(x,y,'o',u,v,'-')
```

(c) Once you have `perchip` and `perspline`, you can use the NCM M-file `interp2dgui` to investigate closed-curve interpolation in two dimensions. You should find that the periodic boundary conditions do a better job of reproducing symmetries of closed curves in the plane.

3.14. (a) Modify `splinetx` so that it forms the full tridiagonal matrix

```
A = diag(a,-1) + diag(b,0) + diag(c,1)
```

and uses backslash to compute the slopes.

(b) Monitor `condest(A)` as the spline knots are varied with `interpgui`. What happens if two of the knots approach each other? Find a data set that makes `condest(A)` large.

3.15. Modify `pchiptx` so that it uses a weighted average of the slopes instead of the weighted harmonic mean.

3.16. (a) Consider

```
x = -1:1/3:1
interpgui(1-x.^2)
```

Which, if any, of the four interpolants `linear`, `spline`, `pchip`, and `polynomial` are the same? Why?

(b) Same questions for

```
interpgui(1-x.^4)
```

3.17. Why does `interpgui(4)` show only three graphs, not four, no matter where you move the points?

3.18. (a) If you want to interpolate census data on the interval $1900 \le t \le 2000$ with a polynomial,
$$P(t) = c_1 t^{10} + c_2 t^9 + \cdots + c_{10} t + c_{11},$$
you might be tempted to use the Vandermonde matrix generated by

```
t = 1900:10:2000
V = vander(t)
```

Why is this a really bad idea?

(b) Investigate *centering* and *scaling* the independent variable. Plot some data, pull down the **Tools** menu on the figure window, select **Basic Fitting**, and find the check box about centering and scaling. What does this check box do?

(c) Replace the variable t with
$$s = \frac{t - \mu}{\sigma}.$$

This leads to a modified polynomial $\tilde{P}(s)$. How are its coefficients related to those of $P(t)$? What happens to the Vandermonde matrix? What values of μ and σ lead to a reasonably well conditioned Vandermonde matrix? One possibility is

```
mu = mean(t)
sigma = std(t)
```

but are there better values?

Chapter 4

Zeros and Roots

This chapter describes several basic methods for computing zeros of functions and then combines three of the basic methods into a fast, reliable algorithm known as '*zeroin*'.

4.1 Bisection

Let's compute $\sqrt{2}$. We will use *interval bisection*, which is a kind of systematic trial and error. We know that $\sqrt{2}$ is between 1 and 2. Try $x = 1\frac{1}{2}$. Because x^2 is greater than 2, this x is too big. Try $x = 1\frac{1}{4}$. Because x^2 is less than 2, this x is too small. Continuing in this way, our approximations to $\sqrt{2}$ are

$$1\frac{1}{2}, \ 1\frac{1}{4}, \ 1\frac{3}{8}, \ 1\frac{5}{16}, \ 1\frac{13}{32}, \ 1\frac{27}{64}, \ \dots .$$

Here is a MATLAB program, including a step counter.

```
M = 2
a = 1
b = 2
k = 0;
while b-a > eps
    x = (a + b)/2;
    if x^2 > M
        b = x
    else
        a = x
    end
    k = k + 1;
end
```

We are sure that $\sqrt{2}$ is in the initial interval [a,b]. This interval is repeatedly cut in half and always brackets the answer. The entire process requires 52 steps. Here are the first few and the last few values.

```
b = 1.50000000000000
a = 1.25000000000000
a = 1.37500000000000
b = 1.43750000000000
a = 1.40625000000000
b = 1.42187500000000
a = 1.41406250000000
b = 1.41796875000000
b = 1.41601562500000
b = 1.41503906250000
b = 1.41455078125000
.....
b = 1.41421356237311
a = 1.41421356237299
a = 1.41421356237305
a = 1.41421356237308
a = 1.41421356237309
b = 1.41421356237310
b = 1.41421356237310
```

Using `format hex`, here are the final values of a and b.

```
a = 3ff6a09e667f3bcc
b = 3ff6a09e667f3bcd
```

They agree up to the last bit. We haven't actually computed $\sqrt{2}$, which is irrational and cannot be represented in floating point. But we have found two *successive* floating-point numbers, one on either side of the theoretical result. We've come as close as we can using floating-point arithmetic. The process takes 52 steps because there are 52 bits in the fraction of an IEEE double-precision number. Each step decreases the interval length by about one bit.

Interval bisection is a slow but sure algorithm for finding a zero of $f(x)$, a real-valued function of a real variable. All we assume about the function $f(x)$ is that we can write a MATLAB program that evaluates it for any x. We also assume that we know an interval $[a, b]$ on which $f(x)$ changes sign. If $f(x)$ is actually a *continuous* mathematical function, then there must be a point x_* somewhere in the interval where $f(x_*) = 0$. But the notion of continuity does not strictly apply to floating-point computation. We might not be able to actually find a point where $f(x)$ is exactly zero. Our goal is as follows:

> *Find a very small interval, perhaps two successive floating-point numbers, on which the function changes sign.*

The MATLAB code for bisection is

```
k = 0;
while abs(b-a) > eps*abs(b)
    x = (a + b)/2;
    if sign(f(x)) == sign(f(b))
```

```
        b = x;
     else
        a = x;
     end
     k = k + 1;
  end
```

Bisection is slow. With the termination condition in the above code, it always takes 52 steps for any function. But it is completely reliable. If we can find a starting interval with a change of sign, then bisection cannot fail to reduce that interval to two successive floating-point numbers that bracket the desired result.

4.2   Newton's Method

Newton's method for solving $f(x) = 0$ draws the tangent to the graph of $f(x)$ at any point and determines where the tangent intersects the x-axis. The method requires one starting value, x_0. The iteration is

$$x_{n+1} = x_n - \frac{f(x_n)}{f'(x_n)}.$$

The MATLAB code is

```
  k = 0;
  while abs(x - xprev) > eps*abs(x)
     xprev = x;
     x = x - f(x)/fprime(x)
     k = k + 1;
  end
```

As a method for computing square roots, Newton's method is particularly elegant and effective. To compute $\sqrt{M}$, find a zero of

$$f(x) = x^2 - M.$$

In this case, $f'(x) = 2x$ and

$$x_{n+1} = x_n - \frac{x_n^2 - M}{2x_n}$$

$$= \frac{1}{2}\left(x_n + \frac{M}{x_n}\right).$$

The algorithm repeatedly averages x and M/x. The MATLAB code is

```
  while abs(x - xprev) > eps*abs(x)
     xprev = x;
     x = 0.5*(x + M/x);
  end
```

Here are the results for $\sqrt{2}$, starting at $x = 1$.

```
1.50000000000000
1.41666666666667
1.41421568627451
1.41421356237469
1.41421356237309
1.41421356237309
```

Newton's method takes only six iterations. In fact, it was done in five, but the sixth iteration was needed to meet the termination condition.

When Newton's method works as it does for square roots, it is very effective. It is the basis for many powerful numerical methods. But, as a general-purpose algorithm for finding zeros of functions, it has three serious drawbacks.

- The function $f(x)$ must be smooth.

- It might not be convenient to compute the derivative $f'(x)$.

- The starting guess must be close to the final result.

In principle, the computation of the derivative $f'(x)$ can be done using a technique known as *automatic differentiation*. A MATLAB function f(x) or a suitable code in any other programming language, defines a mathematical function of its arguments. By combining modern computer science parsing techniques with the rules of calculus, especially the chain rule, it is theoretically possible to generate the code for another function fprime(x), that computes $f'(x)$. However, the actual implementation of such techniques is quite complicated and has not yet been fully realized.

The local convergence properties of Newton's method are very attractive. Let x_* be a zero of $f(x)$ and let $e_n = x_n - x_*$ be the error in the nth iterate. Assume

- $f'(x)$ and $f''(x)$ exist and are continuous,

- x_0 is close to x_*.

Then it is possible to prove [15] that

$$e_{n+1} = \frac{1}{2}\frac{f''(\xi)}{f'(x_n)}e_n^2,$$

where ξ is some point between x_n and x_*. In other words,

$$e_{n+1} = O(e_n^2).$$

This is called *quadratic* convergence. For nice, smooth functions, once you are close enough to the zero, the error is roughly squared with each iteration. The number of correct digits approximately doubles with each iteration. The results we saw for $\sqrt{2}$ are typical.

When the assumptions underlying the local convergence theory are not satisfied, Newton's method might be unreliable. If $f(x)$ does not have continuous, bounded first and second derivatives, or if the starting point is not close enough to the zero, then the local theory does not apply and we might get slow convergence, or even no convergence at all. The next section provides one example of what might happen.

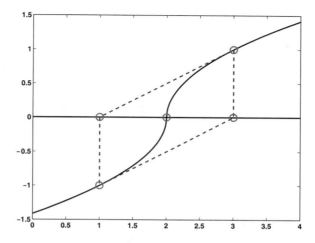

Figure 4.1. *Newton's method in an infinite loop.*

4.3   A Perverse Example

Let's see if we can get Newton's method to iterate forever. The iteration

$$x_{n+1} = x_n - \frac{f(x_n)}{f'(x_n)}$$

cycles back and forth around a point a if

$$x_{n+1} - a = -(x_n - a).$$

This happens if $f(x)$ satisfies

$$x - a - \frac{f(x)}{f'(x)} = -(x - a).$$

This is a separable ordinary differential equation:

$$\frac{f'(x)}{f(x)} = \frac{1}{2(x - a)}.$$

The solution is

$$f(x) = \text{sign}(x - a)\sqrt{|x - a|}.$$

The zero of $f(x)$ is, of course, at $x_* = a$. A plot of $f(x)$, Figure 4.1, with $a = 2$, is obtained with

```
ezplot('sign(x-2)*sqrt(abs(x-2))',0,4)
```

If we draw the tangent to the graph at any point, it intersects the x-axis on the opposite side of $x = a$. Newton's method cycles forever, neither converging nor diverging.

The convergence theory for Newton's method fails in this case because $f'(x)$ is unbounded as $x \to a$. It is also interesting to apply the algorithms discussed in the next sections to this function.

4.4 Secant Method

The secant method replaces the derivative evaluation in Newton's method with a finite difference approximation based on the two most recent iterates. Instead of drawing a tangent to the graph of $f(x)$ at one point, you draw a secant through two points. The next iterate is the intersection of this secant with the x-axis.

The iteration requires two starting values, x_0 and x_1. The subsequent iterates are given by

$$s_n = \frac{f(x_n) - f(x_{n-1})}{x_n - x_{n-1}},$$
$$x_{n+1} = x_n - \frac{f(x_n)}{s_n}.$$

This formulation makes it clear how Newton's $f'(x_n)$ is being replaced with the slope of the secant, s_n. The formulation in the following MATLAB code is a little more compact:

```
while abs(b-a) > eps*abs(b)
    c = a;
    a = b;
    b = b + (b - c)/(f(c)/f(b)-1);
    k = k + 1;
end
```

For $\sqrt{2}$, starting with a = 1 and b = 2, the secant method requires seven iterations, compared with Newton's six.

```
1.33333333333333
1.40000000000000
1.41463414634146
1.41421143847487
1.41421356205732
1.41421356237310
1.41421356237310
```

The secant method's primary advantage over Newton's method is that it does not require code to compute $f'(x)$. Its convergence properties are similar. Again, assuming $f'(x)$ and $f''(x)$ are continuous, it is possible to prove [15] that

$$e_{n+1} = \frac{1}{2} \frac{f''(\xi) f'(\xi_n) f'(\xi_{n-1})}{f'(\xi)^3} e_n e_{n-1},$$

where ξ is some point between x_n and x_*. In other words,

$$e_{n+1} = O(e_n e_{n-1}).$$

This is not quadratic convergence, but it is *superlinear* convergence. It turns out that

$$e_{n+1} = O(e_n^\phi),$$

where ϕ is the golden ratio, $(1 + \sqrt{5})/2$. Once you get close, the number of correct digits is roughly multiplied by 1.6 with each iteration. That's almost as fast as Newton's method and a whole lot faster than the one bit per step produced by bisection.

We leave it to exercise 4.8 to investigate the behavior of the secant method on the perverse function from the previous section:

$$f(x) = \text{sign}(x - a)\sqrt{|x - a|}.$$

4.5 Inverse Quadratic Interpolation

The secant method uses two previous points to get the next one, so why not use three?

Suppose we have three values, a, b, and c, and corresponding function values, $f(a)$, $f(b)$, and $f(c)$. We could interpolate these values by a parabola, a quadratic function of x, and take the next iterate to be the point where the parabola intersects the x-axis. The difficulty is that the parabola might not intersect the x-axis; a quadratic function does not necessarily have real roots. This could be regarded as an advantage. An algorithm known as Muller's method uses the complex roots of the quadratic to produce approximations to complex zeros of $f(x)$. But, for now, we want to avoid complex arithmetic.

Instead of a quadratic in x, we can interpolate the three points with a quadratic function in y. That's a "sideways" parabola, $P(y)$, determined by the interpolation conditions

$$a = P(f(a)), \; b = P(f(b)), \; c = P(f(c)).$$

This parabola always intersects the x-axis, which is $y = 0$. So $x = P(0)$ is the next iterate.

This method is known as *inverse quadratic interpolation*. We will abbreviate it with IQI. Here is MATLAB code that illustrates the idea.

```
k = 0;
while abs(c-b) > eps*abs(c)
    x = polyinterp([f(a),f(b),f(c)],[a,b,c],0)
    a = b;
    b = c;
    c = x;
    k = k + 1;
end
```

The trouble with this "pure" IQI algorithm is that polynomial interpolation requires the abscissae, which in this case are $f(a)$, $f(b)$, and $f(c)$, to be distinct. We have no guarantee that they are. For example, if we try to compute $\sqrt{2}$ using $f(x) = x^2 - 2$ and start with $a = -2, b = 0, c = 2$, we are starting with $f(a) = f(c)$ and the first step is undefined. If we start near this singular situation, say with $a = -2.001, b = 0, c = 1.999$, the next iterate is near $x = 500$.

So IQI is like an immature racehorse. It moves very quickly when it is near the finish line, but its global behavior can be erratic. It needs a good trainer to keep it under control.

4.6   Zeroin

The idea behind the zeroin algorithm is to combine the reliability of bisection with the convergence speed of secant and IQI. T. J. Dekker and colleagues at the Mathematical Center in Amsterdam developed the first version of the algorithm in the 1960s [17]. Our implementation is based on a version by Richard Brent [12]. Here is the outline:

- Start with a and b so that $f(a)$ and $f(b)$ have opposite signs.

- Use a secant step to give c between a and b.

- Repeat the following steps until $|b - a| < \epsilon|b|$ or $f(b) = 0$.

- Arrange a, b, and c so that

    - $f(a)$ and $f(b)$ have opposite signs,
    - $|f(b)| \leq |f(a)|$,
    - c is the previous value of b.

- If $c \neq a$, consider an IQI step.

- If $c = a$, consider a secant step.

- If the IQI or secant step is in the interval $[a, b]$, take it.

- If the step is not in the interval, use bisection.

This algorithm is foolproof. It never loses track of the zero trapped in a shrinking interval. It uses rapidly convergent methods when they are reliable. It uses a slow, but sure, method when it is necessary.

4.7   `fzerotx`

The MATLAB implementation of the zeroin algorithm is called `fzero`. It has several features beyond the basic algorithm. A preamble takes a single starting guess and searches for an interval with a sign change. The values returned by the function `f(x)` are checked for infinities, NaNs, and complex numbers. Default tolerances can be changed. Additional output, including a count of function evaluations, can be requested. Our textbook version of zeroin is `fzerotx`. We have simplified `fzero` by removing most of its additional features while retaining the essential features of zeroin.

We can illustrate the use of `fzerotx` with the zeroth-order Bessel function of the first kind, $J_0(x)$. This function is available in MATLAB as `besselj(0,x)`. The following code finds the first 10 zeros of $J_0(x)$ and produces Figure 4.2 (except for the red 'x', which we will add later).

```
J0 = @(x) besselj(0,x);
for n = 1:10
   z(n) = fzerotx(J0,[(n-1) n]*pi);
end
```

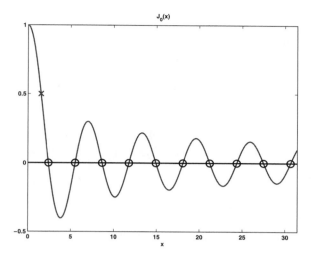

Figure 4.2. *Zeros of $J_0(x)$.*

```
x = 0:pi/50:10*pi;
y = J0(x);
plot(z,zeros(1,10),'o',x,y,'-')
line([0 10*pi],[0 0],'color','black')
axis([0 10*pi -0.5 1.0])
```

You can see from the figure that the graph of $J_0(x)$ is like an amplitude and frequency modulated version of $\cos x$. The distance between successive zeros is close to π.

The function fzerotx takes two arguments. The first specifies the function $F(x)$ whose zero is being sought and the second specifies the interval $[a, b]$ to search. fzerotx is an example of a MATLAB *function function*, which is a function that takes another function as an argument. ezplot is another example. Other chapters of this book—Chapter 6, Quadrature; Chapter 7, Ordinary Differential Equations; and even Chapter 9, Random Numbers—also describe "tx" and "gui" M-files that are function functions.

A function can be passed as an argument to another function in two different ways:

- function handle,

- anonymous function.

A function handle uses the '@' character preceding the name of a built-in function or a function defined in an M-file. Examples include

```
@cos
@humps
@bessj0
```

where bessj0.m is the two-line M-file

```
function y = bessj0(x)
y = besselj(0,x)
```

These handles can then be used as arguments to function functions.

```
z = fzerotx(@bessj0,[0,pi])
```

Note that @besselj is also a valid function handle, but for a function of two arguments. *Anonymous functions* were introduced in MATLAB 7. Examples include

```
F = @(t) cos(pi*t)
G = @(z) z^3-2*z-5
J0 = @(x) besselj(0,x)
```

These objects are called anonymous functions because the construction

```
@(arguments) expression
```

defines a function, but does not give it a name.

M-files and anonymous functions can define functions of more than one argument. In this case, the values of the extra arguments can be passed through fzerotx to the objective function. These values remain constant during the zero finding iteration. This allows us to find where a particular function takes on a specified value y, instead of just finding a zero. For example, consider the equation

$$J_0(\xi) = 0.5.$$

Define an anonymous function with two or three arguments.

```
F = @(x,y) besselj(0,x)-y
```

or

```
B = @(x,n,y) besselj(n,x)-y
```

Then either

```
xi = fzerotx(F,[0,2],.5)
```

or

```
xi = fzerotx(B,[0,2],0,.5)
```

produces

```
xi =
    1.5211
```

The point $(\xi, J_0(\xi))$ is marked with an 'x' in Figure 4.2.
    The preamble for fzerotx is as follows.

```
function b = fzerotx(F,ab,varargin);
%FZEROTX  Textbook version of FZERO.
%   x = fzerotx(F,[a,b]) tries to find a zero of F(x) between
%   a and b.  F(a) and F(b) must have opposite signs.
%   fzerotx returns one endpoint of a small subinterval of
%   [a,b] where F changes sign.
%   Additional arguments, fzerotx(F,[a,b],p1,p2,...),
%   are passed on, F(x,p1,p2,...).
```

The first section of code initializes the variables a, b, and c that characterize the search interval. The function F is evaluated at the endpoints of the initial interval.

```
a = ab(1);
b = ab(2);
   fa = F(a,varargin{:});
   fb = F(b,varargin{:});
if sign(fa) == sign(fb)
   error('Function must change sign on the interval')
end

c = a;
fc = fa;
d = b - c;
e = d;
```

Here is the beginning of the main loop. At the start of each pass through the loop, a, b, and c are rearranged to satisfy the conditions of the zeroin algorithm.

```
while fb ~= 0

   % The three current points, a, b, and c, satisfy:
   %     f(x) changes sign between a and b.
   %     abs(f(b)) <= abs(f(a)).
   %     c = previous b, so c might = a.
   % The next point is chosen from
   %     Bisection point, (a+b)/2.
   %     Secant point determined by b and c.
   %     Inverse quadratic interpolation point determined
   %     by a, b, and c if they are distinct.

   if sign(fa) == sign(fb)
      a = c;   fa = fc;
      d = b - c;   e = d;
   end
   if abs(fa) < abs(fb)
      c = b;     b = a;     a = c;
      fc = fb;   fb = fa;   fa = fc;
   end
```

This section is the convergence test and possible exit from the loop.

```
m = 0.5*(a - b);
tol = 2.0*eps*max(abs(b),1.0);
if (abs(m) <= tol) | (fb == 0.0),
   break
end
```

The next section of code makes the choice between bisection and the two flavors of interpolation.

```
% Choose bisection or interpolation
if (abs(e) < tol) | (abs(fc) <= abs(fb))
   % Bisection
   d = m;
   e = m;
else
   % Interpolation
   s = fb/fc;
   if (a == c)
      % Linear interpolation (secant)
      p = 2.0*m*s;
      q = 1.0 - s;
   else
      % Inverse quadratic interpolation
      q = fc/fa;
      r = fb/fa;
      p = s*(2.0*m*q*(q - r) - (b - c)*(r - 1.0));
      q = (q - 1.0)*(r - 1.0)*(s - 1.0);
   end;
   if p > 0, q = -q; else p = -p; end;
   % Is interpolated point acceptable
   if (2.0*p < 3.0*m*q - abs(tol*q)) & (p < abs(0.5*e*q))
      e = d;
      d = p/q;
   else
      d = m;
      e = m;
   end;
end
```

The final section evaluates F at the next iterate.

```
% Next point
c = b;
fc = fb;
if abs(d) > tol
   b = b + d;
```

```
else
    b = b - sign(b-a)*tol;
end
fb = F(b,varargin{:});
end
```

4.8 fzerogui

The M-file fzerogui demonstrates the behavior of *zeroin* and fzerotx. At each step of
the iteration, you are offered a chance to choose the next point. The choice always includes
the bisection point, shown in red on the computer screen. When there are three distinct
points active, a, b, and c, the IQI point is shown in blue. When $a = c$, so there are only
two distinct points, the secant point is shown in green. A plot of $f(x)$ is also provided as a
dotted line, but the algorithm does not "know" these other function values. You can choose
any point you like as the next iterate. You do not have to follow the *zeroin* algorithm and
choose the bisection or interpolant point. You can even cheat by trying to pick the point
where the dotted line crosses the axis.

We can demonstrate how fzerogui behaves by seeking the first zero of the
Bessel function. It turns out that the first local minimum of $J_0(x)$ is located near $x = 3.83$.
So here are the first few steps of

```
fzerogui('besselj(0,x)',[0 3.83])
```

Initially, $c = b$, so the two choices are the bisection point and the secant point
(Figure 4.3).

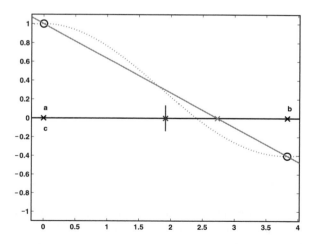

Figure 4.3. *Initially, choose secant or bisection.*

If you choose the secant point, then b moves there and $J_0(x)$ is evaluated at $x = b$.
We then have three distinct points, so the choice is between the bisection point and the IQI
point (Figure 4.4).

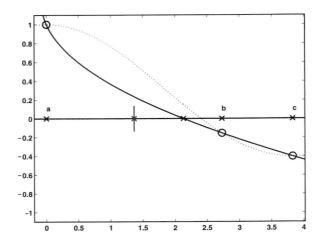

Figure 4.4. *Choose IQI or bisection.*

If you choose the IQI point, the interval shrinks, the GUI zooms in on the reduced interval, and the choice is again between the bisection and secant points, which now happen to be close together (Figure 4.5).

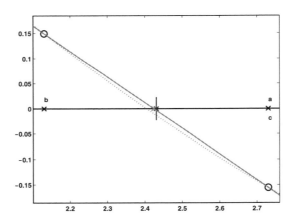

Figure 4.5. *Secant and bisection points nearly coincide.*

You can choose either point, or any other point close to them. After two more steps, the interval shrinks again and the situation shown in Figure 4.6 is reached. This is the typical configuration as we approach convergence. The graph of the function looks nearly like a straight line and the secant or IQI point is much closer to the desired zero than the bisection point. It now becomes clear that choosing secant or IQI will lead to much faster convergence than bisection.

After several more steps, the length of the interval containing a change of sign is reduced to a tiny fraction of the original length, and the algorithm terminates, returning the final b as its result.

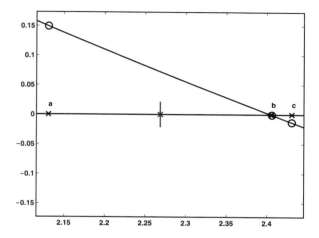

Figure 4.6. *Nearing convergence.*

4.9 Value Finding and Reverse Interpolation

These two problems look very similar.

- Given a function $F(x)$ and a value η, find ξ so that $F(\xi) = \eta$.

- Given data (x_k, y_k) that sample an unknown function $F(x)$, and a value η, find ξ so that $F(\xi) = \eta$.

For the first problem, we are able to evaluate $F(x)$ at any x, so we can use a zero finder on the translated function $f(x) = F(x) - \eta$. This gives us the desired ξ so that $f(\xi) = 0$, and hence $F(\xi) = \eta$.

For the second problem, we need to do some kind of interpolation. The most obvious approach is to use a zero finder on $f(x) = P(x) - \eta$, where $P(x)$ is some interpolant, such as `pchiptx(xk,yk,x)` or `splinetx(xk,yk,x)`. This often works well, but it can be expensive. The zero finder calls for repeated evaluation of the interpolant. With the implementations we have in this book, that involves repeated calculation of the interpolant's parameters and repeated determination of the appropriate interval index.

A sometimes preferable alternative, known as *reverse interpolation*, uses `pchip` or `spline` with the roles of x_k and y_k reversed. This requires monotonicity in the y_k, or at least in a subset of the y_k around the target value η. A different piecewise polynomial, say $Q(y)$, is created with the property that $Q(y_k) = x_k$. Now it is not necessary to use a zero finder. We simply evaluate $\xi = Q(y)$ at $y = \eta$.

The choice between these two alternatives depends on how the data are best approximated by piecewise polynomials. Is it better to use x or y as the independent variable?

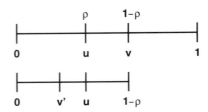

Figure 4.7. *Golden section search.*

4.10   Optimization and `fmintx`

The task of finding maxima and minima of functions is closely related to zero finding. In this
section, we describe an algorithm similar to zeroin that finds a local minimum of a function
of one variable. The problem specification involves a function $f(x)$ and an interval $[a, b]$.
The objective is to find a value of x that gives a local minimum of $f(x)$ on the given interval.
If the function is *unimodular*, that is, has only one local minimum on the interval, then that
minimum will be found. But if there is more than one local minimum, only one of them
will be found, and that one will not necessarily be minimum for the entire interval. It is also
possible that one of the endpoints is a minimizer.

   Interval bisection cannot be used. Even if we know the values of $f(a)$, $f(b)$, and
$f((a + b)/2)$, we cannot decide which half of the interval to discard and still keep the
minimum enclosed.

   Interval trisection is feasible, but inefficient. Let $h = (b - a)/3$, so $u = a + h$ and
$v = b - h$ divide the interval into three equal parts. Assume we find that $f(u) < f(v)$. Then
we could replace b with v, thereby cutting the interval length by a factor of two-thirds, and
still be sure that the minimum is in the reduced interval. However, u would be in the center
of the new interval and would not be useful in the next step. We would need to evaluate the
function twice each step.

   The natural minimization analogue of bisection is *golden section* search. The idea is
illustrated for $a = 0$ and $b = 1$ in Figure 4.7. Let $h = \rho(b - a)$, where ρ is a quantity
a little bit larger than $1/3$ that we have yet to determine. Then the points $u = a + h$ and
$v = b - h$ divide the interval into three unequal parts. For the first step, evaluate both $f(u)$
and $f(v)$. Assume we find that $f(u) < f(v)$. Then we know the minimum is between a
and v. We can replace b with v and repeat the process. If we choose the right value for
ρ, the point u is in the proper position to be used in the next step. After the first step, the
function has to be evaluated only once each step.

   The defining equation for ρ is

$$\frac{\rho}{1 - \rho} = \frac{1 - \rho}{1},$$

or

$$\rho^2 - 3\rho + 1 = 0.$$

The solution is

$$\rho = 2 - \phi = (3 - \sqrt{5})/2 \approx 0.382.$$

Here ϕ is the golden ratio that we used to introduce MATLAB in the first chapter of this book.

With golden section search, the length of the interval is reduced by a factor of $\phi - 1 \approx 0.618$ each step. It would take

$$\frac{-52}{\log_2(\phi - 1)} \approx 75$$

steps to reduce the interval length to roughly `eps`, the size of IEEE double-precision roundoff error, times its original value.

After the first few steps, there is often enough history to give three distinct points and corresponding function values in the active interval. If the minimum of the parabola interpolating these three points is in the interval, then it, rather than the golden section point, is usually a better choice for the next point. This combination of golden section search and parabolic interpolation provides a reliable and efficient method for one-dimensional optimization.

The proper stopping criteria for optimization searches can be tricky. At a minimum of $f(x)$, the first derivative $f'(x)$ is zero. Consequently, near a minimum, $f(x)$ acts like a quadratic with no linear term:

$$f(x) \approx a + b(x - c)^2 + \cdots.$$

The minimum occurs at $x = c$ and has the value $f(c) = a$. If x is close to c, say $x \approx c + \delta$ for small δ, then

$$f(x) \approx a + b\delta^2.$$

Small changes in x are squared when computing function values. If a and b are comparable in size, and nonzero, then the stopping criterion should involve `sqrt(eps)` because any smaller changes in x will not affect $f(x)$. But if a and b have different orders of magnitude, or if either a or c is nearly zero, then interval lengths of size `eps`, rather than `sqrt(eps)`, are appropriate.

MATLAB includes a function function `fminbnd` that uses golden section search and parabolic interpolation to find a local minimum of a real-valued function of a real variable. The function is based upon a Fortran subroutine by Richard Brent [12]. MATLAB also includes a function function, `fminsearch`, that uses a technique known as the Nelder–Meade simplex algorithm to search for a local minimum of a real-valued function of several real variables. The MATLAB Optimization Toolbox is a collection of programs for other kinds of optimization problems, including constrained optimization, linear programming, and large-scale, sparse optimization.

Our NCM collection includes a function `fmintx` that is a simplified textbook version of `fminbnd`. One of the simplifications involves the stopping criterion. The search is terminated when the length of the interval becomes less than a specified parameter `tol`. The default value of `tol` is 10^{-6}. More sophisticated stopping criteria involving relative and absolute tolerances in both x and $f(x)$ are used in the full codes.

The MATLAB demos directory includes a function named `humps` that is intended to illustrate the behavior of graphics, quadrature, and zero-finding routines. The function is

$$h(x) = \frac{1}{(x - 0.3)^2 + 0.01} + \frac{1}{(x - 0.9)^2 + 0.04}.$$

The statements

```
F = @(x) -humps(x)
fmintx(F,-1,2,1.e-4)
```

take the steps shown in Figure 4.8 and in the following output. We see that golden section search is used for the second, third, and seventh steps, and that parabolic interpolation is used exclusively once the search nears the minimizer.

step	x	f(x)
init:	0.1458980337	-25.2748253202
gold:	0.8541019662	-20.9035150009
gold:	-0.2917960675	2.5391843579
para:	0.4492755129	-29.0885282699
para:	0.4333426114	-33.8762343193
para:	0.3033578448	-96.4127439649
gold:	0.2432135488	-71.7375588319
para:	0.3170404333	-93.8108500149
para:	0.2985083078	-96.4666018623
para:	0.3003583547	-96.5014055840
para:	0.3003763623	-96.5014085540
para:	0.3003756221	-96.5014085603

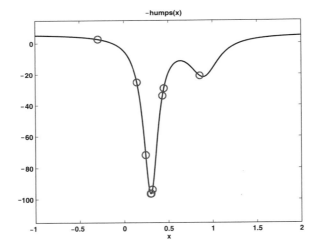

Figure 4.8. *Finding the minimum of* -humps(x).

Exercises

4.1. Use fzerogui to try to find a zero of each of the following functions in the given interval. Do you see any interesting or unusual behavior?

$x^3 - 2x - 5$	$[0, 3]$
$\sin x$	$[1, 4]$
$x^3 - 0.001$	$[-1, 1]$
$\log(x + 2/3)$	$[0, 1]$
$\text{sign}(x - 2)\sqrt{|x - 2|}$	$[1, 4]$
$\text{atan}(x) - \pi/3$	$[0, 5]$
$1/(x - \pi)$	$[0, 5]$

4.2. Here is a little footnote to the history of numerical methods. The polynomial

$$x^3 - 2x - 5$$

was used by Wallis when he first presented Newton's method to the French Academy. It has one real root, between $x = 2$ and $x = 3$, and a pair of complex conjugate roots.
(a) Use the Symbolic Toolbox to find symbolic expressions for the three roots. Warning: The results are not pretty. Convert the expressions to numerical values.
(b) Use the `roots` function in MATLAB to find numerical values for all three roots.
(c) Use `fzerotx` to find the real root.
(d) Use Newton's method starting with a complex initial value to find a complex root.
(e) Can bisection be used to find the complex root? Why or why not?

4.3. Here is a cubic polynomial with three closely spaced real roots:

$$p(x) = 816x^3 - 3835x^2 + 6000x - 3125.$$

(a) What are the exact roots of p?
(b) Plot $p(x)$ for $1.43 \le x \le 1.71$. Show the location of the three roots.
(c) Starting with $x_0 = 1.5$, what does Newton's method do?
(d) Starting with $x_0 = 1$ and $x_1 = 2$, what does the secant method do?
(e) Starting with the interval $[1, 2]$, what does bisection do?
(f) What is `fzerotx(p,[1,2])`? Why?

4.4. What causes `fzerotx` to terminate?

4.5. (a) How does `fzerotx` choose between the bisection point and the interpolant point for its next iterate?
(b) Why is the quantity `tol` involved in the choice?

4.6. Derive the formula that `fzerotx` uses for IQI.

4.7. Hoping to find the zero of $J_0(x)$ in the interval $0 \le x \le \pi$, we might try the statement

```
z = fzerotx(@besselj,[0 pi],0)
```

This is legal usage of a function handle, and of `fzerotx`, but it produces `z = 3.1416`. Why?

4.8. Investigate the behavior of the secant method on the function

$$f(x) = \text{sign}(x - a)\sqrt{|x - a|}.$$

4.9. Find the first ten positive values of x for which $x = \tan x$.

4.10. (a) Compute the first ten zeros of $J_0(x)$. You can use our graph of $J_0(x)$ to estimate their location.

(b) Compute the first ten zeros of $Y_0(x)$, the zeroth-order Bessel function of the second kind.

(c) Compute all the values of x between 0 and 10π for which $J_0(x) = Y_0(x)$.

(d) Make a composite plot showing $J_0(x)$ and $Y_0(x)$ for $0 \leq x \leq 10\pi$, the first ten zeros of both functions, and the points of intersection.

4.11. The *gamma* function is defined by an integral:

$$\Gamma(x+1) = \int_0^\infty t^x e^{-t} dt.$$

Integration by parts shows that, when evaluated at the integers, $\Gamma(x)$ interpolates the factorial function

$$\Gamma(n+1) = n!.$$

$\Gamma(x)$ and $n!$ grow so rapidly that they generate floating-point overflow for relatively small values of x and n. It is often more convenient to work with the logarithms of these functions.

The MATLAB functions gamma and gammaln compute $\Gamma(x)$ and $\log \Gamma(x)$, respectively. The quantity $n!$ is easily computed by the expression

```
prod(1:n)
```

but many people expect there to be a function named factorial, so MATLAB has such a function.

(a) What is the largest value of n for which $\Gamma(n+1)$ and $n!$ can be exactly represented by a double-precision floating-point number?

(b) What is the largest value of n for which $\Gamma(n+1)$ and $n!$ can be approximately represented by a double-precision floating-point number that does not overflow?

4.12. Stirling's approximation is a classical estimate for $\log \Gamma(x+1)$:

$$\log \Gamma(x+1) \sim x \log(x) - x + \frac{1}{2} \log(2\pi x).$$

Bill Gosper [67] has noted that a better approximation is

$$\log \Gamma(x+1) \sim x \log(x) - x + \frac{1}{2} \log(2\pi x + \pi/3).$$

The accuracy of both approximations improves as x increases.

(a) What is the relative error in Stirling's approximation and in Gosper's approximation when $x = 2$?

(b) How large must x be for Stirling's approximation and for Gosper's approximation to have a relative error less than 10^{-6}?

4.13. The statements

```
y = 2:.01:10;
x = gammaln(y);
plot(x,y)
```

produce a graph of the inverse of the log Γ function.

(a) Write a MATLAB function gammalninv that evaluates this function for any x. That is, given x,

```
y = gammalninv(x)
```

computes y so that gammaln(y) is equal to x.

(b) What are the appropriate ranges of x and y for this function?

4.14. Here is a table of the distance, d, that a hypothetical vehicle requires to stop if the brakes are applied when it is traveling with velocity v.

$v(m/s)$	$d(m)$
0	0
10	5
20	20
30	46
40	70
50	102
60	153

What is the speed limit for this vehicle if it must be able to stop in at most 60 m? Compute the speed three different ways.

(a) piecewise linear interpolation,

(b) piecewise cubic interpolation with pchiptx,

(c) reverse piecewise cubic interpolation with pchiptx.

Because these are well-behaved data, the three values are close to each other, but not identical.

4.15. Kepler's model of planetary orbits includes a quantity E, the eccentricity anomaly, that satisfies the equation

$$M = E - e \sin E,$$

where M is the mean anomaly and e is the eccentricity of the orbit. For this exercise, take $M = 24.851090$ and $e = 0.1$.

(a) Use fzerotx to solve for E. You should use an anonymous function

```
M = 24.851090;
e = 0.1;
F = @(E) E - e*sin(E) - M
```

(b) An "exact" formula for E is known:

$$E = M + 2 \sum_{m=1}^{\infty} \frac{1}{m} J_m(me) \sin(mM),$$

where $J_m(x)$ is the Bessel function of the first kind of order m. Use this formula, and besselj(m,x) in MATLAB, to compute E. How many terms are needed? How does this value of E compare to the value obtained with fzerotx?

4.16. Utilities must avoid freezing water mains. If we assume uniform soil conditions, the temperature $T(x,t)$ at a distance x below the surface and time t after the beginning of a cold snap is given approximately by

$$\frac{T(x,t) - T_s}{T_i - T_s} = \text{erf}\left(\frac{x}{2\sqrt{\alpha t}}\right).$$

Here T_s is the constant surface temperature during the cold period, T_i is the initial soil temperature before the cold snap, and α is the thermal conductivity of the soil. If x is measured in meters and t in seconds, then $\alpha = 0.138 \cdot 10^{-6}\,\text{m}^2/\text{s}$. Let $T_i = 20°\,\text{C}$, and $T_s = -15°\,\text{C}$, and recall that water freezes at $0°\,\text{C}$. Use `fzerotx` to determine how deep a water main should be buried so that it will not freeze until at least 60 days' exposure under these conditions.

4.17. Modify `fmintx` to provide printed and graphical output similar to that at the end of section 4.10. Reproduce the results shown in Figure 4.8 for `-humps(x)`.

4.18. Let $f(x) = 9x^2 - 6x + 2$. What is the actual minimizer of $f(x)$? How close to the actual minimizer can you get with `fmintx`? Why?

4.19. Theoretically, `fmintx(@cos,2,4,eps)` should return pi. How close does it get? Why? On the other hand, `fmintx(@cos,0,2*pi)` does return pi. Why?

4.20. If you use `tol = 0` with `fmintx(@F,a,b,tol)`, does the iteration run forever? Why or why not?

4.21. Derive the formulas for minimization by parabolic interpolation used in the following portion of fmintx:

```
r = (x - w) * (fx - fv);
q = (x - v) * (fx - fw);

p = (x - v)*q - (x - w)*r;
s = 2.0*(q - r);
if s > 0.0, p = -p; end
s = abs(s);
% Is the parabola acceptable?
para = ( (abs(p)<abs(0.5*s*e))
        & (p > s*(a - x)) & (p < s*(b - x)) );
if para
  e = d;
  d = p/s;
  newx = x + d;
end
```

4.22. Let $f(x) = \sin(\tan x) - \tan(\sin x)$, $0 \le x \le \pi$.
(a) Plot $f(x)$.
(b) Why is it difficult to compute the minimum of $f(x)$?
(c) What does `fmintx` compute as the minimum of $f(x)$?
(d) What is the limit as $x \to \pi/2$ of $f(x)$?
(e) What is the *glb* or *infimum* of $f(x)$?

Chapter 5

Least Squares

The term *least squares* describes a frequently used approach to solving overdetermined or inexactly specified systems of equations in an approximate sense. Instead of solving the equations exactly, we seek only to minimize the sum of the squares of the residuals.

The least squares criterion has important statistical interpretations. If appropriate probabilistic assumptions about underlying error distributions are made, least squares produces what is known as the *maximum-likelihood* estimate of the parameters. Even if the probabilistic assumptions are not satisfied, years of experience have shown that least squares produces useful results.

The computational techniques for linear least squares problems make use of orthogonal matrix factorizations.

5.1   Models and Curve Fitting

A very common source of least squares problems is curve fitting. Let t be the independent variable and let $y(t)$ denote an unknown function of t that we want to approximate. Assume there are m *observations*, i.e., values of y measured at specified values of t:

$$y_i = y(t_i), \ i = 1, \ldots, m.$$

The idea is to model $y(t)$ by a linear combination of n *basis functions*:

$$y(t) \approx \beta_1 \phi_1(t) + \cdots + \beta_n \phi_n(t).$$

The *design matrix* X is a rectangular matrix of order m by n with elements

$$x_{i,j} = \phi_j(t_i).$$

The design matrix usually has more rows than columns. In matrix-vector notation, the model is

$$y \approx X\beta.$$

The symbol $\approx$ stands for "is approximately equal to." We are more precise about this in the next section, but our emphasis is on *least squares* approximation.

The basis functions $\phi_j(t)$ can be nonlinear functions of t, but the unknown parameters, β_j, appear in the model linearly. The system of linear equations

$$X\beta \approx y$$

is *overdetermined* if there are more equations than unknowns. The MATLAB backslash operator computes a least squares solution to such a system.

```
beta = X\y
```

The basis functions might also involve some nonlinear parameters, $\alpha_1, \ldots, \alpha_p$. The problem is *separable* if it involves both linear and nonlinear parameters:

$$y(t) \approx \beta_1\phi_1(t,\alpha) + \cdots + \beta_n\phi_n(t,\alpha).$$

The elements of the design matrix depend upon both t and α:

$$x_{i,j} = \phi_j(t_i,\alpha).$$

Separable problems can be solved by combining backslash with the MATLAB function `fminsearch` or one of the nonlinear minimizers available in the Optimization Toolbox. The new Curve Fitting Toolbox provides a graphical interface for solving nonlinear fitting problems.

Some common models include the following:

- Straight line: If the model is also linear in t, it is a straight line:

$$y(t) \approx \beta_1 t + \beta_2.$$

- Polynomials: The coefficients β_j appear linearly. MATLAB orders polynomials with the highest power first:

$$\phi_j(t) = t^{n-j}, \quad j = 1, \ldots, n,$$
$$y(t) \approx \beta_1 t^{n-1} + \cdots + \beta_{n-1}t + \beta_n.$$

The MATLAB function `polyfit` computes least squares polynomial fits by setting up the design matrix and using backslash to find the coefficients.

- Rational functions: The coefficients in the numerator appear linearly; the coefficients in the denominator appear nonlinearly:

$$\phi_j(t) = \frac{t^{n-j}}{\alpha_1 t^{n-1} + \cdots + \alpha_{n-1}t + \alpha_n},$$
$$y(t) \approx \frac{\beta_1 t^{n-1} + \cdots + \beta_{n-1}t + \beta_n}{\alpha_1 t^{n-1} + \cdots + \alpha_{n-1}t + \alpha_n}.$$

- Exponentials: The decay rates, λ_j, appear nonlinearly:

$$\phi_j(t) = e^{-\lambda_j t},$$
$$y(t) \approx \beta_1 e^{-\lambda_1 t} + \cdots + \beta_n e^{-\lambda_n t}.$$

- Log-linear: If there is only one exponential, taking logs makes the model linear but changes the fit criterion:

$$y(t) \approx K e^{\lambda t},$$
$$\log y \approx \beta_1 t + \beta_2, \text{ with } \beta_1 = \lambda, \ \beta_2 = \log K.$$

- Gaussians: The means and variances appear nonlinearly:

$$\phi_j(t) = e^{-\left(\frac{t-\mu_j}{\sigma_j}\right)^2},$$
$$y(t) \approx \beta_1 e^{-\left(\frac{t-\mu_1}{\sigma_1}\right)^2} + \cdots + \beta_n e^{-\left(\frac{t-\mu_n}{\sigma_n}\right)^2}.$$

5.2 Norms

The *residuals* are the differences between the observations and the model:

$$r_i = y_i - \sum_1^n \beta_j \phi_j(t_i, \alpha), \ i = 1, \ldots, m.$$

Or, in matrix-vector notation,

$$r = y - X(\alpha)\beta.$$

We want to find the α's and β's that make the residuals as small as possible. What do we mean by "small"? In other words, what do we mean when we use the '$\approx$' symbol? There are several possibilities.

- Interpolation: If the number of parameters is equal to the number of observations, we might be able to make the residuals zero. For linear problems, this will mean that $m = n$ and that the design matrix X is square. If X is nonsingular, the β's are the solution to a square system of linear equations:

$$\beta = X \backslash y.$$

- Least squares: Minimize the sum of the squares of the residuals:

$$\|r\|^2 = \sum_1^m r_i^2.$$

- Weighted least squares: If some observations are more important or more accurate than others, then we might associate different weights, w_j, with different observations and minimize

$$\|r\|_w^2 = \sum_1^m w_i r_i^2.$$

For example, if the error in the ith observation is approximately e_i, then choose $w_i = 1/e_i$.

Any algorithm for solving an unweighted least squares problem can be used to solve a weighted problem by scaling the observations and design matrix. We simply multiply both y_i and the ith row of X by w_i. In MATLAB, this can be accomplished with

```
X = diag(w)*X
y = diag(w)*y
```

• One-norm: Minimize the sum of the absolute values of the residuals:

$$\|r\|_1 = \sum_1^m |r_i|.$$

This problem can be reformulated as a linear programming problem, but it is computationally more difficult than least squares. The resulting parameters are less sensitive to the presence of spurious data points or *outliers*.

• Infinity-norm: Minimize the largest residual:

$$\|r\|_\infty = \max_i |r_i|.$$

This is also known as a Chebyshev fit and can be reformulated as a linear programming problem. Chebyshev fits are frequently used in the design of digital filters and in the development of approximations for use in mathematical function libraries.

The MATLAB Optimization and Curve Fitting Toolboxes include functions for one-norm and infinity-norm problems. We will limit ourselves to least squares in this book.

5.3   censusgui

The NCM program censusgui involves several different linear models. The data are the total population of the United States, as determined by the U.S. Census, for the years 1900 to 2000. The units are millions of people.

t	y
1900	75.995
1910	91.972
1900	105.711
1930	123.203
1940	131.669
1950	150.697
1960	179.323
1970	203.212
1980	226.505
1990	249.633
2000	281.422

The task is to model the population growth and predict the population when $t = 2010$. The default model in censusgui is a cubic polynomial in t:

$$y \approx \beta_1 t^3 + \beta_2 t^2 + \beta_3 t + \beta_4.$$

There are four unknown coefficients, appearing linearly.

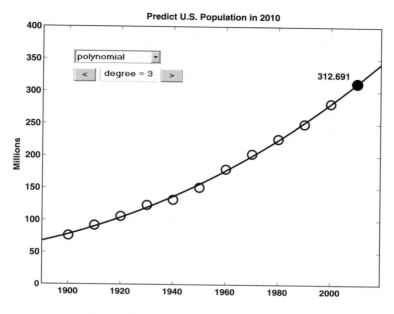

Figure 5.1. censusgui.

Numerically, it's a bad idea to use powers of t as basis functions when t is around 1900 or 2000. The design matrix is badly scaled and its columns are nearly linearly dependent. A much better basis is provided by powers of a translated and scaled t:

$$s = (t - 1950)/50.$$

This new variable is in the interval $-1 \leq s \leq 1$ and the model is

$$y \approx \beta_1 s^3 + \beta_2 s^2 + \beta_3 s + \beta_4.$$

The resulting design matrix is well conditioned.

Figure 5.1 shows the fit to the census data by the default cubic polynomial. The extrapolation to the year 2010 seems reasonable. The push buttons allow you to vary the degree of the polynomial. As the degree increases, the fit becomes more accurate in the sense that $\|r\|$ decreases, but it also becomes less useful because the variation between and outside the observations increases.

The censusgui menu also allows you to choose interpolation by spline and pchip and to see the log-linear fit

$$y \approx K e^{\lambda t}.$$

Nothing in the censusgui tool attempts to answer the all-important question, "Which is the best model?" That's up to you to decide.

5.4 Householder Reflections

Householder reflections are matrix transformations that are the basis for some of the most powerful and flexible numerical algorithms known. We will use Householder reflections in this chapter for the solution of linear least squares problems and in a later chapter for the solution of matrix eigenvalue and singular value problems.

Formally, a Householder reflection is a matrix of the form

$$H = I - \rho u u^T,$$

where u is any nonzero vector and $\rho = 2/\|u\|^2$. The quantity uu^T is a matrix of rank one where every column is a multiple of u and every row is a multiple of u^T. The resulting matrix H is both symmetric and orthogonal, that is,

$$H^T = H$$

and

$$H^T H = H^2 = I.$$

In practice, the matrix H is never formed. Instead, the application of H to a vector x is computed by

$$\tau = \rho u^T x,$$
$$Hx = x - \tau u.$$

Geometrically, the vector x is projected onto u and then twice that projection is subtracted from x.

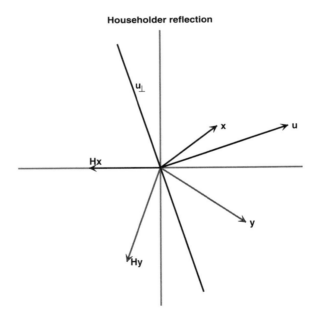

Figure 5.2. *Householder reflection.*

Figure 5.2 shows a vector u and a line labeled $u_\perp$ that is perpendicular to u. It also shows two vectors, x and y, and their images, Hx and Hy, under the transformation H.

The matrix transforms any vector into its mirror image in the line $u_\perp$. For any vector x, the point halfway between x and Hx, that is, the vector

$$x - (\tau/2)u,$$

is actually on the line $u_\perp$. In more than two dimensions, $u_\perp$ is the plane perpendicular to the defining vector u.

Figure 5.2 also shows what happens if u bisects the angle between x and one of the axes. The resulting Hx then falls on that axis. In other words, all but one of the components of Hx are zero. Moreover, since H is orthogonal, it preserves length. Consequently, the nonzero component of Hx is $\pm\|x\|$.

For a given vector x, the Householder reflection that zeros all but the kth component of x is given by

$$\sigma = \pm\|x\|,$$
$$u = x + \sigma e_k,$$
$$\rho = 2/\|u\|^2 = 1/(\sigma u_k),$$
$$H = I - \rho uu^T.$$

In the absence of roundoff error, either sign could be chosen for σ, and the resulting Hx would be on either the positive or the negative kth axis. In the presence of roundoff error, it is best to choose the sign so that

$$\text{sign } \sigma = \text{sign } x_k.$$

Then the operation $x_k + \sigma$ is actually an addition, not a subtraction.

5.5 The QR Factorization

If all the parameters appear linearly and there are more observations than basis functions, we have a linear least squares problem. The design matrix X is m by n with $m > n$. We want to solve

$$X\beta \approx y.$$

But this system is overdetermined—there are more equations than unknowns. So we cannot expect to solve the system exactly. Instead, we solve it in the least squares sense:

$$\min_\beta \|X\beta - y\|.$$

A theoretical approach to solving the overdetermined system begins by multiplying both sides by X^T. This reduces the system to a square, n-by-n system known as the *normal equations*:

$$X^T X\beta = X^T y.$$

If there are thousands of observations and only a few parameters, the design matrix X is quite large, but the matrix $X^T X$ is small. We have projected y onto the space spanned by the columns of X. Continuing with this theoretical approach, if the basis functions are independent, then $X^T X$ is nonsingular and

$$\beta = (X^T X)^{-1} X^T y.$$

This formula for solving linear least squares problems appears in most textbooks on statistics and numerical methods. However, there are several undesirable aspects to this theoretical approach. We have already seen that using a matrix inverse to solve a system of equations is more work and less accurate than solving the system by Gaussian elimination. But, more importantly, the normal equations are always more badly conditioned than the original overdetermined system. In fact, the condition number is squared:

$$\kappa(X^T X) = \kappa(X)^2.$$

With finite-precision computation, the normal equations can actually become singular, and $(X^T X)^{-1}$ nonexistent, even though the columns of X are independent.

As an extreme example, consider the design matrix

$$X = \begin{pmatrix} 1 & 1 \\ \delta & 0 \\ 0 & \delta \end{pmatrix}.$$

If δ is small, but nonzero, the two columns of X are nearly parallel but are still linearly independent. The normal equations make the situation worse:

$$X^T X = \begin{pmatrix} 1 + \delta^2 & 1 \\ 1 & 1 + \delta^2 \end{pmatrix}.$$

If $|\delta| < 10^{-8}$, the matrix $X^T X$ computed with double-precision floating-point arithmetic is exactly singular and the inverse required in the classic textbook formula does not exist.

MATLAB avoids the normal equations. The backslash operator not only solves square, nonsingular systems, but also computes the least squares solution to rectangular, overdetermined systems:

$$\beta = X \backslash y.$$

Most of the computation is done by an *orthogonalization* algorithm known as the QR factorization. The factorization is computed by the built-in function `qr`. The NCM function `qrsteps` demonstrates the individual steps.

The two versions of the QR factorization are illustrated in Figure 5.3. Both versions have

$$X = QR.$$

In the full version, R is the same size as X and Q is a square matrix with as many rows as X. In the economy-sized version, Q is the same size as X and R is a square matrix with as many columns as X. The letter "Q" is a substitute for the letter "O" in "orthogonal" and the letter "R" is for "right" triangular matrix. The Gram–Schmidt process described in many linear algebra texts is a related, but numerically less satisfactory, algorithm that generates the same factorization.

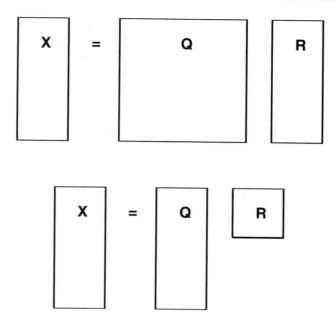

Figure 5.3. *Full and economy QR factorizations.*

A sequence of Householder reflections is applied to the columns of X to produce the matrix R:

$$H_n \cdots H_2 H_1 X = R.$$

The jth column of R is a linear combination of the first j columns of X. Consequently, the elements of R below the main diagonal are zero.

If the same sequence of reflections is applied to the right-hand side, the equations

$$X\beta \approx y$$

become

$$R\beta \approx z,$$

where

$$H_n \cdots H_2 H_1 y = z.$$

The first n of these equations is a small, square, triangular system that can be solved for β by back substitution with the subfunction `backsubs` in `bslashtx`. The coefficients in the remaining $m - n$ equations are all zero, so these equations are independent of β and the corresponding components of z constitute the transformed residual. This approach is preferable to the normal equations because Householder reflections have impeccable numerical credentials and because the resulting triangular system is ready for back substitution.

The matrix Q in the QR factorization is

$$Q = (H_n \cdots H_2 H_1)^T.$$

To solve least squares problems, we do not have to actually compute Q. In other uses of the factorization, it may be convenient to have Q explicitly. If we compute just the first n columns, we have the economy-sized factorization. If we compute all m columns, we have the full factorization. In either case,

$$Q^T Q = I,$$

so Q has columns that are perpendicular to each other and have unit length. Such a matrix is said to have *orthonormal columns*. For the full Q, it is also true that

$$QQ^T = I,$$

so the full Q is an *orthogonal* matrix.

Let's illustrate this with a small version of the census example. We will fit the last six observations with a quadratic:

$$y(s) \approx \beta_1 s^2 + \beta_2 s + \beta_3.$$

The scaled time s = ((1950:10:2000)' - 1950)/50 and the observations y are

```
       s          y
   0.0000    150.6970
   0.2000    179.3230
   0.4000    203.2120
   0.6000    226.5050
   0.8000    249.6330
   1.0000    281.4220
```

The design matrix is X = [s.*s s ones(size(s))].

```
        0           0       1.0000
   0.0400      0.2000       1.0000
   0.1600      0.4000       1.0000
   0.3600      0.6000       1.0000
   0.6400      0.8000       1.0000
   1.0000      1.0000       1.0000
```

The M-file qrsteps shows the steps in the QR factorization.

        qrsteps(X,y)

The first step introduces zeros below the diagonal in the first column of X.

```
  -1.2516     -1.4382      -1.7578
        0      0.1540       0.9119
        0      0.2161       0.6474
        0      0.1863       0.2067
        0      0.0646      -0.4102
        0     -0.1491      -1.2035
```

The same Householder reflection is applied to y.

```
-449.3721
 160.1447
 126.4988
  53.9004
 -57.2197
-198.0353
```

Zeros are introduced in the second column.

```
-1.2516    -1.4382    -1.7578
      0    -0.3627    -1.3010
      0          0    -0.2781
      0          0    -0.5911
      0          0    -0.6867
      0          0    -0.5649
```

The second Householder reflection is also applied to y.

```
-449.3721
-242.3136
 -41.8356
 -91.2045
-107.4973
 -81.8878
```

Finally, zeros are introduced in the third column and the reflection applied to y. This produces the triangular matrix R and a modified right-hand side z.

```
R =
  -1.2516    -1.4382    -1.7578
        0    -0.3627    -1.3010
        0          0     1.1034
        0          0          0
        0          0          0
        0          0          0
z =
-449.3721
-242.3136
 168.2334
  -1.3202
  -3.0801
   4.0048
```

The system of equations $R\beta = z$ is the same size as the original, 6 by 3. We can solve the first three equations exactly (because $R(1:3, 1:3)$ is nonsingular).

```
beta = R(1:3,1:3)\z(1:3)

beta =
     5.7013
   121.1341
   152.4745
```

This is the same solution beta that the backslash operator computes with

```
beta = R\z
```

or

```
beta = X\y
```

The last three equations in $R\beta = z$ cannot be satisfied by any choice of β, so the last three components of z represent the residual. In fact, the two quantities

```
norm(z(4:6))
norm(X*beta - y)
```

are both equal to 5.2219. Notice that even though we used the QR factorization, we never actually computed Q.

The population in the year 2010 can be predicted by evaluating

$$\beta_1 s^2 + \beta_2 s + \beta_3$$

at $s = (2010 - 1950)/50 = 1.2$. This can be done with polyval.

```
p2010 = polyval(beta,1.2)

p2010 =
   306.0453
```

Censusgui itself, fitting a quadratic to more data, predicts 311.5880. Which do you think is going to be closer to the actual result of the 2010 census?

5.6 Pseudoinverse

The definition of the pseudoinverse makes use of the Frobenius norm of a matrix:

$$\|A\|_F = \left(\sum_i \sum_j a_{i,j}^2 \right)^{1/2}.$$

The MATLAB expression norm(X,'fro') computes the Frobenius norm. $\|A\|_F$ is the same as the 2-norm of the long vector formed from all the elements of A.

```
norm(A,'fro') = norm(A(:))
```

The *Moore–Penrose pseudoinverse* generalizes and extends the usual matrix inverse. The pseudoinverse is denoted by a dagger superscript,

$$Z = X^\dagger,$$

and computed by the MATLAB `pinv`.

```
Z = pinv(X)
```

If X is square and nonsingular, then the pseudoinverse and the inverse are the same:

$$X^\dagger = X^{-1}.$$

If X is m by n with $m > n$ and X has full rank, then its pseudoinverse is the matrix involved in the normal equations:

$$X^\dagger = (X^T X)^{-1} X^T.$$

The pseudoinverse has some, but not all, of the properties of the ordinary inverse. $X^\dagger$ is a left inverse because

$$X^\dagger X = (X^T X)^{-1} X^T X = I$$

is the n-by-n identity. But $X^\dagger$ is not a right inverse because

$$XX^\dagger = X(X^T X)^{-1} X^T$$

only has rank n and so cannot be the m-by-m identity.

The pseudoinverse does get as close to a right inverse as possible in the sense that, out of all the matrices Z that minimize

$$\|XZ - I\|_F,$$

$Z = X^\dagger$ also minimizes

$$\|Z\|_F.$$

It turns out that these minimization properties also define a unique pseudoinverse even if X is rank deficient.

Consider the 1-by-1 case. What is the inverse of a real (or complex) number x? If x is not zero, then clearly $x^{-1} = 1/x$. But if x is zero, x^{-1} does not exist. The pseudoinverse takes care of that because, in the scalar case, the unique number that minimizes both

$$|xz - 1| \text{ and } |z|$$

is

$$x^\dagger = \begin{cases} 1/x & : & x \neq 0, \\ 0 & : & x = 0. \end{cases}$$

The actual computation of the pseudoinverse involves the singular value decomposition, which is described in a later chapter. You can `edit pinv` or `type pinv` to see the code.

5.7   Rank Deficiency

If X is rank deficient, or has more columns than rows, the square matrix $X^T X$ is singular and $(X^T X)^{-1}$ does not exist. The formula

$$\beta = (X^T X)^{-1} X^T y$$

obtained from the normal equations breaks down completely.

In these degenerate situations, the least squares solution to the linear system

$$X\beta \approx y$$

is not unique. A *null vector* of X is a nonzero solution to

$$X\eta = 0.$$

Any multiple of any null vector can be added to β without changing how well $X\beta$ approximates y.

In MATLAB, the solution to

$$X\beta \approx y$$

can be computed with either backslash or the pseudoinverse, that is,

```
beta = X\y
```

or

```
beta = pinv(X)*y
```

In the full rank case, these two solutions are the same, although `pinv` does considerably more computation to obtain it. But in degenerate situations these two solutions are not the same.

The solution computed by backslash is called a *basic* solution. If r is the rank of X, then at most r of the components of

```
beta = X\y
```

are nonzero. Even the requirement of a basic solution does not guarantee uniqueness. The particular basic computation obtained with backslash is determined by details of the QR factorization.

The solution computed by `pinv` is the *minimum norm* solution. Out of all the vectors β that minimize $\|X\beta - y\|$, the vector

```
beta = pinv(X)*y
```

also minimizes $\|\beta\|$. This minimum norm solution is unique.

For example, let

$$X = \begin{pmatrix} 1 & 2 & 3 \\ 4 & 5 & 6 \\ 7 & 8 & 9 \\ 10 & 11 & 12 \\ 13 & 14 & 15 \end{pmatrix}$$

and

$$y = \begin{pmatrix} 16 \\ 17 \\ 18 \\ 19 \\ 20 \end{pmatrix}.$$

The matrix X is rank deficient. The middle column is the average of the first and last columns. The vector

$$\eta = \begin{pmatrix} 1 \\ -2 \\ 1 \end{pmatrix}$$

is a null vector.

The statement

```
beta = X\y
```

produces a warning,

```
Warning: Rank deficient, rank = 2   tol =    2.4701e-014.
```

and the solution

```
beta =
    -7.5000
         0
     7.8333
```

As promised, this solution is basic; it has only two nonzero components. However, the vectors

```
beta =
          0
   -15.0000
    15.3333
```

and

```
beta =
   -15.3333
    15.6667
         0
```

are also basic solutions.

The statement

```
beta = pinv(X)*y
```

produces the solution

```
beta =
    -7.5556
     0.1111
     7.7778
```

without giving a warning about rank deficiency. The norm of the pseudoinverse solution

```
norm(pinv(X)*y) = 10.8440
```

is slightly less than the norm of the backslash solution

```
norm(X\y) = 10.8449
```

Out of all the vectors β that minimize $\|X\beta - y\|$, the pseudoinverse has found the shortest. Notice that the difference between the two solutions,

```
X\y - pinv(X)*y =
    0.0556
   -0.1111
    0.0556
```

is a multiple of the null vector η.

If handled with care, rank deficient least squares problems can be solved in a satisfactory manner. Problems that are nearly, but not exactly, rank deficient are more difficult to handle. The situation is similar to square linear systems that are badly conditioned, but not exactly singular. Such problems are not *well posed* numerically. Small changes in the data can lead to large changes in the computed solution. The algorithms used by both backslash and pseudoinverse involve decisions about linear independence and rank. These decisions use somewhat arbitrary tolerances and are particularly susceptible to both errors in the data and roundoff errors in the computation.

Which is "better," backslash or pseudoinverse? In some situations, the underlying criteria of basic solution or minimum norm solution may be relevant. But most problem formulations, particularly those involving curve fitting, do not include such subtle distinctions. The important fact to remember is that the computed solutions are not unique and are not well determined by the data.

5.8   Separable Least Squares

MATLAB provides several functions for solving nonlinear least squares problems. Older versions of MATLAB have one general-purpose, multidimensional, nonlinear minimizer, fmins. In more recent versions of MATLAB, fmins has been updated and renamed fminsearch. The Optimization Toolbox provides additional capabilities, including a minimizer for problems with constraints, fmincon; a minimizer for unconstrained problems, fminunc; and two functions intended specifically for nonlinear least squares, lsqnonlin and lsqcurvefit. The Curve Fitting Toolbox provides a GUI to facilitate the solution of many different linear and nonlinear fitting problems.

In this introduction, we focus on the use of fminsearch. This function uses a direct search technique known as the Nelder–Meade algorithm. It does not attempt to approximate any gradients or other partial derivatives. It is quite effective on small problems involving only a few variables. Larger problems with more variables are better handled by the functions in the Optimization and Curve Fitting Toolboxes.

Separable least squares curve-fitting problems involve both linear and nonlinear parameters. We could ignore the linear portion and use fminsearch to search for all

the parameters. But if we take advantage of the separable structure, we obtain a more efficient, robust technique. With this approach, fminsearch is used to search for values of
the nonlinear parameters that minimize the norm of the residual. At each step of the search
process, the backslash operator is used to compute values of the linear parameters.

Two blocks of MATLAB code are required. One block can be a function, a script, or a
few lines typed directly in the Command Window. It sets up the problem, establishes starting
values for the nonlinear parameters, calls fminsearch, processes the results, and usually
produces a plot. The second block is the objective function that is called by fminsearch.
This function is given a vector of values of the nonlinear parameters, alpha. It should
compute the design matrix X for these parameters, use backslash with X and the observations
to compute values of the linear parameters beta, and return the resulting residual norm.

Let's illustrate all this with expfitdemo, which involves observations of radioactive
decay. The task is to model the decay by a sum of two exponential terms with unknown
rates λ_j:

$$y \approx \beta_1 e^{-\lambda_1 t} + \beta_2 e^{-\lambda_2 t}.$$

Consequently, in this example, there are two linear parameters and two nonlinear parameters.
The demo plots the various fits that are generated during the nonlinear minimization process.
Figure 5.4 shows plots of both the data and the final fit.

The main function begins by specifying 21 observations, t and y.

```
function expfitdemo
t = (0:.1:2)';
y = [5.8955 3.5639 2.5173 1.9790 1.8990 1.3938 1.1359 ...
     1.0096 1.0343 0.8435 0.6856 0.6100 0.5392 0.3946 ...
     0.3903 0.5474 0.3459 0.1370 0.2211 0.1704 0.2636]';
```

The initial plot uses o's for the observations, creates an all-zero placeholder for what
is going to become the evolving fit, and creates a title that will show the values of lambda.
The variable h holds the handles for these three graphics objects.

```
clf
shg
set(gcf,'doublebuffer','on')
h = plot(t,y,'o',t,0*t,'-');
h(3) = title('');
axis([0 2 0 6.5])
```

The vector lambda0 specifies initial values for the nonlinear parameters. In this example,
almost any choice of initial values leads to convergence, but in other situations, particularly
with more nonlinear parameters, the choice of initial values can be much more important.
The call to fminsearch does most of the work. The observations t and y, as well as the
graphics handle h, are passed as extra parameters.

```
lambda0 = [3 6]';
lambda = fminsearch(@expfitfun,lambda0,[],t,y,h)
set(h(2),'color','black')
```

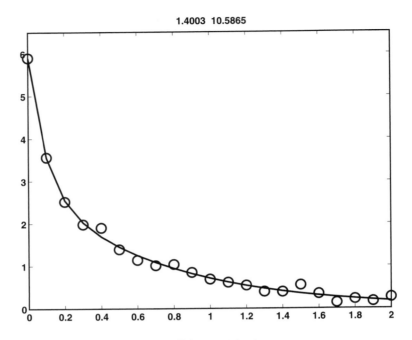

Figure 5.4. expfitdemo.

The objective function is named expfitfun. It can handle n exponential basis functions; we will be using $n = 2$. The first input parameter is a vector provided by fminsearch that contains values of the n decay rates, λ_j. The other parameters are vectors containing the independent and dependent variables, t and y, and the graphics handle. The function computes the design matrix, uses backslash to compute β, evaluates the resulting model, and returns the norm of the residual.

```
function res = expfitfun(lambda,t,y,h)
m = length(t);
n = length(lambda);
X = zeros(m,n);
for j = 1:n
    X(:,j) = exp(-lambda(j)*t);
end
beta = X\y;
z = X*beta;
res = norm(z-y);
```

The objective function also updates the plot of the fit and the title and pauses long enough for us to see the progress of the computation.

```
set(h(2),'ydata',z);
set(h(3),'string',sprintf('%8.4f %8.4f',lambda))
pause(.1)
```

5.9   Further Reading

The reference books on matrix computation [2, 18, 26, 58, 59, 60] discuss least squares. An additional reference is Björck [8].

Exercises

5.1. Let X be the n-by-n matrix generated by

```
[I,J] = ndgrid(1:n);
X = min(I,J) + 2*eye(n,n) - 2;
```

(a) How does the condition number of X grow with n?
(b) Which, if any, of the triangular factorizations `chol(X)`, `lu(X)`, and `qr(X)` reveal the poor conditioning?

5.2. In `censusgui`, change the 1950 population from 150.697 million to 50.697 million. This produces an extreme *outlier* in the data. Which models are the most affected by this outlier? Which models are the least affected?

5.3. If `censusgui` is used to fit the U.S. Census data with a polynomial of degree eight and the fit is extrapolated beyond the year 2000, the predicted population actually becomes zero before the year 2020. On what year, month, and day does that fateful event occur?

5.4. Here are some details that we skipped over in our discussion of Householder reflections. At the same time, we extend the description to include complex matrices. The notation u^T for transpose is replaced with the MATLAB notation u' for complex conjugate transpose. Let x be any nonzero m-by-1 vector and let e_k denote the kth unit vector, that is, the kth column of the m-by-m identity matrix. The sign of a complex number $z = re^{i\theta}$ is

$$\text{sign}(z) = z/|z| = e^{i\theta}.$$

Define σ by

$$\sigma = \text{sign}(x_k)\|x\|.$$

Let

$$u = x + \sigma e_k.$$

In other words, u is obtained from x by adding σ to its kth component.
(a) The definition of ρ uses $\bar{\sigma}$, the complex conjugate of σ:

$$\rho = 1/(\bar{\sigma}u_k).$$

Show that

$$\rho = 2/\|u\|^2.$$

(b) The Householder reflection generated by the vector x is

$$H = I - \rho uu'.$$

Show that
$$H' = H$$

and that
$$H'H = I.$$

(c) Show that all the components of Hx are zero, except for the kth. In other words, show that
$$Hx = -\sigma e_k.$$

(d) For any vector y, let
$$\tau = \rho u'y.$$

Show that
$$Hy = y - \tau u.$$

5.5. Let
$$x = \begin{pmatrix} 9 \\ 2 \\ 6 \end{pmatrix}.$$

(a) Find the Householder reflection H that transforms x into
$$Hx = \begin{pmatrix} -11 \\ 0 \\ 0 \end{pmatrix}.$$

(b) Find nonzero vectors u and v that satisfy
$$Hu = -u,$$
$$Hv = v.$$

5.6. Let
$$X = \begin{pmatrix} 1 & 2 & 3 \\ 4 & 5 & 6 \\ 7 & 8 & 9 \\ 10 & 11 & 12 \\ 13 & 14 & 15 \end{pmatrix}.$$

(a) Verify that X is rank deficient.

Consider three choices for the pseudoinverse of X.

```
Z = pinv(X)        % The actual pseudoinverse
B = X\eye(5,5)     % Backslash
S = eye(3,3)/X     % Slash
```

(b) Compare the values of

$$\|Z\|_F, \quad \|B\|_F, \quad \text{and } \|S\|_F;$$
$$\|XZ - I\|_F, \quad \|XB - I\|_F, \quad \text{and } \|XS - I\|_F;$$
$$\|ZX - I\|_F, \quad \|BX - I\|_F, \quad \text{and } \|SX - I\|_F.$$

Verify that the values obtained with Z are less than or equal to the values obtained with the other two choices. Actually minimizing these quantities is one way of characterizing the pseudoinverse.

(c) Verify that Z satisfies all four of the following conditions, and that B and S fail to satisfy at least one of the conditions. These conditions are known as the Moore–Penrose equations and are another way to characterize a unique pseudoinverse.

$$XZ \text{ is symmetric.}$$
$$ZX \text{ is symmetric.}$$
$$XZX = X.$$
$$ZXZ = Z.$$

5.7. Generate 11 data points, $t_k = (k-1)/10$, $y_k = \text{erf}(t_k)$, $k = 1, \ldots, 11$.

(a) Fit the data in a least squares sense with polynomials of degrees 1 through 10. Compare the fitted polynomial with $\text{erf}(t)$ for values of t between the data points. How does the maximum error depend on the polynomial degree?

(b) Because $\text{erf}(t)$ is an odd function of t, that is, $\text{erf}(x) = -\text{erf}(-x)$, it is reasonable to fit the data by a linear combination of odd powers of t:

$$\text{erf}(t) \approx c_1 t + c_2 t^3 + \cdots + c_n t^{2n-1}.$$

Again, see how the error between data points depends on n.

(c) Polynomials are not particularly good approximants for $\text{erf}(t)$ because they are unbounded for large t, whereas $\text{erf}(t)$ approaches 1 for large t. So, using the same data points, fit a model of the form

$$\text{erf}(t) \approx c_1 + e^{-t^2}(c_2 + c_3 z + c_4 z^2 + c_5 z^3),$$

where $z = 1/(1+t)$. How does the error between the data points compare with the polynomial models?

5.8. Here are 25 observations, y_k, taken at equally spaced values of t.

```
t = 1:25
y = [ 5.0291    6.5099    5.3666    4.1272    4.2948
      6.1261   12.5140   10.0502    9.1614    7.5677
      7.2920   10.0357   11.0708   13.4045   12.8415
     11.9666   11.0765   11.7774   14.5701   17.0440
     17.0398   15.9069   15.4850   15.5112   17.6572]
y = y'; y = y(:)
```

(a) Fit the data with a straight line, $y(t) = \beta_1 + \beta_2 t$, and plot the residuals, $y(t_k) - y_k$. You should observe that one of the data points has a much larger residual than the others. This is probably an *outlier*.

(b) Discard the outlier, and fit the data again by a straight line. Plot the residuals again. Do you see any pattern in the residuals?

(c) Fit the data, with the outlier excluded, by a model of the form

$$y(t) = \beta_1 + \beta_2 t + \beta_3 \sin t.$$

(d) Evaluate the third fit on a finer grid over the interval [0, 26]. Plot the fitted curve, using line style ' – ', together with the data, using line style ' o '. Include the outlier, using a different marker, ' * '.

5.9. *Statistical Reference Datasets.* NIST, the National Institute of Standards and Technology, is the branch of the U.S. Department of Commerce responsible for setting national and international standards. NIST maintains Statistical Reference Datasets, StRD, for use in testing and certifying statistical software. The home page on the Web is [48]. Data sets for linear least squares are under "Linear Regression." This exercise involves two of the NIST reference data sets:

   • `Norris`: linear polynomial for calibration of ozone monitors;

   • `Pontius`: quadratic polynomial for calibration of load cells.

For each of these data sets, follow the Web links labeled

   • Data File (ASCII Format),

   • Certified Values, and

   • Graphics.

Download each ASCII file. Extract the observations. Compute the polynomial coefficients. Compare the coefficients with the certified values. Make plots similar to the NIST plots of both the fit and the residuals.

5.10. *Filip data set.* One of the Statistical Reference Datasets from the NIST is the "Filip" data set. The data consist of several dozen observations of a variable y at different values of x. The task is to model y by a polynomial of degree 10 in x.

This data set is controversial. A search of the Web for "filip strd" will find several dozen postings, including the original page at NIST [48]. Some mathematical and statistical packages are able to reproduce the polynomial coefficients that NIST has decreed to be the "certified values." Other packages give warning or error messages that the problem is too badly conditioned to solve. A few packages give different coefficients without warning. The Web offers several opinions about whether or not this is a reasonable problem. Let's see what MATLAB does with it.

The data set is available from the NIST Web site. There is one line for each data point. The data are given with the first number on the line a value of y, and the second number the corresponding x. The x-values are not monotonically ordered, but it is not necessary to sort them. Let n be the number of data points and $p = 11$ the number of polynomial coefficients.

(a) As your first experiment, load the data into MATLAB, plot it with ' . ' as the line type, and then invoke the **Basic Fitting** tool available under the **Tools** menu on the figure window. Select the 10th-degree polynomial fit. You will be warned that the polynomial is badly conditioned, but ignore that for now. How do the computed coefficients compare with the certified values on the NIST Web page? How does the plotted fit compare with the graphic on the NIST Web page? The basic fitting tool also displays the norm of the residuals, $\|r\|$. Compare this with the NIST quantity "Residual Standard Deviation," which is

$$\frac{\|r\|}{\sqrt{n-p}}.$$

(b) Examine this data set more carefully by using six different methods to compute the polynomial fit. Explain all the warning messages you receive during these computations.

- Polyfit: Use `polyfit(x,y,10)`.

- Backslash: Use `X\y`, where X is the n-by-p truncated Vandermonde matrix with elements

$$X_{i,j} = x_i^{p-j}, \; i = 1, \ldots, n, \; j = 1, \ldots, p.$$

- Pseudoinverse: Use `pinv(X)*y`.

- Normal equations: Use `inv(X'*X)*X'*y`.

- Centering: Let $\mu = \text{mean}(x)$, $\sigma = \text{std}(x)$, $t = (x - \mu)/\sigma$.
  Use `polyfit(t,y,10)`.

- Certified coefficients: Obtain the coefficients from the NIST Web page.

(c) What are the norms of the residuals for the fits computed by the six different methods?

(d) Which one of the six methods gives a very poor fit? (Perhaps the packages that are criticized on the Web for reporting bad results are using this method.)

(e) Plot the five good fits. Use dots, `'.'`, at the data values and curves obtained by evaluating the polynomials at a few hundred points over the range of the x's. The

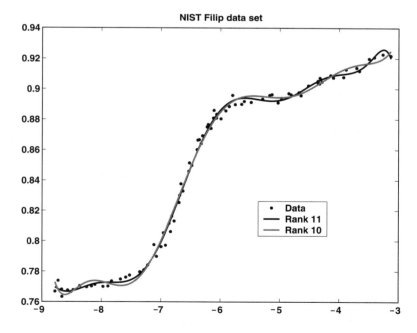

Figure 5.5. *NIST Filip standard reference data set.*

plot should look like Figure 5.5. There are five different plots, but only two visually distinct ones. Which methods produce which plots?

(f) Why do polyfit and backslash give different results?

5.11. *Longley data set.* The Longley data set of labor statistics was one of the first used to test the accuracy of least squares computations. You don't need to go to the NIST Web site to do this problem, but if you are interested in the background, you should see the Longley page at [48]. The data set is available in NCM in the file `longley.dat`. You can bring the data into MATLAB with

```
load longley.dat
y = longley(:,1);
X = longley(:,2:7);
```

There are 16 observations of 7 variables, gathered over the years 1947 to 1962. The variable y and the 6 variables making up the columns of the data matrix X are

y = Total Derived Employment,

x_1 = GNP Implicit Price Deflater,

x_2 = Gross National Product,

x_3 = Unemployment,

x_4 = Size of Armed Forces,

x_5 = Noninstitutional Population Age 14 and Over,

x_6 = Year.

The objective is to predict y by a linear combination of a constant and the six x's:

$$y \approx \beta_0 + \sum_{1}^{6} \beta_k x_k.$$

(a) Use the MATLAB backslash operator to compute $\beta_0, \beta_1, \ldots, \beta_6$. This involves augmenting X with a column of all 1's, corresponding to the constant term.

(b) Compare your β's with the certified values [48].

(c) Use `errorbar` to plot y with error bars whose magnitude is the difference between y and the least squares fit.

(d) Use `corrcoef` to compute the correlation coefficients for X without the column of 1's. Which variables are highly correlated?

(e) Normalize the vector y so that its mean is zero and its standard deviation is one. You can do this with

```
y = y - mean(y);
y = y/std(y)
```

Do the same thing to the columns of X. Now plot all seven normalized variables on the same axis. Include a `legend`.

5.12. *Planetary orbit [30].* The expression $z = ax^2 + bxy + cy^2 + dx + ey + f$ is known as a *quadratic form.* The set of points (x, y), where $z = 0$, is a *conic section.* It can be an ellipse, a parabola, or a hyperbola, depending on the sign of the discriminant $b^2 - 4ac$. Circles and lines are special cases. The equation $z = 0$ can be normalized by dividing the quadratic form by any nonzero coefficient. For example, if $f \neq 0$, we can divide all the other coefficients by f and obtain a quadratic form with the constant term equal to one. You can use the MATLAB `meshgrid` and `contour` functions to plot conic sections. Use `meshgrid` to create arrays X and Y. Evaluate the quadratic form to produce Z. Then use `contour` to plot the set of points where Z is zero.

```
[X,Y] = meshgrid(xmin:deltax:xmax,ymin:deltay:ymax);
Z = a*X.^2 + b*X.*Y + c*Y.^2 + d*X + e*Y + f;
contour(X,Y,Z,[0 0])
```

A planet follows an elliptical orbit. Here are ten observations of its position in the (x, y) plane:

```
x = [1.02 .95 .87 .77 .67 .56 .44 .30 .16 .01]';
y = [0.39 .32 .27 .22 .18 .15 .13 .12 .13 .15]';
```

(a) Determine the coefficients in the quadratic form that fits these data in the least squares sense by setting one of the coefficients equal to one and solving a 10-by-5 overdetermined system of linear equations for the other five coefficients. Plot the orbit with x on the x-axis and y on the y-axis. Superimpose the ten data points on the plot.

(b) This least squares problem is nearly rank deficient. To see what effect this has on the solution, perturb the data slightly by adding to each coordinate of each data point a random number uniformly distributed in the interval $[-.0005, .0005]$. Compute the new coefficients resulting from the perturbed data. Plot the new orbit on the same plot with the old orbit. Comment on your comparison of the sets of coefficients and the orbits.

Chapter 6

Quadrature

The term *numerical integration* covers several different tasks, including numerical evaluation of integrals and numerical solution of ordinary differential equations. So we use the somewhat old-fashioned term *quadrature* for the simplest of these, the numerical evaluation of a definite integral. Modern quadrature algorithms automatically vary an adaptive step size.

6.1 Adaptive Quadrature

Let $f(x)$ be a real-valued function of a real variable, defined on a finite interval $a \leq x \leq b$. We seek to compute the value of the integral,

$$\int_a^b f(x)dx.$$

The word "quadrature" reminds us of an elementary technique for finding this area—plot the function on graph paper and count the number of little squares that lie underneath the curve.

In Figure 6.1, there are 148 little squares underneath the curve. If the area of one little square is $3/512$, then a rough estimate of the integral is $148 \times 3/512 = 0.8672$.

Adaptive quadrature involves careful selection of the points where $f(x)$ is sampled. We want to evaluate the function at as few points as possible while approximating the integral to within some specified accuracy. A fundamental additive property of a definite integral is the basis for adaptive quadrature. If c is any point between a and b, then

$$\int_a^b f(x)dx = \int_a^c f(x)dx + \int_c^b f(x)dx.$$

The idea is that if we can approximate each of the two integrals on the right to within a specified tolerance, then the sum gives us the desired result. If not, we can recursively apply the additive property to each of the intervals $[a, c]$ and $[c, b]$. The resulting algorithm will adapt to the integrand automatically, partitioning the interval into subintervals with fine

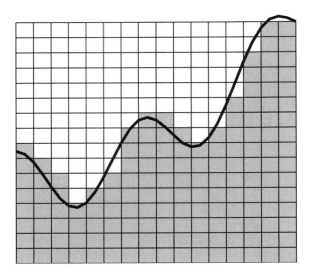

Figure 6.1. *Quadrature.*

spacing where the integrand is varying rapidly and coarse spacing where the integrand is varying slowly.

6.2   Basic Quadrature Rules

The derivation of the quadrature rule used by our MATLAB function begins with two of the basic quadrature rules shown in Figure 6.2: the *midpoint rule* and the *trapezoid rule*. Let $h = b - a$ be the length of the interval. The midpoint rule, M, approximates the integral by the area of a rectangle whose base has length h and whose height is the value of the integrand at the midpoint:

$$M = h f \left(\frac{a + b}{2} \right).$$

The trapezoid rule, T, approximates the integral by the area of a trapezoid with base h and sides equal to the values of the integrand at the two endpoints:

$$T = h \frac{f(a) + f(b)}{2}.$$

The accuracy of a quadrature rule can be predicted in part by examining its behavior on polynomials. The *order* of a quadrature rule is the degree of the lowest degree polynomial that the rule does not integrate exactly. If a quadrature rule of order p is used to integrate a smooth function over a small interval of length h, then a Taylor series analysis shows that the error is proportional to h^p. The midpoint rule and the trapezoid rule are both exact for constant and linear functions of x, but neither of them is exact for a quadratic in x, so they both have order two. (The order of a rectangle rule with height $f(a)$ or $f(b)$ instead of the midpoint is only one.)

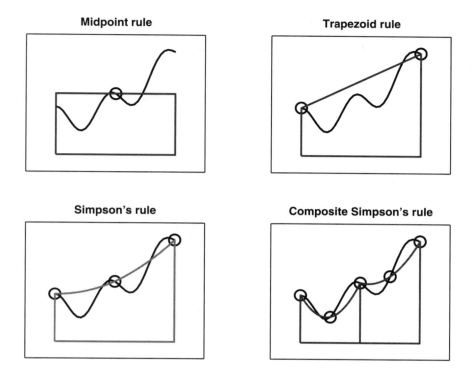

Figure 6.2. *Four quadrature rules.*

The accuracy of the two rules can be compared by examining their behavior on the simple integral

$$\int_0^1 x^2 dx = \frac{1}{3}.$$

The midpoint rule gives

$$M = 1 \left(\frac{1}{2}\right)^2 = \frac{1}{4}.$$

The trapezoid rule gives

$$T = 1\left(\frac{0 + 1^2}{2}\right) = \frac{1}{2}.$$

So the error in M is $1/12$, while the error in T is $-1/6$. The errors have opposite signs and, perhaps surprisingly, the midpoint rule is twice as accurate as the trapezoid rule.

This turns out to be true more generally. For integrating smooth functions over short intervals, M is roughly twice as accurate as T and the errors have opposite signs. Knowing these error estimates allows us to combine the two and get a rule that is usually more accurate than either one separately. If the error in T were exactly -2 times the error in M, then solving

$$S - T = -2(S - M)$$

for S would give us the exact value of the integral. In any case, the solution

$$S = \frac{2}{3}M + \frac{1}{3}T$$

is usually a more accurate approximation than either M or T alone. This rule is known as *Simpson's rule*. It can also be derived by integrating the quadratic function that interpolates the integrand at the two endpoints, a and b, and the midpoint, $c = (a + b)/2$:

$$S = \frac{h}{6}(f(a) + 4f(c) + f(b)).$$

It turns out that S also integrates cubics exactly, but not quartics, so its order is four.

We can carry this process one step further using the two halves of the interval, $[a, c]$ and $[c, b]$. Let d and e be the midpoints of these two subintervals: $d = (a + c)/2$ and $e = (c + b)/2$. Apply Simpson's rule to each subinterval to obtain a quadrature rule over $[a, b]$:

$$S_2 = \frac{h}{12}(f(a) + 4f(d) + 2f(c) + 4f(e) + f(b)).$$

This is an example of a *composite* quadrature rule. See Figure 6.2.

S and S_2 approximate the same integral, so their difference can be used as an estimate of the error:

$$E = (S_2 - S).$$

Moreover, the two can be combined to get an even more accurate approximation, Q. Both rules are of order four, but the S_2 step size is half the S step size, so S_2 is roughly 2^4 times as accurate. Thus, Q is obtained by solving

$$Q - S = 16(Q - S_2).$$

The result is

$$Q = S_2 + (S_2 - S)/15.$$

Exercise 6.2 asks you to express Q as a weighted combination of the five function values $f(a)$ through $f(e)$ and to establish that its order is six. The rule is known as *Weddle's rule*, the sixth-order *Newton–Cotes rule*, and also as the first step of *Romberg integration*. We will simply call it the *extrapolated Simpson's rule* because it uses Simpson's rule for two different values of h and then extrapolates toward $h = 0$.

6.3   quadtx, quadgui

The MATLAB function quad uses the extrapolated Simpson's rule in an adaptive recursive algorithm. Our textbook function quadtx is a simplified version of quad.

The function quadgui provides a graphical demonstration of the behavior of quad and quadtx. It produces a dynamic plot of the function values selected by the adaptive algorithm. The count of function evaluations is shown in the title position on the plot.

The initial portion of quadtx evaluates the integrand $f(x)$ three times to give the first, unextrapolated, Simpson's rule estimate. A recursive subfunction, quadtxstep, is then called to complete the computation.

```
function [Q,fcount] = quadtx(F,a,b,tol,varargin)
%QUADTX   Evaluate definite integral numerically.
%   Q = QUADTX(F,A,B) approximates the integral of F(x)
%   from A to B to within a tolerance of 1.e-6.
%
%   Q = QUADTX(F,A,B,tol) uses tol instead of 1.e-6.
%
%   The first argument, F, is a function handle or
%   an anonymous function that defines F(x).
%
%   Arguments beyond the first four,
%   Q = QUADTX(F,a,b,tol,p1,p2,...), are passed on to the
%   integrand, F(x,p1,p2,..).
%
%   [Q,fcount] = QUADTX(F,...) also counts the number of
%   evaluations of F(x).
%
%   See also QUAD, QUADL, DBLQUAD, QUADGUI.

% Default tolerance
if nargin < 4 | isempty(tol)
   tol = 1.e-6;
end

% Initialization
c = (a + b)/2;
fa = F(a,varargin{:});
fc = F(c,varargin{:});
fb = F(b,varargin{:});

% Recursive call
[Q,k] = quadtxstep(F, a, b, tol, fa, fc, fb, varargin{:});
fcount = k + 3;
```

Each recursive call of quadtxstep combines three previously computed function values with two more to obtain the two Simpson's approximations for a particular interval. If their difference is small enough, they are combined to return the extrapolated approximation for that interval. If their difference is larger than the tolerance, the recursion proceeds on each of the two half intervals.

```
function [Q,fcount] = quadtxstep(F,a,b,tol,fa,fc,fb,varargin)

% Recursive subfunction used by quadtx.

h = b - a;
```

```
c = (a + b)/2;
fd = F((a+c)/2,varargin{:});
fe = F((c+b)/2,varargin{:});
Q1 = h/6 * (fa + 4*fc + fb);
Q2 = h/12 * (fa + 4*fd + 2*fc + 4*fe + fb);
if abs(Q2 - Q1) <= tol
   Q  = Q2 + (Q2 - Q1)/15;
   fcount = 2;
else
   [Qa,ka] = quadtxstep(F, a, c, tol, fa, fd, fc, varargin{:});
   [Qb,kb] = quadtxstep(F, c, b, tol, fc, fe, fb, varargin{:});
   Q  = Qa + Qb;
   fcount = ka + kb + 2;
end
```

The choice of tolerance for comparison with the error estimates is important, but a little tricky. If a tolerance is not specified as the fourth argument to the function, then 10^{-6} is used as the default.

The tricky part is how to specify the tolerance in the recursive calls. How small does the tolerance in each recursive call have to be in order for the final result to have the desired accuracy? One approach would cut the tolerance in half with each level in the recursion. The idea is that if both Qa and Qb have errors less than tol/2, then their sum certainly has an error less than tol. If we did this, the two statements

```
   [Qa,ka] = quadtxstep(F, a, c, tol, fa, fd, fc, varargin{:});
   [Qb,kb] = quadtxstep(F, c, b, tol, fc, fe, fb, varargin{:});
```

would have tol/2 in place of tol.

However, this approach is too conservative. We are estimating the error in the two separate Simpson's rules, not their extrapolated combination. So the actual error is almost always much less than the estimate. More importantly, the subintervals where the actual error is close to the estimate are usually fairly rare. We can allow one of the two recursive calls to have an error close to the tolerance because the other subinterval will probably have a much smaller error. For these reasons, the same value of tol is used in each recursive call.

Our textbook function does have one serious defect: there is no provision for failure. It is possible to try to evaluate integrals that do not exist. For example,

$$\int_0^1 \frac{1}{3x - 1} dx$$

has a nonintegrable singularity. Attempting to evaluate this integral with quadtx results in a computation that runs for a long time and eventually terminates with an error message about the maximum recursion limit. It would be better to have diagnostic information about the singularity.

6.4 Specifying Integrands

MATLAB has several different ways of specifying the function to be integrated by a quadrature routine. The anonymous function facility is convenient for a simple, one-line formula. For example,

$$\int_0^1 \frac{1}{\sqrt{1+x^4}} dx$$

can be computed with the statements

```
f = @(x) 1./sqrt(1+x^4)
Q = quadtx(f,0,1)
```

If we want to compute

$$\int_0^\pi \frac{\sin x}{x} dx,$$

we could try

```
f = @(x) sin(x)/x
Q = quadtx(f,0,pi)
```

Unfortunately, this results in a division by zero message when f(0) is evaluated and, eventually, a recursion limit error. One remedy is to change the lower limit of integration from 0 to the smallest positive floating-point number, realmin.

```
Q = quadtx(f,realmin,pi)
```

The error made by changing the lower limit is many orders of magnitude smaller than roundoff error because the integrand is bounded by one and the length of the omitted interval is less than 10^{-300}.

Another remedy is to use an M-file instead of an anonymous function. Create a file named sinc.m that contains the text

```
function f = sinc(x)
if x == 0
    f = 1;
else
    f = sin(x)/x;
end
```

Then the statement

```
Q = quadtx(@sinc,0,pi)
```

uses a function handle and computes the integral with no difficulty.

Integrals that depend on parameters are encountered frequently. An example is the *beta* function, defined by

$$\beta(z, w) = \int_0^1 t^{z-1}(1 - t)^{w-1} dt.$$

MATLAB already has a `beta` function, but we can use this example to illustrate how to handle parameters. Create an anonymous function with three arguments.

```
F = @(t,z,w) t^(z-1) * (1-t)^(w-1)
```

Or use an M-file with a name like `betaf.m`.

```
function f = betaf(t,z,w)
f = t^(z-1)*(1-t)^(w-1)
```

As with all functions, the order of the arguments is important. The functions used with quadrature routines must have the variable of integration as the first argument. Values for the parameters are then given as extra arguments to `quadtx`. To compute $\beta(8/3, 10/3)$, you should set

```
z = 8/3;
w = 10/3;
tol = 1.e-6;
```

and then use

```
Q = quadtx(F,0,1,tol,z,w);
```

or

```
Q = quadtx(@betaf,0,1,tol,z,w);
```

The function functions in MATLAB itself usually expect the first argument to be in *vectorized* form. This means, for example, that the mathematical expression

$$\frac{\sin x}{1 + x^2}$$

should be specified with MATLAB array notation.

```
sin(x)./(1 + x.^2)
```

Without the two dots,

```
sin(x)/(1 + x^2)
```

calls for linear algebraic vector operations that are not appropriate here. The MATLAB function `vectorize` transforms a scalar expression into something that can be used as an argument to function functions.

Many of the function functions in MATLAB require the specification of an interval of the x-axis. Mathematically, we have two possible notations, $a \le x \le b$ or $[a, b]$.

With MATLAB, we also have two possibilities. The endpoints can be given as two separate arguments, a and b, or can be combined into one vector argument, [a,b]. The quadrature functions quad and quadl use two separate arguments. The zero finder, fzero, uses a single argument because either a single starting point or a two-element vector can specify the interval. The ordinary differential equation solvers that we encounter in the next chapter also use a single argument because a many-element vector can specify a set of points where the solution is to be evaluated. The easy plotting function, ezplot, accepts either one or two arguments.

6.5 Performance

The MATLAB demos directory includes a function named humps that is intended to illustrate the behavior of graphics, quadrature, and zero-finding routines. The function is

$$h(x) = \frac{1}{(x-0.3)^2 + 0.01} + \frac{1}{(x-0.9)^2 + 0.04}.$$

The statement

```
ezplot(@humps,0,1)
```

produces a graph of $h(x)$ for $0 \le x \le 1$. There is a fairly strong peak near $x = 0.3$ and a more modest peak near $x = 0.9$.

The default problem for quadgui is

```
quadgui(@humps,0,1,1.e-4)
```

You can see in Figure 6.3 that with this tolerance, the adaptive algorithm has evaluated the integrand 93 times at points clustered near the two peaks.

With the Symbolic Toolbox, it is possible to analytically integrate $h(x)$. The statements

```
syms x
h = 1/((x-.3)^2+.01) + 1/((x-.9)^2+.04) - 6
I = int(h)
```

produce the indefinite integral

```
I = 10*atan(10*x-3)+5*atan(5*x-9/2)-6*x
```

The statements

```
D = simple(int(h,0,1))
Qexact = double(D)
```

produce a definite integral

```
D = 5*atan(16/13)+10*pi-6
```

and its floating-point numerical value

```
Qexact = 29.85832539549867
```

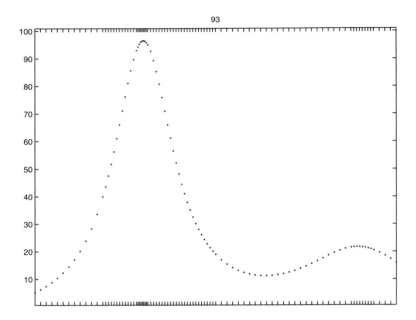

Figure 6.3. *Adaptive quadrature.*

The effort required by a quadrature routine to approximate an integral within a specified accuracy can be measured by counting the number of times the integrand is evaluated. Here is one experiment involving humps and quadtx.

```
for k = 1:12
    tol = 10^(-k);
    [Q,fcount] = quadtx(@humps,0,1,tol);
    err = Q - Qexact;
    ratio = err/tol;
    fprintf('%8.0e %21.14f %7d %13.3e %9.3f\n', ...
        tol,Q,fcount,err,ratio)
end
```

The results are

tol	Q	fcount	err	err/tol
1.e-01	29.83328444174863	25	-2.504e-02	-0.250
1.e-02	29.85791444629948	41	-4.109e-04	-0.041
1.e-03	29.85834299237636	69	1.760e-05	0.018
1.e-04	29.85832444437543	93	-9.511e-07	-0.010
1.e-05	29.85832551548643	149	1.200e-07	0.012
1.e-06	29.85832540194041	265	6.442e-09	0.006
1.e-07	29.85832539499819	369	-5.005e-10	-0.005

1.e-08	29.85832539552631	605	2.763e-11	0.003
1.e-09	29.85832539549603	1061	-2.640e-12	-0.003
1.e-10	29.85832539549890	1469	2.274e-13	0.002
1.e-11	29.85832539549866	2429	-7.105e-15	-0.001
1.e-12	29.85832539549867	4245	0.000e+00	0.000

We see that as the tolerance is decreased, the number of function evaluations increases and the error decreases. The error is always less than the tolerance, usually by a considerable factor.

6.6   Integrating Discrete Data

So far, this chapter has been concerned with computing an approximation to the definite integral of a specified function. We have assumed the existence of a MATLAB program that can evaluate the integrand at any point in a given interval. However, in many situations, the function is only known at a finite set of points, say (x_k, y_k), $k = 1, \ldots, n$. Assume the x's are sorted in increasing order, with

$$a = x_1 < x_2 < \cdots < x_n = b.$$

How can we approximate the integral

$$\int_a^b f(x)dx?$$

Since it is not possible to evaluate $y = f(x)$ at any other points, the adaptive methods we have described are not applicable.

The most obvious approach is to integrate the piecewise linear function that interpolates the data. This leads to the *composite trapezoid rule*

$$T = \sum_{k=1}^{n-1} h_k \frac{y_{k+1} + y_k}{2},$$

where $h_k = x_{k+1} - x_k$. The trapezoid rule can be implemented by a *one-liner*.

```
T = sum(diff(x).*(y(1:end-1)+y(2:end))/2)
```

The MATLAB function `trapz` also provides an implementation.

An example with equally spaced x's is shown in Figure 6.4.

```
x = 1:6
y = [6  8  11  7  5  2]
```

For these data, the trapezoid rule gives

```
T = 35
```

The trapezoid rule is often satisfactory in practice, and more complicated methods may not be necessary. Nevertheless, methods based on higher order interpolation can give

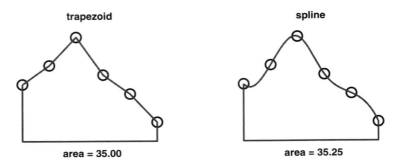

Figure 6.4. *Integrating discrete data.*

other estimates of the integral. Whether or not they are "more accurate" is impossible to decide without further assumptions about the origin of the data.

Recall that both the `spline` and `pchip` interpolants are based on the Hermite interpolation formula:

$$P(x) = \frac{3hs^2 - 2s^3}{h^3} y_{k+1} + \frac{h^3 - 3hs^2 + 2s^3}{h^3} y_k$$
$$+ \frac{s^2(s - h)}{h^2} d_{k+1} + \frac{s(s - h)^2}{h^2} d_k,$$

where $x_k \le x \le x_{k+1}$, $s = x - x_k$, and $h = h_k$. This is a cubic polynomial in s, and hence in x, that satisfies four interpolation conditions, two on function values and two on derivative values:

$$P(x_k) = y_k, \quad P(x_{k+1}) = y_{k+1},$$
$$P'(x_k) = d_k, \quad P'(x_{k+1}) = d_{k+1}.$$

The slopes d_k are computed in `splinetx` or `pchiptx`.

Exercise 6.20 asks you to show that

$$\int_{x_k}^{x_{k+1}} P(x)dx = h_k \frac{y_{k+1} + y_k}{2} - h_k^2 \frac{d_{k+1} - d_k}{12}.$$

Consequently,

$$\int_a^b P(x)dx = T - D,$$

where T is the trapezoid rule and

$$D = \sum_{k=1}^{n-1} h_k^2 \frac{d_{k+1} - d_k}{12}.$$

The quantity D is a higher order correction to the trapezoid rule that makes use of the slopes computed by `splinetx` or `pchiptx`.

If the x's are equally spaced, most of the terms in the sum cancel each other. Then D becomes a simple *end correction* involving just the first and last slopes:

$$D = h^2 \frac{d_n - d_1}{12}.$$

For the sample data shown in Figure 6.4, the area obtained by linear interpolation is 35.00 and by spline interpolation is 35.25. We haven't shown shape-preserving Hermite interpolation, but its area is 35.41667. The integration process averages out the variation in the interpolants, so even though the three graphs might have rather different shapes, the resulting approximations to the integral are often quite close to each other.

6.7 Further Reading

For background on quad and quadl, see Gander and Gautschi [24].

Exercises

6.1. Use quadgui to try to find the integrals of each of the following functions over the given interval and with the given tolerance. How many function evaluations are required for each problem and where are the evaluation points concentrated?

$f(x)$	a	b	tol
humps(x)	0	1	10^{-4}
humps(x)	0	1	10^{-6}
humps(x)	-1	2	10^{-4}
$\sin x$	0	π	10^{-8}
$\cos x$	0	$(9/2)\pi$	10^{-6}
$\sqrt{x}$	0	1	10^{-8}
$\sqrt{x}\log x$	eps	1	10^{-8}
$\tan(\sin x) - \sin(\tan x)$	0	π	10^{-8}
$1/(3x - 1)$	0	1	10^{-4}
$t^{8/3}(1 - t)^{10/3}$	0	1	10^{-8}
$t^{25}(1 - t)^2$	0	1	10^{-8}

6.2. Express Q as a weighted combination of the five function values $f(a)$ through $f(e)$ and establish that its order is six. (See section 6.2.)

6.3. The composite trapezoid rule with n equally spaced points is

$$T_n(f) = \frac{h}{2} f(a) + h \sum_{k=1}^{n-2} f(a + kh) + \frac{h}{2} f(b),$$

where

$$h = \frac{b - a}{n - 1}.$$

Use $T_n(f)$ with various values of n to compute π by approximating

$$\pi = \int_{-1}^{1} \frac{2}{1 + x^2} dx.$$

How does the accuracy vary with n?

6.4. Use `quadtx` with various tolerances to compute π by approximating

$$\pi = \int_{-1}^{1} \frac{2}{1 + x^2} dx.$$

How do the accuracy and the function evaluation count vary with tolerance?

6.5. Use the Symbolic Toolbox to find the exact value of

$$\int_{0}^{1} \frac{x^4(1 - x)^4}{1 + x^2} dx.$$

(a) What famous approximation does this integral bring to mind?
(b) Does numerical evaluation of this integral present any difficulties?

6.6. The error function $\text{erf}(x)$ is defined by an integral:

$$\text{erf}(x) = \frac{2}{\sqrt{\pi}} \int_{0}^{x} e^{-x^2} dx.$$

Use `quadtx` to tabulate $\text{erf}(x)$ for $x = 0.1, 0.2, \ldots, 1.0$. Compare the results with the built-in MATLAB function `erf(x)`.

6.7. The beta function, $\beta(z, w)$, is defined by an integral:

$$\beta(z, w) = \int_{0}^{1} t^{z-1}(1 - t)^{w-1} dt.$$

Write an M-file `mybeta` that uses `quadtx` to compute $\beta(z, w)$. Compare your function with the built-in MATLAB function `beta(z,w)`.

6.8. The gamma function, $\Gamma(x)$, is defined by an integral:

$$\Gamma(x) = \int_{0}^{\infty} t^{x-1} e^{-t} dt.$$

Trying to compute $\Gamma(x)$ by evaluating this integral with numerical quadrature can be both inefficient and unreliable. The difficulties are caused by the infinite interval and the wide variation of values of the integrand.
Write an M-file `mygamma` that tries to use `quadtx` to compute $\Gamma(x)$. Compare your function with the built-in MATLAB function `gamma(x)`. For what x is your function reasonably fast and accurate? For what x does your function become slow or unreliable?

6.9. (a) What is the exact value of

$$\int_{0}^{4\pi} \cos^2 x \, dx?$$

(b) What does `quadtx` compute for this integral? Why is it wrong?
(c) How does `quad` overcome the difficulty?

6.10. (a) Use `ezplot` to plot $x \sin \frac{1}{x}$ for $0 \le x \le 1$.

(b) Use the Symbolic Toolbox to find the exact value of

$$\int_0^1 x \sin \frac{1}{x} dx.$$

(c) What happens if you try

```
quadtx(@(x) x*sin(1/x),0,1)
```

(d) How can you overcome this difficulty?

6.11. (a) Use `ezplot` to plot x^x for $0 \le x \le 1$.

(b) What happens if you try to use the Symbolic Toolbox to find an analytic expression for

$$\int_0^1 x^x dx?$$

(c) Try to find the numerical value of this integral as accurately as you can.

(d) What do you think is the error in the answer you have given?

6.12. Let

$$f(x) = \log(1 + x) \log(1 - x).$$

(a) Use `ezplot` to plot $f(x)$ for $-1 \le x \le 1$.

(b) Use the Symbolic Toolbox to find an analytic expression for

$$\int_{-1}^1 f(x) dx.$$

(c) Find the numerical value of the analytic expression from (b).

(d) What happens if you try to find the integral numerically with

```
quadtx(@(x) log(1+x)*log(1-x),-1,1)
```

(e) How do you work around this difficulty? Justify your solution.

(f) Use `quadtx` and your workaround with various tolerances. Plot error versus tolerance. Plot function evaluation count versus tolerance.

6.13. Let

$$f(x) = x^{10} - 10x^8 + 33x^6 - 40x^4 + 16x^2.$$

(a) Use `ezplot` to plot $f(x)$ for $-2 \le x \le 2$.

(b) Use the Symbolic Toolbox to find an analytic expression for

$$\int_{-2}^2 f(x) dx.$$

(c) Find the numerical value of the analytic expression.

(d) What happens if you try to find the integral numerically with

```
F = @(x) x^10-10*x^8+33*x^6-40*x^4+16*x^2
quadtx(F,-2,2)
```

Why?

(e) How do you work around this difficulty?

6.14. (a) Use quadtx to evaluate

$$\int_{-1}^{2} \frac{1}{\sin(\sqrt{|t|})} dt.$$

(b) Why don't you encounter division-by-zero difficulties at $t = 0$?

6.15. Definite integrals sometimes have the property that the integrand becomes infinite at one or both of the endpoints, but the integral itself is finite. In other words, $\lim_{x \to a} |f(x)| = \infty$ or $\lim_{x \to b} |f(x)| = \infty$, but

$$\int_{a}^{b} f(x) \, dx$$

exists and is finite.

(a) Modify quadtx so that, if an infinite value of $f(a)$ or $f(b)$ is detected, an appropriate warning message is displayed and $f(x)$ is reevaluated at a point very near to a or b. This allows the adaptive algorithm to proceed and possibly converge. (You might want to see how quad does this.)

(b) Find an example that triggers the warning, but has a finite integral.

6.16. (a) Modify quadtx so that the recursion is terminated and an appropriate warning message is displayed whenever the function evaluation count exceeds 10,000. Make sure that the warning message is only displayed once.

(b) Find an example that triggers the warning.

6.17. The MATLAB function quadl uses adaptive quadrature based on methods that have higher order than Simpson's method. As a result, for integrating smooth functions, quadl requires fewer function evaluations to obtain a specified accuracy. The "l" in the function name comes from *Lobatto* quadrature, which uses unequal spacing to obtain higher order. The Lobatto rule used in quadl is of the form

$$\int_{-1}^{1} f(x) \, dx = w_1 f(-1) + w_2 f(-x_1) + w_2 f(x_1) + w_1 f(1).$$

The symmetry in this formula makes it exact for monic polynomials of odd degree $f(x) = x^p$, $p = 1, 3, 5, \ldots$. Requiring the formula to be exact for even degrees x^0, x^2, and x^4 leads to three nonlinear equations in the three parameters w_1, w_2, and x_1. In addition to this basic Lobatto rule, quadl employs even higher order *Kronrod* rules, involving other abscissae, x_k, and weights, w_k.

(a) Derive and solve the equations for the Lobatto parameters w_1, w_2, and x_1.

(b) Find where these values occur in quadl.m.

6.18. Let

$$E_k = \int_{0}^{1} x^k e^{x-1} \, dx.$$

(a) Show that

$$E_0 = 1 - 1/e$$

and that

$$E_k = 1 - k E_{k-1}.$$

(b) Suppose we want to compute $E_1, \ldots, E_n$ for $n = 20$. Which of the following approaches is the fastest and most accurate?

- For each k, use `quadtx` to evaluate E_k numerically.

- Use forward recursion:

$$E_0 = 1 - 1/e;$$

$$\text{for } k = 2, \ldots, n, \ E_k = 1 - kE_{k-1}.$$

- Use backward recursion, starting at $N = 32$ with a completely inaccurate value for E_N:

$$E_N = 0;$$

$$\text{for } k = N, \ldots, 2, \ E_{k-1} = (1 - E_k)/k;$$

$$\text{ignore } E_{n+1}, \ldots, E_N.$$

6.19. An article by Prof. Nick Trefethen of Oxford University in the January/February 2002 issue of *SIAM News* is titled "A Hundred-dollar, Hundred-digit Challenge" [61]. Trefethen's challenge consists of ten computational problems, each of whose answers is a single real number. He asked for each answer to be computed to ten significant digits and offered a $100 prize to the person or group who managed to calculate the greatest number of correct digits. Ninety-four teams from 25 countries entered the computation. Much to Trefethen's surprise, 20 teams scored a perfect 100 points and five more teams scored 99 points. A follow-up book has recently been published [10].

Trefethen's first problem is to find the value of

$$T = \lim_{\epsilon \to 0} \int_\epsilon^1 x^{-1} \cos(x^{-1} \log x) \, dx.$$

(a) Why can't we simply use one of the MATLAB numerical quadrature routines to compute this integral with just a few lines of code?

Here is one way to compute T to several significant digits. Express the integral as an infinite sum of integrals over intervals where the integrand does not change sign:

$$T = \sum_{k=1}^\infty T_k,$$

where

$$T_k = \int_{x_k}^{x_{k-1}} x^{-1} \cos(x^{-1} \log x) dx.$$

Here $x_0 = 1$, and, for $k > 0$, the x_k's are the successive zeros of $\cos(x^{-1} \log x)$, ordered in decreasing order, $x_1 > x_2 > \cdots$. In other words, for $k > 0$, x_k solves the equation

$$\frac{\log x_k}{x_k} = -\left(k - \frac{1}{2}\right)\pi.$$

You can use a zero finder such as `fzerotx` or `fzero` to compute the x_k's. If you have access to the Symbolic Toolbox, you can also use `lambertw` to compute the x_k's. For each x_k, T_k can be computed by numerical quadrature with `quadtx`, `quad`, or `quadl`. The T_k's are alternately positive and negative, and hence the partial sums of the series are alternately greater than and less than the infinite sum. Moreover, the average of two successive partial sums is a more accurate approximation to the final result than either sum by itself.

(b) Use this approach to compute T as accurately as you can with a reasonable amount of computer time. Try to get at least four or five digits. You may be able to get more. In any case, indicate how accurate you think your result is.

(c) Investigate the use of Aitken's δ^2 *acceleration*

$$\tilde{T}_k = T_k - \frac{(T_{k+1} - T_k)^2}{T_{k+1} - 2T_k + T_{k-1}}.$$

6.20. Show that the integral of the Hermite interpolating polynomial

$$P(s) = \frac{3hs^2 - 2s^3}{h^3} y_{k+1} + \frac{h^3 - 3hs^2 + 2s^3}{h^3} y_k$$
$$+ \frac{s^2(s-h)}{h^2} d_{k+1} + \frac{s(s-h)^2}{h^2} d_k$$

over one subinterval is

$$\int_0^h P(s)ds = h\frac{y_{k+1} + y_k}{2} - h^2\frac{d_{k+1} - d_k}{12}.$$

6.21. (a) Modify `splinetx` and `pchiptx` to create `splinequad` and `pchipquad` that integrate discrete data using spline and pchip interpolation.

(b) Use your programs, as well as `trapz`, to integrate the discrete data set

```
x = 1:6
y = [6   8   11   7   5   2]
```

(c) Use your programs, as well as `trapz`, to approximate the integral

$$\int_0^1 \frac{4}{1+x^2} \, dx.$$

Generate random discrete data sets using the statements

```
x = round(100*[0 sort(rand(1,6)) 1])/100
y = round(400./(1+x.^2))/100
```

With infinitely many infinitely accurate points, the integrals would all equal π. But these data sets have only eight points, rounded to only two decimal digits of accuracy.

6.22. This program uses functions in the Spline Toolbox. What does it do?

```
x = 1:6
y = [6   8   11   7   5   2]
```

```
for e = ['c','n','p','s','v']
    disp(e)
    ppval(fnint(csape(x,y,e)),x(end))
end
```

6.23. How large is your hand? Figure 6.5 shows three different approaches to computing the area enclosed by the data that you obtained for exercise 3.3.

Q = 0.3991   **Q = 0.4075**   **Q = 0.4141**

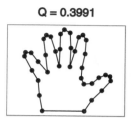
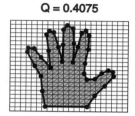
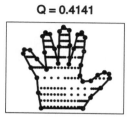

Figure 6.5. *The area of a hand.*

(a) Area of a polygon. Connect successive data points with straight lines and connect the last data point to the first. If none of these lines intersect, the result is a polygon with n vertices, (x_i, y_i). A classic, but little known, fact is that the area of this polygon is

$$(x_1 y_2 - x_2 y_1 + x_2 y_3 - x_3 y_2 + \cdots + x_n y_1 - x_1 y_n)/2.$$

If x and y are column vectors, this can be computed with the MATLAB one-liner

```
(x'*y([2:n 1]) - x([2:n 1])'*y)/2
```

(b) Simple quadrature. The MATLAB function `inpolygon` determines which of a set of points is contained in a given polygonal region in the plane. The polygon is specified by the two arrays x and y containing the coordinates of the vertices. The set of points can be a two-dimensional square grid with spacing h.

```
[u,v] = meshgrid(xmin:h:xmax,ymin:h:ymax)
```

The statement

```
k = inpolygon(u,v,x,y)
```

returns an array the same size as u and v whose elements are one for the points in the polygon and zero for the points outside. The total number of points in the region is the number of nonzeros in k, that is, `nnz(k)`, so the area of the corresponding portion of the grid is

```
h^2*nnz(k)
```

(c) Two-dimensional adaptive quadrature. The *characteristic function* of the region $\chi(u, v)$ is equal to one for points (u, v) in the region and zero for points outside. The area of the region is

$$\iint \chi(u, v) du dv.$$

The MATLAB function `inpolygon(u,v,x,y)` computes the characteristic function if u and v are scalars, or arrays of the same size. But the quadrature functions have one of them a scalar and the other an array. So we need an M-file, `chi.m`, containing

```
function k = chi(u,v,x,y)
if all(size(u) == 1), u = u(ones(size(v))); end
if all(size(v) == 1), v = v(ones(size(u))); end
k = inpolygon(u,v,x,y);
```

Two-dimensional adaptive numerical quadrature is obtained with

```
dblquad(@chi,xmin,xmax,ymin,ymax,tol,[],x,y)
```

This is the least efficient of the three methods. Adaptive quadrature expects the integrand to be reasonably smooth, but $\chi(u, v)$ is certainly not smooth. Consequently, values of `tol` smaller than 10^{-4} or 10^{-5} require a lot of computer time.

Figure 6.5 shows that the estimates of the area obtained by these three methods agree to about two digits, even with fairly large grid sizes and tolerances. Experiment with your own data, use a moderate amount of computer time, and see how close the three estimates can be to each other.

Chapter 7

Ordinary Differential Equations

MATLAB has several different functions for the numerical solution of ordinary differential equations. This chapter describes the simplest of these functions and then compares all of the functions for efficiency, accuracy, and special features. Stiffness is a subtle concept that plays an important role in these comparisons.

7.1 Integrating Differential Equations

The *initial value problem* for an ordinary differential equation involves finding a function $y(t)$ that satisfies

$$\frac{dy(t)}{dt} = f(t, y(t))$$

together with the initial condition

$$y(t_0) = y_0.$$

A numerical solution to this problem generates a sequence of values for the independent variable, $t_0, t_1, \ldots$, and a corresponding sequence of values for the dependent variable, $y_0, y_1, \ldots$, so that each y_n approximates the solution at t_n:

$$y_n \approx y(t_n), \ n = 0, 1, \ldots.$$

Modern numerical methods automatically determine the step sizes

$$h_n = t_{n+1} - t_n$$

so that the estimated error in the numerical solution is controlled by a specified tolerance.

The fundamental theorem of calculus gives us an important connection between differential equations and integrals:

$$y(t + h) = y(t) + \int_t^{t+h} f(s, y(s))ds.$$

We cannot use numerical quadrature directly to approximate the integral because we do not know the function $y(s)$ and so cannot evaluate the integrand. Nevertheless, the basic idea is

185

to choose a sequence of values of h so that this formula allows us to generate our numerical solution.

One special case to keep in mind is the situation where $f(t, y)$ is a function of t alone. The numerical solution of such simple differential equations is then just a sequence of quadratures:

$$y_{n+1} = y_n + \int_{t_n}^{t_{n+1}} f(s)ds.$$

Throughout this chapter, we frequently use "dot" notation for derivatives:

$$\dot{y} = \frac{dy(t)}{dt} \text{ and } \ddot{y} = \frac{d^2 y(t)}{dt^2}.$$

7.2 Systems of Equations

Many mathematical models involve more than one unknown function, and second- and higher order derivatives. These models can be handled by making $y(t)$ a vector-valued function of t. Each component is either one of the unknown functions or one of its derivatives. The MATLAB vector notation is particularly convenient here.

For example, the second-order differential equation describing a simple harmonic oscillator

$$\ddot{x}(t) = -x(t)$$

becomes two first-order equations. The vector $y(t)$ has two components, $x(t)$ and its first derivative $\dot{x}(t)$:

$$y(t) = \begin{bmatrix} x(t) \\ \dot{x}(t) \end{bmatrix}.$$

Using this vector, the differential equation is

$$\dot{y}(t) = \begin{bmatrix} \dot{x}(t) \\ -x(t) \end{bmatrix}$$

$$= \begin{bmatrix} y_2(t) \\ -y_1(t) \end{bmatrix}.$$

The MATLAB function defining the differential equation has t and y as input arguments and should return $f(t, y)$ as a column vector. For the harmonic oscillator, the function could be an M-file containing

```
function ydot = harmonic(t,y)
ydot = [y(2); -y(1)]
```

A more compact version uses matrix multiplication in an anonymous function,

```
f = @(t,y) [0 1; -1 0]*y
```

In both cases, the variable t has to be included as the first argument, even though it is not explicitly involved in the differential equation.

A slightly more complicated example, the *two-body problem*, describes the orbit of one body under the gravitational attraction of a much heavier body. Using Cartesian coordinates, $u(t)$ and $v(t)$, centered in the heavy body, the equations are

$$\ddot{u}(t) = -u(t)/r(t)^3,$$
$$\ddot{v}(t) = -v(t)/r(t)^3,$$

where

$$r(t) = \sqrt{u(t)^2 + v(t)^2}.$$

The vector $y(t)$ has four components:

$$y(t) = \begin{bmatrix} u(t) \\ v(t) \\ \dot{u}(t) \\ \dot{v}(t) \end{bmatrix}.$$

The differential equation is

$$\dot{y}(t) = \begin{bmatrix} \dot{u}(t) \\ \dot{v}(t) \\ -u(t)/r(t)^3 \\ -v(t)/r(t)^3 \end{bmatrix}.$$

The MATLAB function could be

```
function ydot = twobody(t,y)
r = sqrt(y(1)^2 + y(2)^2);
ydot = [y(3); y(4); -y(1)/r^3; -y(2)/r^3];
```

A more compact MATLAB function is

```
ydot = @(t,y) [y(3:4); -y(1:2)/norm(y(1:2))^3]
```

Despite the use of vector operations, the second M-file is not significantly more efficient than the first.

7.3 Linearized Differential Equations

The local behavior of the solution to a differential equation near any point (t_c, y_c) can be analyzed by expanding $f(t, y)$ in a two-dimensional Taylor series:

$$f(t, y) = f(t_c, y_c) + \alpha(t - t_c) + J(y - y_c) + \cdots,$$

where

$$\alpha = \frac{\partial f}{\partial t}(t_c, y_c), \quad J = \frac{\partial f}{\partial y}(t_c, y_c).$$

The most important term in this series is usually the one involving J, the Jacobian. For a system of differential equations with n components,

$$\frac{d}{dt} \begin{bmatrix} y_1(t) \\ y_2(t) \\ \vdots \\ y_n(t) \end{bmatrix} = \begin{bmatrix} f_1(t, y_1, \ldots, y_n) \\ f_2(t, y_1, \ldots, y_n) \\ \vdots \\ f_n(t, y_1, \ldots, y_n) \end{bmatrix},$$

the Jacobian is an n-by-n matrix of partial derivatives:

$$J = \begin{bmatrix} \frac{\partial f_1}{\partial y_1} & \frac{\partial f_1}{\partial y_2} & \cdots & \frac{\partial f_1}{\partial y_n} \\ \frac{\partial f_2}{\partial y_1} & \frac{\partial f_2}{\partial y_2} & \cdots & \frac{\partial f_2}{\partial y_n} \\ \vdots & \vdots & & \vdots \\ \frac{\partial f_n}{\partial y_1} & \frac{\partial f_n}{\partial y_2} & \cdots & \frac{\partial f_n}{\partial y_n} \end{bmatrix}.$$

The influence of the Jacobian on the local behavior is determined by the solution to the linear system of ordinary differential equations

$$\dot{y} = Jy.$$

Let $\lambda_k = \mu_k + i\nu_k$ be the eigenvalues of J and $\Lambda = \text{diag}(\lambda_k)$ the diagonal eigenvalue matrix. If there is a linearly independent set of corresponding eigenvectors V, then

$$J = V\Lambda V^{-1}.$$

The linear transformation

$$Vx = y$$

transforms the local system of equations into a set of decoupled equations for the individual components of x:

$$\dot{x}_k = \lambda_k x_k.$$

The solutions are

$$x_k(t) = e^{\lambda_k(t-t_c)} x(t_c).$$

A single component $x_k(t)$ grows with t if μ_k is positive, decays if μ_k is negative, and oscillates if ν_k is nonzero. The components of the local solution $y(t)$ are linear combinations of these behaviors.

For example, the harmonic oscillator

$$\dot{y} = \begin{bmatrix} 0 & 1 \\ -1 & 0 \end{bmatrix} y$$

is a linear system. The Jacobian is simply the matrix

$$J = \begin{bmatrix} 0 & 1 \\ -1 & 0 \end{bmatrix}.$$

The eigenvalues of J are $\pm i$ and the solutions are purely oscillatory linear combinations of e^{it} and e^{-it}.

A nonlinear example is the two-body problem

$$\dot{y}(t) = \begin{bmatrix} y_3(t) \\ y_4(t) \\ -y_1(t)/r(t)^3 \\ -y_2(t)/r(t)^3 \end{bmatrix},$$

where

$$r(t) = \sqrt{y_1(t)^2 + y_2(t)^2}.$$

In exercise 7.6, we ask you to show that the Jacobian for this system is

$$J = \frac{1}{r^5} \begin{bmatrix} 0 & 0 & r^5 & 0 \\ 0 & 0 & 0 & r^5 \\ 2y_1^2 - y_2^2 & 3y_1 y_2 & 0 & 0 \\ 3y_1 y_2 & 2y_2^2 - y_1^2 & 0 & 0 \end{bmatrix}.$$

It turns out that the eigenvalues of J just depend on the radius $r(t)$:

$$\lambda = \frac{1}{r^{3/2}} \begin{bmatrix} \sqrt{2} \\ i \\ -\sqrt{2} \\ -i \end{bmatrix}.$$

We see that one eigenvalue is real and positive, so the corresponding component of the solution is growing. One eigenvalue is real and negative, corresponding to a decaying component. Two eigenvalues are purely imaginary, corresponding to oscillatory components. However, the overall global behavior of this nonlinear system is quite complicated and is not described by this local linearized analysis.

7.4 Single-Step Methods

The simplest numerical method for the solution of initial value problems is *Euler's* method. It uses a fixed step size h and generates the approximate solution by

$$y_{n+1} = y_n + hf(t_n, y_n),$$
$$t_{n+1} = t_n + h.$$

The MATLAB code would use an initial point t0, a final point tfinal, an initial value y0, a step size h, a function f. The primary loop would simply be

```
t = t0;
y = y0;
while t <= tfinal
    y = y + h*f(t,y)
    t = t + h
end
```

Note that this works perfectly well if y0 is a vector and f returns a vector.

As a quadrature rule for integrating $f(t)$, Euler's method corresponds to a rectangle rule where the integrand is evaluated only once, at the left-hand endpoint of the interval. It is exact if $f(t)$ is constant, but not if $f(t)$ is linear. So the error is proportional to h. Tiny steps are needed to get even a few digits of accuracy. But, from our point of view, the biggest defect of Euler's method is that it does not provide an error estimate. There is no automatic way to determine what step size is needed to achieve a specified accuracy.

If Euler's method is followed by a second function evaluation, we begin to get a viable algorithm. There are two natural possibilities, corresponding to the midpoint rule and the trapezoid rule for quadrature. The midpoint analogue uses Euler to step halfway across the interval, evaluates the function at this intermediate point, then uses that slope to take the actual step:

$$
\begin{aligned}
s_1 &= f(t_n, y_n),\\
s_2 &= f\left(t_n + \frac{h}{2},\, y_n + \frac{h}{2}s_1\right),\\
y_{n+1} &= y_n + hs_2,\\
t_{n+1} &= t_n + h.
\end{aligned}
$$

The trapezoid analogue uses Euler to take a tentative step across the interval, evaluates the function at this exploratory point, then averages the two slopes to take the actual step:

$$
\begin{aligned}
s_1 &= f(t_n, y_n),\\
s_2 &= f(t_n + h,\, y_n + hs_1),\\
y_{n+1} &= y_n + h\frac{s_1 + s_2}{2},\\
t_{n+1} &= t_n + h.
\end{aligned}
$$

If we were to use both of these methods simultaneously, they would produce two different values for y_{n+1}. The difference between the two values would provide an error estimate and a basis for picking the step size. Furthermore, an extrapolated combination of the two values would be more accurate than either one individually.

Continuing with this approach is the idea behind *single-step* methods for integrating ordinary differential equations. The function $f(t, y)$ is evaluated several times for values of t between t_n and t_{n+1} and values of y obtained by adding linear combinations of the values of f to y_n. The actual step is taken using another linear combination of the function values. Modern versions of single-step methods use yet another linear combination of function values to estimate error and determine step size.

Single-step methods are often called *Runge–Kutta* methods, after the two German applied mathematicians who first wrote about them around 1905. The classical Runge–Kutta method was widely used for hand computation before the invention of digital computers and is still popular today. It uses four function evaluations per step:

$$
\begin{aligned}
s_1 &= f(t_n, y_n),\\
s_2 &= f\left(t_n + \frac{h}{2},\, y_n + \frac{h}{2}s_1\right),
\end{aligned}
$$

$$s_3 = f\left(t_n + \frac{h}{2}, \ y_n + \frac{h}{2}s_2\right),$$

$$s_4 = f(t_n + h, \ y_n + hs_3),$$

$$y_{n+1} = y_n + \frac{h}{6}(s_1 + 2s_2 + 2s_3 + s_4),$$

$$t_{n+1} = t_n + h.$$

If $f(t, y)$ does not depend on y, then classical Runge–Kutta has $s_2 = s_3$ and the method reduces to Simpson's quadrature rule.

Classical Runge–Kutta does not provide an error estimate. The method is sometimes used with a step size h and again with step size $h/2$ to obtain an error estimate, but we now know more efficient methods.

Several of the ordinary differential equation solvers in MATLAB, including the textbook solver we describe later in this chapter, are single-step or Runge–Kutta solvers. A general single-step method is characterized by a number of parameters, α_i, $\beta_{i,j}$, γ_i, and δ_i. There are k *stages*. Each stage computes a slope, s_i, by evaluating $f(t, y)$ for a particular value of t and a value of y obtained by taking linear combinations of the previous slopes:

$$s_i = f\left(t_n + \alpha_i h, \ y_n + h\sum_{j=1}^{i-1}\beta_{i,j}s_j\right), \quad i = 1, \ldots, k.$$

The proposed step is also a linear combination of the slopes:

$$y_{n+1} = y_n + h\sum_{i=1}^{k}\gamma_i s_i.$$

An estimate of the error that would occur with this step is provided by yet another linear combination of the slopes:

$$e_{n+1} = h\sum_{i=1}^{k}\delta_i s_i.$$

If this error is less than the specified tolerance, then the step is successful and y_{n+1} is accepted. If not, the step is a failure and y_{n+1} is rejected. In either case, the error estimate is used to compute the step size h for the next step.

The parameters in these methods are determined by matching terms in Taylor series expansions of the slopes. These series involve powers of h and products of various partial derivatives of $f(t, y)$. The *order* of a method is the exponent of the smallest power of h that cannot be matched. It turns out that one, two, three, and four stages yield methods of order one, two, three, and four, respectively. But it takes six stages to obtain a fifth-order method. The classical Runge–Kutta method has four stages and is fourth order.

The names of the MATLAB ordinary differential equation solvers are all of the form odennxx with digits nn indicating the order of the underlying method and a possibly empty xx indicating some special characteristic of the method. If the error estimate is obtained by comparing formulas with different orders, the digits nn indicate these orders. For example, ode45 obtains its error estimate by comparing a fourth-order and a fifth-order formula.

7.5   The BS23 Algorithm

Our textbook function `ode23tx` is a simplified version of the function `ode23` that is included with MATLAB. The algorithm is due to Bogacki and Shampine [9, 53]. The "23" in the function names indicates that two simultaneous single-step formulas, one of second order and one of third order, are involved.

The method has three stages, but there are four slopes s_i because, after the first step, the s_1 for one step is the s_4 from the previous step. The essentials are

$$s_1 = f(t_n, y_n),$$

$$s_2 = f\left(t_n + \frac{h}{2}, y_n + \frac{h}{2}s_1\right),$$

$$s_3 = f\left(t_n + \frac{3}{4}h, y_n + \frac{3}{4}hs_2\right),$$

$$t_{n+1} = t_n + h,$$

$$y_{n+1} = y_n + \frac{h}{9}(2s_1 + 3s_2 + 4s_3),$$

$$s_4 = f(t_{n+1}, y_{n+1}),$$

$$e_{n+1} = \frac{h}{72}(-5s_1 + 6s_2 + 8s_3 - 9s_4).$$

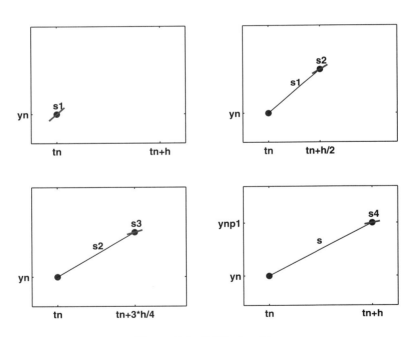

Figure 7.1. *BS23 algorithm.*

The simplified pictures in Figure 7.1 show the starting situation and the three stages. We start at a point (t_n, y_n) with an initial slope $s_1 = f(t_n, y_n)$ and an estimate of a good step size, h. Our goal is to compute an approximate solution y_{n+1} at $t_{n+1} = t_n + h$ that agrees with the true solution $y(t_{n+1})$ to within the specified tolerances.

The first stage uses the initial slope s_1 to take an Euler step halfway across the interval. The function is evaluated there to get the second slope, s_2. This slope is used to take an Euler step three-quarters of the way across the interval. The function is evaluated again to get the third slope, s_3. A weighted average of the three slopes,

$$s = \frac{1}{9}(2s_1 + 3s_2 + 4s_3),$$

is used for the final step all the way across the interval to get a tentative value for y_{n+1}. The function is evaluated once more to get s_4. The error estimate then uses all four slopes:

$$e_{n+1} = \frac{h}{72}(-5s_1 + 6s_2 + 8s_3 - 9s_4).$$

If the error is within the specified tolerance, then the step is successful, the tentative value of y_{n+1} is accepted, and s_4 becomes the s_1 of the next step. If the error is too large, then the tentative y_{n+1} is rejected and the step must be redone. In either case, the error estimate e_{n+1} provides the basis for determining the step size h for the next step.

The first input argument of ode23tx specifies the function $f(t, y)$. This argument can be either

- a function handle, or

- an anonymous function.

The function should accept two arguments—usually, but not necessarily, t and y. The result of evaluating the character string or the function should be a column vector containing the values of the derivatives, dy/dt.

The second input argument of ode23tx is a vector, tspan, with two components, t0 and tfinal. The integration is carried out over the interval

$$t_0 \leq t \leq t_{final}.$$

One of the simplifications in our textbook code is this form of tspan. Other MATLAB ordinary differential equation solvers allow more flexible specifications of the integration interval.

The third input argument is a column vector, y0, providing the initial value of $y_0 = y(t_0)$. The length of y0 tells ode23tx the number of differential equations in the system.

A fourth input argument is optional and can take two different forms. The simplest, and most common, form is a scalar numerical value, rtol, to be used as the relative error tolerance. The default value for rtol is 10^{-3}, but you can provide a different value if you want more or less accuracy. The more complicated possibility for this optional argument is the structure generated by the MATLAB function odeset. This function takes pairs of arguments that specify many different options for the MATLAB ordinary differential equation solvers. For ode23tx, you can change the default values of three quantities: the relative error tolerance, the absolute error tolerance, and the M-file that is called after each successful step. The statement

```
opts = odeset('reltol',1.e-5, 'abstol',1.e-8, ...
              'outputfcn',@myodeplot)
```

creates a structure that specifies the relative error tolerance to be 10^{-5}, the absolute error tolerance to be 10^{-8}, and the output function to be myodeplot.

The output produced by ode23tx can be either graphic or numeric. With no output arguments, the statement

```
ode23tx(F,tspan,y0);
```

produces a dynamic plot of all the components of the solution. With two output arguments, the statement

```
[tout,yout] = ode23tx(F,tspan,y0);
```

generates a table of values of the solution.

7.6 ode23tx

Let's examine the code for ode23tx. Here is the preamble.

```
function [tout,yout] = ode23tx(F,tspan,y0,arg4,varargin)
%ODE23TX   Solve non-stiff differential equations.
%          Textbook version of ODE23.
%
%   ODE23TX(F,TSPAN,Y0) with TSPAN = [T0 TFINAL]
%   integrates the system of differential equations
%   dy/dt = f(t,y) from t = T0 to t = TFINAL.
%   The initial condition is y(T0) = Y0.
%
%   The first argument, F, is a function handle or an
%   anonymous function that defines f(t,y). This function
%   must have two input arguments, t and y, and must
%   return a column vector of the derivatives, dy/dt.
%
%   With two output arguments, [T,Y] = ODE23TX(...)
%   returns a column vector T and an array Y where Y(:,k)
%   is the solution at T(k).
%
%   With no output arguments, ODE23TX plots the solution.
%
%   ODE23TX(F,TSPAN,Y0,RTOL) uses the relative error
%   tolerance RTOL instead of the default 1.e-3.
```

```
%
%     ODE23TX(F,TSPAN,Y0,OPTS) where OPTS = ...
%     ODESET('reltol',RTOL,'abstol',ATOL,'outputfcn',@PLTFN)
%     uses relative error RTOL instead of 1.e-3,
%     absolute error ATOL instead of 1.e-6, and calls PLTFN
%     instead of ODEPLOT after each step.
%
%     More than four input arguments, ODE23TX(F,TSPAN,Y0,
%     RTOL,P1,P2,..), are passed on to F, F(T,Y,P1,P2,..).
%
%     ODE23TX uses the Runge-Kutta (2,3) method of
%     Bogacki and Shampine.
%
%     Example
%        tspan = [0 2*pi];
%        y0 = [1 0]';
%        F = '[0 1; -1 0]*y';
%        ode23tx(F,tspan,y0);
%
%     See also ODE23.
```

Here is the code that parses the arguments and initializes the internal variables.

```
rtol = 1.e-3;
atol = 1.e-6;
plotfun = @odeplot;
if nargin >= 4 & isnumeric(arg4)
   rtol = arg4;
elseif nargin >= 4 & isstruct(arg4)
   if ~isempty(arg4.RelTol), rtol = arg4.RelTol; end
   if ~isempty(arg4.AbsTol), atol = arg4.AbsTol; end
   if ~isempty(arg4.OutputFcn),
        plotfun = arg4.OutputFcn; end
end
t0 = tspan(1);
tfinal = tspan(2);
tdir = sign(tfinal - t0);
plotit = (nargout == 0);
threshold = atol / rtol;
hmax = abs(0.1*(tfinal-t0));
t = t0;
y = y0(:);

% Initialize output.

if plotit
   plotfun(tspan,f,'init');
```

```
else
    tout = t;
    yout = y.';
end
```

The computation of the initial step size is a delicate matter because it requires some knowledge of the overall scale of the problem.

```
s1 = F(t, y, varargin{:});
r = norm(s1./max(abs(y),threshold),inf) + realmin;
h = tdir*0.8*rtol^(1/3)/r;
```

Here is the beginning of the main loop. The integration starts at $t = t_0$ and increments t until it reaches t_{final}. It is possible to go "backward," that is, have $t_{final} < t_0$.

```
while t ~= tfinal

    hmin = 16*eps*abs(t);
    if abs(h) > hmax, h = tdir*hmax; end
    if abs(h) < hmin, h = tdir*hmin; end

    % Stretch the step if t is close to tfinal.

    if 1.1*abs(h) >= abs(tfinal - t)
        h = tfinal - t;
    end
```

Here is the actual computation. The first slope s1 has already been computed. The function defining the differential equation is evaluated three more times to obtain three more slopes.

```
        s2 = F(t+h/2, y+h/2*s1, varargin{:});
        s3 = F(t+3*h/4, y+3*h/4*s2, varargin{:});
        tnew = t + h;
        ynew = y + h*(2*s1 + 3*s2 + 4*s3)/9;
        s4 = F(tnew, ynew, varargin{:});
```

Here is the error estimate. The norm of the error vector is scaled by the ratio of the absolute tolerance to the relative tolerance. The use of the smallest floating-point number, realmin, prevents err from being exactly zero.

```
        e = h*(-5*s1 + 6*s2 + 8*s3 - 9*s4)/72;
        err = norm(e./max(max(abs(y),abs(ynew)),threshold),
                ... inf) + realmin;
```

Here is the test to see if the step is successful. If it is, the result is plotted or appended to the output vector. If it is not, the result is simply forgotten.

```
    if err <= rtol
        t = tnew;
        y = ynew;
```

```
      if plotit
         if plotfun(t,y,'');
            break
         end
      else
         tout(end+1,1) = t;
         yout(end+1,:) = y.';
      end
      s1 = s4; % Reuse final function value to start new step.
   end
```

The error estimate is used to compute a new step size. The ratio `rtol/err` is greater than one if the current step is successful, or less than one if the current step fails. A cube root is involved because the BS23 is a third-order method. This means that changing tolerances by a factor of eight will change the typical step size, and hence the total number of steps, by a factor of two. The factors 0.8 and 5 prevent excessive changes in step size.

```
   % Compute a new step size.
   h = h*min(5,0.8*(rtol/err)^(1/3));
```

Here is the only place where a singularity would be detected.

```
   if abs(h) <= hmin
      warning(sprintf( ...
         'Step size %e too small at t = %e.\n',h,t));
      t = tfinal;
   end
end
```

That ends the main loop. The plot function might need to finish its work.

```
   if plotit
      plotfun([], [], 'done');
   end
```

7.7 Examples

Please sit down in front of a computer running MATLAB. Make sure ode23tx is in your current directory or on your MATLAB path. Start your session by entering

```
   F = @(t,y)  0 ;  ode23tx(F,[0 10],1)
```

This should produce a plot of the solution of the initial value problem

$$\frac{dy}{dt} = 0,$$
$$y(0) = 1,$$
$$0 \le t \le 10.$$

The solution, of course, is a constant function, $y(t) = 1$.

Now you can press the up arrow key, use the left arrow key to space over to the 0, and change it to something more interesting. Here are some examples. At first, we'll change just the 0 and leave the [0 10] and 1 alone.

```
F                          Exact solution
0                          1
t                          1+t^2/2
y                          exp(t)
-y                         exp(-t)
1/(1-3*t)                  1-log(1-3*t)/3    (Singular)
2*y-y^2                    2/(1+exp(-2*t))
```

Make up some of your own examples. Change the initial condition. Change the accuracy by including 1.e-6 as the fourth argument.

Now let's try the harmonic oscillator, a second-order differential equation written as a pair of two first-order equations. First, create a function to specify the equations. Use either

```
F = @(t,y) [y(2); -y(1)];
```

or

```
F = @(t,y) [0 1; -1 0]*y;
```

Use either

```
F = @(t,y) [y(2); -y(1)];
```

or

```
F = @(t,y) [0 1; -1 0]*y;
```

Then the statement

```
ode23tx(F,[0 2*pi],[1; 0])
```

plots two functions of *t* that you should recognize. If you want to produce a *phase plane* plot, you have two choices. One possibility is to capture the output and plot it after the computation is complete.

```
[t,y] = ode23tx(F,[0 2*pi],[1; 0])
plot(y(:,1),y(:,2),'-o')
axis([-1.2 1.2 -1.2 1.2])
axis square
```

The more interesting possibility is to use a function that plots the solution while it is being computed. MATLAB provides such a function in odephas2.m. It is accessed by using odeset to create an options structure.

```
opts = odeset('reltol',1.e-4,'abstol',1.e-6, ...
    'outputfcn',@odephas2);
```

If you want to provide your own plotting function, it should be something like

```
function flag = phaseplot(t,y,job)
persistent p
if isequal(job,'init')
    p = plot(y(1),y(2),'o','erasemode','none');
    axis([-1.2 1.2 -1.2 1.2])
    axis square
    flag = 0;
elseif isequal(job,'')
    set(p,'xdata',y(1),'ydata',y(2))
    drawnow
    flag = 0;
end
```

This is with

```
opts = odeset('reltol',1.e-4,'abstol',1.e-6, ...
    'outputfcn',@phaseplot);
```

Once you have decided on a plotting function and created an options structure, you can compute and simultaneously plot the solution with

```
ode23tx(F,[0 2*pi],[1; 0],opts)
```

Try this with other values of the tolerances.

Issue the command type twobody to see if there is an M-file twobody.m on your path. If not, find the two or three lines of code earlier in this chapter and create your own M-file. Then try

```
ode23tx(@twobody,[0 2*pi],[1; 0; 0; 1]);
```

The code, and the length of the initial condition, indicate that the solution has four components. But the plot shows only three. Why? Hint: Find the zoom button on the figure window toolbar and zoom in on the blue curve.

You can vary the initial condition of the two-body problem by changing the fourth component.

```
y0 = [1; 0; 0; change_this];
ode23tx(@twobody,[0 2*pi],y0);
```

Graph the orbit, and the heavy body at the origin, with

```
y0 = [1; 0; 0; change_this];
[t,y] = ode23tx(@twobody,[0 2*pi],y0);
plot(y(:,1),y(:,2),'-',0,0,'ro')
axis equal
```

You might also want to use something other than 2π for tfinal.

7.8   Lorenz Attractor

One of the world's most extensively studied ordinary differential equations is the Lorenz chaotic attractor. It was first described in 1963 by Edward Lorenz, an M.I.T. mathematician and meteorologist who was interested in fluid flow models of the earth's atmosphere. An excellent reference is a book by Colin Sparrow [57].

We have chosen to express the Lorenz equations in a somewhat unusual way involving a matrix-vector product:

$$\dot{y} = Ay.$$

The vector y has three components that are functions of t:

$$y(t) = \begin{pmatrix} y_1(t) \\ y_2(t) \\ y_3(t) \end{pmatrix}.$$

Despite the way we have written it, this is not a linear system of differential equations. Seven of the nine elements in the 3-by-3 matrix A are constant, but the other two depend on $y_2(t)$:

$$A = \begin{bmatrix} -\beta & 0 & y_2 \\ 0 & -\sigma & \sigma \\ -y_2 & \rho & -1 \end{bmatrix}.$$

The first component of the solution, $y_1(t)$, is related to the convection in the atmospheric flow, while the other two components are related to horizontal and vertical temperature variation. The parameter σ is the Prandtl number, ρ is the normalized Rayleigh number, and β depends on the geometry of the domain. The most popular values of the parameters, $\sigma = 10$, $\rho = 28$, and $\beta = 8/3$, are outside the ranges associated with the earth's atmosphere.

The deceptively simple nonlinearity introduced by the presence of y_2 in the system matrix A changes everything. There are no random aspects to these equations, so the solutions $y(t)$ are completely determined by the parameters and the initial conditions, but their behavior is very difficult to predict. For some values of the parameters, the orbit of $y(t)$ in three-dimensional space is known as a *strange attractor*. It is bounded, but not periodic and not convergent. It never intersects itself. It ranges chaotically back and forth around two different points, or attractors. For other values of the parameters, the solution might converge to a fixed point, diverge to infinity, or oscillate periodically. See Figures 7.2 and 7.3.

Let's think of $\eta = y_2$ as a free parameter, restrict ρ to be greater than one, and study the matrix

$$A = \begin{bmatrix} -\beta & 0 & \eta \\ 0 & -\sigma & \sigma \\ -\eta & \rho & -1 \end{bmatrix}.$$

It turns out that A is singular if and only if

$$\eta = \pm\sqrt{\beta(\rho - 1)}.$$

The corresponding null vector, normalized so that its second component is equal to η, is

$$\begin{pmatrix} \rho - 1 \\ \eta \\ \eta \end{pmatrix}.$$

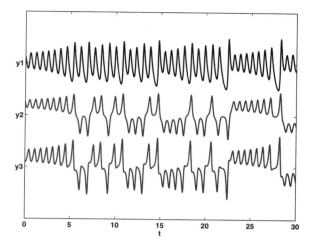

Figure 7.2. *Three components of Lorenz attractor.*

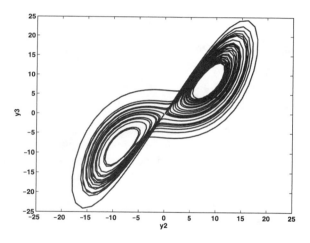

Figure 7.3. *Phase plane plot of Lorenz attractor.*

With two different signs for η, this defines two points in three-dimensional space. These points are fixed points for the differential equation. If

$$y(t_0) = \begin{pmatrix} \rho - 1 \\ \eta \\ \eta \end{pmatrix},$$

then, for all t,

$$\dot{y}(t) = \begin{pmatrix} 0 \\ 0 \\ 0 \end{pmatrix},$$

and so $y(t)$ never changes. However, these points are unstable fixed points. If $y(t)$ does not start at one of these points, it will never reach either of them; if it tries to approach either point, it will be repulsed.

We have provided an M-file, `lorenzgui.m`, that facilitates experiments with the Lorenz equations. Two of the parameters, $\beta = 8/3$ and $\sigma = 10$, are fixed. A `uicontrol` offers a choice among several different values of the third parameter, ρ. A simplified version of the program for $\rho = 28$ would begin with

```
rho = 28;
sigma = 10;
beta = 8/3;
eta = sqrt(beta*(rho-1));
A = [ -beta      0        eta
          0   -sigma    sigma
       -eta     rho       -1  ];
```

The initial condition is taken to be near one of the attractors.

```
yc = [rho-1; eta; eta];
y0 = yc + [0; 0; 3];
```

The time span is infinite, so the integration will have to be stopped by another `uicontrol`.

```
tspan = [0 Inf];
opts = odeset('reltol',1.e-6,'outputfcn',@lorenzplot);
ode45(@lorenzeqn, tspan, y0, opts, A);
```

The matrix A is passed as an extra parameter to the integrator, which sends it on to `lorenzeqn`, the subfunction defining the differential equation. The extra parameter machinery included in the function functions allows `lorenzeqn` to be written in a particularly compact manner.

```
function ydot = lorenzeqn(t,y,A)
A(1,3) = y(2);
A(3,1) = -y(2);
ydot = A*y;
```

Most of the complexity of `lorenzgui` is contained in the plotting subfunction, `lorenzplot`. It not only manages the user interface controls, it must also anticipate the possible range of the solution in order to provide appropriate axis scaling.

7.9   Stiffness

Stiffness is a subtle, difficult, and important concept in the numerical solution of ordinary differential equations. It depends on the differential equation, the initial conditions, and the numerical method. Dictionary definitions of the word "stiff" involve terms like "not easily bent," "rigid," and "stubborn." We are concerned with a computational version of these properties.

*A problem is stiff if the solution being sought varies slowly, but there are nearby
solutions that vary rapidly, so the numerical method must take small steps to
obtain satisfactory results.*

Stiffness is an efficiency issue. If we weren't concerned with how much time a computation
takes, we wouldn't be concerned about stiffness. Nonstiff methods can solve stiff problems;
they just take a long time to do it.

A model of flame propagation provides an example. We learned about this example
from Larry Shampine, one of the authors of the MATLAB ordinary differential equation suite.
If you light a match, the ball of flame grows rapidly until it reaches a critical size. Then it
remains at that size because the amount of oxygen being consumed by the combustion in the
interior of the ball balances the amount available through the surface. The simple model is

$$\dot{y} = y^2 - y^3,$$
$$y(0) = \delta,$$
$$0 \le t \le 2/\delta.$$

The scalar variable $y(t)$ represents the radius of the ball. The y^2 and y^3 terms come from the
surface area and the volume. The critical parameter is the initial radius, δ, which is "small."
We seek the solution over a length of time that is inversely proportional to δ.

At this point, we suggest that you start up MATLAB and actually run our examples.
It is worthwhile to see them in action. We will start with `ode45`, the workhorse of the
MATLAB ordinary differential equation suite. If δ is not very small, the problem is not very
stiff. Try $\delta = 0.01$ and request a relative error of 10^{-4}.

```
delta = 0.01;
F = @(t,y) y^2 - y^3;
opts = odeset('RelTol',1.e-4);
ode45(F,[0 2/delta],delta,opts);
```

With no output arguments, `ode45` automatically plots the solution as it is computed. You
should get a plot of a solution that starts at $y = 0.01$, grows at a modestly increasing rate
until t approaches 100, which is $1/\delta$, then grows rapidly until it reaches a value close to 1,
where it remains.

Now let's see stiffness in action. Decrease δ by three orders of magnitude. (If you
run only one example, run this one.)

```
delta = 0.00001;
ode45(F,[0 2/delta],delta,opts);
```

You should see something like Figure 7.4, although it will take a long time to complete
the plot. If you get tired of watching the agonizing progress, click the stop button in the
lower left corner of the window. Turn on zoom, and use the mouse to explore the solution
near where it first approaches steady state. You should see something like the detail in
Figure 7.4. Notice that `ode45` is doing its job. It's keeping the solution within 10^{-4} of its
nearly constant steady state value. But it certainly has to work hard to do it. If you want an
even more dramatic demonstration of stiffness, decrease the tolerance to 10^{-5} or 10^{-6}.

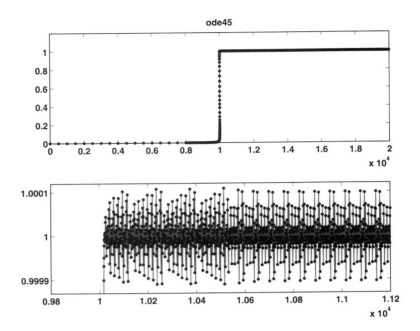

Figure 7.4. *Stiff behavior of* ode45.

This problem is not stiff initially. It only becomes stiff as the solution approaches steady state. This is because the steady state solution is so "rigid." Any solution near $y(t) = 1$ increases or decreases rapidly toward that solution. (We should point out that "rapidly" here is with respect to an unusually long time scale.)

What can be done about stiff problems? You don't want to change the differential equation or the initial conditions, so you have to change the numerical method. Methods intended to solve stiff problems efficiently do more work per step, but can take much bigger steps. Stiff methods are *implicit*. At each step they use MATLAB matrix operations to solve a system of simultaneous linear equations that helps predict the evolution of the solution. For our flame example, the matrix is only 1 by 1, but even here, stiff methods do more work per step than nonstiff methods.

Let's compute the solution to our flame example again, this time with one of the ordinary differential equation solvers in MATLAB whose name ends in "s" for "stiff."

```
delta = 0.00001;
ode23s(F,[0 2/delta],delta,opts);
```

Figure 7.5 shows the computed solution and the zoom detail. You can see that ode23s takes many fewer steps than ode45. This is actually an easy problem for a stiff solver. In fact, ode23s takes only 99 steps and uses just 412 function evaluations, while ode45 takes 3040 steps and uses 20179 function evaluations. Stiffness even affects graphical output. The print files for the ode45 figures are much larger than those for the ode23s figures.

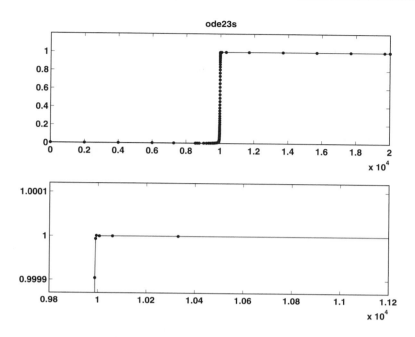

Figure 7.5. *Stiff behavior of* ode23s.

Imagine you are returning from a hike in the mountains. You are in a narrow canyon with steep slopes on either side. An explicit algorithm would sample the local gradient to find the descent direction. But following the gradient on either side of the trail will send you bouncing back and forth across the canyon, as with ode45. You will eventually get home, but it will be long after dark before you arrive. An implicit algorithm would have you keep your eyes on the trail and anticipate where each step is taking you. It is well worth the extra concentration.

This flame problem is also interesting because it involves the Lambert W function, $W(z)$. The differential equation is separable. Integrating once gives an implicit equation for y as a function of t:

$$\frac{1}{y} + \log\left(\frac{1}{y} - 1\right) = \frac{1}{\delta} + \log\left(\frac{1}{\delta} - 1\right) - t.$$

This equation can be solved for y. The exact analytical solution to the flame model turns out to be

$$y(t) = \frac{1}{W(ae^{a-t}) + 1},$$

where $a = 1/\delta - 1$. The function $W(z)$, the Lambert W function, is the solution to

$$W(z)e^{W(z)} = z.$$

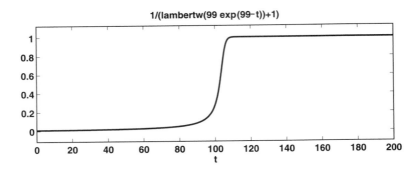

Figure 7.6. *Exact solution for the flame example.*

With MATLAB and the Symbolic Math Toolbox, the statements

```
y = dsolve('Dy = y^2 - y^3','y(0) = 1/100');
y = simplify(y);
pretty(y)
ezplot(y,0,200)
```

produce

```
                1
       ---------------------------
       lambertw(99 exp(99 - t)) + 1
```

and the plot of the exact solution shown in Figure 7.6. If the initial value 1/100 is decreased and the time span $0 \leq t \leq 200$ increased, the transition region becomes narrower.

The Lambert W function is named after J. H. Lambert (1728–1777). Lambert was a colleague of Euler and Lagrange's at the Berlin Academy of Sciences and is best known for his laws of illumination and his proof that π is irrational. The function was "rediscovered" a few years ago by Corless, Gonnet, Hare, and Jeffrey, working on Maple, and by Don Knuth [14].

7.10   Events

So far, we have been assuming that the `tspan` interval, $t_0 \leq t \leq t_{final}$, is a given part of the problem specification, or we have used an infinite interval and a GUI button to terminate the computation. In many situations, the determination of t_{final} is an important aspect of the problem.

One example is a body falling under the force of gravity and encountering air resistance. When does it hit the ground? Another example is the two-body problem, the orbit of one body under the gravitational attraction of a much heavier body. What is the period of the orbit? The *events* feature of the MATLAB ordinary differential equation solvers provides answers to such questions.

Events detection in ordinary differential equations involves two functions, $f(t, y)$ and $g(t, y)$, and an initial condition, (t_0, y_0). The problem is to find a function $y(t)$ and a final value t_* so that

$$\dot{y} = f(t, y),$$
$$y(t_0) = y_0,$$

and

$$g(t_*, y(t_*)) = 0.$$

A simple model for the falling body is

$$\ddot{y} = -1 + \dot{y}^2,$$

with initial conditions $y(0) = 1$, $\dot{y}(0) = 0$. The question is, for what t does $y(t) = 0$? The code for the function $f(t, y)$ is

```
function ydot = f(t,y)
ydot = [y(2); -1+y(2)^2];
```

With the differential equation written as a first-order system, y becomes a vector with two components and so $g(t, y) = y_1$. The code for $g(t, y)$ is

```
function [gstop,isterminal,direction] = g(t,y)
gstop = y(1);
isterminal = 1;
direction = [];
```

The first output, gstop, is the value that we want to make zero. Setting the second output, isterminal, to one indicates that the ordinary differential equation solver should terminate when gstop is zero. Setting the third output, direction, to the empty matrix indicates that the zero can be approached from either direction. With these two functions available, the following statements compute and plot the trajectory shown in Figure 7.7.

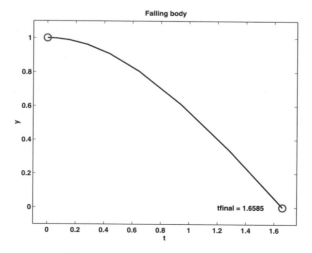

Figure 7.7. *Event handling for falling object.*

```
opts = odeset('events',@g);
y0 = [1; 0];
[t,y,tfinal] = ode45(@f,[0 Inf],y0,opts);
tfinal
plot(t,y(:,1),'-',[0 tfinal],[1 0],'o')
axis([-.1 tfinal+.1 -.1 1.1])
xlabel('t')
ylabel('y')
title('Falling body')
text(1.2, 0, ['tfinal = ' num2str(tfinal)])
```

The terminating value of t is found to be tfinal = 1.6585.

The three sections of code for this example can be saved in three separate M-files, with two functions and one script, or they can all be saved in one function M-file. In the latter case, f and g become subfunctions and have to appear after the main body of code.

Events detection is particularly useful in problems involving periodic phenomena. The two-body problem provides a good example. Here is the first portion of a function M-file, orbit.m. The input parameter is reltol, the desired local relative tolerance.

```
function orbit(reltol)
y0 = [1; 0; 0; 0.3];
opts = odeset('events',@gstop,'reltol',reltol);
[t,y,te,ye] = ode45(@twobody,[0 2*pi],y0,opts,y0);
tfinal = te(end)
yfinal = ye(end,1:2)
plot(y(:,1),y(:,2),'-',0,0,'ro')
axis([-.1 1.05 -.35 .35])
```

The function ode45 is used to compute the orbit. The first input argument is a function handle, @twobody, that references the function defining the differential equations. The second argument to ode45 is any overestimate of the time interval required to complete one period. The third input argument is y0, a 4-vector that provides the initial position and velocity. The light body starts at $(1, 0)$, which is a point with a distance 1 from the heavy body, and has initial velocity $(0, 0.3)$, which is perpendicular to the initial position vector. The fourth input argument is an options structure created by odeset that overrides the default value for reltol and that specifies a function gstop that defines the events we want to locate. The last argument is y0, an "extra" argument that ode45 passes on to both twobody and gstop.

The code for twobody has to be modified to accept a third argument, even though it is not used.

```
function ydot = twobody(t,y,y0)
r = sqrt(y(1)^2 + y(2)^2);
ydot = [y(3); y(4); -y(1)/r^3; -y(2)/r^3];
```

The ordinary differential equation solver calls the gstop function at every step during the integration. This function tells the solver whether or not it is time to stop.

```
function [val,isterm,dir] = gstop(t,y,y0)
d = y(1:2)-y0(1:2);
v = y(3:4);
val = d'*v;
isterm = 1;
dir = 1;
```

The 2-vector d is the difference between the current position and the starting point. The 2-vector v is the velocity at the current position. The quantity val is the inner product between these two vectors. Mathematically, the stopping function is

$$g(t, y) = \dot{d}(t)^T d(t),$$

where

$$d = (y_1(t) - y_1(0), y_2(t) - y_2(0))^T.$$

Points where $g(t, y(t)) = 0$ are the local minimum or maximum of $d(t)$. By setting dir = 1, we indicate that the zeros of $g(t, y)$ must be approached from above, so they correspond to minima. By setting isterm = 1, we indicate that computation of the solution should be terminated at the first minimum. If the orbit is truly periodic, then any minima of d occur when the body returns to its starting point.

Calling orbit with a very loose tolerance

```
orbit(2.0e-3)
```

produces

```
tfinal =
    2.35087197761898

yfinal =
    0.98107659901079   -0.00012519138559
```

and plots Figure 7.8.

You can see from both the value of yfinal and the graph that the orbit does not quite return to the starting point. We need to request more accuracy.

```
orbit(1.0e-6)
```

produces

```
tfinal =
    2.38025846171805

yfinal =
    0.99998593905521    0.00000000032240
```

Now the value of yfinal is close enough to y0 that the graph of the orbit is effectively closed.

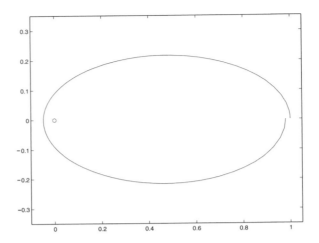

Figure 7.8. *Periodic orbit computed with loose tolerance.*

7.11   Multistep Methods

A single-step numerical method has a short memory. The only information passed from one step to the next is an estimate of the proper step size and, perhaps, the value of $f(t_n, y_n)$ at the point the two steps have in common.

As the name implies, a multistep method has a longer memory. After an initial start-up phase, a pth-order multistep method saves up to perhaps a dozen values of the solution, $y_{n-p+1}, y_{n-p+2}, \ldots, y_{n-1}, y_n$, and uses them all to compute y_{n+1}. In fact, these methods can vary both the order, p, and the step size, h.

Multistep methods tend to be more efficient than single-step methods for problems with smooth solutions and high accuracy requirements. For example, the orbits of planets and deep space probes are computed with multistep methods.

7.12   The MATLAB ODE Solvers

This section is derived from the Algorithms portion of the MATLAB Reference Manual page for the ordinary differential equation solvers.

ode45 is based on an explicit Runge–Kutta (4, 5) formula, the Dormand–Prince pair. It is a one-step solver. In computing $y(t_{n+1})$, it needs only the solution at the immediately preceding time point, $y(t_n)$. In general, ode45 is the first function to try for most problems.

ode23 is an implementation of an explicit Runge–Kutta (2, 3) pair of Bogacki and Shampine's. It is often more efficient than ode45 at crude tolerances and in the presence of moderate stiffness. Like ode45, ode23 is a one-step solver.

ode113 uses a variable-order Adams–Bashforth–Moulton predictor-corrector algorithm. It is often more efficient than ode45 at stringent tolerances and if the ordinary differential equation file function is particularly expensive to evaluate. ode113 is a multistep solver—it normally needs the solutions at several preceding time points to compute the current solution.

The above algorithms are intended to solve nonstiff systems. If they appear to be unduly slow, try using one of the stiff solvers below.

ode15s is a variable-order solver based on the numerical differentiation formulas (NDFs). Optionally, it uses the backward differentiation formulas (BDFs, also known as Gear's method), which are usually less efficient. Like ode113, ode15s is a multistep solver. Try ode15s if ode45 fails or is very inefficient and you suspect that the problem is stiff, or if you are solving a differential-algebraic problem.

ode23s is based on a modified Rosenbrock formula of order two. Because it is a one-step solver, it is often more efficient than ode15s at crude tolerances. It can solve some kinds of stiff problems for which ode15s is not effective.

ode23t is an implementation of the trapezoidal rule using a "free" interpolant. Use this solver if the problem is only moderately stiff and you need a solution without numerical damping. ode23t can solve differential-algebraic equations.

ode23tb is an implementation of TR-BDF2, an implicit Runge–Kutta formula with a first stage that is a trapezoidal rule step and a second stage that is a BDF of order two. By construction, the same iteration matrix is used in evaluating both stages. Like ode23s, this solver is often more efficient than ode15s at crude tolerances.

Here is a summary table from the MATLAB Reference Manual. For each function, it lists the appropriate problem type, the typical accuracy of the method, and the recommended area of usage.

- ode45. Nonstiff problems, medium accuracy. Use most of the time. This should be the first solver you try.

- ode23. Nonstiff problems, low accuracy. Use for large error tolerances or moderately stiff problems.

- ode113. Nonstiff problems, low to high accuracy. Use for stringent error tolerances or computationally intensive ordinary differential equation functions.

- ode15s. Stiff problems, low to medium accuracy. Use if ode45 is slow (stiff systems) or there is a mass matrix.

- ode23s. Stiff problems, low accuracy. Use for large error tolerances with stiff systems or with a constant mass matrix.

- ode23t. Moderately stiff problems, low accuracy. Use for moderately stiff problems where you need a solution without numerical damping.

- ode23tb. Stiff problems, low accuracy. Use for large error tolerances with stiff systems or if there is a mass matrix.

7.13   Errors

Errors enter the numerical solution of the initial value problem from two sources:

- discretization error,

- roundoff error.

Discretization error is a property of the differential equation and the numerical method. If all the arithmetic could be performed with infinite precision, discretization error would be the only error present. Roundoff error is a property of the computer hardware and the program. It is usually far less important than the discretization error, except when we try to achieve very high accuracy.

Discretization error can be assessed from two points of view, local and global. *Local discretization error* is the error that would be made in one step if the previous values were exact and if there were no roundoff error. Let $u_n(t)$ be the solution of the differential equation determined not by the original initial condition at t_0 but by the value of the computed solution at t_n. That is, $u_n(t)$ is the function of t defined by

$$\dot{u}_n = f(t, u_n),$$

$$u_n(t_n) = y_n.$$

The local discretization error d_n is the difference between this theoretical solution and the computed solution (ignoring roundoff) determined by the same data at t_n:

$$d_n = y_{n+1} - u_n(t_{n+1}).$$

Global discretization error is the difference between the computed solution, still ignoring roundoff, and the true solution determined by the original initial condition at t_0, that is,

$$e_n = y_n - y(t_n).$$

The distinction between local and global discretization error can be easily seen in the special case where $f(t, y)$ does not depend on y. In this case, the solution is simply an integral, $y(t) = \int_{t_0}^{t} f(\tau)d\tau$. Euler's method becomes a scheme for numerical quadrature that might be called the "composite lazy man's rectangle rule." It uses function values at the left-hand ends of the subintervals rather than at the midpoints:

$$\int_{t_0}^{t_N} f(\tau)d\tau \approx \sum_{0}^{N-1} h_n f(t_n).$$

The local discretization error is the error in one subinterval:

$$d_n = h_n f(t_n) - \int_{t_n}^{t_{n+1}} f(\tau)d\tau,$$

and the global discretization error is the total error:

$$e_N = \sum_{n=0}^{N-1} h_n f(t_n) - \int_{t_0}^{t_N} f(\tau)d\tau.$$

In this special case, each of the subintegrals is independent of the others (the sum could be evaluated in any order), so the global error is the sum of the local errors:

$$e_N = \sum_{n=0}^{N-1} d_n.$$

In the case of a genuine differential equation where $f(t, y)$ depends on y, the error in any one interval depends on the solutions computed for earlier intervals. Consequently, the relationship between the global error and the local errors is related to the *stability* of the differential equation. For a single scalar equation, if the partial derivative $\partial f/\partial y$ is positive, then the solution $y(t)$ grows as t increases and the global error will be greater than the sum of the local errors. If $\partial f/\partial y$ is negative, then the global error will be less than the sum of the local errors. If $\partial f/\partial y$ changes sign, or if we have a nonlinear system of equations where $\partial f/\partial y$ is a varying matrix, the relationship between e_N and the sum of the d_n can be quite complicated and unpredictable.

Think of the local discretization error as the deposits made to a bank account and the global error as the overall balance in the account. The partial derivative $\partial f/\partial y$ acts like an interest rate. If it is positive, the overall balance is greater than the sum of the deposits. If it is negative, the final error balance might well be less than the sum of the errors deposited at each step.

Our code `ode23tx`, like all the production codes in MATLAB, only attempts to control the local discretization error. Solvers that try to control estimates of the global discretization error are much more complicated, are expensive to run, and are not very successful.

A fundamental concept in assessing the accuracy of a numerical method is its *order*. The order is defined in terms of the local discretization error obtained if the method is applied to problems with smooth solutions. A method is said to be of order p if there is a number C so that

$$|d_n| \leq C h_n^{p+1}.$$

The number C might depend on the partial derivatives of the function defining the differential equation and on the length of the interval over which the solution is sought, but it should be independent of the step number n and the step size h_n. The above inequality can be abbreviated using "big-oh notation":

$$d_n = O(h_n^{p+1}).$$

For example, consider Euler's method:

$$y_{n+1} = y_n + h_n f(t_n, y_n).$$

Assume the local solution $u_n(t)$ has a continuous second derivative. Then, using Taylor series near the point t_n,

$$u_n(t) = u_n(t_n) + (t - t_n)u_n'(t_n) + O((t - t_n)^2).$$

Using the differential equation and the initial condition defining $u_n(t)$,

$$u_n(t_{n+1}) = y_n + h_n f(t_n, y_n) + O(h_n^2).$$

Consequently,

$$d_n = y_{n+1} - u_n(t_{n+1}) = O(h_n^2).$$

We conclude that $p = 1$, so Euler's method is first order. The MATLAB naming conventions for ordinary differential equation solvers would imply that a function using Euler's method by itself, with fixed step size and no error estimate, should be called `ode1`.

Now consider the global discretization error at a fixed point $t = t_f$. As accuracy requirements are increased, the step sizes h_n will decrease, and the total number of steps N required to reach t_f will increase. Roughly, we shall have

$$N = \frac{t_f - t_0}{h},$$

where h is the average step size. Moreover, the global error e_N can be expressed as a sum of N local errors coupled by factors describing the stability of the equations. These factors do not depend in a strong way on the step sizes, and so we can say roughly that if the local error is $O(h^{p+1})$, then the global error will be $N \cdot O(h^{p+1}) = O(h^p)$. This is why $p + 1$ was used instead of p as the exponent in the definition of order.

For Euler's method, $p = 1$, so decreasing the average step size by a factor of 2 decreases the average local error by a factor of roughly $2^{p+1} = 4$, but about twice as many steps are required to reach t_f, so the global error is decreased by a factor of only $2^p = 2$. With higher order methods, the global error for smooth solutions is reduced by a much larger factor.

It should be pointed out that in discussing numerical methods for ordinary differential equations, the word "order" can have any of several different meanings. The order of a differential equation is the index of the highest derivative appearing. For example, $d^2y/dt^2 = -y$ is a second-order differential equation. The order of a system of equations sometimes refers to the number of equations in the system. For example, $\dot{y} = 2y - yz, \dot{z} = -z + yz$ is a second-order system. The order of a numerical method is what we have been discussing here. It is the power of the step size that appears in the expression for the global error.

One way of checking the order of a numerical method is to examine its behavior if $f(t, y)$ is a polynomial in t and does not depend on y. If the method is exact for t^{p-1}, but not for t^p, then its order is not more than p. (The order could be less than p if the method's behavior for general functions does not match its behavior for polynomials.) Euler's method is exact if $f(t, y)$ is constant, but not if $f(t, y) = t$, so its order is not greater than one.

With modern computers, using IEEE floating-point double-precision arithmetic, the roundoff error in the computed solution only begins to become important if very high accuracies are requested or the integration is carried out over a long interval. Suppose we integrate over an interval of length $L = t_f - t_0$. If the roundoff error in one step is of size ϵ, then the worst the roundoff error can be after N steps of size $h = \frac{L}{N}$ is something like

$$N\epsilon = \frac{L\epsilon}{h}.$$

For a method with global discretization error of size Ch^p, the total error is something like

$$Ch^p + \frac{L\epsilon}{h}.$$

For the roundoff error to be comparable with the discretization error, we need

$$h \approx \left(\frac{L\epsilon}{C}\right)^{\frac{1}{p+1}}.$$

The number of steps taken with this step size is roughly

$$N \approx L\left(\frac{C}{L\epsilon}\right)^{\frac{1}{p+1}}.$$

Here are the numbers of steps for various orders p if $L = 20$: $C = 100$, and $\epsilon = 2^{-52}$:

p	N
1	$4.5 \cdot 10^{17}$
3	5,647,721
5	37,285
10	864

These values of p are the orders for Euler's method and for the MATLAB functions ode23 and ode45, and a typical choice for the order in the variable-order method used by ode113. We see that the low-order methods have to take an impractically large number of steps before this worst-case roundoff error estimate becomes significant. Even more steps are required if we assume the roundoff error at each step varies randomly. The variable-order multistep function ode113 is capable of achieving such high accuracy that roundoff error can be a bit more significant with it.

7.14 Performance

We have carried out an experiment to see how all this applies in practice. The differential equation is the harmonic oscillator

$$\ddot{x}(t) = -x(t)$$

with initial conditions $x(0) = 1$, $\dot{x}(0) = 0$, over the interval $0 \leq t \leq 10\pi$. The interval is five periods of the periodic solution, so the global error can be computed simply as the difference between the initial and final values of the solution. Since the solution neither grows nor decays with t, the global error should be roughly proportional to the local error.

The following MATLAB script uses odeset to change both the relative and the absolute tolerances. The refinement level is set so that one step of the algorithm generates one row of output.

```
y0 = [1 0];
for k = 1:13
    tol = 10^(-k);
    opts = odeset('reltol',tol,'abstol',tol,'refine',1);
    tic
    [t,y] = ode23(@harmonic,[0 10*pi],y0',opts);
    time = toc;
    steps = length(t)-1;
    err = max(abs(y(end,:)-y0));
end
```

The differential equation is defined in harmonic.m.

```
function ydot = harmonic(t,y)
ydot = [y(2); -y(1)];
```

The script was run three times, with ode23, ode45, and ode113. The first plot in Figure 7.9 shows how the global error varies with the requested tolerance for the three

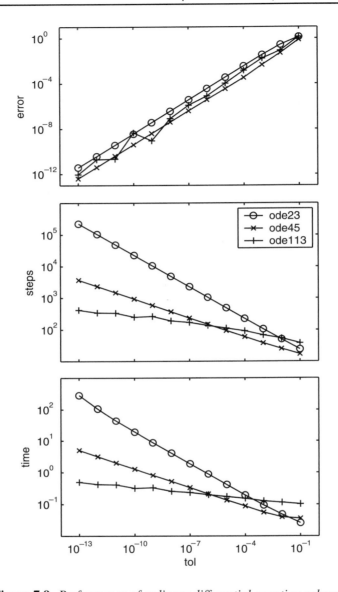

Figure 7.9. *Performance of ordinary differential equation solvers.*

routines. We see that the actual error tracks the requested tolerance quite well. For `ode23`, the global error is about 36 times the tolerance; for `ode45`, it is about 4 times the tolerance; and for `ode113`, it varies between 1 and 45 times the tolerance.

   The second plot in Figure 7.9 shows the numbers of steps required. The results also fit our model quite well. Let τ denote the tolerance 10^{-k}. For `ode23`, the number of steps is about $10\tau^{-1/3}$, which is the expected behavior for a third-order method. For `ode45`, the number of steps is about $9\tau^{-1/5}$, which is the expected behavior for a fifth-order method.

For `ode113`, the number of steps reflects the fact that the solution is very smooth, so the method was often able to use its maximum order, 13.

The third plot in Figure 7.9 shows the execution times, in seconds, on an 800 MHz Pentium III laptop. For this problem, `ode45` is the fastest method for tolerances of roughly 10^{-6} or larger, while `ode113` is the fastest method for more stringent tolerances. The low-order method, `ode23`, takes a very long time to obtain high accuracy.

This is just one experiment, on a problem with a very smooth and stable solution.

7.15 Further Reading

The MATLAB ordinary differential equation suite is described in [54]. Additional material on the numerical solution of ordinary differential equations, and especially stiffness, is available in Ascher and Petzold [4], Brennan, Campbell, and Petzold [11], and Shampine [53].

Exercises

7.1. The standard form of an ODE initial value problem is:

$$\dot{y} = f(t, y), \ y(t_0) = y_0.$$

Express this ODE problem in the standard form.

$$\ddot{u} = \frac{v}{1 + t^2} - \sin r,$$

$$\ddot{v} = \frac{-u}{1 + t^2} + \cos r,$$

where $r = \sqrt{\dot{u}^2 + \dot{v}^2}$. The initial conditions are

$$u(0) = 1, v(0) = \dot{u}(0) = \dot{v}(0) = 0.$$

7.2. You invest \$100 in a savings account paying 6% interest per year. Let $y(t)$ be the amount in your account after t years. If the interest is compounded continuously, then $y(t)$ solves the ODE initial value problem

$$\dot{y} = ry, \ r = .06,$$

$$y(0) = 100.$$

Compounding interest at a discrete time interval, h, corresponds to using a finite difference method to approximate the solution to the differential equation. The time interval h is expressed as a fraction of a year. For example, compounding monthly has $h = 1/12$. The quantity y_n, the balance after n time intervals, approximates the continuously compounded balance $y(nh)$. The banking industry effectively uses Euler's method to compute compound interest.

$$y_0 = y(0),$$

$$y_{n+1} = y_n + hr y_n.$$

This exercise asks you to investigate the use of higher order difference methods to compute compound interest. What is the balance in your account after 10 years with each of the following methods of compounding interest?

Euler's method, yearly.

Euler's method, monthly.

Midpoint rule, monthly.

Trapezoid rule, monthly.

BS23 algorithm, monthly.

Continuous compounding.

7.3. (a) Show experimentally or algebraically that the BS23 algorithm is exact for $f(t, y) = 1$, $f(t, y) = t$, and $f(t, y) = t^2$, but not for $f(t, y) = t^3$.
(b) When is the ode23 error estimator exact?

7.4. The error function erf(x) is usually defined by an integral,

$$\text{erf}(x) = \frac{2}{\sqrt{\pi}} \int_0^x e^{-x^2} dx,$$

but it can also be defined as the solution to the differential equation

$$y'(x) = \frac{2}{\sqrt{\pi}} e^{-x^2},$$

$$y(0) = 0.$$

Use ode23tx to solve this differential equation on the interval $0 \le x \le 2$. Compare the results with the built-in MATLAB function erf(x) at the points chosen by ode23tx.

7.5. (a) Write an M-file named myrk4.m, in the style of ode23tx.m, that implements the classical Runge–Kutta fixed step size algorithm. Instead of an optional fourth argument rtol or opts, the required fourth argument should be the step size h. Here is the proposed preamble.

```
% function [tout,yout] = myrk4(F,tspan,y0,h,varargin)
% MYRK4   Classical fourth-order Runge-Kutta.
% Usage is the same as ODE23TX except the fourth
% argument is a fixed step size h.
% MYRK4(F,TSPAN,Y0,H) with TSPAN = [T0 TF] integrates
% the system of differential equations y' = f(t,y)
```

```
% from t = T0 to t = TF.   The initial condition
% is y(T0) = Y0.
% With no output arguments, MYRK4 plots the solution.
% With two output arguments, [T,Y] = MYRK4(..) returns
% T and Y so that Y(:,k) is the approximate solution at
% T(k). More than four input arguments,
% MYRK4(..,P1,P2,..), are passed on to F,
% F(T,Y,P1,P2,...).
```

(b) Roughly, how should the error behave if the step size h for classical Runge–Kutta is cut in half? (Hint: Why is there a "4" in the name of myrk4?) Run an experiment to illustrate this behavior.

(c) If you integrate the simple harmonic oscillator $\ddot{y} = -y$ over one full period, $0 \le t \le 2\pi$, you can compare the initial and final values of y to get a measure of the global accuracy. If you use your myrk4 with a step size $h = \pi/50$, you should find that it takes 100 steps and computes a result with an error of about 10^{-6}. Compare this with the number of steps required by ode23, ode45, and ode113 if the relative tolerance is set to 10^{-6} and the refinement level is set to one. This is a problem with a very smooth solution, so you should find that ode23 requires more steps, while ode45 and ode113 require fewer.

7.6. The ordinary differential equation problem

$$\dot{y} = -1000(y - \sin t) + \cos t, \ y(0) = 1,$$

on the interval $0 \le t \le 1$ is mildly stiff.

(a) Find the exact solution, either by hand or using dsolve from the Symbolic Toolbox.

(b) Compute the solution with ode23tx. How many steps are required?

(c) Compute the solution with the stiff solver ode23s. How many steps are required?

(d) Plot the two computed solutions on the same graph, with line style '.' for the ode23tx solution and 'o' for the ode23s solution.

(e) Zoom in, or change the axis settings, to show a portion of the graph where the solution is varying rapidly. You should see that both solvers are taking small steps.

(f) Show a portion of the graph where the solution is varying slowly. You should see that ode23tx is taking much smaller steps than ode23s.

7.7. The following problems all have the same solution on $0 \le t \le \pi/2$:

$$\dot{y} = \cos t, \ y(0) = 0,$$
$$\dot{y} = \sqrt{1 - y^2}, \ y(0) = 0,$$
$$\ddot{y} = -y, \ y(0) = 0, \ \dot{y}(0) = 1,$$
$$\ddot{y} = -\sin t, \ y(0) = 0, \ \dot{y}(0) = 1.$$

(a) What is the common solution $y(t)$?

(b) Two of the problems involve second derivatives, $\ddot{y}$. Rewrite these problems as first-order systems, $\dot{y} = f(t, y)$, involving vectors y and f.

(c) What is the Jacobian, $J = \frac{\partial f}{\partial y}$, for each problem? What happens to each Jacobian as t approaches $\pi/2$?

(d) The work required by a Runge–Kutta method to solve an initial value problem $\dot{y} = f(t, y)$ depends on the function $f(t, y)$, not just the solution, $y(t)$. Use odeset to set both reltol and abstol to 10^{-9}. How much work does ode45 require to solve each problem? Why are some problems more work than others?

(e) What happens to the computed solutions if the interval is changed to $0 \le t \le \pi$?

(f) What happens on $0 \le t \le \pi$ if the second problem is changed to

$$\dot{y} = \sqrt{|1 - y^2|}, \quad y(0) = 0.$$

7.8. Use the jacobian and eig functions in the Symbolic Toolbox to verify that the Jacobian for the two-body problem is

$$J = \frac{1}{r^5} \begin{bmatrix} 0 & 0 & r^5 & 0 \\ 0 & 0 & 0 & r^5 \\ 2y_1^2 - y_2^2 & 3y_1 y_2 & 0 & 0 \\ 3y_1 y_2 & 2y_2^2 - y_1^2 & 0 & 0 \end{bmatrix}$$

and that its eigenvalues are

$$\lambda = \frac{1}{r^{3/2}} \begin{bmatrix} \sqrt{2} \\ i \\ -\sqrt{2} \\ -i \end{bmatrix}.$$

7.9. Verify that the matrix in the Lorenz equations

$$A = \begin{bmatrix} -\beta & 0 & \eta \\ 0 & -\sigma & \sigma \\ -\eta & \rho & -1 \end{bmatrix}$$

is singular if and only if

$$\eta = \pm\sqrt{\beta(\rho - 1)}.$$

Verify that the corresponding null vector is

$$\begin{pmatrix} \rho - 1 \\ \eta \\ \eta \end{pmatrix}.$$

7.10. The Jacobian matrix J for the Lorenz equations is not A, but is closely related to A. Find J, compute its eigenvalues at one of the fixed points, and verify that the fixed point is unstable.

7.11. Find the largest value of ρ in the Lorenz equations for which the fixed point is stable.

7.12. All the values of ρ available with lorenzgui except $\rho = 28$ give trajectories that eventually settle down to stable periodic orbits. In his book on the Lorenz equations, Sparrow classifies a periodic orbit by what we might call its *signature*, a sequence of $+$'s and $-$'s specifying the order of the critical points that the trajectory circles during one period. A single $+$ or $-$ would be the signature of a trajectory that circles just one critical point, except that no such orbits exist. The signature '$+-$' indicates

that the trajectory circles each critical point once. The signature '$+++-+---$'
would indicate a very fancy orbit that circles the critical points a total of eight times
before repeating itself.

What are the signatures of the four different periodic orbits generated by
`lorenzgui`? Be careful—each of the signatures is different, and $\rho = 99.65$ is
particularly delicate.

7.13. What are the periods of the periodic orbits generated for the different values of ρ
available with `lorenzgui`?

7.14. The MATLAB demos directory contains an M-file, `orbitode`, that uses `ode45` to
solve an instance of the *restricted three-body problem*. This involves the orbit of a
light object around two heavier objects, such as an Apollo capsule around the earth
and the moon. Run the demo and then locate its source code with the statements

```
orbitode
which orbitode
```

Make your own copy of `orbitode.m`. Find these two statements:

```
tspan = [0 7];
y0 = [1.2; 0; 0; -1.04935750983031990726];
```

These statements set the time interval for the integration and the initial position and
velocity of the light object. Our question is, Where do these values come from? To
answer this question, find the statement

```
[t,y,te,ye,ie] = ode45(@f,tspan,y0,options);
```

Remove the semicolon and insert three more statements after it:

```
te
ye
ie
```

Run the demo again. Explain how the values of `te`, `ye`, and `ie` are related to `tspan`
and `y0`.

7.15. A classical model in mathematical ecology is the Lotka–Volterra predator-prey
model. Consider a simple ecosystem consisting of rabbits that have an infinite supply
of food and foxes that prey on the rabbits for their food. This is modeled by a pair
of nonlinear, first-order differential equations:

$$\frac{dr}{dt} = 2r - \alpha r f, \ r(0) = r_0,$$

$$\frac{df}{dt} = -f + \alpha r f, \ f(0) = f_0,$$

where t is time, $r(t)$ is the number of rabbits, $f(t)$ is the number of foxes, and α is a
positive constant. If $\alpha = 0$, the two populations do not interact, the rabbits do what
rabbits do best, and the foxes die off from starvation. If $\alpha > 0$, the foxes encounter
the rabbits with a probability that is proportional to the product of their numbers.

Such an encounter results in a decrease in the number of rabbits and (for less obvious reasons) an increase in the number of foxes.

The solutions to this nonlinear system cannot be expressed in terms of other known functions; the equations must be solved numerically. It turns out that the solutions are always periodic, with a period that depends on the initial conditions. In other words, for any $r(0)$ and $f(0)$, there is a value $t = t_p$ when both populations return to their original values. Consequently, for all t,

$$r(t + t_p) = r(t), \quad f(t + t_p) = f(t).$$

(a) Compute the solution with $r_0 = 300$, $f_0 = 150$, and $\alpha = 0.01$. You should find that t_p is close to 5. Make two plots, one of r and f as functions of t and one a phase plane plot with r as one axis and f as the other.

(b) Compute and plot the solution with $r_0 = 15$, $f_0 = 22$, and $\alpha = 0.01$. You should find that t_p is close to 6.62.

(c) Compute and plot the solution with $r_0 = 102$, $f_0 = 198$, and $\alpha = 0.01$. Determine the period t_p either by trial and error or with an event handler.

(d) The point $(r_0, f_0) = (1/\alpha, 2/\alpha)$ is a stable equilibrium point. If the populations have these initial values, they do not change. If the initial populations are close to these values, they do not change very much. Let $u(t) = r(t) - 1/\alpha$ and $v(t) = f(t) - 2/\alpha$. The functions $u(t)$ and $v(t)$ satisfy another nonlinear system of differential equations, but if the uv terms are ignored, the system becomes linear. What is this linear system? What is the period of its periodic solutions?

7.16. Many modifications of the Lotka–Volterra predator-prey model (see previous problem) have been proposed to more accurately reflect what happens in nature. For example, the number of rabbits can be prevented from growing indefinitely by changing the first equation as follows:

$$\frac{dr}{dt} = 2\left(1 - \frac{r}{R}\right)r - \alpha r f, \ r(0) = r_0,$$

$$\frac{df}{dt} = -f + \alpha r f, \ y(0) = y_0,$$

where t is time, $r(t)$ is the number of rabbits, $f(t)$ is the number of foxes, α is a positive constant, and R is a positive constant. Because α is positive, $\frac{dr}{dt}$ is negative whenever $r \geq R$. Consequently, the number of rabbits can never exceed R.

For $\alpha = 0.01$, compare the behavior of the original model with the behavior of this modified model with $R = 400$. In making this comparison, solve the equations with $r_0 = 300$ and $f_0 = 150$ over 50 units of time. Make four different plots:

• number of foxes and number of rabbits versus time for the original model,

• number of foxes and number of rabbits versus time for the modified model,

• number of foxes versus number of rabbits for the original model,

• number of foxes versus number of rabbits for the modified model.

For all plots, label all curves and all axes and put a title on the plot. For the last two plots, set the aspect ratio so that equal increments on the x- and y-axes are equal in size.

7.17. An 80-kg paratrooper is dropped from an airplane at a height of 600 m. After 5 s the chute opens. The paratrooper's height as a function of time, $y(t)$, is given by

$$\ddot{y} = -g + \alpha(t)/m,$$
$$y(0) = 600 \text{ m},$$
$$\dot{y}(0) = 0 \text{ m/s},$$

where $g = 9.81$ m/s^2 is the acceleration due to gravity and $m = 80$ kg is the paratrooper's mass. The air resistance $\alpha(t)$ is proportional to the square of the velocity, with different proportionality constants before and after the chute opens.

$$\alpha(t) = \begin{cases} K_1 \dot{y}(t)^2, & t < 5 \text{ s}, \\ K_2 \dot{y}(t)^2, & t \geq 5 \text{ s}. \end{cases}$$

(a) Find the analytical solution for free-fall, $K_1 = 0$, $K_2 = 0$. At what height does the chute open? How long does it take to reach the ground? What is the impact velocity? Plot the height versus time and label the plot appropriately.
(b) Consider the case $K_1 = 1/15$, $K_2 = 4/15$. At what height does the chute open? How long does it take to reach the ground? What is the impact velocity? Make a plot of the height versus time and label the plot appropriately.

7.18. Determine the trajectory of a spherical cannonball in a stationary Cartesian coordinate system that has a horizontal x-axis, a vertical y-axis, and an origin at the launch point. The initial velocity of the projectile in this coordinate system has magnitude v_0 and makes an angle with respect to the x-axis of θ_0 radians. The only forces acting on the projectile are gravity and the aerodynamic drag, D, which depends on the projectile's speed relative to any wind that might be present. The equations describing the motion of the projectile are

$$\dot{x} = v \cos \theta, \quad \dot{y} = v \sin \theta,$$

$$\dot{\theta} = -\frac{g}{v} \cos \theta, \quad \dot{v} = -\frac{D}{m} - g \sin \theta.$$

Constants for this problem are the acceleration of gravity, $g = 9.81$m/s^2, the mass, $m = 15$ kg, and the initial speed, $v_0 = 50$ m/s. The wind is assumed to be horizontal and its speed is a specified function of time, $w(t)$. The aerodynamic drag is proportional to the square of the projectile's velocity relative to the wind:

$$D(t) = \frac{c\rho s}{2} \left((\dot{x} - w(t))^2 + \dot{y}^2 \right),$$

where $c = 0.2$ is the drag coefficient, $\rho = 1.29$ kg/m^3 is the density of air, and $s = 0.25$ m^2 is the projectile's cross-sectional area.
Consider four different wind conditions.

- No wind. $w(t) = 0$ for all t.

- Steady headwind. $w(t) = -10$ m/s for all t.

- Intermittent tailwind. $w(t) = 10$ m/s if the integer part of t is even, and zero otherwise.

- Gusty wind. $w(t)$ is a Gaussian random variable with mean zero and standard deviation 10 m/s.

The integer part of a real number t is denoted by $\lfloor t \rfloor$ and is computed in MATLAB by `floor(t)`. A Gaussian random variable with mean 0 and standard deviation σ is generated by `sigma*randn` (see Chapter 9, Random Numbers).

For each of these four wind conditions, carry out the following computations. Find the 17 trajectories whose initial angles are multiples of 5 degrees, that is, $\theta_0 = k\pi/36$ radians, $k = 1, 2, \ldots, 17$. Plot all 17 trajectories on one figure. Determine which of these trajectories has the greatest downrange distance. For that trajectory, report the initial angle in degrees, the flight time, the downrange distance, the impact velocity, and the number of steps required by the ordinary differential equation solver. Which of the four wind conditions requires the most computation? Why?

7.19. In the 1968 Olympic games in Mexico City, Bob Beamon established a world record with a long jump of 8.90 m. This was 0.80 m longer than the previous world record. Since 1968, Beamon's jump has been exceeded only once in competition, by Mike Powell's jump of 8.95 m in Tokyo in 1991. After Beamon's remarkable jump, some people suggested that the lower air resistance at Mexico City's 2250 m altitude was a contributing factor. This problem examines that possibility.

The mathematical model is the same as the cannonball trajectory in the previous exercise. The fixed Cartesian coordinate system has a horizontal x-axis, a vertical y-axis, and an origin at the takeoff board. The jumper's initial velocity has magnitude v_0 and makes an angle with respect to the x-axis of θ_0 radians. The only forces acting after takeoff are gravity and the aerodynamic drag, D, which is proportional to the square of the magnitude of the velocity. There is no wind. The equations describing the jumper's motion are

$$\dot{x} = v\cos\theta, \quad \dot{y} = v\sin\theta,$$

$$\dot{\theta} = -\frac{g}{v}\cos\theta, \quad \dot{v} = -\frac{D}{m} - g\sin\theta.$$

The drag is

$$D = \frac{c\rho s}{2}\left(\dot{x}^2 + \dot{y}^2\right).$$

Constants for this exercise are the acceleration of gravity, $g = 9.81$ m/s^2, the mass, $m = 80$ kg, the drag coefficient, $c = 0.72$, the jumper's cross-sectional area, $s = 0.50$ m^2, and the takeoff angle, $\theta_0 = 22.5° = \pi/8$ radians.

Compute four different jumps, with different values for initial velocity, v_0, and air density, ρ. The length of each jump is $x(t_f)$, where the air time, t_f, is determined by the condition $y(t_f) = 0$.

(a) "Nominal" jump at high altitude. $v_0 = 10$ m/s and $\rho = 0.94$ kg/m^3.
(b) "Nominal" jump at sea level. $v_0 = 10$ m/s and $\rho = 1.29$ kg/m^3.
(c) Sprinter's approach at high altitude. $\rho = 0.94$ kg/m^3. Determine v_0 so that the length of the jump is Beamon's record, 8.90 m.
(d) Sprinter's approach at sea level. $\rho = 1.29$ kg/m^3 and v_0 is the value determined in (c).

Present your results by completing the following table.

v0	theta0	rho	distance
10.0000	22.5000	0.9400	???
10.0000	22.5000	1.2900	???
???	22.5000	0.9400	8.9000
???	22.5000	1.2900	???

Which is more important, the air density or the jumper's initial velocity?

7.20. A pendulum is a point mass at the end of a weightless rod of length L supported by a frictionless pin. If gravity is the only force acting on the pendulum, its oscillation is modeled by

$$\ddot{\theta} = -(g/L)\sin\theta.$$

Here θ is the angular position of the rod, with $\theta = 0$ if the rod is hanging down from the pin and $\theta = \pi$ if the rod is precariously balanced above the pin. Take $L = 30$ cm and $g = 981$ cm/s^2. The initial conditions are

$$\theta(0) = \theta_0,$$
$$\dot{\theta}(0) = 0.$$

If the initial angle θ_0 is not too large, then the approximation

$$\sin\theta \approx \theta$$

leads to a *linearized* equation

$$\ddot{\theta} = -(g/L)\theta$$

that is easily solved.

(a) What is the period of oscillation for the linearized equation?
If we do not make the assumption that θ_0 is small and do not replace $\sin\theta$ by θ, then it turns out that the period T of the oscillatory motion is given by

$$T(\theta_0) = 4(L/g)^{1/2}K(\sin^2(\theta_0/2)),$$

where $K(s^2)$ is the complete elliptic integral of the first kind, given by

$$K(s^2) = \int_0^1 \frac{dt}{\sqrt{1 - s^2 t^2}\sqrt{1 - t^2}}.$$

(b) Compute and plot $T(\theta_0)$ for $0 \le \theta_0 \le 0.9999\pi$ two different ways. Use the MATLAB function ellipke and also use numerical quadrature with quadtx. Verify that the two methods yield the same results, to within the quadrature tolerance.
(c) Verify that for small θ_0 the linear equation and the nonlinear equation have approximately the same period.
(d) Compute the solutions to the nonlinear model over one period for several different values of θ_0, including values near 0 and near π. Superimpose the phase plane plots of the solutions on one graph.

7.21. What effect does the burning of fossil fuels have on the carbon dioxide in the earth's atmosphere? Even though today carbon dioxide accounts for only about 350 parts per million of the atmosphere, any increase has profound implications for our climate. An informative background article is available at a Web site maintained by the Lighthouse Foundation [39].

A model developed by J. C. G. Walker [65] was brought to our attention by Eric Roden. The model simulates the interaction of the various forms of carbon that are stored in three regimes: the atmosphere, the shallow ocean, and the deep ocean. The five principal variables in the model are all functions of time:

p, partial pressure of carbon dioxide in the atmosphere;

σ_s, total dissolved carbon concentration in the shallow ocean;

σ_d, total dissolved carbon concentration in the deep ocean;

α_s, alkalinity in the shallow ocean;

α_d, alkalinity in the deep ocean.

Three additional quantities are involved in equilibrium equations in the shallow ocean:

h_s, hydrogen carbonate in the shallow ocean;

c_s, carbonate in the shallow ocean;

p_s, partial pressure of gaseous carbon dioxide in the shallow ocean.

The rate of change of the five principal variables is given by five ordinary differential equations. The exchange between the atmosphere and the shallow ocean involves a constant characteristic transfer time d and a source term $f(t)$:

$$\frac{dp}{dt} = \frac{p_s - p}{d} + \frac{f(t)}{\mu_1}.$$

The equations describing the exchange between the shallow and deep oceans involve v_s and v_d, the volumes of the two regimes:

$$\frac{d\sigma_s}{dt} = \frac{1}{v_s}\left((\sigma_d - \sigma_s)w - k_1 - \frac{p_s - p}{d}\mu_2\right),$$

$$\frac{d\sigma_d}{dt} = \frac{1}{v_d}\left(k_1 - (\sigma_d - \sigma_s)w\right),$$

$$\frac{d\alpha_s}{dt} = \frac{1}{v_s}\left((\alpha_d - \alpha_s)w - k_2\right),$$

$$\frac{d\alpha_d}{dt} = \frac{1}{v_d}\left(k_2 - (\alpha_d - \alpha_s)w\right).$$

The equilibrium between carbon dioxide and the carbonates dissolved in the shallow ocean is described by three nonlinear algebraic equations:

$$h_s = \frac{\sigma_s - \left(\sigma_s^2 - k_3\alpha_s(2\sigma_s - \alpha_s)\right)^{1/2}}{k_3},$$

$$c_s = \frac{\alpha_s - h_s}{2},$$

$$p_s = k_4\frac{h_s^2}{c_s}.$$

The numerical values of the constants involved in the model are

$$d = 8.64,$$
$$\mu_1 = 4.95 \cdot 10^2,$$
$$\mu_2 = 4.95 \cdot 10^{-2},$$
$$v_s = 0.12,$$
$$v_d = 1.23,$$
$$w = 10^{-3},$$
$$k_1 = 2.19 \cdot 10^{-4},$$
$$k_2 = 6.12 \cdot 10^{-5},$$
$$k_3 = 0.997148,$$
$$k_4 = 6.79 \cdot 10^{-2}.$$

The source term $f(t)$ describes the burning of fossil fuels in the modern industrial era. We will use a time interval that starts about a thousand years ago and extends a few thousand years into the future:

$$1000 \leq t \leq 5000.$$

The initial values at $t = 1000$,

$$p = 1.00,$$
$$\sigma_s = 2.01,$$
$$\sigma_d = 2.23,$$
$$\alpha_s = 2.20,$$
$$\alpha_d = 2.26,$$

represent preindustrial equilibrium and remain nearly constant as long as the source term $f(t)$ is zero.

The following table describes one scenario for a source term $f(t)$ that models the release of carbon dioxide from burning fossil fuels, especially gasoline. The amounts begin to be significant after 1850, peak near the end of this century, and then decrease until the supply is exhausted.

year	rate
1000	0.0
1850	0.0
1950	1.0
1980	4.0
2000	5.0
2050	8.0
2080	10.0
2100	10.5
2120	10.0
2150	8.0
2225	3.5

2300	2.0
2500	0.0
5000	0.0

Figure 7.10 shows this source term and its effect on the atmosphere and the ocean. The three graphs in the lower half of the figure show the atmospheric, shallow ocean, and deep ocean carbon. (The two alkalinity values are not plotted at all because they are almost constant throughout this entire simulation.) Initially, the carbon in the three regimes is nearly at equilibrium and so the amounts hardly change before 1850. Over the period $1850 \le t \le 2500$, the upper half of Figure 7.10 shows the additional carbon produced by burning fossil fuels entering the system, and the lower half shows the system response. The atmosphere is the first to be affected, showing more than a fourfold increase in 500 years. Almost half of the carbon is then slowly transferred to the shallow ocean and eventually to the deep ocean.

(a) Reproduce Figure 7.10. Use `pchiptx` to interpolate the fuel table and `ode23tx` with the default tolerances to solve the differential equations.

(b) How do the amounts of carbon in the three regimes at year 5000 compare with the amounts at year 1000?

(c) When does the atmospheric carbon dioxide reach its maximum?

(d) These equations are mildly stiff, because the various chemical reactions take place on very different time scales. If you zoom in on some portions of the graphs, you

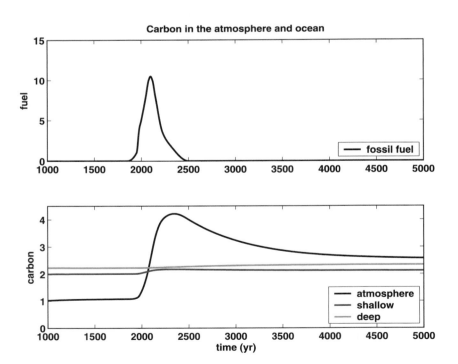

Figure 7.10. *Carbon in the atmosphere and ocean.*

should see a characteristic sawtooth behavior caused by the small time steps required by ode23tx. Find such a region.

(e) Experiment with other MATLAB ordinary differential equation solvers, including ode23, ode45, ode113, ode23s, and ode15s. Try various tolerances and report computational costs by using something like

```
odeset('RelTol',1.e-6,'AbsTol',1.e-6,'stats','on');
```

Which method is preferable for this problem?

7.22. This problem makes use of quadrature, ordinary differential equations, and zero finding to study a nonlinear boundary value problem. The function $y(x)$ is defined on the interval $0 \le x \le 1$ by

$$y'' = y^2 - 1,$$
$$y(0) = 0,$$
$$y(1) = 1.$$

This problem can be solved four different ways. Plot the four solutions obtained on a single figure, using subplot(2,2,1),..., subplot(2,2,4).

(a) Shooting method. Suppose we know the value of $\eta = y'(0)$. Then we could use an ordinary differential equation solver like ode23tx or ode45 to solve the initial value problem

$$y'' = y^2 - 1,$$
$$y(0) = 0,$$
$$y'(0) = \eta.$$

on the interval $0 \le x \le 1$. Each value of η determines a different solution $y(x; \eta)$ and corresponding value for $y(1; \eta)$. The desired boundary condition $y(1) = 1$ leads to the definition of a function of η:

$$f(\eta) = y(1; \eta) - 1.$$

Write a MATLAB function whose argument is η. This function should solve the ordinary differential equation initial problem and return $f(\eta)$. Then use fzero or fzerotx to find a value η_* so that $f(\eta_*) = 0$. Finally, use this η_* in the initial value problem to get the desired $y(x)$. Report the value of η_* you obtain.

(b) Quadrature. Observe that $y'' = y^2 - 1$ can be written

$$\frac{d}{dx}\left(\frac{(y')^2}{2} - \frac{y^3}{3} + y\right) = 0.$$

This means that the expression

$$\kappa = \frac{(y')^2}{2} - \frac{y^3}{3} + y$$

is actually constant. Because $y(0) = 0$, we have $y'(0) = \sqrt{2\kappa}$. So, if we could find the constant κ, the boundary value problem would be converted into an initial value problem. Integrating the equation

$$\frac{dx}{dy} = \frac{1}{\sqrt{2(\kappa + y^3/3 - y)}}$$

gives

$$x = \int_0^y h(y, \kappa)\, dy,$$

where

$$h(y, \kappa) = \frac{1}{\sqrt{2(\kappa + y^3/3 - y)}}.$$

This, together with the boundary condition $y(1) = 1$, leads to the definition of a function $g(\kappa)$:

$$g(\kappa) = \int_0^1 h(y, \kappa)\, dy \; - \; 1.$$

You need two MATLAB functions, one that computes $h(y, \kappa)$ and one that computes $g(\kappa)$. They can be two separate M-files, but a better idea is to make $h(y, \kappa)$ a function within $g(\kappa)$. The function $g(\kappa)$ should use quadtx to evaluate the integral of $h(y, \kappa)$. The parameter κ is passed as an extra argument from g, through quadtx, to h. Then fzerotx can be used to find a value κ_* so that $g(\kappa_*) = 0$. Finally, this κ_* provides the second initial value necessary for an ordinary differential equation solver to compute $y(x)$. Report the value of κ_* you obtain.

(c and d) Nonlinear finite differences. Partition the interval into $n + 1$ equal subintervals with spacing $h = 1/(n + 1)$:

$$x_i = ih, \; i = 0, \ldots, n + 1.$$

Replace the differential equation with a nonlinear system of difference equations involving n unknowns, $y_1, y_2, \ldots, y_n$:

$$y_{i+1} - 2y_i + y_{i-1} = h^2(y_i^2 - 1), \; i = 1, \ldots, n.$$

The boundary conditions are $y_0 = 0$ and $y_{n+1} = 1$.

A convenient way to compute the vector of second differences involves the n-by-n tridiagonal matrix A with -2's on the diagonal, 1's on the super- and subdiagonals, and 0's elsewhere. You can generate a sparse form of this matrix with

```
e = ones(n,1);
A = spdiags([e -2*e e],[-1 0 1],n,n);
```

The boundary conditions $y_0 = 0$ and $y_{n+1} = 1$ can be represented by the n-vector b, with $b_i = 0, i = 1, \ldots, n - 1$, and $b_n = 1$. The vector formulation of the nonlinear difference equation is

$$Ay + b = h^2(y^2 - 1),$$

where y^2 is the vector containing the squares of the elements of y, that is, the MATLAB element-by-element power y.^2. There are at least two ways to solve this system.
(c) Linear iteration. This is based on writing the difference equation in the form

$$Ay = h^2(y^2 - 1) - b.$$

Start with an initial guess for the solution vector y. The iteration consists of plugging the current y into the right-hand side of this equation and then solving the resulting linear system for a new y. This makes repeated use of the sparse backslash operator with the iterated assignment statement

```
y = A\(h^2*(y.^2 - 1) - b)
```

It turns out that this iteration converges linearly and provides a robust method for solving the nonlinear difference equations. Report the value of n you use and the number of iterations required.
(d) Newton's method. This is based on writing the difference equation in the form

$$F(y) = Ay + b - h^2(y^2 - 1) = 0.$$

Newton's method for solving $F(y) = 0$ requires a many-variable analogue of the derivative $F'(y)$. The analogue is the Jacobian, the matrix of partial derivatives

$$J = \frac{\partial F_i}{\partial y_j} = A - h^2 \mathrm{diag}(2y).$$

In MATLAB, one step of Newton's method would be

```
F = A*y + b - h^2*(y.^2 - 1);
J = A - h^2*spdiags(2*y,0,n,n);
y = y - J\F;
```

With a good starting guess, Newton's method converges in a handful of iterations. Report the value of n you use and the number of iterations required.

7.23. The double pendulum is a classical physics model system that exhibits chaotic motion if the initial angles are large enough. The model, shown in Figure 7.11, involves two weights, or *bobs*, attached by weightless, rigid rods to each other and to a fixed pivot. There is no friction, so once initiated, the motion continues forever. The motion is fully described by the two angles θ_1 and θ_2 that the rods make with the negative y-axis.
Let m_1 and m_2 be the masses of the bobs and ℓ_1 and ℓ_2 be the lengths of the rods. The positions of the bobs are

$$x_1 = \ell_1 \sin \theta_1, \quad y_1 = -\ell_1 \cos \theta_1,$$
$$x_2 = \ell_1 \sin \theta_1 + \ell_2 \sin \theta_2, \quad y_2 = -\ell_1 \cos \theta_1 - \ell_2 \cos \theta_2.$$

The only external force is gravity, denoted by g. Analysis based on the Lagrangian formulation of classical mechanics leads to a pair of coupled, second-order, nonlinear

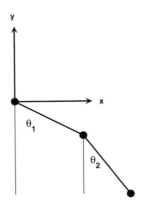

Figure 7.11. *Double pendulum.*

ordinary differential equations for the two angles $\theta_1(t)$ and $\theta_2(t)$:

$$(m_1 + m_2)\ell_1\ddot{\theta}_1 + m_2\ell_2\ddot{\theta}_2 \cos(\theta_1 - \theta_2) = -g(m_1 + m_2)\sin\theta_1$$
$$-m_2\ell_2\dot{\theta}_2^2 \sin(\theta_1 - \theta_2),$$
$$m_2\ell_1\ddot{\theta}_1 \cos(\theta_1 - \theta_2) + m_2\ell_2\ddot{\theta}_2 = -gm_2\sin\theta_2 + m_2\ell_1\dot{\theta}_1^2 \sin(\theta_1 - \theta_2).$$

To rewrite these equations as a first-order system, introduce the 4-by-1 column vector $u(t)$:

$$u = [\theta_1, \theta_2, \dot{\theta}_1, \dot{\theta}_2]^T.$$

With $m_1 = m_2 = \ell_1 = \ell_2 = 1$, $c = \cos(u_1 - u_2)$, and $s = \sin(u_1 - u_2)$, the equations become

$$\dot{u}_1 = u_3,$$
$$\dot{u}_2 = u_4,$$
$$2\dot{u}_3 + c\dot{u}_4 = -g\sin u_1 - su_4^2,$$
$$c\dot{u}_3 + \dot{u}_4 = -g\sin u_2 + su_3^2.$$

Let $M = M(u)$ denote the 4-by-4 *mass matrix*

$$M = \begin{pmatrix} 1 & 0 & 0 & 0 \\ 0 & 1 & 0 & 0 \\ 0 & 0 & 2 & c \\ 0 & 0 & c & 1 \end{pmatrix}$$

and let $f = f(u)$ denote the 4-by-1 nonlinear *force function*

$$f = \begin{pmatrix} u_3 \\ u_4 \\ -g\sin u_1 - su_4^2 \\ -g\sin u_2 + su_3^2 \end{pmatrix}.$$

In matrix-vector notation, the equations are simply

$$M\dot{u} = f.$$

This is an *implicit* system of differential equations involving a nonconstant, nonlinear mass matrix. The double pendulum problem is usually formulated without the mass matrix, but larger problems, with more degrees of freedom, are frequently in implicit form. In some situations, the mass matrix is singular and it is not possible to write the equations in explicit form.

The NCM M-file `swinger` provides an interactive graphical implementation of these equations. The initial position is determined by specifying the starting coordinates of the second bob, (x_2, y_2), either as arguments to `swinger` or by using the mouse. In most situations, this does not uniquely determine the starting position of the first bob, but there are only two possibilities and one of them is chosen arbitrarily. The initial velocities, $\dot{\theta}_1$ and $\dot{\theta}_2$, are zero.

The numerical solution is carried out by `ode23` because our textbook code, `ode23tx`, cannot handle implicit equations. The call to `ode23` involves using `odeset` to specify the functions that generate the mass matrix and do the plotting

```
opts = odeset('mass',@swingmass, ...
        'outputfcn',@swingplot);
ode23(@swingrhs,tspan,u0,opts);
```

The mass matrix function is

```
function M = swingmass(t,u)
c = cos(u(1)-u(2));
M = [1 0 0 0; 0 1 0 0; 0 0 2 c; 0 0 c 1];
```

The driving force function is

```
function f = swingrhs(t,u)
g = 1;
s = sin(u(1)-u(2));
f = [u(3); u(4); -2*g*sin(u(1))-s*u(4)^2;
     -g*sin(u(2))+s*u(3)^2];
```

It would be possible to have just one ordinary differential equation function that returns M\f, but we want to emphasize the implicit facility.

An internal function `swinginit` converts a specified starting point (x, y) to a pair of angles (θ_1, θ_2). If (x, y) is outside the circle

$$\sqrt{x^2 + y^2} > \ell_1 + \ell_2,$$

then the pendulum cannot reach the specified point. In this case, we straighten out the pendulum with $\theta_1 = \theta_2$ and point it in the given direction. If (x, y) is inside the circle of radius two, we return one of the two possible configurations that reach to that point.

Here are some questions to guide your investigation of swinger.

(a) When the initial point is outside the circle of radius two, the two rods start out as one. If the initial angle is not too large, the double pendulum continues to act pretty much like a single pendulum. But if the initial angles are large enough, chaotic motion ensues. Roughly what initial angles lead to chaotic motion?

(b) The default initial condition is

```
swinger(0.862,-0.994)
```

Why is this orbit interesting? Can you find any similar orbits?

(c) Run swinger for a while, then click on its stop button. Go to the MATLAB command line and type get(gcf,'userdata'). What is returned?

(d) Modify swinginit so that, when the initial point is inside the circle of radius two, the other possible initial configuration is chosen.

(e) Modify swinger so that masses other than $m_1 = m_2 = 1$ are possible.

(f) Modify swinger so that lengths other than $\ell_1 = \ell_2 = 1$ are possible. This is trickier than changing the masses because the initial geometry is involved.

(g) What role does gravity play? How would the behavior of a double pendulum change if you could take it to the moon? How does changing the value of g in swingrhs affect the speed of the graphics display, the step sizes chosen by the ordinary differential equation solver, and the computed values of t?

(h) Combine swingmass and swingrhs into one function, swingode. Eliminate the mass option and use ode23tx instead of ode23.

(i) Are these equations stiff?

(j) This is a difficult question. The statement swinger(0,2) tries to delicately balance the pendulum above its pivot point. The pendulum does stay there for a while, but then loses its balance. Observe the value of t displayed in the title for swinger(0,2). What force knocks the pendulum away from the vertical position? At what value of t does this force become noticeable?

Chapter 8

Fourier Analysis

We all use Fourier analysis every day without even knowing it. Cell phones, disc drives, DVDs, and JPEGs all involve fast finite Fourier transforms. This chapter discusses both the computation and the interpretation of FFTs.

The acronym FFT is ambiguous. The first F stands for both "fast" and "finite." A more accurate abbreviation would be FFFT, but nobody wants to use that. In MATLAB the expression fft(x) computes the finite Fourier transform of any vector x. The computation is fast if the integer n = length(x) is the product of powers of small primes. We discuss this algorithm in section 8.6.

8.1 Touch-Tone Dialing

Touch-tone telephone dialing is an example of everyday use of Fourier analysis. The basis for touch-tone dialing is the Dual Tone Multi-Frequency (DTMF) system. The program touchtone demonstrates how DTMF tones are generated and decoded. The telephone dialing pad acts as a 4-by-3 matrix (Figure 8.1). Associated with each row and column is a frequency. These basic frequencies are

```
fr = [697 770 852 941];
fc = [1209 1336 1477];
```

If s is a character that labels one of the buttons on the keypad, the corresponding row index k and column index j can be found with

```
switch s
   case '*', k = 4; j = 1;
   case '0', k = 4; j = 2;
   case '#', k = 4; j = 3;
   otherwise,
      d = s-'0'; j = mod(d-1,3)+1; k = (d-j)/3+1;
end
```

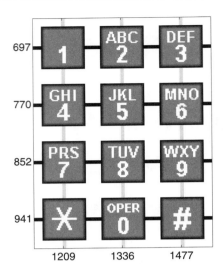

Figure 8.1. *Telephone keypad.*

A key parameter in digital sound is the sampling rate.

```
Fs = 32768
```

A vector of points in the time interval $0 \le t \le 0.25$ at this sampling rate is

```
t = 0:1/Fs:0.25
```

The tone generated by the button in position (k,j) is obtained by superimposing the two
fundamental tones with frequencies fr(k) and fc(j).

```
y1 = sin(2*pi*fr(k)*t);
y2 = sin(2*pi*fc(j)*t);
y = (y1 + y2)/2;
```

If your computer is equipped with a sound card, the MATLAB statement

```
sound(y,Fs)
```

plays the tone.

Figure 8.2 is the display produced by touchtone for the '1' button. The top
subplot depicts the two underlying frequencies and the bottom subplot shows a portion of
the signal obtained by averaging the sine waves with those frequencies.

The data file touchtone.mat contains a recording of a telephone being dialed. Is it
possible to determine the phone number by listening to the signal generated? The statement

```
load touchtone
```

loads both a signal y and a sample rate Fs in the workspace. In order to reduce file size,
the vector y has been saved with 8-bit integer components in the range $-127 \le y_k \le 127$.

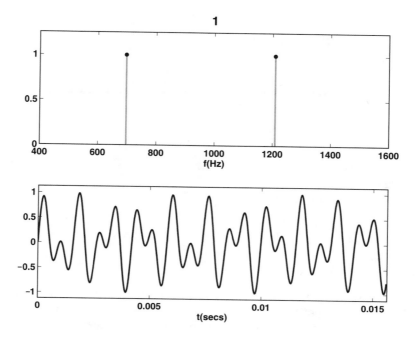

Figure 8.2. *The tone generated by the 1 button.*

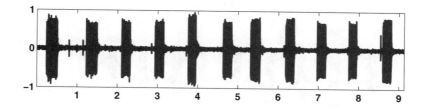

Figure 8.3. *Recording of an 11-digit telephone number.*

The statement

```
y = double(y)/128;
```

rescales the vector and converts it to double precision for later use. The statements

```
n = length(y);
t = (0:n-1)/Fs
```

reproduce the sample times of the recording. The last component of t is 9.1309, indicating that the recording lasts a little over 9 s. Figure 8.3 is a plot of the entire signal.

This signal is noisy. You can even see small spikes on the graph at the times the buttons were clicked. It is easy to see that 11 digits were dialed, but, on this scale, it is impossible to determine the specific digits.

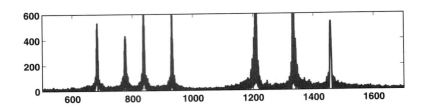

Figure 8.4. *FFT of the recorded signal.*

Figure 8.4 shows the magnitude of the FFT of the signal, which is the key to determining the individual digits.

The plot was produced with

```
p = abs(fft(y));
f = (0:n-1)*(Fs/n);
plot(f,p);
axis([500 1700 0 600])
```

The *x*-axis corresponds to frequency. The `axis` settings limit the display to the range of the DTMF frequencies. There are seven peaks, corresponding to the seven basic frequencies. This overall FFT shows that all seven frequencies are present someplace in the signal, but it does not help determine the individual digits.

The `touchtone` program also lets you break the signal into 11 equal segments and analyze each segment separately. Figure 8.5 is the display from the first segment.

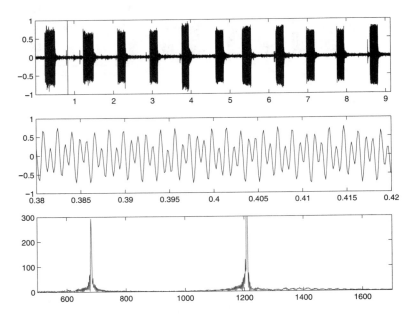

Figure 8.5. *The first segment and its FFT.*

For this segment, there are only two peaks, indicating that only two of the basic frequencies are present in this portion of the signal. These two frequencies come from the `'1'` button. You can also see that the waveform of a short portion of the first segment is similar to the waveform that our synthesizer produces for the `'1'` button. So we can conclude that the number being dialed in `touchtones` starts with a 1. Exercise 8.1 asks you to continue the analysis and identify the complete phone number.

8.2 Finite Fourier Transform

The finite, or discrete, Fourier transform of a complex vector y with n elements is another complex vector Y with n elements

$$Y_k = \sum_{j=0}^{n-1} \omega^{jk} y_j,$$

where ω is a complex nth root of unity:

$$\omega = e^{-2\pi i/n}.$$

In this chapter, the mathematical notation follows conventions common in signal processing literature where $i = \sqrt{-1}$ is the complex unit and j and k are indices that run from 0 to $n - 1$.

The Fourier transform can be expressed with matrix-vector notation:

$$Y = Fy,$$

where the Fourier matrix F has elements

$$f_{k,j} = \omega^{jk}.$$

It turns out that F is nearly its own inverse. More precisely, F^H, the complex conjugate transpose of F, satisfies

$$F^H F = nI,$$

so

$$F^{-1} = \frac{1}{n} F^H.$$

This allows us to invert the Fourier transform:

$$y = \frac{1}{n} F^H Y.$$

Hence

$$y_j = \frac{1}{n} \sum_{k=0}^{n-1} Y_k \bar{\omega}^{jk},$$

where $\bar{\omega}$ is the complex conjugate of ω:

$$\bar{\omega} = e^{2\pi i/n}.$$

We should point out that this is not the only notation for the finite Fourier transform in common use. The minus sign in the definition of ω after the first equation sometimes occurs instead in the definition of $\bar{\omega}$ used in the inverse transform. The $1/n$ scaling factor in the inverse transform is sometimes replaced with $1/\sqrt{n}$ scaling factors in both transforms.

In MATLAB, the Fourier matrix F can be generated for any given n by

```
omega = exp(-2*pi*i/n);
j = 0:n-1;
k = j'
F = omega.^(k*j)
```

The quantity $k*j$ is an *outer product*, an n-by-n matrix whose elements are the products of the elements of two vectors. However, the built-in function fft takes the finite Fourier transform of each column of a matrix argument, so an easier, and quicker, way to generate F is

```
F = fft(eye(n))
```

8.3 fftgui

The GUI fftgui allows you to investigate properties of the finite Fourier transform. If y is a vector containing a few dozen elements,

```
fftgui(y)
```

produces four plots.

```
real(y)             imag(y)
real(fft(y))        imag(fft(y))
```

You can use the mouse to move any of the points in any of the plots, and the points in the other plots respond.

Please run fftgui and try the following examples. Each illustrates some property of the Fourier transform. If you start with no arguments,

```
fftgui
```

all four plots are initialized to zeros(1,32). Click your mouse in the upper left-hand corner of the upper left-hand plot. You are taking the fft of the zeroth unit vector, with one in the first component and zeros elsewhere. This should produce Figure 8.6.

The real part of the result is constant and the imaginary part is zero. You can also see this from the definition

$$Y_k = \sum_{j=0}^{n-1} y_j e^{-2ijk\pi/n}, \ k = 0, \ldots, n-1$$

if $y_0 = 1$ and $y_1 = \cdots = y_{n-1} = 0$. The result is

$$Y_k = 1 \cdot e^0 + 0 + \cdots + 0 = 1 \text{ for all } k.$$

Click y_0 again, hold the mouse down, and move the mouse vertically. The amplitude of the constant result varies accordingly.

Next try the second unit vector. Use the mouse to set $y_0 = 0$ and $y_1 = 1$. This should produce Figure 8.7. You are seeing the graph of

$$Y_k = 0 + 1 \cdot e^{-2ik\pi/n} + 0 + \cdots + 0.$$

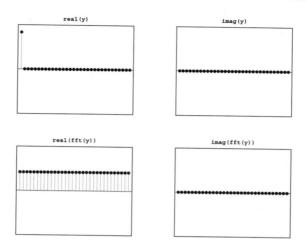

Figure 8.6. *FFT of the first unit vector is constant.*

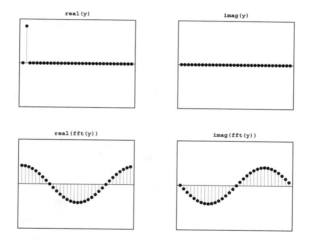

Figure 8.7. *FFT of the second unit vector is a pure sinusoid.*

The nth root of unity can also be written

$$\omega = \cos \delta - i \sin \delta, \text{ where } \delta = 2\pi / n.$$

Consequently, for $k = 0, \ldots, n - 1$,

$$\text{real}(Y_k) = \cos k\delta, \quad \text{imag}(Y_k) = -\sin k\delta.$$

We have sampled two trig functions at n equally spaced points in the interval $0 \le x < 2\pi$. The first sample point is $x = 0$ and the last sample point is $x = 2\pi - \delta$.

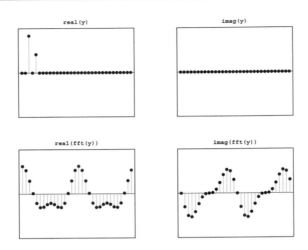

Figure 8.8. *FFT is the sum of two sinusoids.*

Now set $y_2 = 1$ and vary y_4 with the mouse. One snapshot is Figure 8.8. We have graphs of

$$\cos 2k\delta + \eta \cos 4k\delta \text{ and } -\sin 2k\delta - \eta \sin 4k\delta$$

for various values of $\eta = y_4$.

The point just to the right of the midpoint of the x-axis is particularly important. It is known as the *Nyquist point*. With the points numbered from 0 to $n - 1$ for even n, it's the point with index $\frac{n}{2}$. If $n = 32$, it's point number 16. Figure 8.9 shows that the fft of a unit vector at the Nyquist point is a sequence of alternating $+1$'s and -1's.

Now let's look at some symmetries in the FFT. Make several random clicks on the real(y) plot. Leave the imag(y) plot flat zero. Figure 8.10 shows an example. Look carefully at the two fft plots. Ignoring the first point in each plot, the real part is symmetric about the Nyquist point and the imaginary part is antisymmetric about the Nyquist point. More precisely, if y is any real vector of length n and $Y = \text{fft}(y)$, then

$$\text{real}(Y_0) = \sum y_j,$$
$$\text{imag}(Y_0) = 0,$$
$$\text{real}(Y_j) = \text{real}(Y_{n-j}), \quad j = 1, \ldots, n/2,$$
$$\text{imag}(Y_j) = -\text{imag}(Y_{n-j}), \quad j = 1, \ldots, n/2.$$

8.4 Sunspots

For centuries, people have noted that the face of the sun is not constant or uniform in appearance, but that darker regions appear at random locations on a cyclical basis. This activity is correlated with weather and other economically significant terrestrial phenomena. In 1848, Rudolf Wolfer proposed a rule that combined the number and size of these sunspots

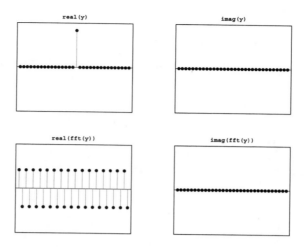

Figure 8.9. *The Nyquist point.*

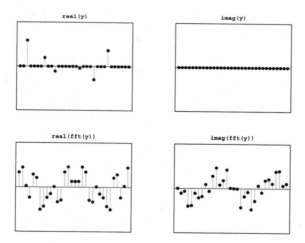

Figure 8.10. *Symmetry about the Nyquist point.*

into a single index. Using archival records, astronomers have applied Wolfer's rule to determine sunspot activity back to the year 1700. Today the sunspot index is measured by many astronomers, and the worldwide distribution of the data is coordinated by the Solar Influences Data Center at the Royal Observatory of Belgium [56].

The text file `sunspot.dat` in the MATLAB demos directory has two columns of numbers. The first column is the years from 1700 to 1987 and the second column is the average Wolfer sunspot number for each year.

```
load sunspot.dat
t = sunspot(:,1)';
```

```
wolfer = sunspot(:,2)';
n = length(wolfer);
```

There is a slight upward trend to the data. A least squares fit gives the trend line.

```
c = polyfit(t,wolfer,1);
trend = polyval(c,t);
plot(t,[wolfer; trend],'-',t,wolfer,'k.')
xlabel('year')
ylabel('Wolfer index')
title('Sunspot index with linear trend')
```

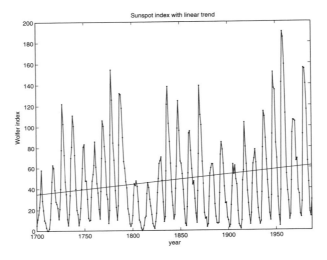

Figure 8.11. *Sunspot index.*

You can definitely see the cyclic nature of the phenomenon (Figure 8.11). The peaks and valleys are a little more than 10 years apart.

Now subtract off the linear trend and take the FFT.

```
y = wolfer - trend;
Y = fft(y);
```

The vector $|Y|^2$ is the *power* in the signal. A plot of power versus frequency is a *periodogram* (Figure 8.12). We prefer to plot $|Y|$, rather than $|Y|^2$, because the scaling is not so exaggerated. The sample rate for these data is one observation per year, so the frequency f has units of cycles per year.

```
Fs = 1;   % Sample rate
f = (0:n/2)*Fs/n;
pow = abs(Y(1:n/2+1));
pmax = 5000;
```

```
plot([f; f],[0*pow; pow],'c-', f,pow,'b.', ...
    'linewidth',2,'markersize',16)
axis([0 .5 0 pmax])
xlabel('cycles/year')
ylabel('power')
title('Periodogram')
```

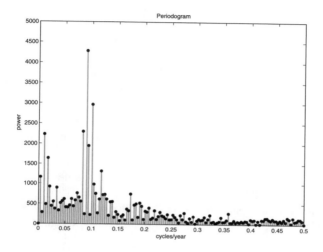

Figure 8.12. *Periodogram of the sunspot index.*

The maximum power occurs near frequency = 0.09 cycles/year. We would like to know the corresponding period in years/cycle. Let's zoom in on the plot and use the reciprocal of frequency to label the x-axis.

```
k = 0:44;
f = k/n;
pow = pow(k+1);
plot([f; f],[0*pow; pow],'c-',f,pow,'b.', ...
    'linewidth',2,'markersize',16)
axis([0 max(f) 0 pmax])
k = 2:3:41;
f = k/n;
period = 1./f;
periods = sprintf('%5.1f|',period);
set(gca,'xtick',f)
set(gca,'xticklabel',periods)
xlabel('years/cycle')
ylabel('power')
title('Periodogram detail')
```

As expected, there is a very prominent cycle with a length of about 11.1 years

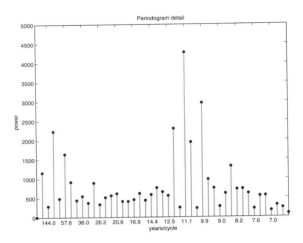

Figure 8.13. *Detail of periodogram shows* 11-*year cycle.*

(Figure 8.13). This shows that, over the last 300 years, the period of the sunspot cycle
has been slightly over 11 years.

The code for this section is in the NCM collection `sunspotstx.m`. The older
version in `toolbox/matlab/demos/sunspots.m` uses slightly different notation.

8.5   Periodic Time Series

The tones generated by a touch-tone telephone and the Wolfer sunspot index are two examples of periodic time series, that is, functions of time that exhibit periodic behavior, at
least approximately. Fourier analysis allows us to estimate the period from a discrete set
of values sampled at a fixed rate. The following table shows the relationship between the
various quantities involved in this analysis.

`y`	data
`Fs`	samples/unit-time
`n = length(y)`	number of samples
`t = (0:n-1)/Fs`	total time
`dt = 1/Fs`	time increment
`Y = fft(y)`	finite Fourier transform
`abs(Y)`	amplitude of FFT
`abs(Y).^2`	power
`f = (0:n-1)*(Fs/n)`	frequency, cycles/unit-time
`(n/2)*(Fs/n) = Fs/2`	Nyquist frequency
`p = 1./f`	period, unit-time/cycle

The periodogram is a plot of the FFT amplitude `abs(Y)`, or power `abs(Y).^2`,
versus the frequency `f`. You only need to plot the first half because the second half is a
reflection of the first half about the Nyquist frequency.

8.6 Fast Finite Fourier Transform

One-dimensional FFTs with a million points and two-dimensional 1000-by-1000 transforms are common. The key to modern signal and image processing is the ability to do these computations rapidly.

Direct application of the definition

$$Y_k = \sum_{j=0}^{n-1} \omega^{jk} y_j, \ k = 0, \ldots, n-1,$$

requires n multiplications and n additions for each of the n components of Y for a total of $2n^2$ floating-point operations. This does not include the generation of the powers of ω. A computer capable of doing one multiplication and addition every microsecond would require a million seconds, or about 11.5 days, to do a million-point FFT.

Several people discovered fast FFT algorithms independently and many people have since contributed to their development, but it was a 1965 paper by John Tukey of Princeton University and John Cooley of IBM Research that is generally credited as the starting point for the modern usage of the FFT.

Modern fast FFT algorithms have computational complexity $O(n \log_2 n)$ instead of $O(n^2)$. If n is a power of 2, a one-dimensional FFT of length n requires fewer than $3n \log_2 n$ floating-point operations. For $n = 2^{20}$, that's a factor of almost 35,000 faster than $2n^2$. Even if $n = 1024 = 2^{10}$, the factor is about 70.

With MATLAB 6.5 and a 700 MHz Pentium laptop, the time required for fft(x) if length(x) is $2^{20} = 1048576$ is about 1 s. The built-in fft function is based on FFTW, "The Fastest Fourier Transform in the West," developed at M.I.T. by Matteo Frigo and Steven G. Johnson [21].

The key to the fast FFT algorithms is the fact that the square of the $2n$th root of unity is the nth root of unity. Using complex notation,

$$\omega = \omega_n = e^{-2\pi i/n},$$

we have

$$\omega_{2n}^2 = \omega_n.$$

The derivation of the fast algorithm starts with the definition of the finite Fourier transform:

$$Y_k = \sum_{j=0}^{n-1} \omega^{jk} y_j, \ k = 0, \ldots, n-1.$$

Assume that n is even and that $k \le n/2 - 1$. Divide the sum into terms with even subscripts and terms with odd subscripts.

$$Y_k = \sum_{even \ j} \omega^{jk} y_j + \sum_{odd \ j} \omega^{jk} y_j$$

$$= \sum_{j=0}^{n/2-1} \omega^{2jk} y_{2j} + \omega^k \sum_{j=0}^{n/2-1} \omega^{2jk} y_{2j+1}.$$

The two sums on the right are components of the FFTs of length $n/2$ of the portions of y with even and odd subscripts. In order to get the entire FFT of length n, we have to do two FFTs of length $n/2$, multiply one of these by powers of ω, and concatenate the results.

The relationship between an FFT of length n and two FFTs of length $n/2$ can be expressed compactly in MATLAB. If n = length(y) is even,

```
omega = exp(-2*pi*i/n);
k = (0:n/2-1)';
w = omega .^ k;
u = fft(y(1:2:n-1));
v = w.*fft(y(2:2:n));
```

then

```
fft(y) = [u+v; u-v];
```

Now, if n is not only even but actually a power of 2, the process can be repeated. The FFT of length n is expressed in terms of two FFTs of length $n/2$, then four FFTs of length $n/4$, then eight FFTs of length $n/8$, and so on until we reach n FFTs of length one. An FFT of length one is just the number itself. If $n = 2^p$, the number of steps in the recursion is p. There is $O(n)$ work at each step, so the total amount of work is

$$O(np) = O(n \log_2 n).$$

If n is not a power of two, it is still possible to express the FFT of length n in terms of several shorter FFTs. An FFT of length 100 is two FFTs of length 50, or four FFTs of length 25. An FFT of length 25 can be expressed in terms of five FFTs of length 5. If n is not a prime number, an FFT of length n can be expressed in terms of FFTs whose lengths divide n. Even if n is prime, it is possible to embed the FFT in another whose length can be factored. We do not go into the details of these algorithms here.

The fft function in older versions of MATLAB used fast algorithms if the length was a product of small primes. Beginning with MATLAB 6, the fft function uses fast algorithms even if the length is prime (see [21]).

8.7 ffttx

Our textbook function ffttx combines the two basic ideas of this chapter. If n is a power of 2, it uses the $O(n \log_2 n)$ fast algorithm. If n has an odd factor, it uses the fast recursion until it reaches an odd length, then sets up the discrete Fourier matrix and uses matrix-vector multiplication.

```
function y = ffttx(x)
%FFTTX Textbook Fast Finite Fourier Transform.
% FFTTX(X) computes the same finite Fourier transform
% as FFT(X).  The code uses a recursive divide and
% conquer algorithm for even order and matrix-vector
% multiplication for odd order.  If length(X) is m*p
% where m is odd and p is a power of 2, the computational
% complexity of this approach is O(m^2)*O(p*log2(p)).
```

```
x = x(:);
n = length(x);
omega = exp(-2*pi*i/n);

if rem(n,2) == 0
    % Recursive divide and conquer
    k = (0:n/2-1)';
    w = omega .^ k;
    u = ffttx(x(1:2:n-1));
    v = w.*ffttx(x(2:2:n));
    y = [u+v; u-v];
else
    % The Fourier matrix
    j = 0:n-1;
    k = j';
    F = omega .^ (k*j);
    y = F*x;
end
```

8.8 fftmatrix

The n-by-n matrix F generated by the MATLAB statement

```
F = fft(eye(n,n))
```

is a complex matrix whose elements are powers of the nth root of unity:

$$\omega = e^{-2\pi i/n}.$$

The statement

```
plot(fft(eye(n,n)))
```

connects the elements of each column of F and thereby generates a subgraph of the graph
on n points. If n is prime, connecting the elements of all columns generates the complete
graph on n points. If n is not prime, the sparsity of the graph of all columns is related to the
speed of the FFT algorithm. The graphs for $n = 8, 9, 10$, and 11 are shown in Figure 8.14.
Because $n = 11$ is prime, the corresponding graph shows all possible connections. But
the other three values of n are not prime. Some of the links in their graphs are missing,
indicating that the FFT of a vector with that many points can be computed more quickly.

The program fftmatrix allows you to investigate these graphs.

```
fftmatrix(n)
```

plots all the columns of the Fourier matrix of order n.

```
fftmatrix(n,j)
```

plots only the j+1st column.

```
fftmatrix
```

defaults to fftmatrix(10,4). In all cases, push buttons allow n, j and the choice
between one or all columns be changed.

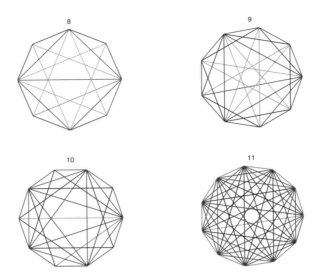

Figure 8.14. *Graphs of FFT matrix.*

8.9   Other Fourier Transforms and Series

We have been studying the finite Fourier transform, which converts one finite sequence of coefficients into another sequence of the same length, n. The transform is

$$Y_k = \sum_{j=0}^{n-1} y_j e^{-2ijk\pi/n}, \ k = 0, \ldots, n-1.$$

The inverse transform is

$$y_j = \frac{1}{n} \sum_{k=0}^{n-1} Y_k e^{2ijk\pi/n}, \ j = 0, \ldots, n-1.$$

The Fourier integral transform converts one complex function into another. The transform is

$$F(\mu) = \int_{-\infty}^{\infty} f(t) e^{-2\pi i \mu t} dt.$$

The inverse transform is

$$f(t) = \int_{-\infty}^{\infty} F(\mu) e^{2\pi i \mu t} d\mu.$$

The variables t and μ run over the entire real line. If t has units of seconds, then μ has units of radians per second. Both of the functions $f(t)$ and $F(\mu)$ are complex valued, but in most applications the imaginary part of $f(t)$ is zero.

Alternative units use $\nu = 2\pi\mu$, which has units of cycles or revolutions per second. With this change of variable, there are no factors of 2π in the exponentials, but there are factors of $1/\sqrt{2\pi}$ in front of the integrals, or a single factor of $1/(2\pi)$ in the inverse transform. The MATLAB Symbolic Toolbox uses this alternative notation with the single factor in the inverse transform.

A Fourier series converts a periodic function into an infinite sequence of Fourier coefficients. Let $f(t)$ be the periodic function and let L be its period, so

$$f(t + L) = f(t) \text{ for all } t.$$

The Fourier coefficients are given by integrals over the period

$$c_j = \frac{1}{L} \int_{-L/2}^{L/2} f(t)e^{-2\pi ijt}dt, \ \ j = \ldots, -1, 0, 1, \ldots.$$

With these coefficients, the complex form of the Fourier series is

$$f(t) = \sum_{j=-\infty}^{\infty} c_j e^{2\pi ijt/L}.$$

A discrete time Fourier transform converts an infinite sequence of data values into a periodic function. Let x_k be the sequence, with the index k taking on all integer values, positive and negative.

The discrete time Fourier transform is the complex-valued periodic function

$$X(e^{i\omega}) = \sum_{k=-\infty}^{\infty} x_k e^{ik\omega}.$$

The sequence can then be represented as

$$x_k = \frac{1}{2\pi} \int_{-\pi}^{\pi} X(e^{i\omega})e^{-ik\omega}d\omega, \ \ k = \ldots, -1, 0, 1, \ldots.$$

The Fourier integral transform involves only integrals. The finite Fourier transform involves only finite sums of coefficients. Fourier series and the discrete time Fourier transform involve both integrals and sequences. It is possible to "morph" any of the transforms into any of the others by taking limits or restricting domains.

Start with a Fourier series. Let L, the length of the period, become infinite and let j/L, the coefficient index scaled by the period length, become a continuous variable, μ. Then the Fourier coefficients c_j become the Fourier transform $F(\mu)$.

Again, start with a Fourier series. Interchanging the roles of the periodic function and the infinite sequence of coefficients leads to the discrete time Fourier transform.

Start with a Fourier series a third time. Now restrict t to a finite number of integral values, k, and restrict j to the same finite number of values. Then the Fourier coefficients become the finite Fourier transform.

In the Fourier integral transform context, Parseval's theorem says

$$\int_{-\infty}^{+\infty} |f(t)|^2 dt = \int_{-\infty}^{+\infty} |F(\mu)|^2 d\mu.$$

This quantity is known as the *total power* in a signal.

8.10   Further Reading

Van Loan [64] describes the computational framework for the fast transforms. A page of links at the FFTW Web site [22] provides useful information.

Exercises

8.1. What is the telephone number recorded in `touchtone.mat` and analyzed by `touchtone.m`?

8.2. Modify `touchtone.m` so that it can dial a telephone number specified by an input argument, such as `touchtone('1-800-555-1212')`.

8.3. Our version of `touchtone.m` breaks the recording into a fixed number of equally spaced segments, each corresponding to a single digit. Modify `touchtone` so that it automatically determines the number and the possibly disparate lengths of the segments.

8.4. Investigate the use of the MATLAB functions `audiorecorder` and `audioplayer`, or some other system for making digital recordings. Make a recording of a phone number and analyze it with your modified version of `touchtone.m`.

8.5. Recall that the Fourier matrix F is the n-by-n complex matrix with elements

$$f_{k,j} = \omega^{jk},$$

where

$$\omega = e^{-2\pi i/n}.$$

Show that $\frac{1}{\sqrt{n}}F$ is unitary. In other words, show that F^H, the complex conjugate transpose of F, satisfies

$$F^H F = nI.$$

The notation here is a little unusual for matrices because the subscripts j and k run from 0 to $n - 1$, instead of from 1 to n.

8.6. What relationship between `n` and `j` causes `fftmatrix(n,j)` to produce a five-point star? What relationship produces a regular pentagon?

8.7. *El Niño.* The climatological phenomenon *el Niño* results from changes in atmospheric pressure in the southern Pacific ocean. The 'Southern Oscillation Index' is the difference in atmospheric pressure between Easter Island and Darwin, Australia, measured at sea level at the same moment. The text file `elnino.dat` contains values of this index measured on a monthly basis over the 14-year period 1962 through 1975.
Your assignment is to carry out an analysis similar to the sunspot example on the *el Niño* data. The unit of time is one month instead of one year. You should find there is a prominent cycle with a period of 12 months and a second, less prominent, cycle with a longer period. This second cycle shows up in about three of the Fourier coefficients, so it is hard to measure its length, but see if you can make an estimate.

8.8. Train whistle. The MATLAB `demos` directory contains several sound samples. One of them is a train whistle. The statement

```
load train
```

gives you a long vector `y` and a scalar `Fs` whose value is the number of samples per second. The time increment is `1/Fs` seconds.

If your computer has sound capabilities, the statement

```
sound(y,Fs)
```

plays the signal, but you don't need that for this problem.

The data do not have a significant linear trend. There are two pulses of the whistle, but the harmonic content of both pulses is the same.

(a) Plot the data with time in seconds as the independent variable.

(b) Produce a periodogram with frequency in cycles/second as the independent variable.

(c) Identify the frequencies of the six peaks in the periodogram. You should find that ratios between these six frequencies are close to ratios between small integers. For example, one of the frequencies is 5/3 times another. The frequencies that are integer multiples of other frequencies are *overtones*. How many of the peaks are fundamental frequencies and how many are overtones?

8.9. Bird chirps. Analyze the `chirp` sound sample from the MATLAB demos directory. By ignoring a short portion at the end, it is possible to segment the signal into eight pieces of equal length, each containing one chirp. Plot the magnitude of the FFT of each segment. Use `subplot(4,2,k)` for `k = 1:8` and the same axis scaling for all subplots. Frequencies in the range from roughly 400 Hz to 800 Hz are appropriate. You should notice that one or two of the chirps have distinctive plots. If you listen carefully, you should be able to hear the different sounds.

Chapter 9

Random Numbers

This chapter describes algorithms for the generation of pseudorandom numbers with both uniform and normal distributions.

9.1 Pseudorandom Numbers

Here is an interesting number:

```
0.95012928514718
```

This is the first number produced by the MATLAB random number generator with its default settings. Start up a fresh MATLAB, set `format long`, type `rand`, and it's the number you get.

If all MATLAB users, all around the world, all on different computers, keep getting this same number, is it really "random"? No, it isn't. Computers are (in principle) deterministic machines and should not exhibit random behavior. If your computer doesn't access some external device, like a gamma ray counter or a clock, then it must really be computing *pseudorandom* numbers. Our favorite definition was given in 1951 by Berkeley professor D. H. Lehmer, a pioneer in computing and, especially, computational number theory:

> A random sequence is a vague notion ... in which each term is unpredictable to the uninitiated and whose digits pass a certain number of tests traditional with statisticians ...

9.2 Uniform Distribution

Lehmer also invented the *multiplicative congruential algorithm*, which is the basis for many of the random number generators in use today. Lehmer's generators involve three integer parameters, a, c, and m, and an initial value, x_0, called the *seed*. A sequence of integers is defined by

$$x_{k+1} = ax_k + c \bmod m.$$

The operation "mod m" means take the remainder after division by m. For example, with $a = 13, c = 0, m = 31$, and $x_0 = 1$, the sequence begins with

$$1, \ 13, \ 14, \ 27, \ 10, \ 6, \ 16, \ 22, \ 7, \ 29, \ 5, \ 3, \ldots.$$

What's the next value? Well, it looks pretty unpredictable, but you've been initiated. So you can compute $(13 \cdot 3)$ mod 31, which is 8. The first 30 terms in the sequence are a permutation of the integers from 1 to 30 and then the sequence repeats itself. It has a period equal to $m - 1$.

If a pseudorandom integer sequence with values between 0 and m is scaled by dividing by m, the result is floating-point numbers uniformly distributed in the interval $[0, 1]$. Our simple example begins with

$$0.0323, \ 0.4194, \ 0.4516, \ 0.8710, \ 0.3226, \ 0.1935, \ 0.5161, \ldots.$$

There is only a finite number of values, 30 in this case. The smallest value is $1/31$; the largest is $30/31$. Each one is equally probable in a long run of the sequence.

In the 1960s, the Scientific Subroutine Package (SSP) on IBM mainframe computers included a random number generator named RND or RANDU. It was a multiplicative congruential with parameters $a = 65539, c = 0$, and $m = 2^{31}$. With a 32-bit integer word size, arithmetic mod 2^{31} can be done quickly. Furthermore, because $a = 2^{16} + 3$, the multiplication by a can be done with a shift and an addition. Such considerations were important on the computers of that era, but they gave the resulting sequence a very undesirable property. The following relations are all taken mod 2^{31}:

$$x_{k+2} = (2^{16} + 3)x_{k+1} = (2^{16} + 3)^2 x_k$$
$$= (2^{32} + 6 \cdot 2^{16} + 9)x_k$$
$$= [6 \cdot (2^{16} + 3) - 9]x_k.$$

Hence

$$x_{k+2} = 6x_{k+1} - 9x_k \quad \text{for all } k.$$

As a result, there is an extremely high correlation among three successive random integers of the sequence generated by RANDU.

We have implemented this defective generator in an M-file `randssp`. A demonstration program `randgui` tries to compute π by generating random points in a cube and counting the fraction that actually lie within the inscribed sphere. With these M-files on your path, the statement

    randgui(@randssp)

will show the consequences of the correlation of three successive terms. The resulting pattern is far from random, but it can still be used to compute π from the ratio of the volumes of the cube and sphere.

For many years, the MATLAB uniform random number function, `rand`, was also a multiplicative congruential generator. The parameters were

$$a = 7^5 = 16807,$$
$$c = 0,$$
$$m = 2^{31} - 1 = 2147483647.$$

These values are recommended in a 1988 paper by Park and Miller [51].

This old MATLAB multiplicative congruential generator is available in the M-file `randmcg`. The statement

    randgui(@randmcg)

shows that the points do not suffer the correlation of the SSP generator. They generate a much better "random" cloud within the cube.

Like our toy generator, `randmcg` and the old version of the MATLAB function `rand` generate all real numbers of the form k/m for $k = 1, \ldots, m - 1$. The smallest and largest are 0.00000000046566 and 0.99999999953434. The sequence repeats itself after $m - 1$ values, which is a little over 2 billion numbers. A few years ago, that was regarded as plenty. But today, an 800 MHz Pentium laptop can exhaust the period in less than half an hour. Of course, to do anything useful with 2 billion numbers takes more time, but we would still like to have a longer period.

In 1995, version 5 of MATLAB introduced a completely different kind of random number generator. The algorithm is based on work of George Marsaglia, a professor at Florida State University and author of the classic analysis of random number generators, "Random numbers fall mainly in the planes" [40].

Marsaglia's generator [43] does not use Lehmer's congruential algorithm. In fact, there are no multiplications or divisions at all. It is specifically designed to produce floating-point values. The results are not just scaled integers. In place of a single seed, the new generator has 35 words of internal memory or *state*. Thirty-two of these words form a cache of floating-point numbers, z, between 0 and 1. The remaining three words contain an integer index i, which varies between 0 and 31, a single random integer j, and a "borrow" flag b. This entire state vector is built up a bit at a time during an initialization phase. Different values of j yield different initial states.

The generation of the ith floating-point number in the sequence involves a "subtract-with-borrow" step, where one number in the cache is replaced with the difference of two others:

$$z_i = z_{i+20} - z_{i+5} - b.$$

The three indices, i, $i + 20$, and $i + 5$, are all interpreted mod 32 (by using just their last five bits). The quantity b is left over from the previous step; it is either zero or a small positive value. If the computed z_i is positive, b is set to zero for the next step. But if the computed z_i is negative, it is made positive by adding 1.0 before it is saved and b is set to 2^{-53} for the next step. The quantity 2^{-53}, which is half of the MATLAB constant `eps`, is called one *ulp* because it is one *unit in the last place* for floating-point numbers slightly less than 1.

By itself, this generator would be almost completely satisfactory. Marsaglia has shown that it has a huge period—almost 2^{1430} values would be generated before it repeated itself. But it has one slight defect. All the numbers are the results of floating-point additions and subtractions of numbers in the initial cache, so they are all integer multiples of 2^{-53}. Consequently, many of the floating-point numbers in the interval [0, 1] are not represented.

The floating-point numbers between $1/2$ and 1 are equally spaced with a spacing of one ulp, and our subtract-with-borrow generator will eventually generate all of them. But numbers less than $1/2$ are more closely spaced and the generator would miss most of them. It would generate only half of the possible numbers in the interval [1/4, 1/2], only a quarter of the numbers in [1/8, 1/4], and so on. This is where the quantity j in the state vector comes in. It is the result of a separate, independent, random number generator based on bitwise logical operations. The floating-point fraction of each z_i is XORed with j to produce the result returned by the generator. This breaks up the even spacing of the numbers less than $1/2$. It is now theoretically possible to generate all the floating-point numbers between 2^{-53} and $1 - 2^{-53}$. We're not sure if they are all actually generated, but we don't know of any that can't be.

Figure 9.1 shows what the new generator is trying to accomplish. For this graph, one ulp is equal to 2^{-4} instead of 2^{-53}.

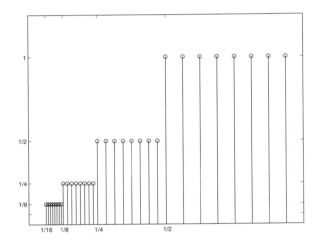

Figure 9.1. *Uniform distribution of floating-point numbers.*

The graph depicts the relative frequency of each of the floating-point numbers. A total of 32 floating-point numbers are shown. Eight of them are between $1/2$ and 1, and they are all equally like to occur. There are also eight numbers between $1/4$ and $1/2$, but, because this interval is only half as wide, each of them should occur only half as often. As we move to the left, each subinterval is half as wide as the previous one, but it still contains the same number of floating-point numbers, so their relative frequencies must be cut in half. Imagine this picture with 2^{53} numbers in each of 2^{32} smaller intervals and you will see what the new random number generator is doing.

With the additional bit fiddling, the period of the new generator becomes something like 2^{1492}. Maybe we should call it the Christopher Columbus generator. In any case, it will run for a very long time before it repeats itself.

9.3 Normal Distribution

Almost all algorithms for generating normally distributed random numbers are based on transformations of uniform distributions. The simplest way to generate an *m*-by-*n* matrix with approximately normally distributed elements is to use the expression

```
sum(rand(m,n,12),3) - 6
```

This works because R = rand(m,n,p) generates a three-dimensional uniformly distributed array and sum(R,3) sums along the third dimension. The result is a two-dimensional array with elements drawn from a distribution with mean $p/2$ and variance $p/12$ that approaches a normal distribution as p increases. If we take $p = 12$, we get a pretty good approximation to the normal distribution and we get the variance to be equal to one without any additional scaling. There are two difficulties with this approach. It requires twelve uniforms to generate one normal, so it is slow. And the finite p approximation causes it to have poor behavior in the tails of the distribution.

Older versions of MATLAB—before MATLAB 5—used the polar algorithm. This generates two values at a time. It involves finding a random point in the unit circle by generating uniformly distributed points in the $[-1, 1] \times [-1, 1]$ square and rejecting any outside the circle. Points in the square are represented by vectors with two components. The rejection portion of the code is

```
r = Inf;
while r > 1
    u = 2*rand(2,1)-1
    r = u'*u
end
```

For each point accepted, the polar transformation

```
v = sqrt(-2*log(r)/r)*u
```

produces a vector with two independent normally distributed elements. This algorithm does not involve any approximations, so it has the proper behavior in the tails of the distribution. But it is moderately expensive. Over 21% of the uniform numbers are rejected if they fall outside of the circle, and the square root and logarithm calculations contribute significantly to the cost.

Beginning with MATLAB 5, the normal random number generator randn uses a sophisticated table lookup algorithm, also developed by George Marsaglia. Marsaglia calls his approach the *ziggurat* algorithm. Ziggurats are ancient Mesopotamian terraced temple mounds that, mathematically, are two-dimensional step functions. A one-dimensional ziggurat underlies Marsaglia's algorithm.

Marsaglia has refined his ziggurat algorithm over the years. An early version is described in Knuth's classic *The Art of Computer Programming* [35]. The version used in MATLAB is described by Marsaglia and W. W. Tsang in [42]. A Fortran version is described in [34, sect. 10.7]. A more recent version is available in the online electronic *Journal of Statistical Software* [41]. We describe this recent version here because it is the most elegant. The version actually used in MATLAB is more complicated, but is based on the same ideas and is just as effective.

The probability density function, or *pdf*, of the normal distribution is the bell-shaped curve

$$f(x) = ce^{-x^2/2},$$

where $c = 1/(2\pi)^{1/2}$ is a normalizing constant that we can ignore. If we generate random points (x, y), uniformly distributed in the plane, and reject any of them that do not fall under this curve, the remaining x's form our desired normal distribution. The ziggurat algorithm covers the area under the pdf by a slightly larger area with n sections. Figure 9.2 has $n = 8$; actual code might use $n = 128$. The top $n - 1$ sections are rectangles. The bottom section is a rectangle together with an infinite tail under the graph of $f(x)$. The right-hand edges of the rectangles are at the points z_k, $k = 2, \ldots, n$, shown with circles in the picture. With $f(z_1) = 1$ and $f(z_{n+1}) = 0$, the height of the kth section is $f(z_k) - f(z_{k+1})$. The key idea is to choose the z_k's so that all n sections, including the unbounded one on the bottom, have the same area. There are other algorithms that approximate the area under the pdf with rectangles. The distinguishing features of Marsaglia's algorithm are the facts that the rectangles are horizontal and have equal areas.

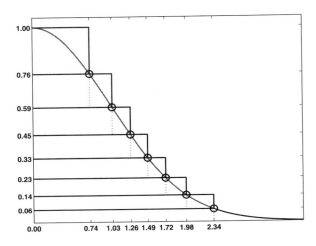

Figure 9.2. *The ziggurat algorithm.*

For a specified number, n, of sections, it is possible to solve a transcendental equation to find z_n, the point where the infinite tail meets the first rectangular section. In our picture with $n = 8$, it turns out that $z_n = 2.34$. In an actual code with $n = 128$, $z_n = 3.4426$. Once z_n is known, it is easy to compute the common area of the sections and the other right-hand endpoints z_k. It is also possible to compute $\sigma_k = z_{k-1}/z_k$, which is the fraction of each section that lies underneath the section above it. Let's call these fractional sections the *core* of the ziggurat. The right-hand edge of the core is the dotted line in our picture. The computation of these z_k's and σ_k's is done in an initialization section of code that is run only once.

After the initialization, normally distributed random numbers can be computed very quickly. The key portion of the code computes a single random integer, j, between 1 and n and a single uniformly distributed random number, u, between -1 and 1. A check is then made to see if u falls in the core of the jth section. If it does, then we know that uz_j is the x-coordinate of a point under the pdf and this value can be returned as one sample from the normal distribution. The code looks something like this.

```
j = ceil(128*rand);
u = 2*rand-1;
```

```
if abs(u) < sigma(j)
    r = u*z(j);
    return
end
```

Most of the σ_j's are greater than 0.98, and the test is true over 97% of the time. One normal random number can usually be computed from one random integer, one random uniform, an if-test, and a multiplication. No square roots or logarithms are required. The point determined by j and u will fall outside the core less than 3% of the time. This happens if $j = 1$ because the top section has no core, if j is between 2 and $n - 1$ and the random point is in one of the little rectangles covering the graph of $f(x)$, or if $j = n$ and the point is in the infinite tail. In these cases, additional computations involving logarithms, exponentials, and more uniform samples are required.

It is important to realize that, even though the ziggurat step function only approximates the probability density function, the resulting distribution is exactly normal. Decreasing n decreases the amount of storage required for the tables and increases the fraction of time that extra computation is required, but does not affect the accuracy. Even with $n = 8$, we would have to do the more costly corrections almost 23% of the time, instead of less than 3%, but we would still get an exact normal distribution.

With this algorithm, MATLAB 6 can generate normally distributed random numbers as fast as it can generate uniformly distributed ones. In fact, MATLAB on an 800 MHz Pentium laptop can generate over 10 million random numbers from either distribution in less than one second.

9.4 randtx, randntx

Our NCM M-file collection includes textbook functions `randtx` and `randntx`. For these two functions, we have chosen to fully reproduce the behavior of the corresponding MATLAB built-in functions `rand` and `randn`. The two textbook functions use the same algorithms and produce the same results (to within roundoff error) as the two built-in functions. All four functions—`rand` with or without an n and with or without a `tx`—have the same usage. With no arguments, the expression `randtx` or `randntx` generates a single uniformly or normally distributed pseudorandom value. With one argument, the expression `randtx(n)` or `randntx(n)` generates an n-by-n matrix. With two arguments, the expression `randtx(m,n)` or `randntx(m,n)` generates an m-by-n matrix.

It is usually not necessary to access or set the internal state of any of the generators. But if you want to repeat a computation using the same sequence of pseudorandom numbers, you can reset the generator state. By default, a generator starts at the state set by `randtx('state',0)` or `randntx('state',0)`. At any point during a computation, you can access the current state with `s = randtx('state')` or `s = randntx('state')`. You can later restore that state with `randtx('state',s)` or `randntx('state',s)`. You can also set the state with `randtx('state',j)` or `randntx('state',j)`, where j is a single integer in the range $0 \le j \le 2^{31} - 1$. The number of states that can be set by a single 32-bit integer is only a tiny fraction of the total number of states.

For the uniform generator `randtx`, the state s is a vector with 35 elements. Thirty-two of the elements are floating-point numbers between 2^{-53} and $1 - 2^{-53}$. The other three elements in s are small integer multiples of `eps`. Although they cannot all be reached from default initial settings, the total number of possible bit patterns in the `randtx` state is $2 \cdot 32 \cdot 2^{32} \cdot 2^{32 \cdot 52}$, which is 2^{1702}.

For the normal generator `randntx`, the state s is a vector with two 32-bit integer elements, so the total number of possible states is 2^{64}.

Both generators have setup calculations that are done only when the generator is first used or reset. For `randtx`, the setup generates the initial floating-point numbers in the state vector one bit at a time. For `randntx`, the setup computes the breakpoints in the ziggurat step function.

After the setup, the principal portion of the uniform generator `randtx` is

```
U = zeros(m,n);
for k = 1:m*n
    x = z(mod(i+20,32)+1) - z(mod(i+5,32)+1) - b;
    if x < 0
        x = x + 1;
        b = ulp;
    else
        b = 0;
    end
    z(i+1) = x;
    i = i+1;
    if i == 32, i = 0; end
    [x,j] = randbits(x,j);
    U(k) = x;
end
```

This takes the difference between two elements in the state, subtracts any carry bit b from the previous calculation, adjusts the result if it is negative, and inserts it into the state. The auxiliary function `randbits` does an XOR operation between the fraction of the floating-point number x and the random integer j.

After the setup, the principal portion of the normal generator `randntx` is

```
R = zeros(m,n);
for k = 1:m*n
    [u,j] = randuni;
    rk = u*z(j+1);
    if abs(rk) < z(j)
        R(k) = rk;
    else
        R(k) = randntips(rk,j,z);
    end
end
```

This uses a subfunction `randuni` to generate a random uniform u and a random integer j. A single multiplication generates a candidate result rk and checks to see if it is within the "core" of the ziggurat. Almost all of the time it is in the core and so becomes an element of the final result. If `rk` is outside the core, then additional computation must be done by the auxiliary subfunction `randtips`.

9.5 Twister

Let's do a run length test using the uniform random number generator that we have described in this chapter and that is implemented in `randtx`.

```
rand('state',0)
x = rand(1,2^24);
delta = .01;
k = diff(find(x<delta));
t = 1:99;
c = histc(k,t);
bar(t,c,'histc')
```

This code sets the generator to its initial state and generates a few million uniformly distributed random numbers. The quantity `delta` is a cutoff tolerance. The quantity `k` is a vector containing the lengths of runs of random numbers that are all greater than the tolerance. The last three statements plot a histogram of the lengths of these sequences. The result is Figure 9.3. The histogram generally confirms our expectation that longer runs are less frequent. But surprisingly, in this experiment, runs of length 27 are only about about half as frequent as they ought to be. You can experiment with other initial states and tolerances and verify that this anomalous behavior is always present.

Why? The gap shown in Figure 9.3 is a property of the "subtract-with-borrow" algorithm employing a cache of length 32 and a generator with offsets 20 and 5,

$$z_i = z_{i+20} - z_{i+5} - b.$$

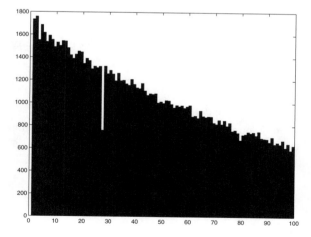

Figure 9.3. *Histogram of run lengths.*

The values 32 and 5 conspire to deplete runs of length 27. This is a curious, but probably serious, property of the algorithm.

Nevertheless, starting with version 7.4 in 2007, the default uniform random number generator in MATLAB uses an algorithm known as the *Mersenne Twister*, developed by M. Matsumoto and T. Nishimura [46]. The generator uses a cache of size 624 and has an incredible period of length $2^{19937} - 1$. It produces floating point values in the closed interval

$$[2^{-53}, 1 - 2^{-53}].$$

In other words, it does not produce an exact 0 or an exact 1. For more details, enter

```
help rand
```

and see the papers referenced on the Mersenne Twister Web page [46].

Exercises

9.1. The number 13 is usually regarded as unlucky. However,

```
rand('state',13)
randgui(@rand)
```

produces a surprisingly lucky result. What is that result?

9.2. Modify `randgui` so that it computes π using a circle inside a square instead of a sphere inside a cube.

9.3. In `randgui`, change the statement

```
x = 2*randfun(3,m)-1;
```

to

```
x = 2*randfun(m,3)'-1;
```

We've interchanged 3 and m, and inserted a matrix transpose operator. With this change,

```
randgui(@randssp)
```

no longer demonstrates the defect in `randssp`. Explain why.

9.4. A very fast random number generator can be based on an irrational number such as the golden ratio

$$\phi = \frac{1 + \sqrt{5}}{2}.$$

The sequence x_n in the interval $0 < x_n < 1$ is generated simply by

$$x_n = \text{fractional part}(n\phi).$$

You can generate this sequence in MATLAB by repeatedly executing the statement

```
x = rem(x + phi, 1)
```

This generator passes a few statistical tests, but does poorly on most.

(a) Write a MATLAB function `randphi`, in the style of `randmcg` and `randssp`, that implements this generator.

(b) Compare the histograms of `randmcg`, `randssp`, and `randphi`. Use 10,000 samples and 50 bins. Which of the generators has the "best" uniform distribution?

(c) How well does

```
randgui(@randphi)
```

compute π? Why?

9.5. The M-files `randtx.m` and `randntx.m` include an internal function `randint` that employs a sequence of bit shifts to produce random integers.

(a) Write a MATLAB function `randjsr`, in the style of `randmcg`, that uses the shift register integer generator to produce uniformly distributed floating-point numbers.

(b) Compare the histogram of your `randjsr` with the histogram of `randtx`. You should find that the two histograms have the same appearance.

(c) Verify that

```
randgui(@randjsr)
```

does a good job of computing π.

9.6. Write an M-file `randnpolar.m` that generates normally distributed random numbers using the polar algorithm described in section 9.3, Normal Distribution. Verify that your function produces the same kind of bell curve shaped histograms as `randn` and `randntx`.

9.7. The NCM M-file `brownian` plots the evolution of a cloud of particles that starts at the origin and diffuses in a two-dimensional random walk, modeling the Brownian motion of gas molecules.

(a) Modify `brownian.m` to keep track of both the average and the maximum particle distance from the origin. Using `loglog` axes, plot both sets of distances as functions of n, the number of steps. You should observe that, on the log-log scale, both plots are nearly linear. Fit both sets of distances with functions of the form $cn^{1/2}$. Plot the observed distances and the fits, using linear axes.

(b) Modify `brownian.m` to model a random walk in three dimensions. Do the distances behave like $n^{1/2}$?

9.8. The term *Monte Carlo simulation* refers to the use of pseudorandom numbers in computational models of stochastic or probabilistic phenomena. The NCM M-file `blackjack` provides an example of such a simulation. The program simulates the card game, either one hand, or thousands of hands, at a time, and collects payoff statistics.

In blackjack, face cards count 10 points, aces count 1 or 11 points, and all other cards count their face value. The objective is to reach, but not exceed, 21 points. If you go over 21, or "bust," before the dealer, you lose your bet on that hand. If you have 21 on the first two cards, and the dealer does not, this is "blackjack" and is worth 1.5 times the bet. If your first two cards are a pair, you may "split" the pair by doubling the bet and use the two cards to start two independent hands. You may "double down" after seeing the first two cards by doubling the bet and receiving just one more card. "Hit" and "draw" mean take another card. "Stand" means stop drawing. "Push" means the two hands have the same total.

The first mathematical analysis of blackjack was published in 1956 by Baldwin, Cantey, Maisel, and McDermott [5]. Their basic strategy, which is also described in many more recent books, makes blackjack very close to a fair game. With basic strategy, the expected win or loss per hand is less than 1% of the bet. The key idea is to avoid going bust before the dealer. The dealer must play a fixed strategy, hitting on 16 or less and standing on 17 or more. Since almost one third of the cards are worth 10 points, you can compare your hand with the dealer's under the assumption that the dealer's hole card is a 10. If the dealer's up card is a 6 or less, she must draw. Consequently, the strategy has you stand on any total over 11 when the dealer is showing a 6 or less. Split aces and split 8's. Do not split anything else. Double down with 11, or with 10 if the dealer is showing a 6 or less. The program displays the recommended basic strategy play for each situation in red. The complete basic strategy is defined by three arrays, HARD, SOFT, and SPLIT, in the code.

A more elaborate strategy, called *card counting*, can provide a definite mathematical advantage. Card-counting players keep track of the cards that have appeared in previous hands, and use that information to alter both the bet and the play as the deck becomes depleted. Our simulation does not involve card counting.

Our blackjack program has two modes. The initial bet for each hand is $10. "Play" mode indicates the basic strategy with color, but allows you to make other choices. "Simulate" mode plays a specified number of hands using the basic strategy and collects statistics. One graph shows the total stake accumulated over the duration of the simulation. Another graph shows the observed probabilities of the ten possible payoffs for each hand. These payoffs include zero for a push, win $15 for a blackjack, win or lose $10 on a hand that has not been split or doubled, win or lose $20 on hands that have been split or doubled once, and win or lose $30 or $40 on hands that have been doubled after a split. The $30 and $40 payoffs occur rarely (and may not be allowed at some casinos) but are important in determining the expected return from the basic strategy. The second graph also displays with $0.\text{xxxx} \pm 0.\text{xxxx}$ the expected fraction of the bet that is won or lost each hand, together with its confidence interval. Note that the expected return is usually negative, but within the confidence interval. The outcome in any session with less than a few million hands is determined more by the luck of the cards than by the expected return.

(a) How many decks of cards are used in our blackjack program? How is the deck represented and how is it shuffled? How are the cards dealt? What role does rand play?

(b) What is the theoretical probability of getting blackjack from a freshly shuffled deck? In other words, the player has 21 on the first two cards and the dealer does not. How does this compare with the probability observed in the simulation?

(c) Modify blackjack so that blackjack pays even money instead of 1.5 times the bet. How does this affect the expected return?

(d) In some casinos, a "push" is regarded as a loss. Modify blackjack to use such a rule. How does this affect the expected return?

(e) Modify `blackjack` to use four artificial 56-card decks that have twice as many aces as usual. How does this affect the expected return?

(f) Modify `blackjack` to use four artificial 48-card decks that do not have any kings. How does this affect the expected return?

Chapter 10

Eigenvalues and Singular Values

This chapter is about eigenvalues and singular values of matrices. Computational algorithms and sensitivity to perturbations are both discussed.

10.1 Eigenvalue and Singular Value Decompositions

An *eigenvalue* and *eigenvector* of a square matrix A are a scalar λ and a nonzero vector x so that

$$Ax = \lambda x.$$

A *singular value* and pair of *singular vectors* of a square or rectangular matrix A are a nonnegative scalar σ and two nonzero vectors u and v so that

$$Av = \sigma u,$$
$$A^H u = \sigma v.$$

The superscript on A^H stands for *Hermitian transpose* and denotes the complex conjugate transpose of a complex matrix. If the matrix is real, then A^T denotes the same matrix. In MATLAB, these transposed matrices are denoted by A'.

The term "eigenvalue" is a partial translation of the German "eigenvert." A complete translation would be something like "own value" or "characteristic value," but these are rarely used. The term "singular value" relates to the distance between a matrix and the set of singular matrices.

Eigenvalues play an important role in situations where the matrix is a transformation from one vector space onto itself. Systems of linear ordinary differential equations are the primary examples. The values of λ can correspond to frequencies of vibration, or critical values of stability parameters, or energy levels of atoms. Singular values play an important role where the matrix is a transformation from one vector space to a different vector space, possibly with a different dimension. Systems of over- or underdetermined algebraic equations are the primary examples.

The definitions of eigenvectors and singular vectors do not specify their normalization. An eigenvector x, or a pair of singular vectors u and v, can be scaled by any nonzero factor without changing any other important properties. Eigenvectors of symmetric matrices are usually normalized to have Euclidean length equal to one, $\|x\|_2 = 1$. On the other hand, the eigenvectors of nonsymmetric matrices often have different normalizations in different contexts. Singular vectors are almost always normalized to have Euclidean length equal to one, $\|u\|_2 = \|v\|_2 = 1$. You can still multiply eigenvectors, or pairs of singular vectors, by -1 without changing their lengths.

The eigenvalue-eigenvector equation for a square matrix can be written

$$(A - \lambda I)x = 0, \ x \neq 0.$$

This implies that $A - \lambda I$ is singular and hence that

$$\det(A - \lambda I) = 0.$$

This definition of an eigenvalue, which does not directly involve the corresponding eigenvector, is the *characteristic equation* or *characteristic polynomial* of A. The degree of the polynomial is the order of the matrix. This implies that an n-by-n matrix has n eigenvalues, counting multiplicities. Like the determinant itself, the characteristic polynomial is useful in theoretical considerations and hand calculations, but does not provide a sound basis for robust numerical software.

Let $\lambda_1, \lambda_2, \ldots, \lambda_n$ be the eigenvalues of a matrix A, let $x_1, x_2, \ldots, x_n$ be a set of corresponding eigenvectors, let Λ denote the n-by-n diagonal matrix with the λ_j on the diagonal, and let X denote the n-by-n matrix whose jth column is x_j. Then

$$AX = X\Lambda.$$

It is necessary to put Λ on the right in the second expression so that each column of X is multiplied by its corresponding eigenvalue. Now make a key assumption that is not true for all matrices—assume that the eigenvectors are linearly independent. Then X^{-1} exists and

$$A = X\Lambda X^{-1},$$

with nonsingular X. This is known as the *eigenvalue decomposition* of the matrix A. If it exists, it allows us to investigate the properties of A by analyzing the diagonal matrix Λ. For example, repeated matrix powers can be expressed in terms of powers of scalars:

$$A^p = X\Lambda^p X^{-1}.$$

If the eigenvectors of A are not linearly independent, then such a diagonal decomposition does not exist and the powers of A exhibit a more complicated behavior.

If T is any nonsingular matrix, then

$$A = TBT^{-1}$$

is known as a *similarity transformation* and A and B are said to be *similar*. If $Ax = \lambda x$ and $x = Ty$, then $By = \lambda y$. In other words, a similarity transformation preserves eigenvalues.

The eigenvalue decomposition is an attempt to find a similarity transformation to diagonal form.

Written in matrix form, the defining equations for singular values and vectors are

$$AV = U\Sigma,$$
$$A^H U = V\Sigma^H.$$

Here Σ is a matrix the same size as A that is zero except possibly on its main diagonal. It turns out that singular vectors can always be chosen to be perpendicular to each other, so the matrices U and V, whose columns are the normalized singular vectors, satisfy $U^H U = I$ and $V^H V = I$. In other words, U and V are *orthogonal* if they are real, or *unitary* if they are complex. Consequently,

$$A = U\Sigma V^H,$$

with diagonal Σ and orthogonal or unitary U and V. This is known as the *singular value decomposition*, or *SVD*, of the matrix A.

In abstract linear algebra terms, eigenvalues are relevant if a square, n-by-n matrix A is thought of as mapping n-dimensional space onto itself. We try to find a basis for the space so that the matrix becomes diagonal. This basis might be complex even if A is real. In fact, if the eigenvectors are not linearly independent, such a basis does not even exist. The SVD is relevant if a possibly rectangular, m-by-n matrix A is thought of as mapping n-space onto m-space. We try to find one change of basis in the domain and a usually different change of basis in the range so that the matrix becomes diagonal. Such bases always exist and are always real if A is real. In fact, the transforming matrices are orthogonal or unitary, so they preserve lengths and angles and do not magnify errors.

If A is m by n with m larger than n, then in the full SVD, U is a large, square m-by-m matrix. The last $m - n$ columns of U are "extra"; they are not needed to reconstruct A. A second version of the SVD that saves computer memory if A is rectangular is known as

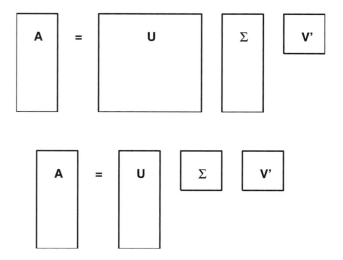

Figure 10.1. *Full and economy SVDs.*

the *economy-sized* SVD. In the economy version, only the first n columns of U and first n rows of Σ are computed. The matrix V is the same n-by-n matrix in both decompositions. Figure 10.1 shows the shapes of the various matrices in the two versions of the SVD. Both decompositions can be written $A = U\Sigma V^H$, even though the U and Σ in the economy decomposition are submatrices of the ones in the full decomposition.

10.2   A Small Example

An example of the eigenvalue and singular value decompositions of a small, square matrix is provided by one of the test matrices from the MATLAB gallery.

```
A = gallery(3)
```

The matrix is

$$A = \begin{pmatrix} -149 & -50 & -154 \\ 537 & 180 & 546 \\ -27 & -9 & -25 \end{pmatrix}.$$

This matrix was constructed in such a way that the characteristic polynomial factors nicely:

$$\det(A - \lambda I) = \lambda^3 - 6\lambda^2 + 11\lambda - 6$$
$$= (\lambda - 1)(\lambda - 2)(\lambda - 3).$$

Consequently, the three eigenvalues are $\lambda_1 = 1$, $\lambda_2 = 2$, and $\lambda_3 = 3$, and

$$\Lambda = \begin{pmatrix} 1 & 0 & 0 \\ 0 & 2 & 0 \\ 0 & 0 & 3 \end{pmatrix}.$$

The matrix of eigenvectors can be normalized so that its elements are all integers:

$$X = \begin{pmatrix} 1 & -4 & 7 \\ -3 & 9 & -49 \\ 0 & 1 & 9 \end{pmatrix}.$$

It turns out that the inverse of X also has integer entries:

$$X^{-1} = \begin{pmatrix} 130 & 43 & 133 \\ 27 & 9 & 28 \\ -3 & -1 & -3 \end{pmatrix}.$$

These matrices provide the eigenvalue decomposition of our example:

$$A = X\Lambda X^{-1}.$$

The SVD of this matrix cannot be expressed so neatly with small integers. The singular values are the positive roots of the equation

$$\sigma^6 - 668737\sigma^4 + 4096316\sigma^2 - 36 = 0,$$

but this equation does not factor nicely. The Symbolic Toolbox statement

```
svd(sym(A))
```

returns exact formulas for the singular values, but the overall length of the result is 822 characters. So we compute the SVD numerically.

```
[U,S,V] = svd(A)
```

produces

```
U =
     -0.2691      -0.6798       0.6822
      0.9620      -0.1557       0.2243
     -0.0463       0.7167       0.6959

S =
   817.7597             0             0
         0        2.4750             0
         0             0        0.0030

V =
      0.6823      -0.6671       0.2990
      0.2287      -0.1937      -0.9540
      0.6944       0.7193       0.0204
```

The expression `U*S*V'` generates the original matrix to within roundoff error.

For `gallery(3)`, notice the big difference between the eigenvalues, 1, 2, and 3, and the singular values, 817, 2.47, and 0.003. This is related, in a way that we will make more precise later, to the fact that this example is very far from being a symmetric matrix.

10.3 eigshow

The function `eigshow` is available in the MATLAB demos directory. The input to `eigshow` is a real, 2-by-2 matrix A, or you can choose an A from a pull-down list in the title. The default A is

$$A = \begin{pmatrix} 1/4 & 3/4 \\ 1 & 1/2 \end{pmatrix}.$$

Initially, `eigshow` plots the unit vector $x = [1, 0]'$, as well as the vector Ax, which starts out as the first column of A. You can then use your mouse to move x, shown in green, around the unit circle. As you move x, the resulting Ax, shown in blue, also moves. The first four subplots in Figure 10.2 show intermediate steps as x traces out a green unit circle. What is the shape of the resulting orbit of Ax? An important, and nontrivial, theorem from linear algebra tells us that the blue curve is an ellipse. `eigshow` provides a "proof by GUI" of this theorem.

The caption for `eigshow` says "Make Ax parallel to x." For such a direction x, the operator A is simply a stretching or magnification by a factor λ. In other words, x is an eigenvector and the length of Ax is the corresponding eigenvalue.

The last two subplots in Figure 10.2 show the eigenvalues and eigenvectors of our 2-by-2 example. The first eigenvalue is positive, so Ax lies on top of the eigenvector x. The length of Ax is the corresponding eigenvalue; it happens to be 5/4 in this example. The

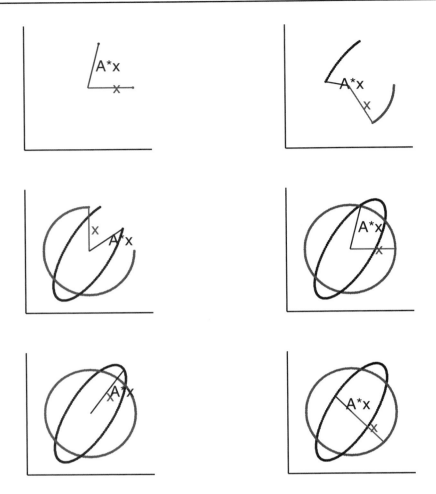

Figure 10.2. `eigshow`.

second eigenvalue is negative, so Ax is parallel to x, but points in the opposite direction. The length of Ax is 1/2, and the corresponding eigenvalue is actually $-1/2$.

You might have noticed that the two eigenvectors are not the major and minor axes of the ellipse. They would be if the matrix were symmetric. The default `eigshow` matrix is close to, but not exactly equal to, a symmetric matrix. For other matrices, it may not be possible to find a real x so that Ax is parallel to x. These examples, which we pursue in the exercises, demonstrate that 2-by-2 matrices can have fewer than two real eigenvectors.

The axes of the ellipse do play a key role in the SVD. The results produced by the `svd` mode of `eigshow` are shown in Figure 10.3. Again, the mouse moves x around the unit circle, but now a second unit vector, y, follows x, staying perpendicular to it. The resulting Ax and Ay traverse the ellipse, but are not usually perpendicular to each other. The goal is to make them perpendicular. If they are, they form the axes of the ellipse. The vectors x

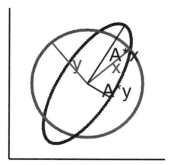

Figure 10.3. `eigshow(svd)`.

and y are the columns of U in the SVD, the vectors Ax and Ay are multiples of the columns of V, and the lengths of the axes are the singular values.

10.4 Characteristic Polynomial

Let A be the 20-by-20 diagonal matrix with $1, 2, \ldots, 20$ on the diagonal. Clearly, the eigenvalues of A are its diagonal elements. However, the characteristic polynomial $\det(A - \lambda I)$ turns out to be

$$\lambda^{20} - 210\lambda^{19} + 20615\lambda^{18} - 1256850\lambda^{17} + 53327946\lambda^{16}$$

$$-1672280820\lambda^{15} + 40171771630\lambda^{14} - 756111184500\lambda^{13}$$

$$+11310276995381\lambda^{12} - 135585182899530\lambda^{11}$$

$$+1307535010540395\lambda^{10} - 10142299865511450\lambda^{9}$$

$$+63030812099294896\lambda^{8} - 311333643161390640\lambda^{7}$$

$$+1206647803780373360\lambda^{6} - 3599979517947607200\lambda^{5}$$

$$+8037811822645051776\lambda^{4} - 12870931245150988800\lambda^{3}$$

$$+13803759753640704000\lambda^{2} - 8752948036761600000\lambda$$

$$+2432902008176640000.$$

The coefficient of $-\lambda^{19}$ is 210, which is the sum of the eigenvalues. The coefficient of λ^{0}, the constant term, is 20!, which is the product of the eigenvalues. The other coefficients are various sums of products of the eigenvalues.

We have displayed all the coefficients to emphasize that doing any floating-point computation with them is likely to introduce large roundoff errors. Merely representing the coefficients as IEEE floating-point numbers changes five of them. For example, the last 3 digits of the coefficient of λ^{4} change from 776 to 392. To 16 significant digits, the exact roots of the polynomial obtained by representing the coefficients in floating point are as follows.

```
    1.00000000000000
    2.00000000000096
    2.99999999986640
    4.00000000495944
    4.99999991473414
    6.00000084571661
    6.99999455544845
    8.00002443256894
    8.99992001186835
   10.00019696490537
   10.99962843024064
   12.00054374363591
   12.99938073455790
   14.00054798867380
   14.99962658217055
   16.00019208303847
   16.99992773461773
   18.00001875170604
   18.99999699774389
   20.00000022354640
```

We see that just storing the coefficients in the characteristic polynomial as double-precision floating-point numbers changes the computed values of some of the eigenvalues in the fifth significant digit.

This particular polynomial was introduced by J. H. Wilkinson around 1960. His perturbation of the polynomial was different than ours, but his point was the same, namely that representing a polynomial in its power form is an unsatisfactory way to characterize either the roots of the polynomial or the eigenvalues of the corresponding matrix.

10.5   Symmetric and Hermitian Matrices

A real matrix is symmetric if it is equal to its transpose, $A = A^T$. A complex matrix is Hermitian if it is equal to its complex conjugate transpose, $A = A^H$. The eigenvalues and eigenvectors of a real symmetric matrix are real. Moreover, the matrix of eigenvectors can be chosen to be orthogonal. Consequently, if A is real and $A = A^T$, then its eigenvalue decomposition is

$$A = X \Lambda X^T,$$

with $X^T X = I = X X^T$. The eigenvalues of a complex Hermitian matrix turn out to be real, although the eigenvectors must be complex. Moreover, the matrix of eigenvectors can be chosen to be unitary. Consequently, if A is complex and $A = A^H$, then its eigenvalue decomposition is

$$A = X \Lambda X^H,$$

with Λ real and $X^H X = I = X X^H$.

For symmetric and Hermitian matrices, the eigenvalues and singular values are obviously closely related. A nonnegative eigenvalue, $\lambda \geq 0$, is also a singular value, $\sigma = \lambda$.

The corresponding vectors are equal to each other, $u = v = x$. A negative eigenvalue, $\lambda < 0$, must reverse its sign to become a singular value, $\sigma = |\lambda|$. One of the corresponding singular vectors is the negative of the other, $u = -v = x$.

10.6 Eigenvalue Sensitivity and Accuracy

The eigenvalues of some matrices are sensitive to perturbations. Small changes in the matrix elements can lead to large changes in the eigenvalues. Roundoff errors introduced during the computation of eigenvalues with floating-point arithmetic have the same effect as perturbations in the original matrix. Consequently, these roundoff errors are magnified in the computed values of sensitive eigenvalues.

To get a rough idea of this sensitivity, assume that A has a full set of linearly independent eigenvectors and use the eigenvalue decomposition

$$A = X\Lambda X^{-1}.$$

Rewrite this as

$$\Lambda = X^{-1}AX.$$

Now let δA denote some change in A, caused by roundoff error or any other kind of perturbation. Then

$$\Lambda + \delta\Lambda = X^{-1}(A + \delta A)X.$$

Hence

$$\delta\Lambda = X^{-1}\delta AX.$$

Taking matrix norms,

$$\|\delta\Lambda\| \leq \|X^{-1}\|\|X\|\|\delta A\| = \kappa(X)\|\delta A\|,$$

where $\kappa(X)$ is the matrix condition number introduced in Chapter 2, Linear Equations. Note that the key factor is the condition of X, the matrix of eigenvectors, not the condition of A itself.

This simple analysis tells us that, in terms of matrix norms, a perturbation $\|\delta A\|$ can be magnified by a factor as large as $\kappa(X)$ in $\|\delta\Lambda\|$. However, since $\delta\Lambda$ is usually not a diagonal matrix, this analysis does not immediately say how much the eigenvalues themselves may be affected. Nevertheless, it leads to the correct overall conclusion:

> *The sensitivity of the eigenvalues is estimated by the condition number of the matrix of eigenvectors.*

You can use the function condest to estimate the condition number of the eigenvector matrix. For example,

```
A = gallery(3)
[X,lambda] = eig(A);
condest(X)
```

yields

```
1.2002e+003
```

A perturbation in `gallery(3)` could result in perturbations in its eigenvalues that are $1.2 \cdot 10^3$ times as large. This says that the eigenvalues of `gallery(3)` are slightly badly conditioned.

A more detailed analysis involves the *left eigenvectors*, which are *row* vectors y^H that satisfy

$$y^H A = \lambda y^H.$$

In order to investigate the sensitivity of an individual eigenvalue, assume that A varies with a perturbation parameter and let $\dot{A}$ denote the derivative with respect to that parameter. Differentiate both sides of the equation

$$Ax = \lambda x$$

to get

$$\dot{A}x + A\dot{x} = \dot{\lambda}x + \lambda\dot{x}.$$

Multiply through by the left eigenvector:

$$y^H \dot{A}x + y^H A\dot{x} = y^H \dot{\lambda}x + y^H \lambda\dot{x}.$$

The second terms on each side of this equation are equal, so

$$\dot{\lambda} = \frac{y^H \dot{A}x}{y^H x}.$$

Taking norms,

$$|\dot{\lambda}| \leq \frac{\|y\|\|x\|}{y^H x}\|\dot{A}\|.$$

Define the *eigenvalue condition number* to be

$$\kappa(\lambda, A) = \frac{\|y\|\|x\|}{y^H x}.$$

Then

$$|\dot{\lambda}| \leq \kappa(\lambda, A)\|\dot{A}\|.$$

In other words, $\kappa(\lambda, A)$ is the magnification factor relating a perturbation in the matrix A to the resulting perturbation in an eigenvalue λ. Notice that $\kappa(\lambda, A)$ is independent of the normalization of the left and right eigenvectors, y and x, and that

$$\kappa(\lambda, A) \geq 1.$$

If you have already computed the matrix X whose columns are the right eigenvectors, one way to compute the left eigenvectors is to let

$$Y^H = X^{-1}.$$

Then, since

$$Y^H A = \Lambda Y^H,$$

the rows of Y^H are the left eigenvectors. In this case, the left eigenvectors are normalized so that

$$Y^H X = I,$$

so the denominator in $\kappa(\lambda, A)$ is $y^H x = 1$ and

$$\kappa(\lambda, A) = \|y\|\|x\|.$$

Since $\|x\| \le \|X\|$ and $\|y\| \le \|X^{-1}\|$, we have

$$\kappa(\lambda, A) \le \kappa(X).$$

The condition number of the eigenvector matrix is an upper bound for the individual eigenvalue condition numbers.

The MATLAB function `condeig` computes eigenvalue condition numbers. Continuing with the `gallery(3)` example,

```
A = gallery(3)
lambda = eig(A)
kappa = condeig(A)
```

yields

```
lambda =
     1.0000
     2.0000
     3.0000

kappa =
   603.6390
   395.2366
   219.2920
```

This indicates that $\lambda_1 = 1$ is slightly more sensitive than $\lambda_2 = 2$ or $\lambda_3 = 3$. A perturbation in `gallery(3)` may result in perturbations in its eigenvalues that are 200 to 600 times as large. This is consistent with the cruder estimate of $1.2 \cdot 10^3$ obtained from `condest(X)`.

To test this analysis, let's make a small random perturbation in A = `gallery(3)` and see what happens to its eigenvalues.

```
format long
delta = 1.e-6;
lambda = eig(A + delta*randn(3,3))

lambda =

   1.00011344999452
   1.99992040276116
   2.99996856435075
```

The perturbation in the eigenvalues is

```
lambda - (1:3)'

ans =
   1.0e-003 *
     0.11344999451923
    -0.07959723883699
    -0.03143564924635
```

This is smaller than, but roughly the same size as, the estimates provided by `condeig` and the perturbation analysis.

```
delta*condeig(A)

ans =
   1.0e-003 *
     0.60363896495665
     0.39523663799014
     0.21929204271846
```

If A is real and symmetric, or complex and Hermitian, then its right and left eigenvectors are the same. In this case,

$$y^H x = \|y\|\|x\|,$$

so, for symmetric and Hermitian matrices,

$$\kappa(\lambda, A) = 1.$$

The eigenvalues of symmetric and Hermitian matrices are perfectly well conditioned. Perturbations in the matrix lead to perturbations in the eigenvalues that are roughly the same size. This is true even for multiple eigenvalues.

At the other extreme, if λ_k is a multiple eigenvalue that does not have a corresponding full set of linearly independent eigenvectors, then the previous analysis does not apply. In this case, the characteristic polynomial for an n-by-n matrix can be written

$$p(\lambda) = \det(A - \lambda I) = (\lambda - \lambda_k)^m q(\lambda),$$

where m is the multiplicity of λ_k and $q(\lambda)$ is a polynomial of degree $n - m$ that does not vanish at λ_k. A perturbation in the matrix of size δ results in a change in the characteristic polynomial from $p(\lambda) = 0$ to something like

$$p(\lambda) = O(\delta).$$

In other words,

$$(\lambda - \lambda_k)^m = O(\delta)/q(\lambda).$$

The roots of this equation are

$$\lambda = \lambda_k + O(\delta^{1/m}).$$

This mth root behavior says that multiple eigenvalues without a full set of eigenvectors are extremely sensitive to perturbation.

As an artificial, but illustrative, example, consider the 16-by-16 matrix with 2's on the main diagonal, 1's on the superdiagonal, δ in the lower left-hand corner, and 0's elsewhere:

$$A = \begin{pmatrix} 2 & 1 & & & \\ & 2 & 1 & & \\ & & \ddots & \ddots & \\ & & & 2 & 1 \\ \delta & & & & 2 \end{pmatrix}.$$

The characteristic equation is

$$(\lambda - 2)^{16} = \delta.$$

If $\delta = 0$, this matrix has an eigenvalue of multiplicity 16 at $\lambda = 2$, but there is only 1 eigenvector to go along with this multiple eigenvalue. If δ is on the order of floating-point roundoff error, that is, $\delta \approx 10^{-16}$, then the eigenvalues are on a circle in the complex plane with center at 2 and radius

$$(10^{-16})^{1/16} = 0.1.$$

A perturbation on the size of roundoff error changes the eigenvalue from 2.0000 to 16 different values, including 1.9000, 2.1000, and 2.0924 + 0.0383i. A tiny change in the matrix elements causes a much larger change in the eigenvalues.

Essentially the same phenomenon, but in a less obvious form, explains the behavior of another MATLAB gallery example,

```
A = gallery(5)
```

The matrix is

```
A =
           -9          11         -21          63        -252
           70         -69         141        -421        1684
         -575         575       -1149        3451      -13801
         3891       -3891        7782      -23345       93365
         1024       -1024        2048       -6144       24572
```

The computed eigenvalues, obtained from `lambda = eig(A)`, are

```
lambda =
  -0.0408
  -0.0119 + 0.0386i
  -0.0119 - 0.0386i
   0.0323 + 0.0230i
   0.0323 - 0.0230i
```

How accurate are these computed eigenvalues?

The gallery(5) matrix was constructed in such a way that its characteristic equation is

$$\lambda^5 = 0.$$

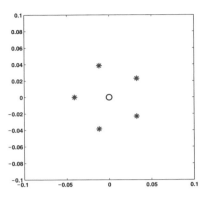

Figure 10.4. `plot(eig(gallery(5)))`.

You can confirm this by noting that A^5, which is computed without any roundoff error, is the zero matrix. The characteristic equation can easily be solved by hand. All five eigenvalues are actually equal to zero. The computed eigenvalues give little indication that the "correct" eigenvalues are all zero. We certainly have to admit that the computed eigenvalues are not very accurate.

The MATLAB `eig` function is doing as well as can be expected on this problem. The inaccuracy of the computed eigenvalues is caused by their sensitivity, not by anything wrong with `eig`. The following experiment demonstrates this fact. Start with

```
A = gallery(5)
e = eig(A)
plot(real(e),imag(e),'r*',0,0,'ko')
axis(.1*[-1 1 -1 1])
axis square
```

Figure 10.4 shows that the computed eigenvalues are the vertices of a regular pentagon in the complex plane, centered at the origin. The radius is about 0.04.

Now repeat the experiment with a matrix where each element is perturbed by a single roundoff error. The elements of `gallery(5)` vary over four orders of magnitude, so the correct scaling of the perturbation is obtained with

```
e = eig(A + eps*randn(5,5).*A)
```

Put this statement, along with the `plot` and `axis` commands, on a single line and use the up arrow to repeat the computation several times. You will see that the pentagon flips orientation and that its radius varies between 0.03 and 0.07, but that the computed eigenvalues of the perturbed problems behave pretty much like the computed eigenvalues of the original matrix.

The experiment provides evidence for the fact that the computed eigenvalues are the exact eigenvalues of a matrix $A + E$, where the elements of E are on the order of roundoff error compared to the elements of A. This is the best we can expect to achieve with floating-point computation.

10.7 Singular Value Sensitivity and Accuracy

The sensitivity of singular values is much easier to characterize than the sensitivity of eigenvalues. The singular value problem is always perfectly well conditioned. A perturbation analysis would involve an equation like

$$\Sigma + \delta\Sigma = U^H(A + \delta A)V.$$

But, since U and V are orthogonal or unitary, they preserve norms. Consequently, $\|\delta\Sigma\| = \|\delta A\|$. Perturbations of any size in any matrix cause perturbations of roughly the same size in its singular values. There is no need to define condition numbers for singular values because they would always be equal to one. The MATLAB function svd always computes singular values to full floating-point accuracy.

We have to be careful about what we mean by "same size" and "full accuracy." Perturbations and accuracy are measured relative the norm of the matrix or, equivalently, the largest singular value:

$$\|A\|_2 = \sigma_1.$$

The accuracy of the smaller singular values is measured relative to the largest one. If, as is often the case, the singular values vary over several orders of magnitude, the smaller ones might not have full accuracy relative to themselves. In particular, if the matrix is singular, then some of the σ_i must be zero. The computed values of these σ_i will usually be on the order of $\epsilon\|A\|$, where ϵ is eps, the floating-point accuracy parameter.

This can be illustrated with the singular values of gallery(5). The statements

```
A = gallery(5)
format long e
svd(A)
```

produce

```
1.010353607103610e+005
1.679457384066496e+000
1.462838728086172e+000
1.080169069985612e+000
4.988578262459575e-014
```

The largest element of A is 93365, and we see that the largest singular value is a little larger, about 10^5. There are three singular values near 10^0. Recall that all the eigenvalues of this matrix are zero, so the matrix is singular and the smallest singular value should theoretically be zero. The computed value is somewhere between ϵ and $\epsilon\|A\|$.

Now let's perturb the matrix. Let this infinite loop run for a while.

```
while 1
   clc
   svd(A+eps*randn(5,5).*A)
   pause(.25)
end
```

This produces varying output like this.

```
1.010353607103610e+005
1.67945738406****e+000
1.46283872808****e+000
1.08016906998****e+000
*.***************-0**
```

The asterisks show the digits that change as we make the random perturbations. The 15-digit format does not show any changes in σ_1. The changes in σ_2, σ_3, and σ_4 are smaller than $\epsilon \|A\|$, which is roughly 10^{-11}. The computed value of σ_5 is all roundoff error, less than 10^{-11}.

The `gallery(5)` matrix was constructed to have very special properties for the eigenvalue problem. For the singular value problem, its behavior is typical of any singular matrix.

10.8   Jordan and Schur Forms

The eigenvalue decomposition attempts to find a diagonal matrix Λ and a nonsingular matrix X so that

$$A = X \Lambda X^{-1}.$$

There are two difficulties with the eigenvalue decomposition. A theoretical difficulty is that the decomposition does not always exist. A numerical difficulty is that, even if the decomposition exists, it might not provide a basis for robust computation.

The solution to the nonexistence difficulty is to get as close to diagonal as possible. This leads to the Jordan canonical form (JCF). The solution to the robustness difficulty is to replace "diagonal" with "triangular" and to use orthogonal and unitary transformations. This leads to the Schur form.

A *defective* matrix is a matrix with at least one multiple eigenvalue that does not have a full set of linearly independent eigenvectors. For example, `gallery(5)` is defective; zero is an eigenvalue of multiplicity five that has only one eigenvector.

The JCF is the decomposition

$$A = X J X^{-1}.$$

If A is not defective, then the JCF is the same as the eigenvalue decomposition. The columns of X are the eigenvectors and $J = \Lambda$ is diagonal. But if A is defective, then X consists of eigenvectors and *generalized* eigenvectors. The matrix J has the eigenvalues on the diagonal and ones on the superdiagonal in positions corresponding to the columns of X that are not ordinary eigenvectors. The rest of the elements of J are zero.

The function `jordan` in the MATLAB Symbolic Toolbox uses unlimited-precision rational arithmetic to try to compute the JCF of small matrices whose entries are small integers or ratios of small integers. If the characteristic polynomial does not have rational roots, the Symbolic Toolbox regards all the eigenvalues as distinct and produces a diagonal JCF.

The JCF is a discontinuous function of the matrix. Almost any perturbation of a defective matrix can cause a multiple eigenvalue to separate into distinct values and eliminate the ones on the superdiagonal of the JCF. Matrices that are nearly defective have badly conditioned sets of eigenvectors, and the resulting similarity transformations cannot be used for reliable numerical computation.

A numerically satisfactory alternative to the JCF is provided by the Schur form. Any matrix can be transformed to upper triangular form by a unitary similarity transformation:

$$B = T^H A T.$$

The eigenvalues of A are on the diagonal of its Schur form B. Since unitary transformations are perfectly well conditioned, they do not magnify any errors.

For example,

```
A = gallery(3)
[T,B] = schur(A)
```

produces

```
A =
  -149   -50   -154
   537   180    546
   -27    -9    -25
T =
    0.3162   -0.6529    0.6882
   -0.9487   -0.2176    0.2294
    0.0000    0.7255    0.6882
B =
    1.0000   -7.1119  -815.8706
         0    2.0000   -55.0236
         0         0     3.0000
```

The diagonal elements of B are the eigenvalues of A. If A were symmetric, B would be diagonal. In this case, the large off-diagonal elements of B measure the lack of symmetry in A.

10.9 The QR Algorithm

The QR algorithm is one of the most important, widely used, and successful tools we have in technical computation. Several variants of it are in the mathematical core of MATLAB. They compute the eigenvalues of real symmetric matrices, real nonsymmetric matrices, and pairs of complex matrices, and the singular values of general matrices. These functions are used, in turn, to find zeros of polynomials, to solve special linear systems, and to assess stability, and for many other tasks in various toolboxes.

Dozens of people have contributed to the development of the various QR algorithms. The first complete implementation and an important convergence analysis are due to J. H. Wilkinson. Wilkinson's book, *The Algebraic Eigenvalue Problem* [56], as well as two fundamental papers, was published in 1965.

The QR *algorithm* is based on repeated use of the QR *factorization* that we described in Chapter 5, Least Squares. The letter "Q" denotes orthogonal and unitary matrices and the letter "R" denotes right, or upper, triangular matrices. The qr function in MATLAB factors any matrix, real or complex, square or rectangular, into the product of a matrix Q with orthonormal columns and matrix R that is nonzero only its upper, or right, triangle.

Using the `qr` function, a simple variant of the QR algorithm, known as the single-shift algorithm, can be expressed as a MATLAB one-liner. Let A be any square matrix. Start with

```
n = size(A,1)
I = eye(n,n)
```

Then one step of the single-shift QR iteration is given by

```
s = A(n,n);   [Q,R] = qr(A - s*I);   A = R*Q + s*I
```

If you enter this on one line, you can use the up arrow key to iterate. The quantity s is the shift; it accelerates convergence. The QR factorization makes the matrix triangular:

$$A - sI = QR.$$

Then the reverse-order multiplication RQ restores the eigenvalues because

$$RQ + sI = Q^T(A - sI)Q + sI = Q^T A Q,$$

so the new A is orthogonally similar to the original A. Each iteration effectively transfers some "mass" from the lower to the upper triangle while preserving the eigenvalues. As the iterations are repeated, the matrix often approaches an upper triangular matrix with the eigenvalues conveniently displayed on the diagonal.

For example, start with A = `gallery(3)`.

```
-149      -50      -154
 537      180       546
 -27       -9       -25
```

The first iterate,

```
 28.8263 -259.8671   773.9292
  1.0353   -8.6686    33.1759
 -0.5973    5.5786   -14.1578
```

already has its largest elements in the upper triangle. After five more iterations, we have

```
  2.7137  -10.5427 -814.0932
 -0.0767    1.4719  -76.5847
  0.0006   -0.0039    1.8144
```

As we know, this matrix was contrived to have its eigenvalues equal to 1, 2, and 3. We can begin to see these three values on the diagonal. Five more iterations gives

```
  3.0716   -7.6952  802.1201
  0.0193    0.9284  158.9556
 -0.0000    0.0000    2.0000
```

One of the eigenvalues has been computed to full accuracy and the below-diagonal element adjacent to it has become zero. It is time to deflate the problem and continue the iteration on the 2-by-2 upper left submatrix.

The QR algorithm is never practiced in this simple form. It is always preceded by a reduction to Hessenberg form, in which all the elements below the subdiagonal are zero. This reduced form is preserved by the iteration, and the factorizations can be done much more quickly. Furthermore, the shift strategy is more sophisticated and is different for various forms of the algorithm.

The simplest variant involves real, symmetric matrices. The reduced form in this case is tridiagonal. Wilkinson provided a shift strategy that allowed him to prove a global convergence theorem. Even in the presence of roundoff error, we do not know of any examples that cause the implementation in MATLAB to fail.

The SVD variant of the QR algorithm is preceded by a reduction to a bidiagonal form that preserves the singular values. It has the same guaranteed convergence properties as the symmetric eigenvalue iteration.

The situation for real, nonsymmetric matrices is much more complicated. In this case, the given matrix has real elements, but its eigenvalues may well be complex. Real matrices are used throughout, with a double-shift strategy that can handle two real eigenvalues, or a complex conjugate pair. Even thirty years ago, counterexamples to the basic iteration were known and Wilkinson introduced an 'ad hoc' shift to handle them. But no one has been able to prove a complete convergence theorem. In principle, it is possible for the eig function in MATLAB to fail with an error message about lack of convergence.

10.10 **eigsvdgui**

Figures 10.5 and 10.6 are snapshots of the output produced by eigsvdgui showing steps in the computation of the eigenvalues of a nonsymmetric matrix and of a symmetric matrix. Figure 10.7 is a snapshot of the output produced by eigsvdgui showing steps in the computation of the singular values of a nonsymmetric matrix.

The first phase in the computation shown in Figure 10.5 of the eigenvalues of a real, nonsymmetric, n-by-n matrix is a sequence of $n - 2$ orthogonal similarity transformations. The kth transformation uses Householder reflections to introduce zeros below the subdiagonal in the kth column. The result of this first phase is known as a Hessenberg matrix; all the elements below the first subdiagonal are zero.

```
for k = 1:n-2
   u = A(:,k);
   u(1:k) = 0;

   sigma = norm(u);
   if sigma ~= 0
      if u(k+1) < 0, sigma = -sigma; end
      u(k+1) = u(k+1) + sigma;
      rho = 1/(sigma*u(k+1));
      v = rho*A*u;
      w = rho*(u'*A)';
```

 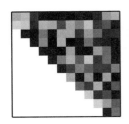 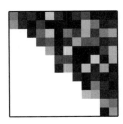

Figure 10.5. eigsvdgui, *nonsymmetric matrix.*

```
    gamma = rho/2*u'*v;
    v = v - gamma*u;
    w = w - gamma*u;
    A = A - v*u' - u*w';
    A(k+2:n,k) = 0;
  end
end
```

The second phase uses the QR algorithm to introduce zeros in the first subdiagonal. A real, nonsymmetric matrix will usually have some complex eigenvalues, so it is not possible to completely transform it to the upper triangular Schur form. Instead, a real Schur form with 1-by-1 and 2-by-2 submatrices on the diagonal is produced. Each 1-by-1 matrix is a real eigenvalue of the original matrix. The eigenvalues of each 2-by-2 block are a pair of complex conjugate eigenvalues of the original matrix.

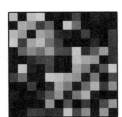 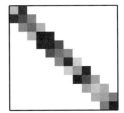 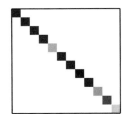

Figure 10.6. eigsvdgui, *symmetric matrix.*

The computation of the eigenvalues of a symmetric matrix shown in Figure 10.6 also has two phases. The result of the first phase is a matrix that is both symmetric and Hessenberg, so it is tridiagonal. Then, since all the eigenvalues of a real, symmetric matrix are real, the QR iterations in the second phase can completely zero the subdiagonal and produce a real, diagonal matrix containing the eigenvalues.

Figure 10.7 shows the output produced by eigsvdgui as it computes the singular values of a nonsymmetric matrix. Multiplication by any orthogonal matrix preserves singular values, so it is not necessary to use similarity transformations. The first phase uses a Householder reflection to introduce zeros below the diagonal in each column, then a different Householder reflection to introduce zeros to the right of the first superdiagonal in

 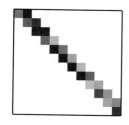 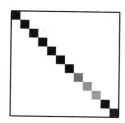

Figure 10.7. `eigsvdgui`, *SVD*.

the corresponding row. This produces an upper bidiagonal matrix with the same singular values as the original matrix. The QR iterations then zero the superdiagonal to produce a diagonal matrix containing the singular values.

10.11   Principal Components

Principal component analysis, or PCA, approximates a general matrix by a sum of a few "simple" matrices. By "simple" we mean rank one; all of the rows are multiples of each other, and so are all of the columns. Let A be any real m-by-n matrix. The economy-sized SVD

$$A = U \Sigma V^T$$

can be rewritten

$$A = E_1 + E_2 + \cdots + E_p,$$

where $p = \min(m, n)$. The component matrices E_k are rank one outer products:

$$E_k = \sigma_k u_k v_k^T.$$

Each column of E_k is a multiple of u_k, the kth column of U, and each row is a multiple of v_k^T, the transpose of the kth column of V. The component matrices are orthogonal to each other in the sense that

$$E_j E_k^T = 0, \ j \neq k.$$

The norm of each component matrix is the corresponding singular value

$$\|E_k\| = \sigma_k.$$

Consequently, the contribution each E_k makes to reproducing A is determined by the size of the singular value σ_k.

If the sum is truncated after $r < p$ terms,

$$A_r = E_1 + E_2 + \cdots + E_r,$$

the result is a rank r approximation to the original matrix A. In fact, A_r is the closest rank r approximation to A. It turns out that the error in this approximation is

$$\|A - A_r\| = \sigma_{r+1}.$$

Since the singular values are in decreasing order, the accuracy of the approximation increases as the rank increases.

PCA is used in a wide range of fields, including statistics, earth sciences, and archaeology. The description and notation also vary widely. Perhaps the most common description is in terms of eigenvalues and eigenvectors of the cross-product matrix $A^T A$. Since

$$A^T A V = V \Sigma^2,$$

the columns of V are the eigenvectors $A^T A$. The columns of U, scaled by the singular values, can then be obtained from

$$U \Sigma = A V.$$

The data matrix A is frequently *standardized* by subtracting the means of the columns and dividing by their standard deviations. If this is done, the cross-product matrix becomes the correlation matrix.

Factor analysis is a closely related technique that makes additional statistical assumptions about the elements of A and modifies the diagonal elements of $A^T A$ before computing the eigenvalues and eigenvectors.

For a simple example of PCA on the unmodified matrix A, suppose we measure the height and weight of six subjects and obtain the following data.

```
A =
      47       15
      93       35
      53       15
      45       10
      67       27
      42       10
```

The dark bars in Figure 10.8 plot this data.

We expect height and weight to be strongly correlated. We believe there is one underlying component—let's call it "size"—that predicts both height and weight. The statement

```
[U,S,V] = svd(A,0)
sigma = diag(S)
```

produces

```
U =
    0.3153      0.1056
    0.6349     -0.3656
    0.3516      0.3259
    0.2929      0.5722
    0.4611     -0.4562
    0.2748      0.4620

V =
    0.9468      0.3219
```

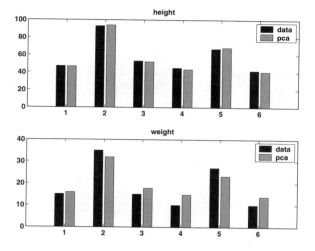

Figure 10.8. *PCA of data.*

```
    0.3219    -0.9468

sigma =
  156.4358
    8.7658
```

Notice that σ_1 is much larger than σ_2. The rank one approximation to A is

```
E1 = sigma(1)*U(:,1)*V(:,1)'

E1 =
   46.7021    15.8762
   94.0315    31.9657
   52.0806    17.7046
   43.3857    14.7488
   68.2871    23.2139
   40.6964    13.8346
```

In other words, the single underlying principal component is

```
size = sigma(1)*U(:,1)

size =
   49.3269
   99.3163
   55.0076
   45.8240
   72.1250
   42.9837
```

The two measured quantities are then well approximated by

```
height  ≈  size*V(1,1)
weight  ≈  size*V(2,1)
```

The light bars in Figure 10.8 plot these approximations.

A larger example involves digital image processing. The statements

```
load detail
subplot(2,2,1)
image(X)
colormap(gray(64))
axis image, axis off
r = rank(X)
title(['rank = ' int2str(r)])
```

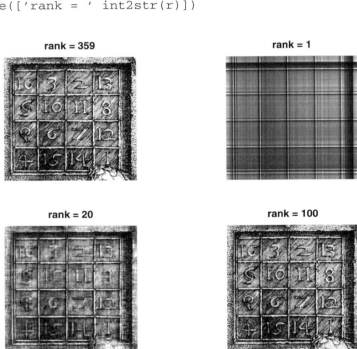

Figure 10.9. *Principal components of Dürer's magic square.*

produce the first subplot in Figure 10.9. The matrix X obtained with the load statement is 359 by 371 and is numerically of full rank. Its elements lie between 1 and 64 and serve as indices into a gray-scale color map. The resulting picture is a detail from Albrecht Dürer's etching "Melancolia II," showing a 4-by-4 magic square. The statements

```
[U,S,V] = svd(X,0);
sigma = diag(S);
semilogy(sigma,'.')
```

produce the logarithmic plot of the singular values of X shown in Figure 10.10. We see that the singular values decrease rapidly. There are one greater than 10^4 and only six greater than 10^3.

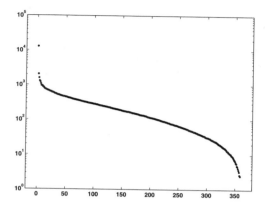

Figure 10.10. *Singular values (log scale).*

The other three subplots in Figure 10.9 show the images obtained from principal component approximations to X with $r = 1$, $r = 20$, and $r = 100$. The rank one approximation shows the horizontal and vertical lines that result from a single outer product, $E_1 = \sigma_1 u_1 v_1^T$. This checkerboard-like structure is typical of low-rank principal component approximations to images. The individual numerals are recognizable in the $r = 20$ approximation. There is hardly any visible difference between the $r = 100$ approximation and the full-rank image.

Although low-rank matrix approximations to images do require less computer storage and transmission time than the full-rank image, there are more effective data compression techniques. The primary uses of PCA in image processing involve feature recognition.

10.12 Circle Generator

The following algorithm was used to plot circles on some of the first computers with graphical displays. At the time, there was no MATLAB and no floating-point arithmetic. Programs were written in machine language and arithmetic was done on scaled integers. The circle-generating program looked something like this.

```
      x = 32768
      y = 0
   L: load y
      shift right 5 bits
      add x
      store in x
      change sign
      shift right 5 bits
      add y
      store in y
```

```
plot x y
go to L
```

Why does this generate a circle? In fact, does it actually generate a circle? There are no trig functions, no square roots, no multiplications or divisions. It's all done with shifts and additions.

The key to this algorithm is the fact that the new x is used in the computation of the new y. This was convenient on computers at the time because it meant you needed only two storage locations, one for x and one for y. But, as we shall see, it is also why the algorithm comes close to working at all.

Here is a MATLAB version of the same algorithm.

```
h = 1/32;
x = 1;
y = 0;
while 1
    x = x + h*y;
    y = y - h*x;
    plot(x,y,'.')
    drawnow
end
```

The M-file circlegen lets you experiment with various values of the step size h. It provides an actual circle in the background. Figure 10.11 shows the output for the carefully chosen default value, h = 0.20906. It's not quite a circle. However, circlegen(h) generates better circles with smaller values of h. Try circlegen(h) for various h yourself.

If we let (x_n, y_n) denote the nth point generated, then the iteration is

$$x_{n+1} = x_n + hy_n,$$
$$y_{n+1} = y_n - hx_{n+1}.$$

The key is the fact that x_{n+1} appears on the right in the second equation. Substituting the first equation into the second gives

$$x_{n+1} = x_n + hy_n,$$
$$y_{n+1} = -hx_n + (1 - h^2)y_n.$$

Let's switch to matrix-vector notation. Let x_n now denote the 2-vector specifying the nth point and let A be the *circle generator* matrix

$$A = \begin{pmatrix} 1 & h \\ -h & 1 - h^2 \end{pmatrix}.$$

With this notation, the iteration is simply

$$x_{n+1} = Ax_n.$$

This immediately leads to

$$x_n = A^n x_0.$$

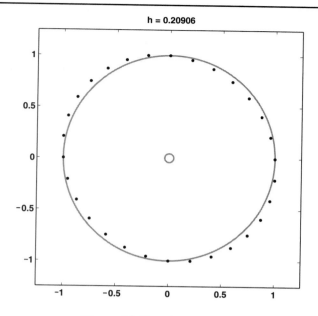

Figure 10.11. `circlegen`.

So, the question is, for various values of h, how do powers of the circle generator matrix behave?

For most matrices A, the behavior of A^n is determined by its *eigenvalues*. The MATLAB statement

```
[X,Lambda] = eig(A)
```

produces a *diagonal* eigenvalue matrix Λ and a corresponding eigenvector matrix X so that

$$AX = X\Lambda.$$

If X^{-1} exists, then

$$A = X\Lambda X^{-1}$$

and

$$A^n = X\Lambda^n X^{-1}.$$

Consequently, the powers A^n remain bounded if the eigenvector matrix is nonsingular and the eigenvalues λ_k, which are the diagonal elements of Λ, satisfy

$$|\lambda_k| \leq 1.$$

Here is an easy experiment. Enter the line

```
h = 2*rand, A = [1 h; -h 1-h^2], lambda = eig(A), abs(lambda)
```

Repeatedly press the up arrow key, then the Enter key. You should eventually become convinced, at least experimentally, of the following:

For any h in the interval $0 < h < 2$, the eigenvalues of the circle generator matrix A are complex numbers with absolute value 1.

The Symbolic Toolbox provides some assistance in actually proving this fact.

```
syms h
A = [1 h; -h 1-h^2]
lambda = eig(A)
```

creates a symbolic version of the iteration matrix and finds its eigenvalues.

```
A =
[    1,      h]
[   -h,  1-h^2]

lambda =
[ 1-1/2*h^2+1/2*(-4*h^2+h^4)^(1/2)]
[ 1-1/2*h^2-1/2*(-4*h^2+h^4)^(1/2)]
```

The statement

```
abs(lambda)
```

does not do anything useful, in part because we have not yet made any assumptions about the symbolic variable h.

We note that the eigenvalues will be complex if the quantity involved in the square root is negative, that is, if $|h| < 2$. The determinant of a matrix should be the product of its eigenvalues. This is confirmed with

```
d = det(A)
```

or

```
d = simple(prod(lambda))
```

Both produce

```
d =
1
```

Consequently, if $|h| < 2$, the eigenvalues, λ, are complex and their product is 1, so they must satisfy $|\lambda| = 1$.

Because

$$\lambda = 1 - h^2/2 \pm h\sqrt{-1 + h^2/4},$$

it is plausible that, if we define θ by

$$\cos\theta = 1 - h^2/2$$

or

$$\sin\theta = h\sqrt{1 - h^2/4},$$

then

$$\lambda = \cos\theta \pm i\sin\theta.$$

The Symbolic Toolbox confirms this with

```
theta = acos(1-h^2/2);
Lambda = [cos(theta)-i*sin(theta); cos(theta)+i*sin(theta)]
diff = simple(lambda-Lambda)
```

which produces

```
Lambda =
[ 1-1/2*h^2-1/2*i*(4*h^2-h^4)^(1/2)]
[ 1-1/2*h^2+1/2*i*(4*h^2-h^4)^(1/2)]

diff =
[ 0]
[ 0]
```

In summary, this proves that, if $|h| < 2$, the eigenvalues of the circle generator matrix are

$$\lambda = e^{\pm i\theta}.$$

The eigenvalues are distinct, and hence X must be nonsingular and

$$A^n = X \begin{pmatrix} e^{in\theta} & 0 \\ 0 & e^{-in\theta} \end{pmatrix} X^{-1}.$$

If the step size h happens to correspond to a value of θ that is $2\pi/p$, where p is an integer, then the algorithm generates only p discrete points before it repeats itself.

How close does our circle generator come to actually generating circles? In fact, it generates ellipses. As the step size h gets smaller, the ellipses get closer to circles. The *aspect ratio* of an ellipse is the ratio of its major axis to its minor axis. It turns out that the aspect ratio of the ellipse produced by the generator is equal to the *condition number* of the matrix of eigenvectors, X. The condition number of a matrix is computed by the MATLAB function `cond(X)` and is discussed in more detail in Chapter 2, Linear Equations.

The solution to the 2-by-2 system of ordinary differential equations

$$\dot{x} = Qx,$$

where

$$Q = \begin{pmatrix} 0 & 1 \\ -1 & 0 \end{pmatrix},$$

is a circle

$$x(t) = \begin{pmatrix} \cos t & \sin t \\ -\sin t & \cos t \end{pmatrix} x(0).$$

So the iteration matrix

$$\begin{pmatrix} \cos h & \sin h \\ -\sin h & \cos h \end{pmatrix}$$

generates perfect circles. The Taylor series for $\cos h$ and $\sin h$ show that the iteration matrix for our circle generator,

$$A = \begin{pmatrix} 1 & h \\ -h & 1 - h^2 \end{pmatrix},$$

approaches the perfect iterator as h gets small.

10.13   Further Reading

The reference books on matrix computation [2, 18, 26, 58, 59, 60] discuss eigenvalues. In addition, the classic by Wilkinson [68] is still readable and relevant. ARPACK, which underlies the sparse `eigs` function, is described in [38].

Exercises

10.1. Match the following matrices to the following properties. For each matrix, choose the most descriptive property. Each property can be matched to one or more of the matrices.

```
magic(4)                     Symmetric
hess(magic(4))               Defective
schur(magic(5))              Orthogonal
pascal(6)                    Singular
hess(pascal(6))              Tridiagonal
schur(pascal(6))             Diagonal
orth(gallery(3))             Hessenberg form
gallery(5)                   Schur form
gallery('frank',12)          Jordan form
[1 1 0; 0 2 1; 0 0 3]
[2 1 0; 0 2 1; 0 0 2]
```

10.2. (a) What is the largest eigenvalue of `magic(n)`? Why?
      (b) What is the largest singular value of `magic(n)`? Why?

10.3. As a function of n, what are the eigenvalues of the n-by-n Fourier matrix, `fft(eye(n))`?

10.4. Try this:

```
n = 101;
d = ones(n-1,1);
A = diag(d,1) + diag(d,-1);
e = eig(A)
plot(-(n-1)/2:(n-1)/2,e,'.')
```

Do you recognize the resulting curve? Can you guess a formula for the eigenvalues of this matrix?

10.5. Plot the trajectories in the complex plane of the eigenvalues of the matrix A with elements

$$a_{i,j} = \frac{1}{i - j + t}$$

as t varies over the interval $0 < t < 1$. Your plot should look something like Figure 10.12.

10.6. (a) In theory, the elements of the vector obtained from

```
condeig(gallery(5))
```

should be infinite. Why?

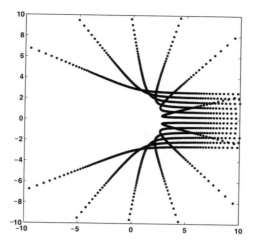

Figure 10.12. *Eigenvalue trajectories.*

(b) In practice, the computed values are only about 10^{10}. Why?

10.7. This exercise uses the Symbolic Toolbox to study a classic eigenvalue test matrix, the Rosser matrix.

(a) You can compute the eigenvalues of the Rosser matrix exactly and order them in increasing order with

```
R = sym(rosser)
e = eig(R)
[ignore,k] = sort(double(e))
e = e(k)
```

Why can't you just use e = sort(eig(R))?

(b) You can compute and display the characteristic polynomial of R with

```
p = poly(R)
f = factor(p)
pretty(f)
```

Which terms in f correspond to which eigenvalues in e?

(c) What does each of these statements do?

```
e = eig(sym(rosser))
r = eig(rosser)
double(e) - r
double(e - r)
```

(d) Why are the results in (c) on the order of 10^{-12} instead of eps?

(e) Change R(1,1) from 611 to 612 and compute the eigenvalues of the modified matrix. Why do the results appear in a different form?

10.8. Both of the matrices

```
P = gallery('pascal',12)
F = gallery('frank',12)
```

have the property that, if λ is an eigenvalue, so is $1/\lambda$. How well do the computed eigenvalues preserve this property? Use `condeig` to explain the different behavior for the two matrices.

10.9. Compare these three ways to compute the singular values of a matrix.

```
svd(A)
sqrt(eig(A'*A))
Z = zeros(size(A)); s = eig([Z A; A' Z]); s = s(s>0)
```

10.10. Experiment with `eigsvdgui` on random symmetric and nonsymmetric matrices, `randn(n)`. Choose values of n appropriate for the speed of your computer and investigate the three variants `eig`, `symm`, and `svd`. The title in the `eigsvdgui` shows the number of iterations required. Roughly, how does the number of iterations for the three different variants depend upon the order of the matrix?

10.11. Pick a value of n and generate a matrix with

```
A = diag(ones(n-1,1),-1) + diag(1,n-1);
```

Explain any atypical behavior you observe with each of the following.

```
eigsvdgui(A,'eig')
eigsvdgui(A,'symm')
eigsvdgui(A,'svd')
```

10.12. The NCM file `imagesvd.m` helps you investigate the use of PCA in digital image processing. If you have them available, use your own photographs. If you have access to the MATLAB Image Processing Toolbox, you may want to use its advanced features. However, it is possible to do basic image processing without the toolbox. For an m-by-n color image in JPEG format, the statement

```
X = imread('myphoto.jpg');
```

produces a three-dimensional m-by-n-by-3 array X with m-by-n integer subarrays for the red, green, and blue intensities. It would be possible to compute three separate m-by-n SVDs of the three colors. An alternative that requires less work involves altering the dimensions of X with

```
X = reshape(X,m,3*n)
```

and then computing one m-by-$3n$ SVD.
(a) The primary computation in `imagesvd` is done by

```
[V,S,U] = svd(X',0)
```

How does this compare with

    [U,S,V] = svd(X,0)

(b) How does the choice of approximating rank affect the visual qualities of the images? There are no precise answers here. Your results will depend upon the images you choose and the judgments you make.

10.13. This exercise investigates a model of the human gait developed by Nikolaus Troje at the Bio Motion Lab of Ruhr University in Bochum, Germany. Their Web page provides an interactive demo [7]. Two papers describing the work are also available on the Web [62, 63].

Troje's data result from motion capture experiments involving subjects wearing reflective markers walking on a treadmill. His model is a five-term Fourier series with vector-valued coefficients obtained by principal component analysis of the experimental data. The components, which are also known as *postures* or *eigenpostures*, correspond to static position, forward motion, sideways sway, and two hopping/bouncing movements that differ in the phase relationship between the upper and lower portions of the body. The model is purely descriptive; it does not make any direct use of physical laws of motion.

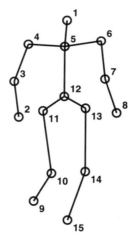

Figure 10.13. *Walker at rest.*

The moving position $v(t)$ of the human body is described by 45 functions of time, which correspond to the location of 15 points in three-dimensional space. Figure 10.13 is a static snapshot. The model is

$$v(t) = v_1 + v_2 \sin \omega t + v_3 \cos \omega t + v_4 \sin 2\omega t + v_5 \cos 2\omega t.$$

If the postures $v_1, \ldots, v_5$ are regarded as the columns of a single 45-by-5 matrix V, the calculation of $v(t)$ for any t involves a matrix-vector multiplication. The resulting vector can then be reshaped into a 15-by-3 array that exposes the spatial coordinates. For example, at $t = 0$, the time-varying coefficients form the vector w = [1 0 1 0 1]'. Consequently, reshape(V*w,15,3) produces the coordinates of the initial position.

The five postures for an individual subject are obtained by a combination of principal component and Fourier analysis. The individual characteristic frequency ω is an independent speed parameter. If the postures are averaged over the subjects with a particular characteristic, the result is a model for the "typical" walker with that characteristic. The characteristics available in the demo on the Web page include male/female, heavy/light, nervous/relaxed, and happy/sad.

Our M-file walker.m is based on the postures for a typical female walker, $f_1, \ldots, f_5$, and a typical male walker, $m_1, \ldots, m_5$. Slider s_1 varies the time increment and hence the apparent walking speed. Sliders $s_2, \ldots, s_5$ vary the amount that each component contributes to the overall motion. Slider s_6 varies a linear combination of the female and male walkers. A slider setting greater than 1.0 overemphasizes the characteristic. Here is the complete model, including the sliders:

$$f(t) = f_1 + s_2 f_2 \sin \omega t + s_3 f_3 \cos \omega t + s_4 f_4 \sin 2\omega t + s_5 f_5 \cos 2\omega t,$$

$$m(t) = m_1 + s_2 m_2 \sin \omega t + s_3 m_3 \cos \omega t + s_4 m_4 \sin 2\omega t + s_5 m_5 \cos 2\omega t,$$

$$v(t) = (f(t) + m(t))/2 + s_6 (f(t) - m(t))/2.$$

(a) Describe the visual differences between the gaits of the typical female and male walkers.

(b) File walkers.mat contains four data sets. F and M are the postures of the typical female and typical male obtained by analyzing all the subjects. A and B are the postures of two individual subjects. Are A and B male or female?

(c) Modify walker.m to add a waving hand as an additional, artificial, posture.

(d) What does this program do?

```
load walkers
F = reshape(F,15,3,5);
M = reshape(M,15,3,5);
for k = 1:5
    for j = 1:3
        subplot(5,3,j+3*(k-1))
        plot([F(:,j,k) M(:,j,k)])
        ax = axis;
        axis([1 15 ax(3:4)])
    end
end
```

(e) Change walker.m to use a Fourier model parametrized by amplitude and phase. The female walker is

$$f(t) = f_1 + s_2 a_1 \sin(\omega t + s_3 \phi_1) + s_4 a_2 \sin(2\omega t + s_5 \phi_2).$$

A similar formulation is used for the male walker. The linear combination of the two walkers using s_6 is unchanged. The amplitude and phase are given by

$$a_1 = \sqrt{f_2^2 + f_3^2},$$
$$a_2 = \sqrt{f_4^2 + f_5^2},$$
$$\phi_1 = \tan^{-1}(f_3/f_2),$$
$$\phi_2 = \tan^{-1}(f_5/f_4).$$

10.14. In English, and in many other languages, vowels are usually followed by consonants and consonants are usually followed by vowels. This fact is revealed by a principal component analysis of the digraph frequency matrix for a sample of text. English text uses 26 letters, so the digraph frequency matrix is a 26-by-26 matrix, A, with counts of pairs of letters. Blanks and all other punctuation are removed from the text and the entire sample is thought of as circular or periodic, so the first letter follows the last letter. The matrix entry $a_{i,j}$ is the number of times the ith letter is followed by the jth letter in the text. The row and column sums of A are the same; they count the number of times individual letters occur in the sample. So the fifth row and fifth column usually have the largest sums because the fifth letter, which is "E," is usually the most frequent.

A principal component analysis of A produces a first component,

$$A \approx \sigma_1 u_1 v_1^T,$$

that reflects the individual letter frequencies. The first right- and left-singular vectors, u_1 and v_1, have elements that are all of the same sign and that are roughly proportional to the corresponding frequencies. We are primarily interested in the second principle component,

$$A \approx \sigma_1 u_1 v_1^T + \sigma_2 u_2 v_2^T.$$

The second term has positive entries in vowel-consonant and consonant-vowel positions and negative entries in vowel-vowel and consonant-consonant positions. The NCM collection contains a function `digraph.m` that carries out this analysis. Figure 10.14 shows the output produced by analyzing Lincoln's Gettysburg Address with

```
digraph('gettysburg.txt')
```

The ith letter of the alphabet is plotted at coordinates $(u_{i,2}, v_{i,2})$. The distance of each letter from the origin is roughly proportional to its frequency, and the sign patterns cause the vowels to be plotted in one quadrant and the consonants to be plotted in the opposite quadrant. There is even a little more detail. The letter "N" is usually preceded by a vowel and often followed by another consonant, like "D" or "G," and so it shows up in a quadrant pretty much by itself. On the other hand, "H" is often preceded by another consonant, namely "T," and followed by a vowel, "E," so it also gets its own quadrant.

(a) Explain how `digraph` uses `sparse` to count letter pairs and create the matrix. `help sparse` should be useful.

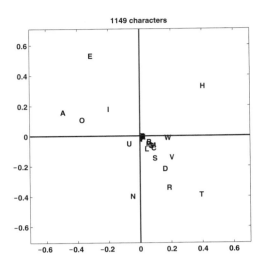

Figure 10.14. *The second principal component of a digraph matrix.*

(b) Try `digraph` on other text samples. Roughly how many characters are needed to see the vowel-consonant frequency behavior?

(c) Can you find any text with at least several hundred characters that does not show the typical behavior?

(d) Try `digraph` on M-files or other source code. Do computer programs typically have the same vowel-consonant behavior as prose?

(e) Try `digraph` on samples from other languages. Hawaiian and Finnish are particularly interesting. You may need to modify `digraph` to accommodate more or fewer than 26 letters. Do other languages show the same vowel-consonant behavior as English?

10.15. Explain the behavior of `circlegen` for each of the following values of the step size h. What, if anything, is special about these particular values? Is the orbit a discrete set of points? Does the orbit stay bounded, grow linearly, or grow exponentially? If necessary, increase the axis limits in `circlegen` so that it shows the entire orbit. Recall that $\phi = (1 + \sqrt{5})/2$ is the golden ratio:

$$h = \sqrt{2 - 2\cos(2\pi/30)} \text{ (the default)},$$
$$h = 1/\phi,$$
$$h = \phi,$$
$$h = 1.4140,$$
$$h = \sqrt{2},$$
$$h = 1.4144,$$
$$h < 2,$$
$$h = 2,$$
$$h > 2.$$

10.16. (a) Modify `circlegen` so that both components of the new point are determined from the old point, that is,

$$x_{n+1} = x_n + h y_n,$$
$$y_{n+1} = y_n - h x_n.$$

(This is the *explicit Euler's method* for solving the circle ordinary differential equation.) What happens to the "circles"? What is the iteration matrix? What are its eigenvalues?

(b) Modify `circlegen` so that the new point is determined by solving a 2-by-2 system of simultaneous equations:

$$x_{n+1} - h y_{n+1} = x_n,$$
$$y_{n+1} + h x_{n+1} = y_n.$$

(This is the *implicit Euler's method* for solving the circle ordinary differential equation.) What happens to the "circles"? What is the iteration matrix? What are its eigenvalues?

10.17. Modify `circlegen` so that it keeps track of the maximum and minimum radius during the iteration and returns the ratio of these two radii as the value of the function. Compare this computed aspect ratio with the eigenvector condition number, `cond(X)`, for various values of `h`.

Chapter 11

Partial Differential Equations

A wide variety of partial differential equations occurs in technical computing. We cannot begin to cover them all in this book. In this chapter, we limit ourselves to three model problems for second-order partial differential equations in one or two space dimensions.

11.1 Model Problems

All the problems we consider involve the Laplacian operator, which is

$$\triangle = \frac{\partial^2}{\partial x^2}$$

in one space dimension and

$$\triangle = \frac{\partial^2}{\partial x^2} + \frac{\partial^2}{\partial y^2}$$

in two space dimensions. We let $\vec{x}$ denote the single variable x in one dimension and the pair of variables (x, y) in two dimensions.

The first model problem is the Poisson equation. This *elliptic* equation does not involve a time variable, and so describes the steady state, quiescent behavior of a model variable:

$$\triangle u = f(\vec{x}).$$

There are no initial conditions.

The second model problem is the heat equation. This *parabolic* equation occurs in models involving diffusion and decay:

$$\frac{\partial u}{\partial t} = \triangle u - f(\vec{x}).$$

The initial condition is

$$u(\vec{x}, 0) = u_0(\vec{x}).$$

The third model problem is the wave equation. This *hyperbolic* equation describes how a disturbance travels through matter. If the units are chosen so that the wave propagation speed is equal to one, the amplitude of a wave satisfies

$$\frac{\partial^2 u}{\partial t^2} = \triangle u.$$

Typical initial conditions specify the initial amplitude and take the initial velocity to be zero:

$$u(\vec{x}, 0) = u_0(\vec{x}), \quad \frac{\partial u}{\partial t}(\vec{x}, 0) = 0.$$

In one dimension, all the problems take place on a finite interval on the x-axis. In more than one space dimension, geometry plays a vital role. In two dimensions, all the problems take place in a bounded region Ω in the (x, y) plane. In all cases, $f(\vec{x})$ and $u_0(\vec{x})$ are given functions of $\vec{x}$. All the problems involve boundary conditions where the value of u or some partial derivative of u is specified on the boundary of Ω. Unless otherwise specified, we will take the boundary values to be zero.

11.2   Finite Difference Methods

Basic finite difference methods for approximating solutions to these problems use a uniform mesh with spacing h. In one dimension, for the interval $a \leq x \leq b$, the spacing is $h = (b - a)/(m + 1)$ and the mesh points are

$$x_i = a + ih, \ i = 0, \ldots, m + 1.$$

The second derivative with respect to x is approximated by the 3-point centered second difference:

$$\triangle_h u(x) = \frac{u(x + h) - 2u(x) + u(x - h)}{h^2}.$$

In two dimensions, the mesh is the set of points

$$(x_i, y_j) = (ih, jh)$$

that lie within the region Ω. Approximating the partial derivatives with centered second differences gives the 5-point discrete Laplacian

$$\triangle_h u(x, y) = \frac{u(x + h, y) - 2u(x, y) + u(x - h, y)}{h^2}$$
$$+ \frac{u(x, y + h) - 2u(x, y) + u(x, y - h)}{h^2}.$$

Alternative notation uses $P = (x, y)$ for a mesh point and $N = (x, y + h)$, $E = (x + h, y)$, $S = (x, y - h)$, and $W = (x - h, y)$ for its four neighbors in the four compass directions. The discrete Laplacian is

$$\triangle_h u(P) = \frac{u(N) + u(W) + u(E) + u(S) - 4u(P)}{h^2}.$$

The finite difference Poisson problem involves finding values of u so that

$$\triangle_h u(\vec{x}) = f(\vec{x})$$

for each point $\vec{x}$ on the mesh.

If the source term $f(\vec{x})$ is zero, Poisson's equation is called Laplace's equation:

$$\triangle_h u(x) = 0.$$

In one dimension, Laplace's equation has only trivial solutions. The value of u at a mesh point x is the average of the values of u at its left and right neighbors, so $u(x)$ must be a linear function of x. Taking the boundary conditions into consideration implies that $u(x)$ is the linear function connecting the two boundary values. If the boundary values are zero, then $u(x)$ is identically zero. In more than one dimension, solutions to Laplace's equation are called *harmonic* functions and are not simply linear functions of $\vec{x}$.

The finite difference heat and wave equations also make use of first and second differences in the t direction. Let δ denote the length of a time step. For the heat equation, we use a difference scheme that corresponds to Euler's method for ordinary differential equations:

$$\frac{u(\vec{x}, t + \delta) - u(\vec{x}, t)}{\delta} = \triangle_h u(\vec{x}).$$

Starting with the initial conditions $u(\vec{x}, 0) = u_0(\vec{x})$, we can step from any value of t to $t + \delta$ with

$$u(\vec{x}, t + \delta) = u(\vec{x}, t) + \delta \triangle_h u(\vec{x}, t)$$

for all of the mesh points $\vec{x}$ in the region. The boundary conditions supply values on the boundary or outside the region. This method is *explicit* because each new value of u can be computed directly from values of u at the previous time step. More complicated methods are *implicit* because they involve the solution of systems of equations at each step.

For the wave equation, we can use a centered second difference in t:

$$\frac{u(\vec{x}, t + \delta) - 2u(\vec{x}, t) + u(\vec{x}, t - \delta)}{\delta^2} = \triangle_h u(\vec{x}, t).$$

This requires two "layers" of values of the solution, one at $t - \delta$ and one at t. In our simple model problem, the initial condition

$$\frac{\partial u}{\partial t}(\vec{x}, 0) = 0$$

allows us to start with both $u(\vec{x}, 0) = u_0(\vec{x})$ and $u(\vec{x}, \delta) = u_0(\vec{x})$. We compute subsequent layers with

$$u(\vec{x}, t + \delta) = 2u(\vec{x}, t) - u(\vec{x}, t - \delta) + \delta^2 \triangle_h u(\vec{x}, t)$$

for all of the mesh points $\vec{x}$ in the region. The boundary conditions supply values on the boundary or outside the region. Like our scheme for the heat equation, this method for solving the wave equation is *explicit*.

11.3   Matrix Representation

If a one-dimensional mesh function is represented as a vector, the one-dimensional difference operator $\triangle_h$ becomes the tridiagonal matrix

$$\frac{1}{h^2}\begin{pmatrix} -2 & 1 & & & & \\ 1 & -2 & 1 & & & \\ & 1 & -2 & 1 & & \\ & & \ddots & \ddots & \ddots & \\ & & & 1 & -2 & 1 \\ & & & & 1 & -2 \end{pmatrix}.$$

This matrix is symmetric. (It is also *negative definite*.) Most importantly, even if there are thousands of interior mesh points, there are at most three nonzero elements in each row and column. Such matrices are the prime examples of *sparse* matrices. When computing with sparse matrices, it is important to use data structures that store only the locations and values of the nonzero elements.

With u represented as a vector and $h^2\triangle_h$ as a matrix A, the Poisson problem becomes

$$Au = b,$$

where b is a vector (the same size as u) containing the values of $h^2 f(x)$ at the interior mesh points. The first and last components of b would also include any nonzero boundary values.

In MATLAB, the solution to the discrete Poisson problem is computed using sparse backslash, which takes advantage of the sparsity in A:

    u = A\b

The situation for meshes in two dimensions is more complicated. Let's number the interior mesh points in Ω from top to bottom and from left to right. For example, the numbering of an L-shaped region would be

```
L =
    0    0    0    0    0    0    0    0    0    0    0
    0    1    5    9   13   17   21   30   39   48    0
    0    2    6   10   14   18   22   31   40   49    0
    0    3    7   11   15   19   23   32   41   50    0
    0    4    8   12   16   20   24   33   42   51    0
    0    0    0    0    0    0   25   34   43   52    0
    0    0    0    0    0    0   26   35   44   53    0
    0    0    0    0    0    0   27   36   45   54    0
    0    0    0    0    0    0   28   37   46   55    0
    0    0    0    0    0    0   29   38   47   56    0
    0    0    0    0    0    0    0    0    0    0    0
```

The zeros are points on the boundary or outside the region. With this numbering, the values of any function defined on the interior of the region can be reshaped into a long column vector. In this example, the length of the vector is 56.

If a two-dimensional mesh function is represented as a vector, the finite difference Laplacian becomes a matrix. For example, at point number 43,

$$h^2 \triangle_h u(43) = u(34) + u(42) + u(44) + u(52) - 4u(43).$$

If A is the corresponding matrix, then its 43rd row would have five nonzero elements:

$$a_{43,34} = a_{43,42} = a_{43,44} = a_{43,52} = 1, \text{ and } a_{43,43} = -4.$$

A mesh point near the boundary has only two or three interior neighbors, so the corresponding row of A has only three or four nonzero entries.

The complete matrix A has -4's on its diagonal, four 1's off the diagonal in most of its rows, two or three 1's off the diagonal in some of its rows, and zeros elsewhere. For the example region above, A would be 56 by 56. Here is A if there are only 16 interior points.

```
A =
   -4   1   1   0   0   0   0   0   0   0   0   0   0   0   0   0
    1  -4   0   1   0   0   0   0   0   0   0   0   0   0   0   0
    1   0  -4   1   1   0   0   0   0   0   0   0   0   0   0   0
    0   1   1  -4   0   1   0   0   0   0   0   0   0   0   0   0
    0   0   1   0  -4   1   1   0   0   0   0   0   0   0   0   0
    0   0   0   1   1  -4   0   1   0   0   0   0   0   0   0   0
    0   0   0   0   1   0  -4   1   0   0   0   1   0   0   0   0
    0   0   0   0   0   1   1  -4   1   0   0   0   1   0   0   0
    0   0   0   0   0   0   0   1  -4   1   0   0   0   1   0   0
    0   0   0   0   0   0   0   0   1  -4   1   0   0   0   1   0
    0   0   0   0   0   0   0   0   0   1  -4   0   0   0   0   1
    0   0   0   0   0   0   1   0   0   0   0  -4   1   0   0   0
    0   0   0   0   0   0   0   1   0   0   0   1  -4   1   0   0
    0   0   0   0   0   0   0   0   1   0   0   0   1  -4   1   0
    0   0   0   0   0   0   0   0   0   1   0   0   0   1  -4   1
    0   0   0   0   0   0   0   0   0   0   1   0   0   0   1  -4
```

This matrix is symmetric, negative definite, and sparse. There are at most five nonzero elements in each row and column.

MATLAB has two functions that involve the discrete Laplacian, del2 and delsq. If u is a two-dimensional array representing a function $u(x, y)$, then del2(u) computes $\triangle_h u$, scaled by $h^2/4$, at interior points, and uses one-sided formulas at points near the boundary. For example, the function $u(x, y) = x^2 + y^2$ has $\triangle u = 4$. The statements

```
h = 1/20;
[x,y] = meshgrid(-1:h:1);
u = x.^2 + y.^2;
d = (4/h^2) * del2(u);
```

produce an array d, the same size as x and y, with all the elements equal to 4.

If G is a two-dimensional array specifying the numbering of a mesh, then A = -delsq(G) is the matrix representation of the operator $h^2 \triangle_h$ on that mesh. The mesh numbering for several specific regions is generated by numgrid. For example,

```
m = 5
L = numgrid('L',2*m+1)
```

generates the L-shaped mesh with 56 interior points shown above. And

```
m = 3
A = -delsq(numgrid('L',2*m+1))
```

generates the 16-by-16 matrix A shown above.

The function `inregion` can also generate mesh numberings. For example, the coordinates of the vertices of the L-shaped domain are

```
xv = [0   0   1   1  -1  -1   0];
yv = [0  -1  -1   1   1   0   0];
```

The statement

```
[x,y] = meshgrid(-1:h:1);
```

generates a square grid of width h. The statement

```
[in,on] = inregion(x,y,xv,yv);
```

generates arrays of zeros and ones that mark the points that are contained in the domain, including the boundary, as well as those that are strictly on the boundary. The statements

```
p = find(in-on);
n = length(p);
L = zeros(size(x));
L(p) = 1:n;
```

number the n interior points from top to bottom and left to right. The statement

```
A = -delsq(L);
```

generates the n-by-n sparse matrix representation of the discrete Laplacian on the mesh.

With u represented as a vector with n components, the Poisson problem becomes

$$Au = b,$$

where b is a vector (the same size as u) containing the values of $h^2 f(x, y)$ at the interior mesh points. The components of b that correspond to mesh points with neighbors on the boundary or outside the region also include any nonzero boundary values.

As in one dimension, the solution to the discrete Poisson problem is computed using sparse backslash.

```
u = A\b
```

11.4 Numerical Stability

The time-dependent heat and wave equations generate a sequence of vectors, $u^{(k)}$, where the k denotes the kth time step. For the heat equation, the recurrence is

$$u^{(k+1)} = u^{(k)} + \sigma A u^{(k)},$$

where

$$\sigma = \frac{\delta}{h^2}.$$

This can be written

$$u^{(k+1)} = Mu^{(k)},$$

where

$$M = I + \sigma A.$$

In one dimension, the iteration matrix M has $1 - 2\sigma$ on the diagonal and one or two σ's off the diagonal in each row. In two dimensions, M has $1 - 4\sigma$ on the diagonal and two, three, or four σ's off the diagonal in each row. Most of the row sums in M are equal to 1; a few are less than 1. Each element of $u^{(k+1)}$ is a linear combination of elements of $u^{(k)}$ with coefficients that add up to 1 or less. Now here is the key observation. If the elements of M are nonnegative, then the recurrence is stable. In fact, it is dissipative. Any error or noise in $u^{(k)}$ is not magnified in $u^{(k+1)}$. But if the diagonal elements of M are negative, then the recurrence can be unstable. Error and noise, including roundoff error and noise in the initial conditions, can be magnified with each time step. Requiring $1 - 2\sigma$ or $1 - 4\sigma$ to be positive leads to a very important *stability condition* for this explicit method for the heat equation. In one dimension,

$$\sigma \le \frac{1}{2}.$$

And, in two dimensions,

$$\sigma \le \frac{1}{4}.$$

If this condition is satisfied, the iteration matrix has positive diagonal elements and the method is stable.

Analysis of the wave equation is a little more complicated because it involves three levels, $u^{(k+1)}$, $u^{(k)}$, and $u^{(k-1)}$. The recurrence is

$$u^{(k+1)} = 2u^{(k)} - u^{(k-1)} + \sigma A u^{(k)},$$

where

$$\sigma = \frac{\delta^2}{h^2}.$$

The diagonal elements of the iteration matrix are now $2 - 2\sigma$, or $2 - 4\sigma$. In one dimension, the stability condition is

$$\sigma \le 1.$$

And, in two dimensions,

$$\sigma \le \frac{1}{2}.$$

These stability conditions are known as the *CFL conditions*, after Courant, Friedrichs and Lewy, who wrote a paper in 1928 that used finite difference methods to prove existence of solutions to the partial differential equations of mathematical physics. Stability conditions are restrictions on the size of the time step, δ. Any attempt to speed up the computation by taking larger time steps is likely to be disastrous. For the heat equation, the stability condition is particularly severe—the time step must be smaller than the *square* of the space mesh width. More sophisticated methods, often involving some implicit equation solving at each step, have less restrictive or unlimited stability conditions.

The M-file `pdegui` illustrates the concepts discussed in this chapter by offering the choice among several domains and among the model partial differential equations. For Poisson's equation, `pdegui` uses sparse backslash to solve

$$\triangle_h u = 1$$

in the chosen domain. For the heat and wave equations, the stability parameter σ can be varied. If the critical value, 0.25 for the heat equation and 0.50 for the wave equation, is exceeded by even a small amount, the instability rapidly becomes apparent.

You will find much more powerful capabilities in the MATLAB Partial Differential Equation Toolbox.

11.5   The L-Shaped Membrane

Separating out periodic time behavior in the wave equation leads to solutions of the form

$$u(\vec{x}, t) = \cos\left(\sqrt{\lambda}\, t\right) v(\vec{x}).$$

The functions $v(\vec{x})$ depend upon λ. They satisfy

$$\triangle v + \lambda v = 0$$

and are zero on the boundary. The quantities λ that lead to nonzero solutions are the *eigenvalues*, and the corresponding functions $v(\vec{x})$ are the *eigenfunctions* or *modes*. They are determined by the physical properties and the geometry of each particular situation. The square roots of the eigenvalues are resonant frequencies. A periodic external driving force at one of these frequencies generates an unboundedly strong response in the medium.

Any solution of the wave equation can be expressed as a linear combination of these eigenfunctions. The coefficients in the linear combination are obtained from the initial conditions.

In one dimension, the eigenvalues and eigenfunctions are easily determined. The simplest example is a violin string, held fixed at the ends of the interval of length π. The eigenfunctions are

$$v_k(x) = \sin\left(kx\right).$$

The eigenvalues are determined by the boundary condition, $v_k(\pi) = 0$. Hence, k must be an integer and

$$\lambda_k = k^2.$$

If the initial condition, $u_0(x)$, is expanded in a Fourier sine series,

$$u_0(x) = \sum_k a_k \sin\left(kx\right),$$

then the solution to the wave equation is

$$\begin{aligned}
u(x, t) &= \sum_k a_k \cos\left(kt\right) \sin\left(kx\right) \\
&= \sum_k a_k \cos\left(\sqrt{\lambda_k}\, t\right) v_k(x).
\end{aligned}$$

In two dimensions, an L-shaped region formed from three unit squares is interesting for several reasons. It is one of the simplest geometries for which solutions to the wave equation cannot be expressed analytically, so numerical computation is necessary. Furthermore, the 270° nonconvex corner causes a singularity in the solution. Mathematically, the gradient of the first eigenfunction is unbounded near the corner. Physically, a membrane stretched over such a region would rip at the corner. This singularity limits the accuracy of finite difference methods with uniform grids. The MathWorks has adopted a surface plot of the first eigenfunction of the L-shaped region as the company logo. The computation of this eigenfunction involves several of the numerical techniques we have described in this book.

Simple model problems involving waves on an L-shaped region include an L-shaped membrane, or L-shaped tambourine, and a beach towel blowing in the wind, constrained by a picnic basket on one fourth of the towel. A more practical example involves ridged microwave waveguides. One such device, shown in Figure 11.1, is a waveguide-to-coax adapter. The active region is the channel with the H-shaped cross section visible at the end of the adapter. The ridges increase the bandwidth of the guide at the expense of higher attenuation and lower power-handling capability. Symmetry of the H about the dotted lines shown in the contour plot of the electric field implies that only one quarter of the domain needs to be considered and that the resulting geometry is our L-shaped region. The boundary conditions are different than our membrane problem, but the differential equation and the solution techniques are the same.

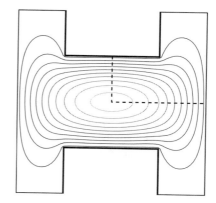

Figure 11.1. *A double-ridge microwave-to-coax adapter and its H-shaped region. Photo courtesy Advanced Technical Materials, Inc.* [1].

Eigenvalues and eigenfunctions of the L-shaped domain can be computed by finite difference methods. The MATLAB statements

```
m = 200
h = 1/m
A = delsq(numgrid('L',2*m+1))/h^2
```

set up the 5-point finite difference approximation to the Laplacian on an 200-by-200 mesh in each of the three squares that make up the domain. The resulting sparse matrix A has order 119201 and 594409 nonzero entries. The statement

```
lambda = eigs(A,6,0)
```

uses Arnoldi's method from the MATLAB implementation of ARPACK to compute the first
six eigenvalues. It takes less than 2 min on a 1.4 GHz Pentium laptop to produce

```
lambda =
    9.64147
   15.19694
   19.73880
   29.52033
   31.91583
   41.47510
```

The exact values are

```
    9.63972
   15.19725
   19.73921
   29.52148
   31.91264
   41.47451
```

You can see that even with this fine mesh and large matrix calculation, the computed eigenvalues are accurate to only three or four significant digits. If you try to get more accuracy
by using a finer mesh and hence a larger matrix, the computation requires so much memory
that the total execution time is excessive.

For the L-shaped domain and similar problems, a technique using analytic solutions to
the underlying differential equation is much more efficient and accurate than finite difference
methods. The technique involves polar coordinates and fractional-order Bessel functions.
With parameters α and λ, the functions

$$v(r, \theta) = J_\alpha(\sqrt{\lambda}\, r) \sin(\alpha\, \theta)$$

are exact solutions to the polar coordinate version of the eigenfunction equation

$$\frac{\partial^2 v}{\partial r^2} + \frac{1}{r}\frac{\partial v}{\partial r} + \frac{1}{r^2}\frac{\partial^2 v}{\partial \theta^2} + \lambda v = 0.$$

For any value of λ, the functions $v(r, \theta)$ satisfy the boundary conditions

$$v(r, 0) = 0 \text{ and } v(r, \pi/\alpha) = 0$$

on the two straight edges of a circular sector with angle π/α. If $\sqrt{\lambda}$ is chosen to be a
zero of the Bessel function, $J_\alpha(\sqrt{\lambda}) = 0$, then $v(r, \theta)$ is also zero on the circle, $r = 1$.
Figure 11.2 shows a few of the eigenfunctions of the circular sector with angle $3\pi/2$. The
eigenfunctions have been chosen to illustrate symmetry about $3\pi/4$ and $\pi/2$.

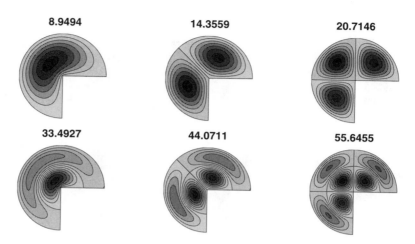

Figure 11.2. *Eigenfunctions of the three-quarter disc.*

We approximate the eigenfunctions of the L-shaped domain and other regions with corners by linear combinations of the circular sector solutions:

$$v(r, \theta) = \sum_j c_j J_{\alpha_j}(\sqrt{\lambda}\, r) \sin(\alpha_j\, \theta).$$

The angle of the reentrant 270° corner in the L-shaped region is $3\pi/2$, or $\pi/(2/3)$, so the values of α are integer multiples of $2/3$:

$$\alpha_j = \frac{2j}{3}.$$

These functions $v(r, \theta)$ are exact solutions to the eigenfunction differential equation. There is no finite difference mesh involved. The functions also satisfy the boundary conditions on the two edges that meet at the reentrant corner. All that remains is to pick the parameter λ and the coefficients c_j so that the boundary conditions on the remaining edges are satisfied.

A least squares approach involving the SVD is used to determine λ and the c_j. Pick m points, (r_i, θ_i), on the remaining edges of the boundary. Let n be the number of fundamental solutions to be used. Generate an m-by-n matrix A with elements that depend upon λ:

$$A_{i,j}(\lambda) = J_{\alpha_j}(\sqrt{\lambda}\, r_i) \sin(\alpha_j\, \theta_i), \quad i = 1, \ldots, m, \quad j = 1, \ldots, n.$$

Then, for any vector c, the vector Ac is the vector of boundary values, $v(r_i, \theta_i)$. We want to make $||Ac||$ small without taking $||c||$ small. The SVD provides the solution.

Let $\sigma_n(A(\lambda))$ denote the smallest singular value of the matrix $A(\lambda)$. and let λ_k denote a value of λ that produces a local minimum of the smallest singular value:

$$\lambda_k = k\text{th minimizer}(\sigma_n(A(\lambda))).$$

Each λ_k approximates an eigenvalue of the region. The corresponding right singular vector provides the coefficients for the linear combination $c = V(:,n)$.

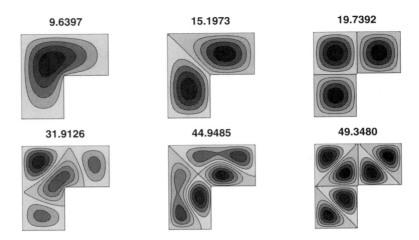

Figure 11.3. *Eigenfunctions of the L-shaped region.*

It is worthwhile to take advantage of symmetries. It turns out that the eigenfunctions fall into three symmetry classes:

- symmetric about the center line at $\theta = 3\pi/4$, so $v(r, \theta) = v(r, 3\pi/2 - \theta)$;

- antisymmetric about the center line at $\theta = 3\pi/4$, so $v(r, \theta) = -v(r, 3\pi/2 - \theta)$;

- eigenfunction of the square, so $v(r, \pi/2) = 0$ and $v(r, \pi) = 0$.

These symmetries allow us to restrict the values of α_j used in each expansion:

- $\alpha_j = \frac{2j}{3}$, j odd and not a multiple of 3;

- $\alpha_j = \frac{2j}{3}$, j even and not a multiple of 3;

- $\alpha_j = \frac{2j}{3}$, j a multiple of 3.

The M-file `membranetx` in the NCM directory computes eigenvalues and eigenfunctions of the L-membrane using these symmetries and a search for local minima of $\sigma_n(A(\lambda))$. The M-file `membrane`, distributed with MATLAB in the `demos` directory, uses an older version of the algorithm based on the QR decomposition instead of the SVD. Figure 11.3 shows six eigenfunctions of the L-shaped region, with two from each of the three symmetry classes. They can be compared with the eigenfunctions of the sector shown in Figure 11.2. By taking the radius of the sector to be $2/\sqrt{\pi}$, both regions have the same area and the eigenvalues are comparable.

The `demo` M-file `logo` makes a `surf` plot of the first eigenfunction, then adds lighting and shading to create The MathWorks logo. After being so careful to satisfy the boundary conditions, the logo uses only the first two terms in the circular sector expansion. This artistic license gives the edge of the logo a more interesting curved shape.

Exercises

11.1. Let n be an integer and generate n-by-n matrices A, D, and I with the statements

```
e = ones(n,1);
I = spdiags(e,0,n,n);
D = spdiags([-e e],[0 1],n,n);
A = spdiags([e -2*e e],[-1 0 1],n,n);
```

(a) For an appropriate value of h, the matrix $(1/h^2)A$ approximates $\triangle_h$ for the interval $0 \leq x \leq 1$. Is that value of h equal to $1/(n-1)$, $1/n$, or $1/(n+1)$?
(b) What does $(1/h)D$ approximate?
(c) What are $D^T D$ and $D D^T$?
(d) What is A^2?
(e) What is kron(A,I)+kron(I,A)?
(f) Describe the output produced by plot(inv(full(-A))).

11.2. (a) Use finite differences to compute a numerical approximation to the solution $u(x)$ to the one-dimensional Poisson problem

$$\frac{d^2 u}{dx^2} = \exp(-x^2)$$

on the interval $-1 \leq x \leq 1$. The boundary conditions are $u(-1) = 0$ and $u(1) = 0$. Plot your solution.
(b) If you have access to dsolve in the Symbolic Toolbox, or if you are very good at calculus, find the analytic solution of the same problem and compare it with your numerical approximation.

11.3. Reproduce the contour plot in Figure 11.1 of the first eigenfunction of the H-shaped ridge waveguide formed from four L-shaped regions.

11.4. Let $h(x)$ be the function defined by the M-file humps(x). Solve four different problems involving $h(x)$ on the interval $0 \leq x \leq 1$.
(a) One-dimensional Poisson problem with humps as the source term:

$$\frac{d^2 u}{dx^2} = -h(x),$$

with boundary conditions

$$u(0) = 0, \; u(1) = 0.$$

Make plots, similar to Figure 11.4, of $h(x)$ and $u(x)$. Compare diff(u,2) with humps(x).
(b) One-dimensional heat equation with humps as the source term:

$$\frac{\partial u}{\partial t} = \frac{\partial^2 u}{\partial x^2} + h(x),$$

with initial value

$$u(0, x) = 0$$

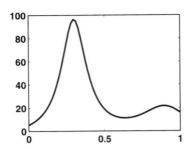 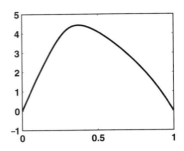

Figure 11.4. *h(x) and u(x).*

and boundary conditions

$$u(0, t) = 0, \ u(1, t) = 0.$$

Create an animated plot of the solution as a function of time. What is the limit as $t \to \infty$ of $u(x, t)$?

(c) One-dimensional heat equation with humps as the initial value:

$$\frac{\partial u}{\partial t} = \frac{\partial^2 u}{\partial x^2},$$

with initial value

$$u(x, 0) = h(x)$$

and boundary conditions

$$u(0, t) = h(0), \ u(1, t) = h(1).$$

Create an animated plot of the solution as a function of time. What is the limit as $t \to \infty$ of $u(x, t)$?

(d) One-dimensional wave equation with humps as the initial value:

$$\frac{\partial^2 u}{\partial t^2} = \frac{\partial^2 u}{\partial x^2},$$

with initial values

$$u(x, 0) = h(x),$$
$$\frac{\partial u}{\partial t}(x, 0) = 0,$$

and boundary conditions

$$u(0, t) = h(0), \ u(1, t) = h(1).$$

Create an animated plot of the solution as a function of time. For what values of t does $u(x, t)$ return to its initial value $h(x)$?

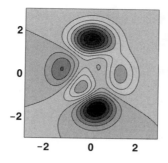 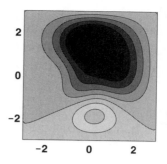

Figure 11.5. $p(x, y)$ and $u(x, y)$.

11.5. Let $p(x, y)$ be the function defined by the M-file `peaks (x,y)`. Solve four different problems involving $p(x, y)$ on the square $-3 \le x \le 3$, $-3 \le y \le 3$.

(a) Two-dimensional Poisson problem with `peaks` as the source term:

$$\frac{\partial^2 u}{\partial x^2} + \frac{\partial^2 u}{\partial y^2} = p(x, y),$$

with boundary conditions

$$u(x, y) = 0 \text{ if } |x| = 3 \text{ or } |y| = 3.$$

Make contour plots, similar to Figure 11.5, of $p(x, y)$ and $u(x, y)$.

(b) Two-dimensional heat equation with `peaks` as the source term:

$$\frac{\partial u}{\partial t} = \frac{\partial^2 u}{\partial x^2} + \frac{\partial^2 u}{\partial y^2} - p(x, y),$$

with initial value

$$u(x, y, 0) = 0$$

and boundary conditions

$$u(x, y, t) = 0 \text{ if } |x| = 3 \text{ or } |y| = 3.$$

Create an animated contour plot of the solution as a function of time. What is the limit as $t \to \infty$ of $u(x, t)$?

(c) Two-dimensional heat equation with `peaks` as the initial value:

$$\frac{\partial u}{\partial t} = \frac{\partial^2 u}{\partial x^2},$$

with initial value

$$u(x, y, 0) = p(x, y)$$

and boundary conditions

$$u(x, y, t) = p(x, y) \text{ if } |x| = 3 \text{ or } |y| = 3.$$

Create an animated contour plot of the solution as a function of time. What is the limit as $t \to \infty$ of $u(x, t)$?

(d) Two-dimensional wave equation with `peaks` as the initial value:

$$\frac{\partial^2 u}{\partial t^2} = \frac{\partial^2 u}{\partial x^2},$$

with initial values

$$u(x, y, 0) = p(x, y),$$
$$\frac{\partial u}{\partial t}(x, y, 0) = 0$$

and boundary conditions

$$u(x, y, t) = p(x, y) \text{ if } |x| = 3 \text{ or } |y| = 3.$$

Create an animated contour plot of the solution as a function of time. Does the limit as $t \to \infty$ of $u(x, t)$ exist?

11.6. The *method of lines* is a convenient technique for solving time-dependent partial differential equations. Replace all the spatial derivatives with finite differences, but leave the time derivatives intact. Then use a stiff ordinary differential equation solver on the resulting system. In effect, this is an implicit time-stepping finite difference algorithm with the time step determined automatically and adaptively by the ODE solver. For our model heat and wave equations, the ODE systems are simply

$$\dot{\mathbf{u}} = (1/h^2)A\mathbf{u}$$

and

$$\ddot{\mathbf{u}} = (1/h^2)A\mathbf{u}.$$

The matrix $(1/h^2)A$ represents $\triangle_h$, and $\mathbf{u}$ is the vector-valued function of t formed from all the elements $u(x_i, t)$ or $u(x_i, y_j, t)$ at the mesh points.

(a) The MATLAB function `pdepe` implements the method of lines in a general setting. Investigate its use for our one- and two-dimensional model heat equations.

(b) If you have access to the Partial Differential Equation Toolbox, investigate its use for our two-dimensional model heat and wave equations.

(c) Implement your own method of lines solutions for our model equations.

11.7. Answer the following questions about `pdegui`.

(a) How does the number of points n in the grid depend upon the grid size h for the various regions?

(b) How does the time step for the heat equation and for the wave equation depend upon the grid size h?

(c) Why are the contour plots of the solution to the Poisson problem and the eigenvalue problem with `index = 1` similar?

(d) How do the contour plots produced by `pdegui` of the eigenfunctions of the L-shaped domain compare with those produced by

```
contourf(membranetx(index))
```

(e) Why are the regions Drum1 and Drum2 interesting? Search the Web for "isospec-tral" and "Can you hear the shape of a drum?" You should find many articles and papers, including ones by Gordon, Webb, and Wolpert [28] and Driscoll [19].

11.8. Add the outline of your hand that you obtained in exercise 3.4 as another region to pdegui. Figure 11.6 shows one of the eigenfunctions of my hand.

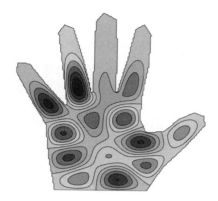

Figure 11.6. *An eigenfunction of a hand.*

11.9. The electrostatic capacity of a region Ω is the quantity

$$\int \int_\Omega u(x, y) dx dy,$$

where $u(x, y)$ is the solution to the Poisson problem

$$\triangle u = -1 \text{ in } \Omega$$

and $u(x, y) = 0$ on the boundary of Ω.
(a) What is the capacity of the unit square?
(b) What is the capacity of the L-shaped domain?
(c) What is the capacity of your hand?

11.10. The statements

```
load penny
P = flipud(P)
contour(P,1:12:255)
colormap(copper)
axis square
```

access a file in the MATLAB demos directory and produce Figure 11.7. The data were obtained in 1984 at what was then the National Bureau of Standards by an instrument that makes precise measurements of the depth of a mold used to mint the U.S. one cent coin.

The NCM function pennymelt uses this penny data as the initial condition, $u(x, y, 0)$, for the heat equation and produces an animated, evolving plot of the

Figure 11.7. *The depth of a mold used to mint the U.S. one cent coin.*

solution, $u(x, y, t)$. You can choose either a lighted, surface plot or a contour plot. You can choose the time step δ with uicontrols or with `pennymelt(delta)`. You can also choose a time-stepping algorithm know as the *ADI* or *alternating direction implicit* method. Each time step involves two half-steps, one implicit in the x direction and the other implicit in the y direction.

$$-\sigma u^{(k+1/2)}(N) + (1 + 2\sigma)u^{(k+1/2)}(P) - \sigma u^{(k+1/2)}(S)$$
$$= \sigma u^{(k)}(E) + (1 - 2\sigma)u^{(k)}(P) + \sigma u^{(k)}(W),$$
$$-\sigma u^{(k+1)}(E) + (1 + 2\sigma)u^{(k+1)}(P) - \sigma u^{(k+1)}(W)$$
$$= \sigma u^{(k+1/2)}(N) + (1 - 2\sigma)u^{(k+1/2)}(P) + \sigma u^{(k+1/2)}(S).$$

Solving these implicit equations on an m-by-n grid requires the solution of m tridiagonal systems of order n for the first half-step and then n tridiagonal systems of order m for the second half-step.

Answer these questions about `pennymelt`.

(a) What is the limiting behavior of $u(x, y, t)$ as $t \to \infty$?

(b) For what values of δ is the explicit time-stepping algorithm stable?

(c) Demonstrate that the ADI method is stable for any value of δ.

11.11. Let $p(x, y)$ be the function defined on a 128-by-128 square by the penny data described in the previous exercise.

(a) Make a contour plot of $p(x, y)$ and make a lighted surface plot using the section of code in `pennymelt.m`.

(b) Solve the discrete Poisson problem

$$\triangle_h u = p$$

with $u(x, y) = 0$ outside the square, and plot the solution $u(x, y)$.

(c) Use `del2` to compute

$$f = \triangle_h u,$$

and compare $f(x, y)$ with $p(x, y)$.

11.12. Modify `pennymelt.m` to solve the wave equation instead of the heat equation.

11.13. Modify `waves.m` to use nine eigenfunctions instead of four.

11.14. The eigenvalues and eigenfunctions of the unit square are

$$\lambda_{m,n} = (m^2 + n^2)\pi^2,$$
$$u_{m,n} = \sin mx \sin ny.$$

If the $\lambda_{m,n}$ are indexed with one subscript and listed in increasing order, we have

$$\lambda_k = (2, 5, 5, 8, 10, 10, 13, 13, 17, 17, 18, 20, 20, \ldots)\pi^2.$$

We see that λ_1, λ_4, and λ_{11} are simple eigenvalues, but that most of the eigenvalues are double.

(a) What is the smallest triple eigenvalue of the unit square and what is its index? In other words, what is the smallest integer that can be written as the sum of two squares in three different ways?

(b) What is the smallest quadruple eigenvalue of the unit square?

11.15. By reflecting the eigenfunctions of the unit square twice, we obtain some of the eigenfunctions of the L-shaped domain. The indexing is different because the L also has eigenfunctions that are not derived from the square. For example, λ_3 of the L is $2\pi^2$ because it is equal to λ_1 of the square. And $\lambda_8 = \lambda_9$ of the L is a double eigenvalue, $5\pi^2$, corresponding to $\lambda_2 = \lambda_3$ of the square.

(a) Roughly what fraction of the eigenvalues of the L-shaped region are also eigenvalues of the square?

(b) What is the smallest triple eigenvalue of the L-shaped region and what is its index?

(c) What is the smallest quadruple eigenvalue of the L-shaped region?

(d) Neither `membranetx` nor `pdegui` uses the $\sin mx \sin ny$ representation of eigenfunctions of the square. This is OK because these eigenfunctions are not unique and can have other representations. How do `membranetx` and `pdegui` compute eigenfunctions? How do they get a set of linearly independent eigenfunctions for eigenvalues with multiplicity greater than one?

11.16. Enter the commands

```
ncmlogo
cameratoolbar
```

Or, just enter the command `ncmlogo` and then select **Camera Toolbar** from the **View** tab on the figure window. Experiment with the various icons available on the new toolbar. What do they all do?

11.17. Make your own copy of `ncmlogo` and modify it to create a logo for your own book or company.

Bibliography

[1] ADVANCED TECHNICAL MATERIALS, INC.
http://www.atmmicrowave.com

[2] E. ANDERSON, Z. BAI, C. BISCHOF, S. BLACKFORD, J. DEMMEL, J. DONGARRA, J. DU
CROZ, A. GREENBAUM, S. HAMMARLING, A. MCKENNEY, AND D. SORENSEN, *LAPACK
Users' Guide*, Third Edition, SIAM, Philadelphia, 1999.
http://www.netlib.org/lapack

[3] A. ARASU, J. NOVAK, A. TOMKINS, AND J. TOMLIN, *PageRank Computation and the
Structure of the Web*.
http://www2002.org/CDROM/poster/173.pdf

[4] U. M. ASCHER AND L. R. PETZOLD, *Computer Methods for Ordinary Differential
Equations and Differential-Algebraic Equations*, SIAM, Philadelphia, 1998.

[5] R. BALDWIN, W. CANTEY, H. MAISEL, AND J. MCDERMOTT, *The optimum strategy in
blackjack*, Journal of the American Statistical Association, 51 (1956), pp. 429–439.

[6] M. BARNSLEY, *Fractals Everywhere*, Academic Press, Boston, 1993.

[7] BIO MOTION LAB.
http://www.biomotionlab.ca

[8] A. BJÖRCK, *Numerical Methods for Least Squares Problems*, SIAM, Philadelphia,
1996.

[9] P. BOGACKI AND L. F. SHAMPINE, *A* 3(2) *pair of Runge–Kutta formulas*, Applied
Mathematics Letters, 2 (1989), pp. 1–9.

[10] F. BORNEMANN, D. LAURIE, S. WAGON, AND J. WALDVOGEL, *The SIAM* 100-*Digit
Challenge: A Study in High-Accuracy Numerical Computing*, SIAM, Philadelphia,
2004.

[11] K. E. BRENAN, S. L. CAMPBELL, AND L. R. PETZOLD, *Numerical Solution of Initial-
Value Problems in Differential-Algebraic Equations*, SIAM, Philadelphia, 1996.

[12] R. P. BRENT, *Algorithms for Minimization without Derivatives*, Prentice–Hall,
Englewood Cliffs, NJ, 1973.

[13] J. W. COOLEY AND J. W. TUKEY, *An algorithm for the machine calculation of complex Fourier series*, Mathematics of Computation, 19 (1965), pp. 297–301.

[14] R. M. CORLESS, G. H. GONNET, D. E. G. HARE, D. J. JEFFREY, AND D. E. KNUTH, *On the Lambert W function*, Advances in Computational Mathematics, 5 (1996), pp. 329–359.
     http://www.apmaths.uwo.ca/~rcorless/frames/PAPERS/LambertW

[15] G. DAHLQUIST AND A. BJÖRCK, *Numerical Methods*, Prentice–Hall, Englewood Cliffs, NJ, 1974.

[16] C. DE BOOR, *A Practical Guide to Splines*, Springer-Verlag, New York, 1978.

[17] T. J. DEKKER, *Finding a zero by means of successive linear interpolation*, in Constructive Aspects of the Fundamental Theorem of Algebra, B. Dejon and P. Henrici (editors), Wiley-Interscience, New York, 1969, pp. 37–48.

[18] J. W. DEMMEL, *Applied Numerical Linear Algebra*, SIAM, Philadelphia, 1997.

[19] T. A. DRISCOLL, *Eigenmodes of isospectral drums*, SIAM Review, 39 (1997), pp. 1–17.
     http://www.math.udel.edu/~driscoll/pubs/drums.pdf

[20] G. FORSYTHE, M. MALCOLM, AND C. MOLER, *Computer Methods for Mathematical Computations*, Prentice–Hall, Englewood Cliffs, NJ, 1977.

[21] M. FRIGO AND S. G. JOHNSON, *FFTW: An adaptive software architecture for the FFT*, in Proceedings of the 1998 IEEE International Conference on Acoustics Speech and Signal Processing, 3 (1998), pp. 1381–1384.
     http://www.fftw.org

[22] M. FRIGO AND S. G. JOHNSON, *Links to FFT-related resources.*
     http://www.fftw.org/links.html

[23] F. N. FRITSCH AND R. E. CARLSON, *Monotone piecewise cubic interpolation*, SIAM Journal on Numerical Analysis, 17 (1980), pp. 238–246.

[24] W. GANDER AND W. GAUTSCHI, *Adaptive Quadrature—Revisited*, BIT Numerical Mathematics, 40 (2000), pp. 84–101.
     http://www.inf.ethz.ch/personal/gander

[25] J. R. GILBERT, C. MOLER, AND R. SCHREIBER, *Sparse matrices in MATLAB: Design and implementation*, SIAM Journal on Matrix Analysis and Applications, 13 (1992), pp. 333–356.

[26] G. H. GOLUB AND C. F. VAN LOAN, *Matrix Computations*, Third Edition, The Johns Hopkins University Press, Baltimore, 1996.

[27] GOOGLE, *Google Technology.*
     http://www.google.com/technology/index.html

[28] C. GORDON, D. WEBB, AND S. WOLPERT, *Isospectral plane domains and surfaces via Riemannian orbifolds*, Inventiones Mathematicae, 110 (1992), pp. 1–22.

[29] D. C. Hanselman and B. Littlefield, *Mastering MATLAB 6, A Comprehensive Tutorial and Reference*, Prentice–Hall, Upper Saddle River, NJ, 2000.

[30] M. T. Heath, *Scientific Computing: An Introductory Survey*, McGraw–Hill, New York, 1997.

[31] D. J. Higham and N. J. Higham, *MATLAB Guide*, SIAM, Philadelphia, 2000.

[32] N. J. Higham, and F. Tisseur, *A block algorithm for matrix 1-norm estimation, with an application to 1-norm pseudospectra*, SIAM Journal on Matrix Analysis and Applications, 21 (2000), pp. 1185–1201.

[33] N. J. Higham, *Accuracy and Stability of Numerical Algorithms*, SIAM, Philadelphia, 2002.

[34] D. Kahaner, C. Moler, and S. Nash, *Numerical Methods and Software*, Prentice–Hall, Englewood Cliffs, NJ, 1989.

[35] D. E. Knuth, *The Art of Computer Programming: Volume 2, Seminumerical Algorithms*, Addison–Wesley, Reading, MA, 1969.

[36] J. Lagarias, *The $3x + 1$ problem and its generalizations*, American Mathematical Monthly, 92 (1985), pp. 3–23.
http://www.cecm.sfu.ca/organics/papers/lagarias

[37] A. N. Langville and C. D. Meyer, *Google's PageRank and Beyond*, Princeton University Press, Princeton, NJ, 2006.

[38] R. B. Lehoucq, D. C. Sorensen, and C. Yang, *ARPACK Users' Guide: Solution of Large-Scale Eigenvalue Problems with Implicitly Restarted Arnoldi Methods*, SIAM, Philadelphia, 1998.
http://www.caam.rice.edu/software/ARPACK

[39] Lighthouse Foundation.
http://www.lighthouse-foundation.org

[40] G. Marsaglia, *Random numbers fall mainly in the planes*, Proceedings of the National Academy of Sciences, 61 (1968), pp. 25–28.

[41] G. Marsaglia and W. W. Tsang, *The ziggurat method for generating random variables*, Journal of Statistical Software, 5 (2000), pp. 1–7.
http://www.jstatsoft.org/v05/i08

[42] G. Marsaglia and W. W. Tsang, *A fast, easily implemented method for sampling from decreasing or symmetric unimodal density functions*, SIAM Journal on Scientific and Statistical Computing 5 (1984), pp. 349–359.

[43] G. Marsaglia and A. Zaman, *A new class of random number generators*, Annals of Applied Probability, 3 (1991), pp. 462–480.

[44] THE MATHWORKS, INC., *Getting Started with MATLAB*.
     `http://www.mathworks.com/access/helpdesk/help/techdoc`
        `/learn_matlab/learn_matlab.shtml`

[45] THE MATHWORKS, INC., List of MATLAB-based books.
     `http://www.mathworks.com/support/books/index.jsp`

[46] M. MATSUMOTO AND T. NISHIMURA, Mersenne Twister Home Page.
     `http://www.math.sci.hiroshima-u.ac.jp/~m-mat/MT/emt.html`

[47] C. MOLER, *Numerical Computing with MATLAB*,
     Electronic edition: The MathWorks, Inc., Natick, MA, 2004.
     `http://www.mathworks.com/moler`
     Print edition: SIAM, Philadelphia, 2004.
     `http://www.ec-securehost.com/SIAM/ot87.html`

[48] NATIONAL INSTITUTE OF STANDARDS AND TECHNOLOGY, *Statistical Reference
     Datasets*.
     `http://www.itl.nist.gov/div898/strd`
     `http://www.itl.nist.gov/div898/strd/lls/lls.shtml`
     `http://www.itl.nist.gov/div898/strd/lls/data/Longley.shtml`

[49] M. OVERTON, *Numerical Computing with IEEE Floating Point Arithmetic*, SIAM,
     Philadelphia, 2001.

[50] L. PAGE, S. BRIN, R. MOTWANI, AND T. WINOGRAD, *The PageRank Citation Ranking:
     Bringing Order to the Web*.
     `http://dbpubs.stanford.edu:8090/pub/1999-66`

[51] S. K. PARK AND K. W. MILLER, *Random number generators: Good ones are hard to
     find*, Communications of the ACM, 31 (1988), pp. 1192–1201.

[52] I. PETERSON, *Prime Spirals*, Science News Online, 161 (2002).
     `http://www.sciencenews.org/20020504/mathtrek.asp`

[53] L. F. SHAMPINE, *Numerical Solution of Ordinary Differential Equations*, Chapman
     and Hall, New York, 1994.

[54] L. F. SHAMPINE AND M. W. REICHELT, *The MATLAB ODE suite*, SIAM Journal on
     Scientific Computing, 18 (1997), pp. 1–22.

[55] K. SIGMON AND T. A. DAVIS, *MATLAB Primer*, Sixth Edition, Chapman and Hall/CRC,
     Boca Raton, FL, 2002.

[56] SOLAR INFLUENCES DATA CENTER, *Sunspot archive and graphics*.
     `http://sidc.oma.be`

[57] C. SPARROW, *The Lorenz Equations: Bifurcations, Chaos, and Strange Attractors*,
     Springer-Verlag, New York, 1982.

[58] G. W. STEWART, *Introduction to Matrix Computations*, Academic Press, New York, 1973.

[59] G. W. STEWART, *Matrix Algorithms: Basic Decompositions*, SIAM, Philadelphia, 1998.

[60] L. N. TREFETHEN AND D. BAU, III, *Numerical Linear Algebra*, SIAM, Philadelphia, 1997.

[61] L. N. TREFETHEN, *A hundred-dollar, hundred-digit challenge*, SIAM News, 35 (1) (2002).
http://www.siam.org/pdf/news/388.pdf
http://www.siam.org/books/100digitchallenge
http://web.comlab.ox.ac.uk/oucl/work/nick.trefethen/hundred.html

[62] N. TROJE.
http://journalofvision.org/2/5/2

[63] N. TROJE.
http://www.biomotionlab.de/Text/WDP2002_Troje.pdf

[64] C. VAN LOAN, *Computational Frameworks for the Fast Fourier Transform*, SIAM, Philadelphia, 1992.

[65] J. C. G. WALKER, *Numerical Adventures with Geochemical Cycles*, Oxford University Press, New York, 1991.

[66] E. WEISSTEIN, *World of Mathematics, Prime Spiral*,
http://mathworld.wolfram.com/PrimeSpiral.html

[67] E. WEISSTEIN, *World of Mathematics, Stirling's Approximation*.
http://mathworld.wolfram.com/StirlingsApproximation.html

[68] J. WILKINSON, *The Algebraic Eigenvalue Problem*, Clarendon Press, Oxford, 1965.

Index